THE LDS GOSPEL TOPICS SERIES

THE LDS GOSPEL TOPICS SERIES

A SCHOLARLY ENGAGEMENT

EDITED BY
MATTHEW L. HARRIS AND NEWELL G. BRINGHURST

AFTERWORD BY
ARMAND L. MAUSS

SIGNATURE BOOKS | 2020 | SALT LAKE CITY

In memory of Armand L. Mauss

The opinions expressed in this book are not necessarily those of the publisher.

Cover design by Jason Francis.

The cover image is a portrait of Lucy Mack Smith painted by Sutcliffe Maudsley circa 1842.

FIRST EDITION | 2020

LIBRARY OF CONGRESS CATALOGING-IN-PUBLICATION DATA

Names: Harris, Matthew L., editor. | Bringhurst, Newell G., editor. | Mauss, Armand L., writer of afterword.

Title: The LDS gospel topics series : a scholarly engagement / edited by Matthew L. Harris and Newell G. Bringhurst ; afterword by Armand L. Mauss.

Description: First edition. | Salt Lake City : Signature Books, 2020. | Includes index. | Summary: "This anthology provides a scholarly, in-depth analysis of the thirteen Gospel Topics essays issued by the Church of Jesus Christ of Latter-day Saints from December 2013 to October 2015. The contributors reflect a variety of faith traditions, including the LDS Church, Community of Christ, Catholic, and Evangelical Christian. Each contributor is an experienced, thoughtful scholar, many having written widely on religious thought in general and Mormon history in particular. The writers probe the strengths and weaknesses of each of the Gospel Topics essays, providing a forthright discussion on the relevant issues in LDS history and doctrine. The editors hope that these analyses will spark a healthy discussion about the Gospel Topics essays, as well as stimulate further discussion in the field of Mormon Studies"—provided by publisher.

Identifiers: LCCN 2020025699 (print) | LCCN 2020025700 (ebook) | ISBN 9781560852872 (paperback) | ISBN 9781560853862 (ebook)

Subjects: LCSH: Church of Jesus Christ of Latter-day Saints—Doctrines. | Gospel topics (Church of Jesus Christ of Latter-day Saints) | Mormon Church—Doctrines.

Classification: LCC BX8637 .L37 2020 (print) | LCC BX8637 (ebook) | DDC 230/.9332—dc23

LC record available at https://lccn.loc.gov/2020025699
LC ebook record available at https://lccn.loc.gov/2020025700

CONTENTS

ACKNOWLEDGMENTS

Many people made this volume possible. First, and foremost, is Travis Stratford of New York City, who graciously shared his experiences behind-the-scenes encouraging officials of the Church of Jesus Christ of Latter-day Saints to release the Gospel Topics Essays. Stratford also shared copies of his "Faith Crisis" reports, which were indispensable to the release of the essays. (Travis is discussed at greater length in the introduction.)

We are also indebted to the many church historians and archivists who shared their expertise discussing a variety of questions raised in this volume. Our thanks to Reid L. Nielson, Matthew J. Grow, and most especially LDS Church Historian Steven E. Snow (now retired), who was warmly encouraging after we presented some of the ideas in the introduction at the Mormon History Association Conference in St. Louis, Missouri, in 2017. We should stress that all errors of fact and judgment in the introduction are entirely our own.

We are especially grateful to the scholars who contributed essays to this volume. Their professionalism, sensitivity, and honesty make this a much better book than it would be if we were its only authors. Our thanks, also, to Signature Books for making the press a warm, hospitable place to publish our work.

Finally, we thank our wives—Courtney A. Harris and Mary Ann Bringhurst—who continue to tolerate our fascination with the Mormon past. We are grateful for their love and support.

INTRODUCTION
WHY THE GOSPEL TOPICS ESSAYS?

Matthew L. Harris and Newell G. Bringhurst

On a chilly evening in November 2010, some 600 Swedish Latter-day Saints met at an LDS chapel in Stockholm to discuss their concerns about difficult theological questions in the LDS Church. It was not an ordinary church fireside. High-ranking officials from church headquarters in Salt Lake City had been sent to meet with them. "They had a remarkably frank and sometimes testy exchange, especially about [Joseph] Smith and polygamy," the *New York Times* noted. The meeting was requested by a well-respected Swedish Latter-day Saint named Hans Mattsson, a one-time "Area Authority Seventy" for the LDS Church in Europe. Mattsson expressed alarm concerning certain controversial LDS teachings discovered on the internet. "I felt like I had an earthquake under my feet," Mattsson explained. "Everything I'd been taught, everything I'd been proud to preach about and witness about just crumbled under my feet. It was such a terrible psychological and nearly physical disturbance."[1]

Dubbed "the Swedish Rescue" mission, this "special fireside" was led by LDS Church Historian/Recorder and general authority Marlin K. Jensen and Assistant Church Historian/Recorder Richard E. Turley Jr.[2] Jensen explained that the purpose of the

---

1. Laurie Goodstein, "Some Mormons Search the Web and Find Doubt," *New York Times*, July 20, 2013. See also John Dehlin's interview with "Hans Mattsson—Former LDS Area Authority Seventy (Sweden)," *Mormon Stories* (July 22, 2013), at www.mormonstories.org/hans-mattsson.

2. "Special Fireside for Disaffected Latter-day Saints in Sweden": Guest speakers Elder Marlin K. Jensen, Church Historian and Recorder, and Richard E. Turley Jr., Assistant Church Historian, Vasterhaninge Chapel, Stockholm, Sweden, Nov. 28, 2010, copy of audio and transcript https://www.youtube.com/watch?v=j_2Ht4d9R5g.

fireside was to "offer some information in a reliable and loving way that will be responsive to some of the questions that you have." He further stated that "we're going to invite you to share with us your most pressing questions," adding, "I know the Church is true and my prayer tonight is that those of you who may be in doubt may have some of your doubt removed."[3]

The fireside quickly turned testy. After Jensen's opening statement quoting scripture and bearing testimony, one of the members asked: "Is it okay to ask questions now?" For the next three and a half hours, they asked Jensen and Turley questions concerning polygamy/polyandry, the ancient authenticity of the Book of Abraham, the translation of the Book of Mormon, and other controversial doctrinal and historical matters. Turley and Jensen tried to answer them. During one tense moment, a participant chided the two men for what he perceived was an obfuscating answer about the Book of Mormon. "That is amazing," he noted, unimpressed with Turley's answer. "But those are not the questions we want."[4]

Jensen and Turley, well-aware of the crisis at hand, had been previously apprised of some of the questions the Swedes might ask. They brought a handout recommending five websites favorable to the church and implored the participants to spend more time on these faith-affirming sites rather than on "anti-Mormon websites." They further stated that senior church apostle Boyd K. Packer had directed the church history department to put "together a committee to create answers to difficult gospel questions," in what would later be called the Gospel Topics Essays. "We are working on those now," Jensen stated, "and we're also giving thought to how we will disseminate these answers to the world. But we'll give you our best answers. We wanted you to know tonight there are answers."[5]

The answers could not come fast enough. A year after Turley and Jensen met with Swedish Latter-day Saints, Travis Stratford, a

---

3. Ibid., 3–4, 12.

4. Ibid., 11, 26–27. At another point in the meeting, Turley asked his interlocutors, "Let's stop interrupting and just keep going through very, very quickly" (ibid., 36). According to Hans Mattsson, the meeting lasted three and a half hours. Mattsson, Email to Matthew L. Harris, Feb. 5, 2017, Harris files.

5. "Special Fireside for Disaffected Latter-day Saints in Sweden," 9, 20–21.

middle-aged brand strategist from New York City, was experiencing a faith crisis of his own. Having served an LDS proselytizing mission in Sweden, graduated from LDS-owned Brigham Young University, and married in the LDS temple, Stratford had come of age in an orthodox LDS environment. But over the years his faith had waivered, affected by websites he discovered discussing and challenging LDS truth claims. After learning about the Swedish Rescue fireside, he contacted Mattsson, hoping for a collaborative effort to use his research skills and Mattsson's connections "to help the Brethren understand how Faith Crisis is destroying [LDS] families." In May 2011, Mattsson scheduled a meeting with Marlin Jensen, perceiving him as "the most qualified to understand the issue." With the Swedish Fireside still fresh on his mind, Jensen agreed to meet with Mattsson and Stratford in New York City in October of that year. Included in the discussion was LDS scholar Gregory A. Prince. Jensen attended with the blessing of Apostle Packer.[6]

In preparation for the meeting, Stratford compiled data to present to Jensen. He asked his friend John Dehlin to assemble a team of LDS professionals to conduct a qualitative ethnographic survey on "Why Mormons Question." (Dehlin, a therapist-in-training, specialized in navigating LDS faith crises.) The team surveyed several thousand disaffected Latter-day Saints, receiving 3,086 responses. Though not strictly scientific, the survey revealed that Latter-day Saints became disaffected due to a loss of belief in LDS doctrine and theology. Many respondents questioned the prophetic role of Joseph Smith, founder of the LDS Church, and the Book of Mormon as a divine text. A significant number of respondents questioned the translation of the Book of Abraham, LDS teachings on polygamy, blacks and the priesthood, DNA and Book of Mormon peoples, and quasi-Masonic aspects of the LDS temple endowment ceremony.[7]

---

6. Our thanks to Travis Stratford for providing details about the events in a document he created titled "LDS Faith Crisis Timeline." This and subsequent material in this introductory essay derive from this document, as well as from emails and correspondence from Stratford to Harris, summer 2017. Jensen informed Stratford that Boyd K. Packer gave him permission to meet in New York City. As recalled in Stratford, Email to Matthew L. Harris, Aug. 13, 2017.

7. John Dehlin, "Understanding Mormon Disbelief: Why Do Some Mormons Lose Their Testimony, and What Happens to Them When They Do?," results from

Dehlin's research, which was eventually published on the internet in March 2012, represented the first systematic effort within the LDS Church to attempt to quantify why individual Latter-day Saints were experiencing a faith crisis. Notably, his work challenged the popular perception that Latter-day Saints became disaffected largely because of sin, pride, spiritual inertia, or personal conflicts with leadership. The study showed convincingly that Latter-day Saints tended to leave due to a crisis of faith, triggered by controversial aspects of church history and doctrine compounded by official attempts to minimize or obfuscate.[8]

At the New York City meeting, Jensen expressed shock at the survey's findings. "Why Mormons Question" indicated a much more extensive faith crisis than Jensen initially believed. But more important, the crisis affected well-educated, LDS professionals. "Our best and our brightest" are leaving the church, Jensen noted, prompting him to call for "reconciliation strategies" to remedy the problem. He further acknowledged that an "internal team" at LDS headquarters was already working on "position papers" to address concerns raised in the survey. But he opined that the team did not have the "political capital" to get the papers published. To this end,

---

an online survey administered in 2011, published in March 2012 on website entitled "Why Mormons Question": www.whymormonsquestion.org. A recent and more reliable study avers that the top reasons for LDS disaffection include the notion that Latter-day Saints could not reconcile their values with the church's, loss of belief in the church's exclusive truth claims as the "one true church," and the church leadership's not telling the truth regarding doctrinal and historical issues. See Jana Riess, *The Next Mormons: How Millennials Are Changing the LDS Church* (New York: Oxford University Press, 2019), 223–28 (quote at 224). See also E. Marshall Brooks, *Disenchanted Lives: Apostasy and Ex-Mormonism among the Latter-day Saints* (New Brunswick, New Jersey: Rutgers University Press, 2018); and David B. Ostler, *Bridges: Ministering to Those Who Question* (Salt Lake City: Kofford Books, 2019). Of the studies on LDS disaffection, Riess's is the most comprehensive and scholarly.

8. Dehlin, "Understanding Mormon Disbelief." The LDS orthodox position why Latter-day Saints leave the faith is typically associated with their desire to sin and/or personal conflicts they experienced at church. See Bruce R. McConkie, *Mormon Doctrine* (Salt Lake City: Bookcraft, 1958), 41; Edward L. Kimball, ed., *The Teachings of Spencer W. Kimball* (Salt Lake City: Bookcraft, 1982), 155, 335–36; Gordon B. Hinckley, "Stay the Course—Keep the Faith," *Ensign,* Nov. 1995, 72; David A. Bednar, "And Nothing Shall Offend Them," *Conference Report* (Oct. 2005), at www.lds.org/general-conference/2006/10/and-nothing-shall-offend-them?lang=eng; and Boyd K. Packer, *Mine Errand from the Lord* (Salt Lake City: Deseret Book Co., 2008), 394–96.

4

he invited Stratford to Salt Lake City to present his work to other church authorities hoping that senior leaders would see the urgent need to release the "position papers" when they were completed.[9]

While arrangements were underway for Stratford to visit Salt Lake City, Jensen expressed his views about LDS disaffection. In a meeting with LDS students at Utah State University in January 2012, he acknowledged that Latter-day Saints were finding information online that was not flattering to the church.[10] Jensen said that church-correlated efforts to present a faith-promoting version of LDS history seemed not to be serving the church well, particularly those aspects that conflicted with conflicting information on the internet. "Everything [is] out there for them to consume if they want to Google it," he proffered. At one critical point, a student asked if leaders of the church knew that members are "leaving in droves," and Jensen noted that "we are aware." He confided that "Not since Kirtland [Ohio, in the 1830s] have we seen such an exodus of the Church's best and brightest leaders."[11]

Jensen's admission concerning LDS disaffection initiated a wave of news coverage. The *Washington Post* described a former BYU student who "spiritually imploded" when confronted with challenging material on LDS history and doctrine at the church university. Similarly, the *Salt Lake Tribune* reported that "more and more members of the Utah-based Church of Jesus Christ of Latter-day Saints" are leaving the "fold, ... feeling betrayed" by what they find online. A "special [Reuters] report" stated that

9. Stratford, "LDS Faith Crisis Timeline."

10. Peter Henderson and Kristina Cooke, "Special Report: Mormonism Besieged by the Modern Age," *Reuters,* Jan. 31, 2012, at www.uk.reuters.com/article/2012/01/30/uk-mormonchurch-idUKTRE80T1CP20120130. According to Gregory Prince, who had firsthand knowledge, Jensen learned about the Dehlin survey in "late 2011" (Prince, Email to Matthew L. Harris, Jan. 5, 2017). Stratford pinpoints the exact date on October 24, 2011, when Jensen met with Stratford in New York City to discuss Stratford and Dehlin's "Faith Crisis" survey (Stratford timeline in Harris files). See also Riess, *The Next Mormons,* 218–19.

11. As quoted in Henderson and Cooke, "Special Report: Mormonism Besieged by the Modern Age." A student made an audiotape transcript of Jensen's discussion with Utah State University students and posted it online. Before it was taken down, Harris heard it. It was initially posted at www.fileswap.com/dl/5iKOuShH9D/ElderJensenQandAInterlacedEdited.mp3.

"Mormonism [is being] besieged by the modern age."[12] In response, Terryl Givens, a respected LDS scholar, conceded "that this is a real crisis. It is an epidemic." Joanna Brooks, another prominent LDS scholar, declared that the time has arrived for Latter-day Saints to "Come to Terms with Church History."[13]

As such stories circulated on the internet, Stratford met with a dozen or so officials at church headquarters in February 2012 to present data from Dehlin's survey and to discuss the impact of faith crisis on LDS families. LDS public relations leaders, Church Education System employees, and other church officials attended the meeting, which included Jensen and Michael Otterson, Managing Director of LDS Public Affairs. The participants agreed to "proactively promote empathy towards those in Faith Crisis and push to make the 'position papers' available."[14] Most significantly, Otterson shared Stratford's PowerPoint presentation with Apostles L. Tom Perry and Quentin L. Cook—both in charge of LDS public affairs. But bureaucratic inertia, coupled with the anxieties of certain church leaders, stalled progress for a year. Seeking to push the process forward, Stratford, with Jensen's support, put together a hardbound report of the faith crisis findings, which included data from Dehlin's survey and the PowerPoint presentation he made in Salt Lake City. In turn, Jensen shared the expanded "LDS Faith Crisis" report with First Presidency counselor Dieter F. Uchtdorf, considered the most open and sensitive LDS leader on faith crisis issues.[15]

---

12. Carrie Sheffield, "A Mormon Church in Need of Reform," *Washington Post*, Jan. 29, 2012; Peggy Fletcher Stack, "Mormons Tackling Tough Questions in Their History," *Salt Lake Tribune*, Feb. 3, 2012; Henderson and Cooke, "Special Report: Mormonism Besieged by the Modern Age."

13. Terryl Givens, as quoted in Stack, "Mormons Tackling Tough Questions in Their History"; Joanna Brooks, "Time for Mormons to Come to Terms with Church History" (blog), *Religion Dispatches*, Jan. 31, 2012, at www.religiondispatches.org/dispatches/joannabrooks/5635/time_for_mormons_to_come_to_terms_with_church_history. Givens's most important books in Mormon Studies include his two-volume history of Mormon theology: *Wrestling the Angel: The Foundations of Mormon Thought: Cosmos, God, Humanity* (New York: Oxford University Press, 2015), and *Feeding the Flock: The Foundations of Mormon Thought: Church and Praxis* (New York: Oxford University Press, 2017). Brooks is best known for *The Book of Mormon Girl: Stories from an American Faith* (New York: Free Press, 2012).

14. Stratford, "LDS Crisis Timeline."

15. Stratford, "LDS Faith Crisis Timeline"; Stratford, "LDS Personal Faith Crisis," Apr. 2013, Harris files.

The "LDS Faith Crisis" report presented significant challenges to the church's top leadership. It called the church to be more open and honest about its history and doctrine, warning that "unless bold measures are taken to treat those in Faith Crisis and to mitigate the challenge for future generations, significantly more LDS families will become impaired and the future success of the Church will be put at risk." The report further stated that "Mitigating Faith Crisis for future generations is possible but will require bold steps. The key is to ensure future generations no longer become shocked by gaps between our official LDS narrative and our uncorrelated history."[16]

Stratford's report laid bare what was at stake—there was a significant chasm between correlated, hagiographic church history in LDS books and manuals and unfiltered, less-than-edifying accounts on the internet. Certain leaders responded to the "Faith Crisis" report skeptically, declining to admit what seemed obvious to others: the internet was causing the church to lose control over its narrative.[17] In particular, Apostle Cook warned Latter-day Saints about the dangers of using the internet to research church history. Cook addressed the issue in an LDS general conference sermon in October 2012, some six months after receiving a copy of Stratford's presentation. He stated, "Some have immersed themselves in Internet materials that magnify, exaggerate, and, in some cases, invent shortcomings of early Church leaders," further warning that church members could "draw incorrect conclusions that can affect testimony." Cook counseled, "Any who have made these choices can repent and be spiritually renewed."[18]

---

16. Stratford, "LDS Personal Faith Crisis," 123–24.

17. LDS historian David Whittaker notes that in "the age of the internet it is no longer possible for any one person or organization to control how the history of the Church of Jesus Christ of Latter-day Saints is either studied or written about." In Whittaker, "Mormon Studies as an Academic Discipline," in Terryl L. Givens and Philip L. Barlow, eds., *The Oxford Handbook of Mormonism* (New York: Oxford University Press, 2015), 102. See also Joseph Walker, "Mormons Navigate Faith and Doubt in the Digital Age," *Deseret News*, July 26, 2013; and Blair G. Van Dyke and Lloyd Isao Erickson, eds., *Perspectives on Mormon Theology: Apologetics* (Salt Lake City: Greg Kofford Books, 2017).

18. Cook, "Can Ye Feel So Now," *LDS Conference Report* (Oct. 2012), at www.lds.org/general-conference/2012/10/can-ye-feel-so-now?lang=eng.

Cook's failure to grasp the larger issues of faith crisis frustrated Stratford. For Latter-day Saints afflicted by doubt, things were not that simple. The apostle's sermon ignored Dehlin's data about why Latter-day Saints were leaving the church and did not address the fact that the church had not been forthcoming about its history. Still, Stratford remained undeterred. As he contemplated his next move, a prominent LDS business professor recommended conducting another survey "capturing first-hand experiences" of Latter-day Saints enduring a faith crisis. Stratford and the professor hoped that personal, real-life stories detailing LDS disaffection would prompt church leaders to take faith crisis more seriously. Thus, in the spring of 2013, Stratford, along with two prominent LDS members, designed and published a second survey called "Faith Crisis Chronicles." The team collected and analyzed over 1,500 stories, creating a compelling narrative explaining why Latter-day Saints were leaving the faith.[19]

One anonymous respondent, "a fully-active Latter-day Saint," claimed that after consulting the controversial website "Mormonthink.org," she "began reading voraciously and was shocked at what I discovered. ... I became obsessed with getting to the bottom of it and finding out about the real Joseph Smith. The biggest shockers were that Joseph translated the Book of Mormon without the plates, with his head in a hat that contained a seer stone, and also that there were several versions of the First Visions," adding "I never knew that the texts contained in the Pearl of Great Price were not literal translations of the scrolls that Joseph obtained." Another anonymous respondent, "a fully active, full-tithe paying member," expressed anguish when he "watched an interview between [LDS Church] President [Gordon B.] Hinckley and a German reporter where the Prophet was asked why the Blacks were denied the Priesthood until 1978. President Hinckley looked the reporter in the eyes [and] said, 'I don't know.' I was floored," the respondent explained. "Surely this man who had been a peer of the likes of [prominent LDS theologian and

---

19. Stratford, "LDS Crisis Timeline"; Stratford et al., eds., "LDS Faith Chronicles," May 2013, Harris files. Due to privacy concerns, we do not reveal the other participants in the "Faith Chronicles" project.

apostle] Bruce R. McConkie knew of the teachings of the mark of Cain and yet here he was flatly denying them. To me, this was a bald-faced lie. The idea that a Prophet of God would lie to a reporter shook me to the core."[20]

Affected by such stories, Stratford and his associates decided to share the "Faith Crisis Chronicles" with church leaders. In August 2013, Stratford personally delivered a hard copy to Uchtdorf's office at LDS headquarters—supplementing the "Faith Crisis Report" that Jensen had shared with him two months earlier.[21] At the same time, Stratford pursued another tactic to get officials to release the "position papers." Earlier in the spring of 2013, he arranged for Mattsson to visit New York City to interview with Laurie Goodstein of the *New York Times* to promote greater transparency by church leaders.[22] Goodstein's article, "Some Mormons Search the Web and Find Doubt," appeared on July 20, 2013 and was subsequently republished throughout the United States and abroad. Mattsson's interview provided a sobering assessment revealing that even leaders within the faith were not immune from unsettling material on the internet. Goodstein explained that when Mattsson "discovered credible evidence that the church's founder, Joseph Smith, was a polygamist and that the Book of Mormon and other scriptures were rife with historical anomalies … , he felt that the foundation on which he had built his life began to crumble." She continued: The "Mormon Church is grappling with a wave of doubt and disillusionment among members who encountered information on the Internet that sabotaged what they were taught about their faith. …"[23]

Alarmed by the *New York Times* story, and clearly influenced by the two Faith Crisis reports, Uchtdorf publicly acknowledged the problem of Mormon disaffection. In a landmark October 2013 LDS conference address, Uchtdorf admitted that "there have been some things said and done [by LDS leaders] that could

---

20. Stratford, "Faith Crisis Chronicles," Aug. 2013, 96, 150, Harris files.

21. In an email to Matthew Harris, Jan. 5, 2017, Gregory Prince, who has "direct knowledge" of the situation, said that Uchtdorf was given a "hard copy" of Dehlin's survey in June 2013, as it was summarized and outlined in Stratford's "Faith Crisis Report."

22. Stratford, "LDS Faith Crisis Timeline."

23. Goodstein, "Some Mormons Search the Web and Find Doubt."

cause people to question." He further confessed: "And, to be perfectly frank, there have been times when members or leaders in the Church have simply made mistakes. There may be have been things said or done that were not in harmony with our values, principles, or doctrine." Uchtdorf also rejected the notion that Latter-day Saints leave the church "because they have been offended, or [are] lazy or sinful. Actually, it is not that simple," he explained. There "is not just one reason that applies to the variety of situations."[24] Although Uchtdorf did not name a specific doctrine or teaching when church leaders may have erred, his remarks revealed an intuitive awareness that controversial LDS teachings were pushing many members away from "the Church they once loved."[25] His concerns were well-founded. According to statistical reports, church growth was 1.7% in 2015, the lowest since 1937. By comparison, in 1979, the year following the black priesthood revelation, the growth rate stood at 6.7 percent.[26]

Uchtdorf's acknowledgment that general authorities had "said or done things" that caused disaffection revealed that church leaders were beginning to take seriously the Faith Crisis reports. Stratford's work, with Jensen's guidance and support, produced the desired results. In December 2013, some two months after Uchtdorf's general conference address, the LDS church published the first of what became known as the "Gospel Topics Essays." Several

---

24. Dieter F. Uchtdorf, "Come, Join with Us," *Conference Report* (Oct. 2013), at www.lds.org/general-conference/2013/10/come-join-with-us?lang=eng.

25. Uchtdorf, "Come, Join with Us." See also Laurie Goodstein, "A Top Mormon Leader Acknowledges the Church 'Made Mistakes,'" *New York Times*, Oct. 5, 2013. Despite Uchtdorf's acknowledgment about LDS leadership's culpability in LDS disaffection, some LDS writers continue to place the onus on rank-and-file members. See, for example, Robert L. Millett, *Whatever Happened to Faith?* (Salt Lake City: Deseret Book Co., 2017), chap. 5 ("Why People Leave").

26. For the 2016 statistical report, see "2015 Statistical Report for April 2016 General Conference," *LDS Newsroom*, Apr. 2, 2016, at www.mormonnewsroom.org/article/2015-statistical-report-April-2016-general-conference. For the 1937 statistical report, see Jana Riess, "Mormon Growth Slows to Its Lowest Level Since 1937, *Colorado Springs Gazette*, Apr. 19, 2016; and Riess, *The Next Mormons*, 6. The best source for LDS membership growth is David G. Stewart Jr. and Matt Martinich, *Reaching the Nations: International LDS Church Growth Almanac 2014 edition*, 3 vols. (Privately published by David G. Stewart, 2013).

general authorities communicated to Stratford that his work had pushed the "position papers" forward.[27]

———

Other factors hastened the release of the "Gospel Topics Essays." Uchtdorf, along with other LDS leaders, expressed unease about "sensitive issues" affecting the church's growth rate. Church scholars, primarily BYU professors, had addressed the topic through numerous publications. In 1998, Deseret Book, the church's press, published *Answers: Straightforward Answers to Tough Gospel Questions.* Six years later Deseret Book published *Getting at the Truth: Responding to Difficult Questions about LDS Beliefs,* followed by *No Weapon Shall Prosper: New Light on Sensitive Issues* (2011). After Dehlin and Stratford's surveys, Deseret Book published four additional books: *The Crucible of Doubt: Reflections on the Quest for Faith* (2014); *Planted: Belief and Belonging in an Age of Doubt* (2015); *A Reason for Faith: Navigating LDS Doctrine and Church History* (2016); and *Letters to a Young Mormon* (2018). Likewise, the church has relied on apologetic websites like *FAIRMORMON: Critical Questions, Faithful Answers, The Interpreter Foundation,* and *The Neal A. Maxwell Institute of Religious Scholarship* at BYU to address problematic historical and doctrinal issues.[28]

---

27. Stratford, "LDS Faith Crisis Timeline." An LDS general authority (whom we have chosen not to identify by name) also conveyed to Matthew Harris that Stratford played a significant role in getting the "Gospel Topics Essays" released.

28. Joseph Fielding McConkie, *Answers: Straightforward Answers to Tough Gospel Questions* (Salt Lake City: Deseret Book Co., 1998); Robert L. Millet, *Getting at the Truth: Responding to Difficult Questions about LDS Beliefs* (Salt Lake City: Deseret Book Co., 2004); Robert L. Millet, ed., *No Weapon Shall Prosper: New Light on Sensitive Issues* (Salt Lake City: Deseret Book Co., 2011); Terryl Givens and Fiona Givens, *The Crucible of Doubt: Reflections On the Quest for Faith* (Salt Lake City: Deseret Book Co., 2014); Patrick Q. Mason, *Planted: Belief and Belonging in an Age of Doubt* (Salt Lake City: Deseret Book Co. and Neal A. Maxwell Institute, 2015); Laura Harris Hales, ed., *A Reason for Doubt: Navigating LDS Doctrine and Church History* (Provo/Salt Lake City: BYU Religious Studies Center/Deseret Book Co., 2016); Adam S. Miller, *Letters to a Young Mormon,* 2nd ed. (Salt Lake City: Deseret Book Co. and Neal A. Maxwell Institute, 2018). The church has also relied on apologetic websites like *FAIRMORMON: Critical Questions, Faithful Answers* (www.fairmormon.org), *The Interpreter Foundation* (www.interpreterfoundation.org) and *The Neal A. Maxwell Institute of Religious Scholarship* at BYU (formerly part of the Foundation of Ancient Research and Mormon Studies; www.maxwellinstitute.byu.edu).

All such efforts notwithstanding, Latter-day Saints continue to leave the church in significant numbers, especially millennials, disturbed by controversial information found online. "Never before have we had this information age with social networking and bloggers publishing unvetted points of view," Marlin Jensen candidly observed.[29] According to a report prepared for general authorities in 2008, the activity rate of "young single adults" was 30 percent in North America and 20 percent internationally. The overall activity rate was 25 percent, the report noted, indicating that Mormon millennials were leaving the church on a level comparable to their Evangelical, Protestant, and Catholic counterparts.[30] With the proliferation of websites critical of the LDS Church, the activity rate among millennials has dipped even further since 2008. "Only 64 percent of Mormon millennials are sticking with the faith," *Salt Lake Tribune* religion reporter Peggy Fletcher Stack noted in 2016. "That's down dramatically from the 90 percent reported three and four decades ago and has steadily slipped from 72 percent in the early 2000s to 70 percent in 2007."[31] In an

---

29. Jenson, quoted in Stack, "Mormons Tackling Tough Questions in Their History." Latter-day Saints are not the only faith group feeling the effects of the modern age. For a study of the internet on Catholic faith communities, see Patricia Wittberg, *Building Strong Church Communities: A Sociological Overview* (Mahwah, New Jersey: Paulist Press, 2012).

30. In 2008, BYU professor and former LDS mission president Alan Wilkins made a private presentation to general authorities discussing youth activity rates in the church. This presentation was subsequently leaked to the public. Jana Riess, "Worldwide, Only 25 Percent of Young Single Mormons Are Active in the LDS Church," *Religious News Service*, Oct. 5, 2016, at www.religionnews.com/2016/10/05/leaked-worldwide-only-25-of-young-single-mormons-are-active-in-the-lds-church; "What's in the Leaked Videos of Meetings with Senior LDS Church Leaders?" *Deseret News*, Oct. 2, 2016; Matt Canham et al., "A Brief Look at What's in Leaked Mormon Videos," *Salt Lake Tribune*, Oct. 4, 2016; Riess, *The Next Mormons*, 7. On religious disaffection among Protestant, Catholic, and Evangelical millennials, see Robert D. Putnam and David E. Campbell, *American Grace: How Religion Divides and Unites Us* (New York: Simon and Schuster, 2010), 100–11, 120–33; and Robert P. Jones, Daniel Cox, Betsy Cooper, and Rachel Lienesch, "Exodus: Why Americans are Leaving Religion—and Why They're Unlikely to Come Back," report of the Public Religion Research Institute (Sept. 22, 2016), at www.prri.org/research/prri-rns-poll-nones-atheist-leaving-religion.

31. Stack, "More Mormon Millennials Are Delaying Marriage, Leaving Their Faith," *Salt Lake Tribune*, Apr. 15, 2016. See also Jana Riess, "Are Mormons in Their 20s and 30s Leaving the LDS Church?" *Religious News Service*, Apr. 14, 2016, at www.religionnews.com/2016/04/14/mormons-20s-30s-leaving-lds-church. See also [no

interview with *BYU Magazine* in 2014, BYU history professor and newly named director of the Maxwell Institute Spencer Fluhman addressed the problem, admitting that "Latter-day Saints have experienced crises of faith throughout the history of the Church, but the number of those asking hard questions or finding themselves in faith crisis has increased with the advent of the Internet." He further explained that the "information explosion exposed Latter-day Saints to a wider range of information about their faith and about their past." Fellow BYU religion professor Rachel Cope concurred: "More students are coming across information on the Internet that they haven't been exposed to before. They do not know how to process these new details and in many cases feel a betrayal of trust." The two professors also noted "the issues that most often come up [in class] include polygamy, women and the priesthood, race and the priesthood restriction before 1978, sexual orientation, and the translations of the Book of Mormon and the Book of Abraham."[32]

Four websites, in particular, have provided the impetus for LDS disaffection. One of the most influential sites is Jeremy Runnells's *Letter to a CES Director.* Runnells, himself an LDS millennial, was an orthodox member of the LDS Church until he encountered information on the internet disclosing controversial aspects of LDS origins and practices. Anguished over such disclosures, he reached out to family and church leaders in expressing his doubts. When such efforts failed to assuage his concerns, he assembled a lengthy list of questions and sent them in the form of a letter to a Church Education System director who promised a response. The director's lack of response prompted Runnells to go public. In April 2013, he posted his "CES Letter" online, and within days it went viral, generating thousands of hits.[33]

author] "America's Changing Religious Landscape," *Pew Research Center,* May 12, 2015, at www.pewforum.org/2015/05/12/americas-changing-religious-landscape; David Masci, "Why Millennials Are Less Religious than Older Americans," *Pew Research Center,* Jan. 8, 2016, at www.pewresearch.org/fact-tank/2016/01/08/qa-why-millennials-are-less-religious-than-older-americans.

32. Fluhman and Cope, as quoted in Sue M. Bergin, "Keeping the Faith," *BYU Magazine,* Spring 2014, at www.magazine.byu.edu/?act=view&a=3306.

33. "Letters to a CES Director": http://cesletter.com. In 2016, Runnells resigned from the LDS Church before church officials took punitive action against him for

Concurrently, a second, more heavily-trafficked website, elicited attention. *Ex-Mormon Reddit*, founded in 2009, contains hundreds of stories explaining why Latter-day Saints leave the church or are in the process of leaving. Edgy and provocative, the site offers a platform for Latter-day Saints to express their doubts about LDS teachings and policies, often in a jocular way. It publishes "leaked" LDS-oriented documents providing fodder to critics who believe that the church is hiding its history.[34] When the site began tracking subscribers in 2012, it had over 5,000. Four years later in 2016, the website traffic swelled to over 50,000 viewers, a ten-fold increase.[35]

MormonThink and *Mormon Stories*, both of which Hans Mattsson reviewed prior to his departure from the LDS Church, are also influential websites.[36] Established in 2008, *MormonThink* touts itself as "neither anti-Mormon" nor apologetic, but "rather concerned with truth." It purports to offer "the strongest and most compelling arguments and explanations from both the critics and the defenders of the Church." Neatly arranged into several categories, the site includes information on an array of topics, from polygamy to church finances. Accompanying each topic is a brief commentary challenging the official church explanation. Today, *MormonThink* continues to have a following, though arguably it has been superseded by *Letter to a CES Director* and *Ex-Mormon Reddit* as the preferred sites for disaffected Latter-day Saints.[37]

Mormon Stories, by contrast, is a lively and controversial podcast started by John Dehlin in 2005. For over ten years, Dehlin has interviewed dozens of Latter-day Saints who have discussed their

---

promoting controversial LDS teachings. Peggy Fletcher Stack, "Author of 'Letter to a CES Director' Resigns from Mormon Church," *Salt Lake Tribune*, Apr. 18, 2016.

34. *Ex-Mormon Reddit*: www.reddit.com/r/exmormon. See "Mormon File Leaks," www.reddit.com/r/Mormonleaks; Laurie Goodstein, "Leaked Videos Pull Back Curtain on Mormon Leadership," *New York Times*, Oct. 6, 2016; and Peggy Fletcher Stack, "New Website Plans to Showcase Leaked Mormon Documents," *Salt Lake Tribune*, Dec. 17, 2016.

35. For data on Ex-Mormon Reddit, see "exmormon metrics," at www.reddit-metrics.com/r/exmormon.

36. Mattsson, Email to Harris, Jan. 30, 2017.

37. *MormonThink*, at www.mormonthink.com. See also D. Jeff Burton's interview with the founder of *MormonThink*, in "Anonymous Confessions of an LDS Webmaster," *Sunstone*, July 2008, 67–69. Website traffic for *MormonThink* is not available.

"faith crisis" on his podcast, allowing listeners to forge connections and sympathies as they shared their concerns about the church.[38] The most prominent podcasters include Kate Kelley of the Ordain Women Movement, who was excommunicated in 2014 and Christine Jeppsen Clark, the daughter of LDS general authority Malcolm Jeppsen, who resigned her membership in 2014. Also popular is Laura Roper Andreasen, the granddaughter of Apostle Russell Ballard, who resigned from the LDS Church in 2015. And finally, Hans Mattsson of Swedish Rescue fame, explained his struggles with the church, motivated by the discovery of books and internet sites causing him to question his LDS faith.[39]

As these websites gained traction over the years, the church responded, urging members to combat the negative websites by flooding "the earth through social media." In a devotional address at Brigham Young University in 2014, Apostle David A. Bednar instructed Saints to provide positive and uplifting stories about the church on their Facebook pages, twitter accounts, and blog sites. "Our messages should seek to edify and uplift rather than to argue, debate, condemn, or belittle," the apostle urged. Latter-day Saints should share "the gospel with genuine love and concern for

---

38. For more information about *Mormon Stories*, see www.mormonstories.org/about. For Mattson's interview, see *Mormon Stories*, July 22, 2013, at www.mormonstories.org/hans-mattsson. Like Jeremy Runnells, John Dehlin was also forced out of the LDS Church. He was excommunicated in 2015 in part because of his "internet presence" challenging "the doctrines of the church." Peggy Fletcher Stack, "Mormon Critic John Dehlin Is Excommunicated," *Salt Lake Tribune*, Feb. 10, 2015.

39. "Neil Ransom and Kate Kelley—After Kate's Excommunication," *Mormon Stories*, July 26, 2014, at www.mormonstories.org/neil-ransom-and-kate-kelly-after-kates-excommunication; "Christine Jeppsen Clark, Daughter of General Authority Malcolm Jeppsen," ibid., July 7, 2014, at www.mormonstories.org/christine-jeppsen-clark-daughter-of-general-authority-malcolm-jeppsen; "Laura Roper Andreasen—Granddaughter of LDS Apostle M. Russell Ballard," ibid., Nov. 18, 2015, at www.mormonstories.org/laura-roper-andreasen-granddaughter-m-russell-ballard; "Hans Mattsson—Former LDS Area Authority Seventy (Sweden)," ibid., July 22, 2013, at www.mormonstories.org/hans-mattsson. The site also includes stories from faithful Latter-day Saints, including Columbia University historian Richard Bushman and BYU law professor Edward L. Kimball, son of LDS President Spencer W. Kimball. "Richard Bushman, Part 1—Experiences as a Mormon Historian," ibid., Jan. 22, 2007, at www.mormonstories.org/richard-bushman-and-rough-stone-rolling-part-1-experiences-as-a-mormon-historian; "Edward L. Kimball, Son of Spencer W. Kimball, Parts 1 and 2," ibid., Mar. 31, 2010, at www.mormonstories.org/137-138-edward-kimball-son-of-spencer-w-kimball-parts-1-2.

others. Be courageous and bold but not overbearing in sustaining and defending our beliefs, and avoid contention."[40] The First Presidency and Quorum of the Twelve echoed Bednar's call, tweeting uplifting stories and faith-promoting experiences. Members can now "Follow the Brethren on Social Media" through an official LDS website at churchofjesuschrist.org.[41]

Meanwhile, as orthodox and discontented Latter-day Saints discussed their faith on the internet, church president Thomas S. Monson, who was keenly aware of LDS disaffection, oversaw a strategy to counter it. As late as 2008, he made reclaiming those disgruntled Latter-day Saints the central focus of his ministry, aptly summed up in the title of his biography *To the Rescue*.[42] During Monson's presidency, the First Presidency and other general authorities initiated a carefully-orchestrated campaign to produce a more honest, accurate history. They commissioned a number of projects designed to promote greater transparency.[43] With funding from private donors, they supported a multi-volume project to publish the Joseph Smith Papers, both in print

---

40. Bednar, BYU Education Week devotional address, Aug. 19, 2014, "Flood the Earth Through Social Media," *Liahona*, Aug. 2015, at www.lds.org/liahona/2015/08/youth/flood-the-earth-through-social-media?lang=eng. Patrick Q. Mason, "Mormon Blogs, Mormon Studies, and the Mormon Mind," *Dialogue: A Journal of Mormon Thought* 45 (Fall 2012): 12–25, offers a brief analysis of important LDS blogs. However, more work needs to be done with blog sites critical of the LDS faith and the affect they have on orthodox Latter-day Saints.

41. "Follow the Brethren on Social Media," *LDS.org*, at www.lds.org/prophets-and-apostles/unto-all-the-world/social-media-and-the-brethren?lang=eng; Lindsey Williams, "LDS General Authorities Reflect on Conference through Social Media Posts," *Deseret News*, Apr. 5, 2016.

42. Heidi S. Swinton, *To the Rescue: The Biography of Thomas S. Monson* (Salt Lake City: Deseret Book Co., 2010). In addition, Marlin Jensen identified Monson's focus in reclaiming disaffected members as a "rescue." For this point, see Henderson and Cooke, "Special Report: Mormonism Besieged by the Modern Age." See also Thomas S. Monson, "Reach Out to Rescue," *Teachings of Thomas S. Monson* (Salt Lake City: Church of Jesus Christ of Latter-day Saints, 2013), at www.lds.org/prophets-and-apostles/unto-all-the-world/monson-encourages-members-to-reach-out?lang=eng.

43. J. B. Haws, *The Mormon Image in the American Mind: Fifty Years of Public Perception* (New York: Oxford University Press, 2013), 188–90; Marlin K. Jensen, "Minding the House of Church History: Reflections of a Church Historian at the End of His Time," *Journal of Mormon History* 39 (Spring 2013): 85–87; and Robert D. McFadden, "Thomas Monson, President of the Mormon Church, Dies at 90," *New York Times*, Jan. 3, 2018, who explained: "Mr. Monson displayed a new openness to scholars of Mormonism, … allowing them remarkable access to church records."

and online.[44] To facilitate access to materials previously unavailable to scholars, leaders sanctioned the digitization of unpublished manuscripts on the Church History Library webpage.[45] The First Presidency and Quorum of the Twelve also approved the publication of the previously-restricted Council of Fifty Minutes as well as certain unpublished documents chronicling the early turbulent years of the Relief Society.[46] Further, they allowed inclusion of several First Vision accounts into a new Church Museum video and cooperated in the publication of books dealing with sensitive issues involving early church leaders.[47] In addition, senior church leaders released a photograph and supported the publication of

---

44. As of 2020, twenty-two volumes have been published. Twenty-seven volumes are expected to be published altogether (www.josephsmithpapers.org/articles/published-volumes). Utah philanthropists and Latter-day Saints Larry and Gayle Miller helped to fund the Smith Papers project. Tad Walch, "Miller Funding Joseph Smith Project," *Deseret News*, Apr. 5, 2005. Scholars have already begun to make copious use of the Smith papers. See Mark Ashurst-McGee, Robin Jensen, and Sharalyn D. Howcroft, eds., *Foundational Texts of Mormonism: Examining Major Early Sources* (New York: Oxford University Press, 2018).

45. R. Scott Lloyd, "Millions of LDS Documents Images Now Online," *Deseret News*, June 29, 2012; "Online Resources," Church History Library (Feb. 24, 2015), at www.history.lds.org/article/web-resources?lang=eng.

46. R. Scott Lloyd, "Council of Fifty Minutes to Be Published in Joseph Smith Papers," *Church News*, Sept. 20, 2016, at www.lds.org/church/news/council-of-fifty-minutes-to-be-published-in-joseph-smith-papers-release?lang=eng; Matthew J. Grow et al., eds., *The Joseph Smith Papers, Administrative Records, Council of Fifty Minutes: March 1844-January 1846*, vol. 9 (Salt Lake City: Church Historian's Press, 2016); Jill Mulvay Derr et. al., eds., *The First Fifty Years of Relief Society: Key Documents in Latter-day Saint Women's History* (Salt Lake City: Church Historian's Press, 2016).

47. Jannalee Rosner, "Elder Holland: Several First Vision Accounts Used in New Church Museum Video," *LDS Living* (2015), at www.ldsliving.com/Elder-Holland-Several-First-Vision-Accounts-Used-in-New-Church-Museum-Video/s/80121. Richard Lyman Bushman, *Joseph Smith: Rough Stone Rolling* (New York: Alfred A. Knopf, 2005); Ronald W. Walker, Richard E. Turley Jr., Glen M. Leonard, *Massacre at Mountain Meadows* (New York: Oxford University Press, 2011); John G. Turner, *Brigham Young: Pioneer Prophet* (Cambridge, Massachusetts: Harvard University Press, 2012); Carol Cornwall Madsen, *Emmeline B. Wells: An Intimate History* (Salt Lake City: University of Utah Press, 2016); Laurel Thatcher Ulrich, *A House Full of Females: Plural Marriage and Women's Rights in Early Mormonism, 1835–1870* (New York: Alfred A. Knopf, 2017); Steven C. Harper, *First Vision: Memory and Mormon Origins* (New York: Oxford University Press, 2019); Terryl Givens (with Brian Hauglid), *The Pearl of Greatest Price: Mormonism's Most Controversial Scripture* (New York: Oxford University Press, 2019). See also Haws, *Mormon Image*, 189. Deseret Book Company, the official LDS publishing house, also deserves some credit for improving transparency within LDS biography. See, for example, Edward L. Kimball, *Lengthen Your Stride: The Presidency of Spencer W. Kimball* (Salt Lake City: Deseret Book Co.,

an article and book showcasing a controversial seer stone that Joseph Smith had used in translating the Book of Mormon.[48]

Most importantly, church leaders commissioned and participated in the production of a series of thirteen essays acknowledging openly and candidly thorny issues that had once been considered taboo by earlier church leaders.[49] This involved a collaborative effort of church historians, outside scholars, and general authorities, in which the church revised its "Gospel Topics" section on the church's official website. Its intended purpose was to provide a resource for Latter-day Saints struggling with challenging LDS teachings.[50] General authority Steven E. Snow, who replaced

---

2005); and Robert I. Eaton and Henry J. Eyring, *I Will Lead You Along: The Life of Henry B. Eyring* (Salt Lake City: Deseret Book Co., 2013).

48. Peggy Fletcher Stack, "Mormon Church Releases Photos of 'Seer Stones' Used by Church Founder Joseph Smith," *Salt Lake Tribune*, Sept. 13, 2015; R. Scott Lloyd, "Book of Mormon Printer's Manuscript, Photos of Seer Stone Featured in New Book," *Church News*, Aug. 6, 2015, at www.lds.org/church/news/book-of-mormon-printers-manuscript-photos-of-seer-stone-featured-in-new-book?lang=eng; Richard E. Turley Jr. et al., "Joseph the Seer," *Ensign*, Oct. 2015, at www.lds.org/ensign/2015/10/joseph-the-seer?lang=eng; Michael Hubbard MacKay and Nicholas J. Frederick, *Joseph Smith's Seer Stones* (Provo/Salt Lake City: BYU Religious Studies Center/Deseret Book Co., 2016).

49. The essays are published as "Gospel Topics Essays" on the official LDS website: www.lds.org/topics/essays?lang=eng. The challenge of writing LDS history within LDS institutional constraints is discussed in Gregory A. Prince, *Leonard Arrington and the Writing of Mormon History* (Salt Lake City: University of Utah Press, 2016); Leonard J. Arrington, *Adventures of a Church Historian* (Urbana: University of Illinois Press, 1998); Ronald W. Walker, David J. Whittaker, James B. Allen, *Mormon History* (Urbana: University of Illinois Press, 2001); George D. Smith, ed., *Faithful History: Essays on Writing Mormon History* (Salt Lake City: Signature Books, 1992); D. Michael Quinn, ed., *The New Mormon History: Revisionist Essays on the Past* (Salt Lake City: Signature Books, 1992); Richard Lyman Bushman, *On the Road with Joseph Smith: An Author's Diary* (Salt Lake City: Greg Kofford Books, 2007); Alexander L. Baugh and Reid L. Neilson, eds., *Conversations with Mormon Historians* (Salt Lake City: Deseret Book Co., 2015); and James B. Allen, "On Writing Church History: Personal Reflections on Writing, Publishing, and Republishing *The Story of the Latter-day Saints*," *Journal of Mormon History* 41 (Jan. 2015): 45–63.

50. Michael Otterson, managing director of LDS Public Affairs, acknowledged the collaborative effort. "None of these essays are the product of a single author," he explained. Each "is the product of multiple contributors and a rigorous editing and revision process, with ultimate review and approval conducted by the First Presidency and the Quorum of the Twelve Apostles." Otterson, Email to Matthew L. Harris, Feb. 24, 2014. See also Tad Walch, "LDS Church Enhances Web Pages on its History, Doctrine," *Deseret News*, Dec. 9, 2013; and the "gospel topics" page link titled "What About Historical Questions." There Snow describes the

Marlin Jensen as Church Historian and Recorder in 2012, noted that the essays will "provide a series of answers that will help our members better understand these chapters in our history." The "Gospel Topics Essays," he further explained, will provide Latter-day Saints with answers to difficult "gospel" questions. General authority Paul B. Pieper added that the essays would "strengthen their testimony and deepen their conversion."[51]

The first essay appeared coincidentally online on November 20, 2013, a month after Uchtdorf's controversial general conference sermon, and the final one posted nearly two years later on October 23, 2015.[52] The essays cover virtually every major issue that respondents expressed concern about in the Dehlin and Stratford surveys, specifically multiple accounts of the First Vision, the translation of the Book of Mormon, the ancient historicity of the Book of Abraham, the priesthood and temple restriction for black people, polygamy/polyandry, the Mountain Meadows Massacre, blood atonement, women and the priesthood, and changing positions of science and DNA within the church. Three controversial topics not covered are the possible connections between Masonry and LDS temple rituals, the ancient historicity of the Book of Mormon, and issues involving LBGTQ people and the church.[53]

---

collaboration among scholars, church historians, and general authorities (www.lds.org/topics#media=11373505780672488714-eng).

51. Snow and Pieper both quoted in Tad Walch, "LDS Church Enhances Web Pages on Its History, Doctrine," *Deseret News*, Dec. 9, 2014.

52. "New Essays Address Topics on Women, Priesthood, Mother in Heaven: Essays Complete Series of 13 Begun in 2013," *LDS Newsroom* (Oct. 23, 2015), at www.mormonnewsroom.org/article/new-church-essays-women-priesthood-mother-in-heaven.

53. On Mormons and Masonry, see Michael W. Homer, "'Similarity of Priesthood in Masonry': The Relationship between Freemasonry and Mormonism," *Dialogue: A Journal of Mormon Thought* 27 (Fall 1994): 1–113; Michael W. Homer, *Joseph's Temples: The Dynamic Relationship Between Freemasonry and Mormonism* (Salt Lake City: University of Utah Press, 2014). For scholarship on the historicity of the Book of Mormon, see Terryl L. Givens, *By the Hand of Mormon: The American Scripture that Launched a New World Religion* (New York: Oxford University Press, 2002); Elizabeth Fenton and Jared Hickman, eds., *Americanist Approaches to the Book of Mormon* (New York: Oxford University Press, 2019); and William L. Davis, *Visions in a Seer Stone: Joseph Smith and the Making of the Book of Mormon* (Chapel Hill: University of North Carolina Press, 2020). For an appraisal of LDS sexuality, especially LGBT issues, see D. Michael Quinn, *Same-Sex Dynamics Among Nineteenth-Century Americans: A Mormon Example* (Urbana: University of Illinois Press, 2001); Gregory A. Prince, *Gay Rights and the Mormon Church: Intended Actions, Unintended Consequences* (Salt Lake City: University

The public rollout of the essays was deliberately low-keyed, demonstrating LDS leaders' ambivalence in exposing church members to controversial topics. Apart from a handful of interviews that Steven Snow gave to journalists, there were "no news releases and no fanfare."[54] Church officials strategically buried the essays on the church website in an effort to downplay them—according to reliable sources involved with the process.[55] The First Presidency and the Quorum of the Twelve, moreover, declined to sign the essays or publish them in the *Ensign*, the official church magazine. The essays received no exposure in general conference and minimal exposure in ward meetinghouses. The only acknowledgment that senior leaders made during the first year of the rollout involved a 2014 statement from the LDS Church newsroom along with a private memorandum from the church priesthood department to "General Authorities, Area Seventies, Stake, Mission, and District Presidents, Bishops and Branch Presidents." Leaders asserted that the "purpose of the Gospel Topics section is to provide accurate and transparent information on church history and doctrine within the framework of faith when church members have questions regarding [LDS] history and doctrine."[56]

Not surprisingly, the low-keyed release of the essays posed challenges for Latter-day Saints who tried to utilize them in teaching Sunday school classes. "Few Mormons seem to know about them," one report noted. Other church members rejected the idea that they bore the imprimatur of the church.[57] This, in

---

of Utah Press, 2019); Taylor G. Petrey, "Toward a Post-Heterosexual Mormon Theology," *Dialogue: A Journal of Mormon Thought* 44 (Winter 2011): 106–141; Taylor G. Petrey, *Tabernacles of Clay: Sexuality and Gender in Modern Mormonism* (Chapel Hill: University of North Carolina Press, 2020); and Riess, *The Next Mormons*, 140–46.

54. Peggy Fletcher Stack, "Mormon Leaders Spread Word about Controversial Essays," *Salt Lake Tribune*, Oct. 21, 2014.

55. This has been confirmed to us by three sources with direct knowledge of the layout of the essays.

56. "Church Provides Context for Recent Media Coverage on Gospel Topics Pages," LDS Newsroom (Nov. 11, 2014), at www.mormonnewsroom.org/article/church-provides-context-gospel-topics-pages; "LDS Church Responds to National Media Coverage of Gospel Topics Pages," *Deseret News*, Nov. 11, 2014; Stack, "Mormon Leaders Spread Word."

57. Stack, "Mormon Leaders Spread Word"; Stack, "New Mormon Mission: How to Teach Members the Messy Part of LDS History, Theology," *Salt Lake Tribune*, Mar. 8, 2015.

turn, led to confusion within the church, as when a Sunday school teacher in Hawaii taught from one of the essays, which raised the ire of his local ward bishop who released the hapless teacher from teaching, accusing him of using unauthorized sources. Similarly, a group of BYU professors and students "met ... resistance from fellow Mormons" who derided the essays "as not official but merely Public Affairs pieces."[58] These are not isolated incidences. Scores of comparable stories on LDS blog sites prompted journalist Peggy Fletcher Stack to write: "Memo to Mormons: Those Essays Have Been Approved by the Faith's Highest Leaders."[59]

As late as 2015, church leaders recognized this problem and began taking measures to address it. In September of that year, Apostle Russell M. Ballard promoted the essays at a regional conference in Utah explaining that the "Church is dedicated to transparency and has donated precious resources to provide new insights and offer even more context to the story of the Restoration through the Joseph Smith Papers website and the Gospel Topics Essays on LDS.org." Five months later in February 2016, Ballard endorsed the essays to a group of Church Education System teachers counseling them to learn "these Essays like you know the back of your hand," adding that "Gone are the days when a student asked an honest question and a teacher responded, 'Don't worry about it!'"[60] That same year, church officials continued to promote the essays as "background reading" for students at Brigham

---

58. Peggy Fletcher Stack, "This Mormon Sunday School Teacher Was Dismissed for Using Church's Own Race Essay in Lesson," *Salt Lake Tribune*, May 5, 2015; Stack, "New Mormon Mission."

59. Peggy Fletcher Stack, "Memo to Mormons: Those Essays Have Been Approved by the Faith's Highest Leaders," *Salt Lake Tribune*, June 26, 2015.

60. Ballard, "To the Saints in the Utah South Area," address given to 235 stakes in Utah South Area, Sept. 13, 2015, at www.lds.org/prophets-and-apostles/unto-all-the-world/to-the-saints-in-the-utah-south-area?lang=eng; Ballard, "The Opportunities and Responsibilities of CES Teachers in the 21st Century," address to CES Religious Educators, Feb. 26, 2016, at www.lds.org/broadcasts/article/evening-with-a-general-authority/2016/02/the-opportunities-and-responsibilities-of-ces-teachers-in-the-21st-century?lang=eng. See also Peggy Fletcher Stack, "Apostle Tells Mormon Educators: Don't Duck Tough Questions—Whether about Polygamy, Priesthood or Other Topics," *Salt Lake Tribune*, Mar. 4, 2016; Marianne Holman Prescott, "An Evening with a General Authority: Elder Ballard," *Deseret News*, Feb. 27, 2016.

Young University and in the Church Education System, providing supplemental material to the lesson manual. Moreover, church officials authorized a revised curriculum for LDS young adults dealing with "sensitive issues"[61] and commissioned scholars to incorporate essential elements of the essays into "Mormon [Sunday school] lessons" as well as a new four-volume history of the church.[62] Church leaders also addressed the "different accounts" of the First Vision during firesides for college-aged youth. Ultimately, in 2016, leaders mandated a Gospel Essays app to enable church members to utilize the essays quickly and expeditiously.[63]

In addressing the issue of why the church was not doing more to promote the essays, Church Historian Steven Snow frankly admitted it "was a soft roll out. There wasn't an announcement saying 'You can go to this website to learn everything weird about the

---

61. For the revised curriculum, see "Foundations of the Restoration—Religion C-225," May 2017, Harris files (courtesy of J. B. Haws, BYU religion department); *Foundations of the Restoration Teacher Manual* (Salt Lake City: Church of Jesus Christ of Latter-day Saints, 2015), at www.lds.org/manual/foundations-of-the-restoration-teacher-manual?lang=eng; *Teachings in the Savior's Way* (Salt Lake City: Church of Jesus Christ of Latter-day Saints, 2016), at www.lds.org/manual/teaching-in-the-saviors-way?lang=eng. See also "New LDS Church History Seminary Manual Addresses Sensitive Issues," *Utah Valley 360,* Feb. 13, 2014, at www.utahvalley360.com/2014/02/13/new-lds-church-history-seminary-manual-addresses-sensitive-issues.

62. The essays are published in *Revelations in Context* (Salt Lake City: Church of Jesus Christ of Latter-day Saints, 2016), at www.history.lds.org/section/revelations?lang=eng; "Revelations in Context Provides the Stories Behind D&C Sections," *Church News,* Dec. 21, 2016, at www.lds.org/church/news/revelations-in-context-provides-the-stories-behind-dc-sections?lang=eng; Peggy Fletcher Stack, "New Scholarship Coming to Mormon Lessons, but Will Instructions Really Teach It?" *Salt Lake Tribune,* Dec. 21, 2016. For the four-volume history, see "Church Historian Announces New Four-Volume History of the Church," *Church News,* June 4, 2017, at www.lds.org/church/news/church-historian-announces-new-4-volume-history-of-the-church?lang=eng. Two volumes in the "Saints" series have already been published: Scott A. Hales et al., *The Standard of Truth, 1815–1846* (Salt Lake City: Church of Jesus Christ of Latter-day Saints, 2018); and Scott A. Hales et al., *No Unhallowed Hand, 1846–1893* (Salt Lake City: Church of Jesus Christ of Latter-day Saints, 2019). The last two volumes will be published in 2020 and 2021, respectively.

63. Richard J. Maynes, "The Truth Restored," address for young adults, Salt Lake Tabernacle, May 1, 2016, at www.lds.org/broadcasts/article/worldwide-devotionals/2016/01/the-truth-restored?lang=eng. See also Marianne Holman Prescott, "LDS Leader Speaks to Young Adults about Different Accounts of Church Founder's First Vision," *Deseret News,* May 1, 2016; David Noyce, "Mormon Leader; Differing Versions of Joseph Smith's 'First Vision' Make It the 'Best-Documented in History,'" *Salt Lake Tribune,* May 2, 2016; Tad Walch, "Essays on Mormon History, Doctrine Find New Visibility in Official App, Sunday School," *Deseret News,* Dec. 31, 2016.

Mormon church you ever wanted to learn.'" Snow and his fellow general authorities understood the controversial content of the essays, some of which repudiated teachings from earlier leaders, others acknowledging troubling episodes in early church history that had been previously downplayed or completely ignored. Snow stated, "I don't think you are gonna see a well-publicized campaign to tell you to go to these sites." The Essays, he further conceded, were commissioned for the "rising generation [to] inoculate" them from troubling information found online. "We were losing young people particularly," Snow confessed. "And we felt we owed a safe place for people to go to get [their questions] answered."[64]

But spreading the essays generated some concern among rank-and-file members. A BYU-Idaho student became disturbed after reading the essay explaining how "Joseph Smith had translated the Book of Mormon by looking at a stone in a hat." He believed that it was "false doctrine" and vowed "to pull up some primary sources" to prove the teaching wrong. He continued: "Once I started searching, I came across this recently published essay on LDS. org. It talked openly about the translation process of the Book of Mormon. It shocked me. My issue with it was that the narrative it laid out was completely different from the one I'd grown up learning about. I frantically searched the footnotes of the essay for some sort of an explanation. However, the more I searched the more confused I became." Before long, the young man became disillusioned and left the church, wondering "Why wasn't I ever told [about] any of this?"[65]

A one-time LDS bishop in New Zealand also found the essays

---

64. John Dehlin, "BONUS: Elder Steven E. Snow Candidly Explains Why the LDS Gospel Topics Essays Are Not Publicized by the Church," *Mormon Stories*, July 16, 2016, at www.mormonstories.org/elder-steven-e-snow-lds-gospel-topics-essays-not-advertisex; Walch, "Essays on Mormon History, Doctrine." See also Rick Bennett, "Elder Snow's Role with the Gospel Topics Essays," *Gospel Tangents*, July 30, 2019, at www.gospeltangents.com/category/gospel-topics-essays.

65. Austin Hales, "A Parting of Ways: Why I Decided to Leave Mormonism" (blog), July 17, 2016, at www.medium.com/@austinhale/a-parting-of-ways-why-I-decided-to-leave-mormonism-44824a3b2d63#.kdnwvohd6. Thanks to Julie Reidhead for providing this reference. See also Colleen McDannell, *Sister Saints: Mormon Women Since the End of Polygamy* (New York: Oxford University Press, 2019), 190, who wrote: "The new historical honesty unsettled many Mormon women and some even felt deceived."

troubling. "Though I haven't left the church, this shift to more transparency is a challenge for me. ... Not because I don't welcome these revisions. They seem very fair and thoroughly researched. But like my fellow high priests, I too used these now discarded explanations and doctrines throughout my leadership to teach—and now I'm left to wonder." He continued: "As a former Bishop I am perplexed. I have repeated stories to my ward to justify particular church practices. I have given the hard line on church policies and doctrines and have held people accountable. ... All of this has caused me to grapple with my own questions. Is it possible that I have hurt people with doctrines and dogmas that in the light of these essays seem to sit on shaky ground? I understand how essential it is to 'sustain' the Brethren but these days I live with a caution that those ideals that I believe today could be dismissed by future First Presidencies."[66]

Another Latter-day Saint opined: "Given that they [church leaders] were wrong and it has taken the Brethren this long to admit it, what do we accept now as doctrine that might be repudiated in a few years' time? Where are the curriculum lessons that address our need to deal with institutional and even prophetic error?"[67] Another Latter-day Saint asked: "Where do we draw the line between prophet and man?"[68]

Notwithstanding these admissions, other Latter-day Saints extolled the essays as "a real blessing," reflecting "a maturing church" that is both refreshing and invigorating.[69] LDS historian Richard Bushman, author of an acclaimed biography on Joseph Smith, praised them, commending church leaders for their candor and openness. The "best way to prevent" Latter-day Saints from discovering challenging material online is to tell "the whole story

---

66. Ganesh Cherian, "A Former Bishop's Doctrinal Dilemmas" (blog), posted on *KiwiMormon,* Feb. 12, 2014, at www.patheos.com/blogs/kiwimormon/2014/02/a-former-bishops-doctrinal-dilemmas.

67. Gina Colvin, "Mormons, Mandela, and the Race and Priesthood Statement" (blog), *KiwiMormon,* Dec. 8, 2013, at www.patheos.com/blogs/kiwimormon/2013/12/mormons-mandela-and-the-race-and-priesthood-statement.

68. Janan Russell, quoted in Peggy Fletcher Stack, "On 37th Anniversary of Priesthood Ban's End, Black Mormons Say Race Issues Still Need Attention," *Salt Lake Tribune,* June 8, 2015.

69. Mason, *Planted,* 1.

from the beginning," he noted. "If the disruptive facts are worked into the history Latter-day Saints hear as they grow up, they won't be turned upside down when they come across something else." LDS scholar Terryl Givens agreed, speculating that "if you tell a 12-year-old child that Joseph Smith used a 'peep stone' in a hat to translate the Book of Mormon, he'll think that's cool or interesting. But if they find out about that on the Internet at the age of 50," Givens continued, "they'll ask, 'Why didn't the church tell me?'"[70]

Perhaps First Presidency counselor Uchtdorf put it best when he explained: "Truth and transparency complement each other. We always need to remember that transparency and openness keep us clear of the negative side effects of secrecy or the cliché of faith-promoting rumors."[71]

――――――

The contributors to this volume examine the thirteen Gospel Topics essays published by the Church of Jesus Christ of Latter-day Saints. Each contributor is an experienced, thoughtful scholar; many have written widely on religious thought in general and Mormon history in particular. The writers probe the strengths and weaknesses of the Gospel Topics essays to provide a trenchant, illuminating discussion on salient issues in Mormon history and doctrine. The contributors' use of the Gospel Topics essays reflects the version of the essays posted at the time on the church's lds.org address (since renamed churchofjesuschrist.org) and may not reference changes made to the essays subsequently. The Topics essays have been, and presumably will continue to be, silently revised since they were first published.

We hope that the reflective, wide-ranging essays that follow will spark further discussion about important issues facing the LDS Church today.

---

70. Bushman and Givens, quoted in Stack, "Mormons Tackling Tough Questions in Their History."

71. Uchtdorf, quoted in Catherine Reese Newton, "LDS Leader Tells Mormons to Embrace Their History, Keep Their Faith," *Salt Lake Tribune*, Mar. 17, 2014.

1. ARE MORMONS CHRISTIAN?

Craig L. Blomberg

Views of Mormonism in the broader world have fluctuated considerably over the years.[1] In the last half-century alone, just in the United States, one can trace the ups and downs from when Michigan Governor George W. Romney was a contender for the Republican nomination for a US presidential candidate in 1968 to when his son, Mitt, received that same nomination in 2012. In the late 1960s, Governor Romney's Mormonism was not a major factor in his political successes and failures. When Mitt withdrew from the race in 2008, it was a significant factor, though somewhat less so in 2012. The primary question people were asking across the country was not if Mormons were Christians, but rather if Mormonism was just too "weird" for us to trust someone for president who truly believed all that they believed. Or else people raised concerns about a Mormon candidate having to answer to LDS authorities in Salt Lake City. But in many Evangelical Christian circles, the question of whether Mormons were *bona fide* Christians did seem to matter, because many claimed that they would not vote for a non-Christian candidate.[2]

The question may be raised in its most public form during political campaigns, but it is a question of perennial interest for Evangelicals and, at times, other Protestants, and even for Catholic and Orthodox believers. As liberal and ecumenical as the National Council of Churches is (along with the parent organization, the

---

1. Although the preferred term today is the Church of Jesus Christ of Latter-day Saints, the Gospel Topics essay uses "Mormon" to refer both to the church and to its members (Mormons).

2. See the excellent study by J. B. Haws, *The Mormon Image in the American Mind: Fifty Years of Public Perception* (New York: Oxford University Press, 2013).

World Council of Churches), repeated investigations into the acceptance of baptism in the LDS Church as transferrable to other denominations, along with questions about membership of the LDS in the NCC or WCC, have yet to yield the conclusion that the LDS are similar enough to be considered another fully legitimate form of Christianity.[3]

During the 1980s, arriving at dispassionate opinions was made particularly difficult by the film and book, *The Godmakers*, a scaremongering, sensationalizing, and at times simply inaccurate portrayal of the Mormon faith, which became widely known within the Evangelical community.[4] This was also the era in which Walter Martin's books, some of which were published earlier, were reaching their zenith in popularity and impact.[5] While not nearly as scaremongering or sensationalizing (though his live talks could be), there were still places where his information was inaccurate. At least he did not, nor did other countercult writings and ministries in the last quarter of the twentieth century, tend to distinguish much between what was official LDS doctrine (found in the church's canonized Standard Works) and what was unofficial Mormon folklore or what was semiofficial teaching of respected LDS authorities but not part of Mormon scripture.

As the twentieth century was coming to a close, two major trends began to burgeon that continue to this day. First, individuals in all kinds of churches were creating their own potluck or potpourri of religious beliefs, akin to what Robert Bellah and his colleagues in 1985 reported on as "Sheilaism," after a woman they interviewed named Sheila Larson who described her religion with that term, as she picked and chose whatever resonated most with her personally in her "inner voice."[6] Questions of logical

---

3. A fairly striking observation given the breadth of what the NCC and WCC have been willing to include.

4. Ed Decker and Dave Hunt's movie by that name was released in 1982 and was subsequently made into a book with the same name (Eugene, Oregon: Harvest House, 1984).

5. Most notably, *The Kingdom of the Cults* (Minneapolis: Bethany House, 1965), which has now gone through five editions. But compare also his *The Maze of Mormonism* (Ventura, California: Regal, 1978).

6. Robert N. Bellah et al., *Habits of the Heart: Individualism and Commitment in American Religious Life* (Berkeley: University of California Press, 1985), 221.

consistency of the beliefs that individuals combined together were seldom asked, and, if they were, the answers did not always matter much! When "Sheilaism" was first described, it seemed extreme and unusual; today it sounds commonplace. Second, the 1990s was the decade when the internet became a household word and central fixture in most homes and almost all businesses. Of course, it had always been possible to produce "yellow journalism," to privately disseminate distorted propaganda or to find established publishers with ideologies that drastically skewed what they would or would not publish. But once anyone could set up a website, a blog, or respond to others who published legitimate or illegitimate reports, the quality control over what many people believed to be true plummeted. Every year saw the amount of information added to the worldwide web increase, but every year saw the amount of misinformation skyrocket as well. And what civil courtesies remained in the public square seemed to all but vanish entirely with the potential anonymity of online blogging.[7]

Little wonder, then, that the LDS Church authorities prefaced their online presentation of Gospel Topics with the following explanation: "Recognizing that today so much information about The Church of Jesus Christ of Latter-day Saints can be obtained from questionable and often inaccurate sources, officials of the Church began in 2013 to publish straightforward, in-depth essays on a number of topics." The topics are then listed in alphabetical order, so that the very first one is "Are Mormons Christian?"[8] Had the topics been listed in order of importance, beginning with the most important, this would probably still have been the first essay nonetheless.

Asking what makes a person or a movement Christian is a fascinating question, one which has received a wide variety of answers throughout church history. Probably the most common answer has been one of self-identification. Individuals and churches that call themselves Christian should be taken at face value.[9] But even that

---

7. For an excellent manifesto of what the culture needs to acquire, see Richard J. Mouw, *Uncommon Decency: Christian Civility in an Uncivil World,* 2nd ed. (Downers Grove, Iillinois: Intervarsity Press, 2010).

8. See www.lds.org/topics/christians?lang=eng.

9. This is the approach, for example, that is routinely taken by those investigating the number of adherents of Christianity worldwide or in a given location. See, e.g., David B.

answer gives rise to the question of what those using the moniker mean by it. The oldest known uses of the word, in the three New Testament passages in which it appears (Acts 11:36, 26:28; 1 Pet. 4:16), suggest that it was first applied to followers of Jesus by outsiders to their young movement, possibly with a hint of disparagement.[10] The *–ianos* suffix was attached to the proper noun *Christos* ("Christ") in Greek, just as it was to the dynastic name "Herod" to denote followers of the Herods–Herodians. Maybe the closest contemporary analogy is our use of –ite (or –ian) when we affix it to a name to refer to a small collection of "groupies" of a famous individual. A Russian supporter of the current regime might be called a Putinite, a follower of megachurch pastor John MacArthur could be dubbed a MacArthurite, or an investor who imitated Bill Gates on a smaller scale might be labeled a Gatesian. There are not any inherently negative connotations, but, in some contexts, there can be.

Of course, over the centuries, the church split into different groups. Roman Catholics separated from Eastern Orthodox, which had already begun to create national Orthodox entities and would continue to do so. The Protestant Reformation led to a plethora of churches over time. Every one called him-/herself Christian; every one drew on aspects of Jesus' life as depicted in the New Testament. But certain groups or certain wings of certain groups appeared to deviate so much from the historic teaching and practice of the churches they broke away from that the parent congregations were often suspicious. The breakaway children returned the favor, and, in some cases, they were the first ones to reject the authentic Christianity of the group they broke away from.

The identification of church and state in numerous European countries (though not always the same branch of the church) led to language developing that spoke about Christian *countries*. This made it possible for some individuals to call themselves Christian and mean by it nothing more than that they were citizens of a

---

Barrett, *World Christian Encyclopedia: A Comparative Survey of Churches and Religions in the Modern World, A.D. 1900–2000* (New York: Oxford University Press, 1982).

10. Compare Horst Balz and Gerhard Schneider, eds., *Exegetical Dictionary of the New Testament* (Grand Rapids, Michigan: Eerdmans, 1993), 3: 477–78.

Christian country. Ironically, this kind of language today is more common in countries in which Islam dominates than in countries where Christianity does or, at least, once did. Thus, many Middle-Eastern Muslims will equate the descriptor "Christian" with a Caucasian person who permanently resides in a Western nation, especially the United States, irrespective of their personal theological beliefs, ethical practices, or lack thereof.

The theological liberalism that intruded into many Protestant denominations in the nineteenth century and into large parts of Roman Catholicism in the twentieth century led the more conservative Christians of those traditions to begin to reserve "Christian" or "true Christian" for those who retained the historic teachings of the faith—who believed in a supernatural Triune God; the virgin birth, sinless life, atoning death, and bodily resurrection of Jesus who will one day return to this earth and usher in final judgment; salvation by grace through faith not based on good works but producing good works; and the like. "Christian" and "Evangelical Christian" were thus used interchangeably in some circles.[11]

The coming of age of most Baby Boomers in the U.S.—the mid-1960s through the early 1980s—was also a period of booming growth for parachurch organizations.[12] Founded to serve numerous functions, they all recognized that there were important tasks for Christians to do that established churches were either not in a good position to carry out or for some other reason simply were

---

11. The most widely cited and lauded definition of "Evangelical" is probably that of David W. Bebbington, *Evangelicalism in Modern Britain: A History from the 1730s to the 1980s*, rev. ed. (London: Allen & Unwin, 1989), 2–3: "*conversionism*, the belief that lives need to be changes; *activism*, the expression of the gospel in effort; *biblicism*, a particular regard for the Bible; and what may be called *crucicentrism*, a stress on the sacrifice of Christ on the cross." Contrast that with a doctrinal basis like that of the Evangelical Theological Society, a largely American organization, which was originally founded with one statement—on the inerrancy of the Bible (to bridge the denominational divides in conservative Protestantism), and to which was later added a second statement, explicitly to exclude evangelical Catholics, Mormons, Jehovah's Witnesses, etc.: "The Bible alone, and the Bible in its entirety, is the Word of God written and is therefore inerrant in the autographs. God is a Trinity, Father, Son, and Holy Spirit, each an uncreated person, one in essence, equal in power and glory" (www.etsjets.org/about).

12. Wesley K. Willmer and J. David Schmidt, *The Prospering Parachurch: Enlarging the Boundaries of God's Kingdom* (San Francisco: Josey-Bass, 1998).

not doing well. Evangelism and missions in many circles seemed to be one of these premier tasks, especially on high school, college, and university campuses, and Youth for Christ, Young Life, Campus Crusade for Christ, InterVarsity Christian Fellowship, the Navigators, and Fellowship of Christian Athletes all stood in the gap. Precisely because these organizations were not churches, they wanted to appeal to as broad a cross-section of the Christian populace as they could while remaining true to what they understood to be the fundamentals of the faith, as sketched out above. The result is that the biggest divide, especially in the Protestant world, over the last forty to fifty years has been between theologically conservative and theologically liberal individuals and organizations *within* most major Protestant denominations, rather than the differences *among* the different Protestant denominations.

Parachurch organizations, then, found Baptists, Lutherans, Presbyterians, Methodists, and many others comfortably working and worshiping together, and doing so far more readily than the conservative Missouri Synod Lutheran Church could ever do with its liberal counterparts in the 1960s and 1970s—the Lutheran Church in America and the American Lutheran Church.[13] Southern Baptists and American Baptists (formerly Northern Baptists) had less in common with each other than Southern Baptists did with the Evangelical Free Church in America (a denomination that never had a liberal rift in it). American Baptists, United Methodists, and the Presbyterian Church USA cooperated in all kinds of ecumenical efforts that the Free Methodists, Baptist General Conference, and Presbyterian Church of America (all more Evangelical groups), along with many others, could never join in with. Not surprisingly, each side, but especially the conservative side, in these divisions increasingly began to speak of only their own as true Christians.

The past half-century of American Evangelical Christianity has

---

13. These two Lutheran groups, with remarkably similar names, reflected Scandinavian and German roots, respectively. They merged, along with a small liberal wing of Missouri Synod Lutherans to form what is today called the Evangelical Lutheran Church in America. But "Evangelical" here represents the German *evangelische*, which is more or less a synonym for Protestant. When Germans want to speak of what Americans typically mean by Evangelical, they use the word *evangelikal*.

thus been taught to evaluate carefully any new religious movement it encountered (even if it was new only to them). Preeminently they were taught to ask others, "Have you received Jesus Christ as your Lord and Savior?" This was a carryover from the divide between conservatives and liberals within the historic Christian churches, especially at the time of the fundamentalist-modernist controversy in the 1920s. In general, liberals would not attest to having had such a "born again" experience, to use the term Chuck Colson appropriated from John 3:3 and 5 and popularized,[14] so that Evangelicals would know where and with whom to start in sharing their faith. But members of the so-called cults, sects, or new religious movements would often say, "Oh, yes, I know Jesus," but then go on to say things that sounded more like Hinduism, Buddhism, or ancient paganism. The Bible itself talked about those who preached "another Jesus" (2 Cor. 11:4) or "another gospel" (Gal. 1:6–9), who were diabolically rather than divinely inspired. So it made sense to ask a follow-up question: "Which Jesus do you know?" Or "What do you believe about this Jesus?" or "What do you value most about him?" Conservative Christians would listen to find out if they ever said anything like, "I believe Jesus is fully God and fully human," "I believe he is part of the Triune God of Father, Son and Holy Spirit," or "I believe he died for the sins of mankind and was bodily resurrected from the dead." This language comes from the early creeds of Christianity, but there is clear biblical support for every one of these formulations.[15] I should add that Evangelicals also cherished (and still cherish) hearing others acknowledge the Bible as their full and final authority for belief and practice.[16]

To show the ongoing influence of this mindset forty years after 1976, which *Newsweek* dubbed "The Year of the Evangelical,"[17] one need only turn to the gathering of a couple thousand Evangelical leaders in the summer of 2016 to listen to Donald Trump as he

---

14. Charles Colson, *Born Again* (Old Tappan, New Jersey: Chosen Books, 1976).

15. See especially Alister McGrath, *"I Believe": Exploring the Apostles' Creed*, 2nd ed. (Downers Grove, Illinois: Intervarsity Press, 1997).

16. See especially D. A. Carson, ed., *The Enduring Authority of the Christian Scriptures* (Grand Rapids, Michigan: Eerdmans, 2016).

17. Kenneth L. Woodward, "Born Again: The Year of the Evangelical," *Newsweek*, Oct. 25, 1976, 68–78.

campaigned for the US presidency. During the question-and-answer time, he was asked what being a Christian meant to him, and he responded by talking about being inspired by the life and values of Jesus.[18] But he said none of the things above that might have led his listeners to believe he was truly one of them. Perhaps most telling was a year earlier, when asked if he had ever "repented," he said he did not think so. Rather, when he made mistakes, he just tried to learn from them and do better the next time.[19] Candidate Trump could hardly have sent any clearer signals to his audience that he was not an Evangelical, that he did not even understand Evangelical faith. In retrospect, it seems unlikely that everyone was listening very carefully.

How does all this affect Mormon understanding of other historically Christian movements and their understanding of the LDS? It has really only been in the last twenty years or so that Mormons and other Christians, especially Evangelicals, have engaged in sustained theological dialogues. A ground-breaking work, it seems, was my dialogue with Brigham Young University professor of New Testament, Stephen Robinson, in a co-authored volume entitled *How Wide the Divide? A Mormon and an Evangelical in Conversation*.[20] From 2000 to 2020, Richard Mouw, longtime president of the evangelical Fuller Seminary in Pasadena, California, and Robert Millet, longtime BYU religious studies professor and occupier of various roles in interfaith dialogues, convened gatherings of Evangelical and LDS academics in numerous venues and with various formats to discuss a broad

---

18. Specifically, "Jesus to me is somebody I can think about for security and confidence. Somebody I can revere in terms of bravery and in terms of courage and, because I consider the Christian religion so important, somebody I can totally rely on in my own mind." Kimberly Winston, "Trump Tackles Christianity's Big Question: Who Is Jesus?" *Religion News Service*, June 8, 2016, at www.religionnews.com/2016/06/08/trump-tackles-who-is-jesus.

19. "I am not sure I have. I just go on and try to do a better job from there. I don't think so," he said. "I think if I do something wrong, I think, I just try and make it right. I don't bring God into that picture. I don't." Eugene Scott, "Trump Believes in God, But Hasn't Sought Forgiveness," *CNN Politics*, July 18, 2015, at www.cnn.com/2015/07/18/politics/trump-has-never-sought-forgiveness.

20. Stephen E. Robinson and Craig L. Blomberg, *How Wide the Divide? A Mormon and an Evangelical in Conversation* (Downers Grove, Illinois: Intervarsity Press, 1997).

range of topics of mutual interest.[21] Other co-authored works have appeared at both the more academic level[22] and the more popular level of writing and speaking.[23] Something of a liberal Christian counterpart to these undertakings led to a book of essays comparing and contrasting LDS thought with "contemporary Christian theologies," and containing contributions by both LDS and liberal Christian scholars.[24] A conference at BYU in the mid-2000s led to an anthology of perspectives on salvation from Orthodox, Catholic, liberal, and conservative Protestant and multiple LDS perspectives, published by the BYU Religious Studies Center.[25] But there are still plenty of people in all of these circles who are aware of none of this. So I am grateful for this opportunity to respond as a representative Evangelical to "Are Mormons Christian?" writing from the perspective of one who has been uniquely privileged to participate in many of these developments.

The LDS Gospel Topics essay "Are Mormons Christian?" begins by affirming the majority of what the typical believer faithful to the historic roots of Christianity holds dear. Mormons, we are told, "worship God the Eternal Father in the name of Jesus Christ." Joseph Smith himself defined the fundamentals of his belief system as the testimony of the apostles and prophets to the death, burial, resurrection, and ascension of Jesus. The Quorum of the Twelve in this millennium have reiterated that "Jesus is the Living Christ" and "the immortal Son of God," and that his is the way that leads to perfect happiness and eternal life. Mormons therefore unabashedly declare themselves to be Christian. But they note three recurring counterclaims in recent decades that the

---

21. A work that discloses much of the fruit of this dialogue is Robert L. Millet and Richard J. Mouw, eds., *Talking Doctrine: Mormons and Evangelicals in Conversation* (Downers Grove, Illinois: Intervarsity Press, 2015).

22. For example, Robert L. Millet and Gerald R. McDermott, *Claiming Christ: A Mormon-Evangelical Debate* (Grand Rapids, Michigan: Brazos, 2007).

23. For example, Robert L. Millet and Gregory C. V. Johnson, *Bridging the Divide: A Continuing Conversation between a Mormon and an Evangelical* (Rhinebeck, New York: Monkfish, 2007).

24. David L. Paulsen and Donald W. Musser, eds., *Mormonism in Dialogue with Contemporary Christian Theologies* (Macon, Georgia: Mercer University Press, 2007).

25. Roger R. Keller and Robert L. Millet, eds., *Salvation in Christ: Comparative Christian Views* (Provo, Utah: Brigham Young University Religious Studies Center, 2005).

rest of the document proceeds to address. First, LDS do not accept the creeds and confessions of post-New Testament Christianity. Second, they do not "descend from" any one of the three lines of historical Christianity—Eastern Orthodoxy, Roman Catholicism, or Protestantism. Third, scripture for the LDS includes not just the Bible but the Book of Mormon, the Doctrine and Covenants, and the Pearl of Great Price.

In responding to the first complaint, the "Are Mormons Christian?" essay stresses the long-held LDS belief that even the earliest Christian creeds in the second century, after the completion of the New Testament, were influenced in part by Greco-Roman philosophy and therefore are not reliable guides to authentic first-century Christian teachings. This is the beginning of what other LDS leaders and writers have often called the Great Apostasy of the Christian church. The Reformation improved matters some, but only the nineteenth-century Mormon Restoration brought back the full expression of authoritative, original Christianity.[26]

That Restoration explains why Mormons are neither Orthodox nor Catholic nor Protestant is the second complaint the document addresses. All branches of Christianity had, to some extent, become corrupt; what was needed was the re-establishment of the original, pristine form. There was a diversity in pre-creedal Christianity, moreover, that makes it inappropriate to consider Mormons non-Christian. Several of the distinctive tenets of LDS faith do, in fact, find some precedent in certain early Christian teaching. One thinks here, for example, of the deification of the believer or the corporeality of God.[27]

Finally, to the charge that Mormons add scripture to the Bible, the essay counters by noting that the Bible itself nowhere excludes the possibility of God inspiring further scripture. What is more, every branch of Christianity *de facto* adds authoritative teaching to the Bible, whether it is the teachings of a pope or patriarch, the traditions of the particular denomination, certain historic creeds

---

26. Compare, for example, Kent P. Jackson, *From Apostasy to Restoration* (Salt Lake City: Deseret Book Co., 1996).

27. Compare, for example, Stephen E. Robinson, *Are Mormons Christians?* (Salt Lake City: Deseret Book Co., 1991), 60–65, 79–87.

or councils, or the pronouncements of the most respected biblical linguists and scholars of the day. The additional scripture of the LDS, it is asserted, is thoroughly Christ-centered, and therefore should pose no problem for other Christians.

"Are Mormons Christians?" concludes with an appeal for Christians of all stripes to work together in the social and moral arenas to counter the unethical and anti-family malaise of our modern world. It asks others to judge the LDS by their overall fruits (in the spirit of Matt. 7:16–20) rather than by certain distinctive, possibly divisive doctrines. It stresses that the Mormon faith can enrich whatever existing spirituality people already have. Overall, the document is written in a very irenic tone, a far cry from Joseph Smith's own statement, canonized in the Pearl of Great Price, that all the creeds of the rest of Christendom "were an abomination in his sight; that those professors [i.e., those who profess the creeds] were all corrupt" (JS—H 1:19).

A thoughtful Christian layperson or pastor fifty-five years of age or older, reading "Are Mormons Christian?" without any detailed firsthand exposure to Mormonism is likely to react in several ways in light of the shared history and experiences of Baby Boomers sketched earlier in this chapter. To the extent that this generation has passed on their convictions to their children, a number of younger adults will probably react in similar fashion. First, they will likely observe that the document does not address the most basic concerns that Evangelical Christians typically have. Above all, do the LDS teach salvation by grace through faith sufficiently, so that their adherents are not trying to gain God's favor by good works—the very distortion of the gospel that Paul anathematized in Galatians 1:6–9?[28] A common second question would probably ask, "Yes, they say they follow Jesus, but is it the Jesus of the Bible?" Clearly false teachers even in New Testament times were promoting "another Jesus" who could not save his followers (2 Cor. 11:4).[29]

These typical Christians will be familiar with key New Testament texts like Christ's Great Commission to his followers to "go and

---

28. Compare Millet and McDermott, *Claiming Christ,* 163–91.

29. Hence Robert Millet's *A Different Jesus? The Christ of the Latter-day Saints* (Grand Rapids, Michigan: Eerdmans, 2006).

make disciples of all nations, baptizing them in the [singular] name of the Father and of the Son and of the Holy Spirit."[30] They may have concluded many prayer meetings and Bible studies with Paul's formulation at the end of 2 Corinthians, "the grace of the Lord Jesus Christ, and the love of God, and the fellowship of the Holy Spirit be with you all" (13:14). Whether or not they can cite chapter and verse, they will know that there are many passages that equate Jesus with God and the Holy Spirit with God, and that the New Testament nevertheless continues to affirm that there is only one God.[31] They may grant that the issues of the day at the time of the writings of the creeds and councils colored the way concepts were framed and worded, but they will fail to see how the basic principle of the Trinity—one God in three persons—can be called post–New Testament. So if the Jesus of the LDS is not the second person of the Trinity, they will wonder how it can possibly be the Jesus of the New Testament.

The average but reasonably educated Evangelical will also have questions about the Mormon Restoration. If they know little of Mormonism, they will probably puzzle over what it was that the Reformation did not restore. If told that it was fundamentally the priesthood authority, they will ask, where is that in the New Testament? If the answer is Matthew 16:16–19, they may say, "No, that's a Catholic (or maybe Orthodox) understanding of authority." Nothing in Christ's calling Peter a rock or giving him keys to the kingdom implies anything about him holding an office with unique authority that must be passed on to subsequent generations.[32] That is why Martin Luther turned to 1 Peter 2:5 to stress

---

30. In Hellenistic Greek, to use a singular noun modified by multiple nominal expressions in the genitive case suggests that all those expressions together define one entity. This is part of Granville Sharp's Rule. See, for example, Daniel B. Wallace, *Greek Grammar beyond the Basics* (Grand Rapids, Michigan: Zondervan, 1996), 270–90. For an entire book on *Granville Sharp's Canon and Its Kin: Semantics and Significance*, see Daniel B. Wallace's volume so-entitled (New York: Peter Lang, 2009).

31. For examples, see Millard J. Erickson, *Christian Theology*, 3rd ed. (Grand Rapids, Michigan: Baker, 2013), 291–313, 623–42, 771–87. Compare also Millard J. Erickson, *God in Three Persons: A Contemporary Interpretation of the Trinity* (Grand Rapids, Michigan: Baker, 1995).

32. Compare Joseph A. Burgess (*History of the Exegesis of Matthew 16:17–19 from 1781 to 1965* [Ann Arbor, Michigan: Edwards Bros., 1966]), who shows how even Catholic exegetes were often convinced of this during much of the period after the Council of Trent and before Vatican II, even while many others still upheld conciliar dicta.

the priesthood of all believers. Catholics had created a magisterium to bestow different levels of authority on different persons and offices within the church. Protestants, admittedly, have not always shed themselves of all the vestiges of this structure. But if a priest in the Old Testament was foremost someone who mediated God's forgiveness to an individual worshipper by declaring his animal sacrifices efficacious, then, with Christ's once-for-all sacrifice, there is no longer any need for an intermediary between God and humanity—neither popes nor priests, pastors, prophets, nor presidents of any church.[33]

As for an expanded canon, the average Evangelical will (wrongly) cite Revelation 21:18–19 about God damning anyone who adds or deletes words from John's Apocalypse. Not recalling that in context this could refer only to the book of Revelation, and because Revelation is the last book of the canon, they will assume that it applies to the whole Bible.[34] But they will (rightly) note that while creeds, confessions, church tradition, and scholarly opinion can have great impact on a person's or church's beliefs, all Protestant denominations acknowledge in their own documents and live out in their best moments the commitment to *sola scriptura*. Try introducing a novel belief into any of these churches by saying, "It seems to me that the logical outgrowth of the Nicene Creed (or the Westminster Confession of Faith, or the doctrinal statement

---

33. For an excellent treatment of what Luther did and did not mean by the "priesthood of believers" and what may fairly be concluded from 1 Peter 2:5 itself, see John H. Elliott, *1 Peter* (New York: Doubleday, 2001), 449–55.

34. Indeed, to argue for a closed canon is to implicitly adopt the Catholic notion that the church determines and therefore can close the canon, rather than the Protestant concept of the canon as self-attesting. As Bruce M. Metzger (*The Canon of the New Testament: Its Origin, Development and Significance* [Oxford: Oxford University Press, 1987], 282–84) phrases it, the biblical canon is "a collection of authoritative texts," not an "authoritative collection of (authoritative) texts." Nevertheless, there were criteria of canonicity either explicit or implicit in the early church's consideration of various books, including apostolicity, catholicity and consistency. With the conviction that God's speaking through Christ was the final, decisive revelation of God to humanity prior to Judgment Day (Heb. 1:1–4), and the requirement that books for inclusion be widely valued in all major segments of the Christian world, it is hard to see how writings of later centuries could every qualify for canonization, however valuable they might otherwise be. See further Michael J. Kruger, *Canon Revisited: Establishing the Origins and Authority of the New Testament Books* (Wheaton, Illinois: Crossway, 2012).

of Focus on the Family) is …" and the congregation will typically respond, "Show it to us in the Bible and then we'll consider it." The same holds true for the other ancient creeds, Reformation-era confessions of faith, and modern doctrinal statements of various churches and parachurch organizations.

Of course plenty of Evangelical believers are not this thoughtful. But these are questions and comments that are heard over and over again in Evangelical churches and schools.[35]

One could hope that someday the LDS leadership might produce a revised, expanded edition of (or a new document similar to) "Are Mormons Christians?" to put forward *five* common concerns and then offer their replies. To the three charges they have already addressed, they could add something along the lines of "4. Latter-day Saints are a religion of works, not grace, and therefore no more successfully qualify as genuinely Christian than did most medieval Catholics," and "5. Latter-day Saints do not believe that Jesus provided a full and final atonement for the sins of humanity, because they are constantly urging their people to do more and more good works and participate in temple rituals, so that they can achieve the highest levels of heaven in the life to come." These concerns can no doubt be worded more simply and clearly, but they address the important issues.

In responding to point 4, such a hypothetical revised document, in my opinion, should refer to the kinds of teachings one finds in Robert Millet's *Grace Works* or in the 2015 LDS general conference address by Dieter F. Uchtdorf, second counselor in the First Presidency of the LDS Church.[36] Works are absolutely essential but as the outflow of one's salvation by grace, not as a contributor to it. Second Nephi 25:23 remains a sticking point for many people; a straightforward reading suggests that faithful Latter-day Saints

---

35. They are also representative of the typical responses in Evangelical literature about the LDS, even when it is not overtly countercult in nature. See, for example, Andrew Jackson, *Mormonism Explained: What Latter-day Saints Teach and Practice* (Wheaton, Michigan: Crossway, 2008); Ross Anderson, *Understanding the Book of Mormon* (Grand Rapids, Michigan: Zondervan, 2009); and Ross Anderson *Understanding Your Mormon Neighbor* (Grand Rapids, Michigan: Zondervan, 2011).

36. Robert L. Millet, *Grace Works: After All We Can Do* (Salt Lake City: Deseret Book Co., 2003); Dieter F. Uchtdorf, "The Gift of Grace," *Conference Report* (Apr. 2015), at www.lds.org/general-conference/2015/04/the-gift-of-grace?lang=eng&_r=1.

do everything they possibly can and then God graciously steps in and supplies grace for what remains. This sounds exactly like the teaching of the Judaizers in Galatia whom Paul condemned. Even if it did not, it should offer hope to no one, because no one ever does all one could have done. We miss opportunities daily for doing more good. But when one learns that the passage may take this fact into account and mean "after all you can do, which can never add up to anything that would satisfy God, we are saved by grace" or "after all, there is nothing you could ever do to merit God's favor, so God saves us wholly by his grace," then the believer from any denomination should acknowledge this as a thoroughly Christian concept.[37]

It is unfortunate that most Latter-day Saints have come across a historic aberration of Evangelical thought sometimes referred to as the free-grace movement (as if any Evangelical did *not* believe in free grace).[38] This is linked, in turn, with the notion that one can accept Jesus' free gift of salvation and have him as one's Savior without having him also as one's Lord or Master. The desire behind this theology is well-intended: making Christ Lord may easily sound as if there were a certain level of performance or accomplishments one has to achieve to be accepted by him. But this is not what the New Testament means when it refers to confessing Jesus as Lord. It means rather that one is not coming to Christ consciously withholding certain areas of one's life from his influence. An ancient master had the right to command his servants to do anything he wanted in any dimension of life. To use a simple but paradoxical summary, "salvation is absolutely free, but it will cost you your life."[39] True biblical teaching never suggests one can accept Jesus, go out and live like the devil without any qualms of

---

37. Compare further Stephen E. Robinson, *Following Christ: The Parable of the Divers and More Good News* (Salt Lake City: Deseret Book Co., 1995), 87: "In fact, having faith in the Savior, repenting, entering the covenant, and staying put therein are 'all we *can* do' (2 Nephi 25:23)."

38. Associated particularly with the many writings of Zane Hodges, a longtime professor at Dallas Seminary until his death in 2008; and Robert N. Wilkin, president of the Grace Evangelical Society. See also Joseph Dillow, *Final Destiny: The Future Reign of the Servant Kings,* 2nd ed. (Woodlands, Texas: Grace Theology Press, 2015).

39. Compare especially Darrell L. Bock, "A Review of *the Gospel according to Jesus* by John F. MacArthur," *Bibliotheca Sacra* 146 (1989): 21–40.

conscience or repentance, and be saved. Evangelicals are not opposed to good works; they just insist on not putting the cart before the horse. They are our response to Christ's atonement offered to us as wholly undeserving sinners.[40]

The issue gets complicated, however, because Evangelicals and LDS regularly use "salvation" to mean two slightly different things. For Evangelicals, it is the all-inclusive term for what happens when one is converted, accepts Jesus, and is made right with God. It means that if you die, you go to heaven in the presence of the Triune Godhead, awaiting the resurrection of the body at the Day of Judgment, with the new heavens and new earth as the eternal state following that.[41] For Mormons, it often means that one will be resurrected and not sent to hell, but one still awaits assignment to one of the three kingdoms—the celestial, terrestrial, or telestial.[42] Committed Mormons aspire, of course, to the celestial kingdom, which tends to be referred to as "exaltation" on top of mere "salvation." And here is where faithfulness and obedience come in again, and where traditional Christians see the specter of works-based righteousness.

While not addressing all of the differences between the two belief systems, one helpful form of rapprochement would be for the LDS to compare their convictions to the common Evangelical notion of rewards in heaven. While we do not separate the afterlife into three distinct kingdoms, confining God's presence (as opposed to Jesus') to the highest realm, many Evangelicals, especially of a more Calvinist bent, believe that while salvation is entirely by grace, the nature of our experience of the new heavens and new earth will depend on the extent to which we have obeyed God in this life. Some appeal to the New Testament language of crowns and think of degrees of glory or honor. Others talk about

---

40. For an excellent, courteous response to the "free grace" movement, see Wayne Grudem, *"Free Grace" Theology: 5 Ways It Diminishes the Gospel* (Wheaton, Michigan: Crossway, 2016).

41. Compare R. E. O. White, "Salvation," in Walter A. Elwell, ed., *Evangelical Dictionary of Theology*, 2nd ed., (Grand Rapids, Michigan: Baker, 2001), 967–69.

42. Compare Robert L. Millet, "Salvation," in Robert L. Millet, Camille Fronk Olson, Andrew C. Skinner, and Brent L. Top, eds., *LDS Beliefs: A Doctrinal Reference* (Salt Lake City: Deseret Book Co., 2011), 556; with Brent L. Top, "Exaltation," in *LDS Beliefs*, 198–99.

opportunities for service, in keeping with the parable of the talents (Matt. 25:14–30), while still others liken the differences to capacities for enjoying and appreciating eternal life.[43] Still others reject entirely this vestige of Roman Catholicism that carried over into various wings of the Reformation, but they are in the minority among Evangelicals in so doing.[44] And those who hold such views are certainly no less godly for doing so. If that issue does not have to divide Evangelicals, then it should not be a "defeater" in their dialogue and co-operation with the LDS.

Responding to complaint 5 would follow similar tracks. Mormons can in good conscience stress that Christ did make full and final atonement for our salvation, and that we stand purified before God solely on the basis of "the merits, and mercy, and grace of the Holy Messiah" (2 Ne. 2:8). LDS apostle Jeffrey Holland's 2015 general conference talk on the Atonement is a powerful example of the kind of teaching that should warm every Evangelical's heart.[45] Using the illustration of someone hanging on to the edge of a cliff, unable to pull himself up, Holland envisioned God as the rescuer at the top of the cliff who requires the person to let go, reach out to their rescuer, and trust that they will be caught and placed safely on the top. The renewed focus in many LDS circles of a theology of the cross is most welcome and should continue to be highlighted in any revised or expanded version of "Are Mormons Christian?" or any similar document drafted in the future. The obvious absence of any cross atop Mormon churches is an iconic distinction that deserves brief comment. Whatever the historic reasons for this architecture, if it is true that an adequate explanation today for its absence is to stress the resurrection rather

---

43. See, for example, Erickson, *Christian Theology*, 1132–33.

44. For Luther's and my views, see Craig L. Blomberg, "Degrees of Reward in the Kingdom of Heaven?" *Journal of the Evangelical Theological Society* 35 (1992): 159–72. For the doctrine as a leftover from Catholic thought, see Emma Disley, "Degrees of Glory: Protestant Doctrine and the Concept of Rewards Hereafter," *Journal of Theological Studies* 42 (1991): 77–105.

45. Jeffrey R. Holland, "Where Justice, Love and Mercy Meet," *Conference Report* (Apr. 2015), at www.lds.org/general-conference/2015/04/where-justice-love-and-mercy-meet?lang=eng&_r=1. Compare also Robert L. Millet, *What Happened to the Cross?* (Salt Lake City: Deseret Book Co., 2007).

than the crucifixion,[46] then it is important to highlight that the *empty* cross of Protestant architecture and iconography intends to make the identical statement. A crucifix—the cross with Jesus still hanging on it—is itself by no means a denial of the resurrection, but within Roman Catholicism tends to visually emphasize the weakness and powerlessness of Jesus rather than his conquest of death and powerful life reigning at the right hand of the Father. That complaint cannot be made of the Protestant empty cross, so Mormons should have no objection to highlighting the cross more than they sometimes have done.[47]

If we turn back now to the original three issues that "Are Mormons Christian?" presented and replied to, we may make a few additional comments about the kind of responses that would reassure outsiders even more that the LDS represent a bona fide version of Christianity. In principle, most Evangelicals should have no problem accepting a person who says, "I believe in every word of the Bible; I simply do not accept the later creeds." This was, after all, the position of the Stone-Campbell movement that birthed the uniquely American denominations, the Disciples of Christ, the so-called Independent Christian Churches, and the Church of Christ.[48] Churches in the Evangelical Lutheran Church in America today often do not recite "He descended into hell" as part of the Apostles' Creed,[49] because the best biblical scholarship is in agreement that the passages traditionally cited in support of that belief do not teach it at all.[50] Moreover, that one clause was not formally included in the creed until about the eighth century, almost a full half a millennium after the standardization of much of the rest of

---

46. See Gordon B. Hinckley, "The Symbol of Our Faith," *Ensign,* Apr. 2005, at www.lds.org/ensign/2005/04/the-symbol-of-our-faith?lang=eng.

47. This should be true, irrespective of the emphasis that is or is not placed on Gethsemane in the process of the atonement, on which, see especially Andrew C. Skinner, *Gethsemane* (Salt Lake City: Deseret Book Co., 2002).

48. On which, see especially D. Newell Williams, Douglas A. Foster, and Paul M. Blowers, eds., *The Stone-Campbell Movement: A Global History* (St. Louis: Chalice, 2013).

49. Hymnals sometimes indicate with an asterisk that this clause is optional or that it may be translated differently.

50. See especially William J. Dalton, *Christ's Proclamation to the Spirits: A Study of 1 Peter 3:18–4:6,* 2nd ed. (Rome: Gregorian and Biblical Press, 1989).

the creed.[51] Pastors in various (not all) Presbyterian denominations have the option of indicating their disagreement with a limited number of specific statements within the Westminster Confession without it calling into question their ordination.[52]

In other words, the creeds do not actually function as an authority on a par with scripture, however it may seem at times that they do. The Bible can still trump the creeds.

So for LDS simply to say that they do not accept the creeds does not really get to the heart of the matter. The key question is which parts of the creeds they do not believe in. Take the oldest and most widely utilized creed of all, the Apostles' Creed. It reads,

> I believe in God the Father Almighty, Maker of heaven and earth.
>
> And in Jesus Christ, his only Son, our Lord, who was conceived by the Holy Ghost, born of the Virgin Mary, suffered under Pontius Pilate, was crucified, dead and buried; he descended into hell. The third day he rose from the dead. He ascended into heaven and sitteth on the right hand of God the Father Almighty. From thence [sic] he shall come to judge the quick and the dead.
>
> I believe in the Holy Ghost, the holy catholic church,[53] the communion of saints, the forgiveness of sins, the resurrection of the body, and the life everlasting.[54]

Exactly which part of this do LDS not believe? Stephen Robinson said he could affirm all of it, as long as he was allowed to define "holy catholic church" as "true Christianity," as he understood many Evangelicals also defined it.[55]

The real sticking point comes in the fourth-century Nicene Creed with its more explicit articulation of Trinitarian doctrine.[56]

---

51. Phillip Schaff, *The Creeds of Christendom*, 3 vols., 6th ed., rev. David S. Schaff (Grand Rapids, Michigan: Baker, 1998), 1:21.

52. This is the policy, for example, of the Presbytery of the West of the Evangelical Presbyterian Church, for whom I have functioned as a biblical and theological consultant.

53. Some versions of the creed substitute "Christian" for "catholic." Others explain that "catholic" in this context means merely "universal."

54. Schaff, *Creeds of Christendom*, 1: 21.

55. Robinson and Blomberg, *How Wide the Divide?* 219–20n8.

56. "We believe in one God the Father Almighty, Maker of heaven and earth, and of all things visible and invisible. And in one Lord Jesus Christ, the only-begotten Son of God, begotten of the Father before all worlds, God of God, Light of Light,

But in most conversations with LDS friends about what it is they reject about the classic Christian belief in the Trinity, Evangelicals hear them reject modalism, just as historic Christianity rejected it. In other words, Latter-day Saints reject the idea that God can present himself at one moment as the Father, at another as the Son, and at another as the Holy Spirit. They want to safeguard the fact that when Christ prayed to the Father, he was not praying to himself; that when he was the incarnate Son of God on earth, the Father was still ruling the universe from his heavenly throne.[57] All this is historic, orthodox Christianity. Of course the vision and revelation to Joseph Smith that the Father and not just the Son had a body is distinctively Mormon. But as long as Mormon theology stresses that God is invisibly omnipresent even while visibly embodied (as classic Christian thought stresses of Jesus),[58] this distinction need contradict nothing even in the Nicene Creed.

Part of the problem is that LDS and historic Christians alike think almost exclusively in the categories of systematic rather than biblical theology in discussing the Trinity. With the Nicene Creed, the fourth-century church sought to put their beliefs about God, Jesus, and the Holy Spirit into meaningful language for the Greco-Roman culture they found themselves in, although this point can be easily overstated. The debates built on earlier ones in previous centuries, especially with Gnosticism, and often centered on what did or did not logically follow from having a God who was the Eternal Father, with whom Jesus and the Holy Spirit were

very God of very God, begotten, not made being of one substance with the Father, by whom all things were made; Who, for us men, and for our salvation, came down from heaven, and was incarnate by the Holy Ghost of the Virgin Mary, and was made man. He was crucified for us under Pontius Pilate, and suffered and was buried. And the third day he rose again, according to the Scriptures, and ascended into heaven, and sitteth on the right hand of the Father; and he shall come again, with glory, to judge the quick and the dead, whose kingdom shall have no end. And we believe in the Holy Ghost, the Lord and giver of life, who proceedeth from the Father and the Son, who with the Father and the Son together is worshiped and glorified, who spake by the prophets. We believe in one holy catholic and apostolic church. We acknowledge one baptism for the remission of sins; and we look for the resurrection of the dead, and the life of the world to come." Schaff, *Creeds of Christendom*, 1: 27–28.

57. For example, Robert L. Millet, *The Vision of Mormonism: Pressing the Boundaries of Christianity* (St. Louis: Paragon House, 2007), 65–73.

58. Millet, "God," in *LDS Beliefs*, 262.

to be equated. In other words, what emerged as orthodoxy was not nearly as radically contextualized as the views that were rejected.[59] LDS nevertheless think that all branches of the early church distorted biblical teaching in the process; other Christians think that not all did. So one needs to move from the fourth century back to the first and phrase things historically rather than philosophically. The first-century Jew, Jesus of Nazareth, said and did many things that his followers could not explain apart from ascribing to him the language of deity. He fulfilled prophecy and worked miracles, he made astonishing claims for himself and backed them up by his actions, and above all he was raised from the dead to life unending.[60] Despite being staunch Jewish monotheists, his apostles could not adequately account for what they had seen and heard without using language of divinity in speaking of Jesus.[61] Based on their experience of the Holy Spirit from Pentecost onward, they had no choice but to speak of him not only in the divine language they inherited from their scriptures (God's Spirit) but in personal terms as well.[62] But the Spirit was clearly empowering them when Jesus was no longer bodily present. And when Jesus was present, he was clearly not all there was to God. Preserve these truths and one has the heart of Christian trinitarian thinking, whatever specific language one chooses to encapsulate it with.[63]

To the second of the three issues that "Are Mormons Christian?" addresses, two additional points could be made. First, the Restoration did not occur in a vacuum. The Stone-Campbell movement was already using the language of restoration rather than reformation. It was radically anti-Calvinist. It was part of the euphoria of

59. See especially Donald Fairbairn, *Life in the Trinity: An Introduction to Theology with the Help of the Church Fathers* (Downers Grove, Illinois: Intervarsity Press, 2009), 38–58.

60. See especially Ben Witherington III, *The Christology of Jesus* (Minneapolis: Fortress, 1990).

61. Larry W. Hurtado, *Lord Jesus Christ: Devotion to Jesus in Earliest Christianity* (Grand Rapids, Michigan: Eerdmans, 2003), 53–78.

62. See especially James D. G. Dunn, *Jesus and the Spirit: A Study of the Religious and Charismatic Experience of Jesus and the First Christians as Reflected in the New Testament* (London: SCM, 1975).

63. Compare further Larry W. Hurtado, *How on Earth Did Jesus Become a God? Historical Questions about Earliest Devotion to Jesus* (Grand Rapids, Michigan: Eerdmans, 2005).

the day that God was creating something new on the American continent that would usher in the end of human history as we know it. There are at least nineteen major similarities between Alexander Campbell's distinctive teaching and practice and the early Joseph Smith's, mediated most likely by Sidney Rigdon who was a Campbellite leader prior to his conversion to Mormonism.[64] As in religious taxonomies that include the LDS among other Western Protestant sects, there is a sense in which it may be fairly stated that Mormonism descended from Protestantism, even if they moved farther away from it than other nineteenth-century sects.[65]

On the other hand, and second, the extent to which Mormons wish to continue to dissociate themselves from any of the three major branches of Christianity makes it harder for them to credibly claim to be Christian at the same time. Imagine a young man raised in a not overly devout LDS home today who begins to go around describing a vision he had received in which he saw three identical looking men who identified themselves as Father, Son, and Holy Ghost. They instructed him to associate with no existing church but to await further revelation. Eventually an angel guides him to dig up silver tiles that are covered with writing he cannot read but looks a little like pictographs on totem poles. Later he announces he has been enabled by God's Spirit to translate them. They tell the story of a group of Mormons who migrated to the Yukon in the late nineteenth century and who mingled with the Inuit there until they were all killed off except for one who had buried these tiles with their story engraved on them.

Later God reveals to this young man extensive instructions for the founding of a new group restoring the original Mormonism of Joseph Smith, which had begun to be corrupted by Brigham Young,

---

64. Blomberg, "Is Mormonism Christian?" in Carl Mosser, Paul Owen and Frank T. Beckwith, eds., *The New Mormon Challenge* (Grand Rapids, Michigan: Zondervan, 2002), 322–23.

65. George B. Arbaugh, *Revelation in Mormonism* (Chicago: University of Chicago Press, 1932). Compare also David F. Holland, *Continuing Revelation and Canonical Restraint in Early America* (New York: Oxford University Press, 2011). Holland discusses the twin trends of adding authoritative sources to the Bible (at least *de facto* if not *de jure*) and putting limits on what could be added (whether or not formally canonized). All the movements he discusses are Protestant or have their roots, to one degree or another, in Protestantism.

lost its moorings considerably in the mid-twentieth century, was reformed and improved by LDS church president Ezra Taft Benson
but still needs a full restoration. After all, Joseph Smith died before
he could pass on his authority to his divinely ordained successor,
so no existing Mormons have true priesthood authority. The Salt
Lake City-based Mormons, the rural Utah fundamentalist Mormons, and the Community of Christ (formerly the Reorganized
Church of Jesus Christ of Latter-day Saints) are all illegitimate,
and it is time to restore original Mormonism under the leadership
of this upstart young man. Anyone who wants to be in God's best
graces has to be baptized into the new church this man is organizing, which is to be called the Restored Church of our Holy Lord
Jesus Christ of Last-day Disciples. Existing Mormon baptisms are
not good enough for membership in his church. Indeed, this new
Restored Church is the one true church on the entire planet. At the
same time, it wants to call itself Mormon and be treated as fully
Mormon by the Quorum of the Twelve and the First Presidency in
Salt Lake City, by all the renegade fundamentalist Mormons, and
by the Community of Christ. What is the likelihood that *anyone*
in these three groups would agree? Yet that is very close to how the
rest of Christendom perceives, rightly or wrongly, the desires of the
Church of Jesus Christ of Latter-day Saints.[66]

Of course, my example is deliberately extreme and absurd. I
mean no offense to anyone by it. I use it simply to try, with however poor an analogy, to show how people without a pervasive
knowledge of Mormonism could respond to the "Are Mormons
Christian?" essay. My years of study and dialogue actually make
me much more hopeful about the genuinely Christian nature of
at least a significant and growing portion of the LDS Church, especially where views on the Atonement and on grace match those
we have mentioned earlier. I thoroughly support joint efforts to
combat unhealthy moral and social trends, the plea with which
the essay ends. I find it unfortunate that Evangelicals of my generation have largely resisted such cooperation, typically because
they think it will confuse others into imagining that we are all

---

66. I used a similar (and probably better!) example about a break away movement
from Islam in "Is Mormonism Christian?" 324–25.

alike.[67] In my experience, that seldom actually happens, and, even allowing for very rare instances in which it might, is it not worth the risk for the sake of the good that would be accomplished in the process? And do not those fears of confusing the two movements somehow imply that both LDS and Evangelicals would be mute in the process of whatever projects they jointly undertook, telling no one who the people were who were involved or why they were doing what they were doing? And what are the odds of *that* ever happening? Among millennials of both communities, however, I find much less fear of such efforts and even some enthusiasm for them. It may require the generation of those sixty and over to largely die off first (though I hope not, since I fall into that age bracket!), but I believe the day will come fairly soon when such cooperation can and will happen if people continue to lobby for it.

I conclude by alluding to Stephen H. Webb's book, *Mormon Christianity: What Other Christians Can Learn from the Latter-day Saints*. In it, Webb distinguishes between what he calls the evangelical and metaphysical traditions within contemporary Mormonism, which he associates, respectively, with Robert Millet and with David Paulsen, longtime philosophy professor at BYU though now retired.[68] While he does not take sides but simply assesses the strengths and weaknesses of each strand of thought, my conclusion, not surprisingly, is that the evangelical tradition should be the wave of the future that the LDS embrace. Then future documents of the genre of "Are Mormons Christian?" will be more persuasive and the goals and dreams for cooperation with which the essay ends will come to fruition more readily.

---

67. Precisely the main arguments given to me repeatedly by countercult ministry leaders Sandra Tanner and Bill McKeever in private communication and oral conversation after the publication of Robinson and Blomberg, *How Wide the Divide?*

68. New York: Oxford University Press, 2013, 160–61.

2. BECOMING LIKE GOD
A CRITIQUE

Richard Sherlock

If those of us who are traditional Christians were limited in our assessment of the Church of Jesus Christ of Latter-day Saints to the theology found in the Book of Mormon, we could reasonably conclude that Mormonism is a somewhat robust version of the free will Baptist theology that was pervasive in early America. For example, the Book of Mormon's rather vitriolic attack on infant baptism is mirrored in many Baptist tracts of the period (Moro. 8:9–15). Catholics such as I would find many things to contest in this theology, but we could not say that the theology was out of the broad Christian orbit.[1] The Catholic Church considers a baptism in a Baptist church to be a Christian baptism. Imperfect though Catholics would find Book of Mormon theology to be, we might well see it as broadly Christian.[2]

Of course, non-Mormons do not find the story of the coming forth of the Book of Mormon at all persuasive. Nor do we accept the picture of the Father and the Son as separate physical beings as seen in Joseph Smith's account of his "first vision." Catholics especially reject the idea that the early church went astray in a vast, profound apostasy such that the Christian church required a wholesale restoration, not merely a reformation as Luther and Calvin thought.

Where Mormonism seriously diverges from the Christian tradition, such that most Christians, myself included, cannot call it,

---

1. I converted to Roman Catholicism from the LDS Church in 2010.

2. I owe this insight to Carl Mosser. I emphasize that this point applies only to the actual theology of the book, not to claims about the ancient Americas that are central to the historical veracity of the book.

even broadly, Christian, is the theology and practice that Smith introduced in the 1840s: plural marriage, temple rituals, and the teaching about God and humankind. These all come from the Nauvoo period of Mormonism, and they lead to a serious conclusion that the difference between Mormonism and Christianity is a difference of kind not of degree.

In recent years the LDS Church has sought to confront its more controversial beliefs in essays designed to present them in their most favorable, yet still honest, light. Other contributors to the present compilation assess the credibility of others of the church's recent Gospel Topics essays. The subject of this chapter, the Gospel Topics essay "Becoming like God," however, is, in my opinion, a misleading remake of one of Joseph Smith's most important and for Christians most heretical documents, the so-called "King Follett Sermon."[3] The sermon was given orally on April 7, 1844, two months before a mob murdered Smith and his brother Hyrum, and has been published officially by the LDS Church twice since 1970. In the Church's magazine for adults, the *Ensign*, in 1971, Smith's sermon was called "one of the classics of Church literature."[4]

I

"Becoming like God" makes so many contestable claims that one chapter cannot treat all of them. In what follows I concentrate on four elements. First, I discuss the manner in which the essay selectively quotes and sometimes misinterprets biblical and patristic sources for the idea that man can become a god or "like God." Scholars generally refer to this idea as "deification." Second, I contest the LDS claim that creation ex nihilo is a belief that did not emerge until the second century of the Christian era. Third, I examine how the essay avoids any serious discussion of Smith's claim that "as man is God once was." Fourth, I show how the essay tames the traditional LDS claim that the telos, or ultimate aim, of

---

3. "Becoming Like God," at www.lds.org/topics/becoming-like-god?lang=eng.

4. For various accounts of "The King Follett Sermon," see *The Papers of Joseph Smith*, www.josephsmithpapers.org/site/accounts-of-the-king-follett-sermon. Joseph Smith, "The King Follett Sermon," *Ensign*, Apr. 1971: www.lds.org/ensign/1971/04/the-king-follett-sermon?lang=eng. This is the account I use.

human existence is not merely to become like God, but to become a god and rule one's own "kingdom." Along the way I note places where the LDS Church is open about its beliefs and their differences from the general Christian tradition.

II

As is more fully explained below, the problems with the Gospel Topics essay begin with the title: "Becoming like God." There is a long Christian tradition articulating the telos (deification) of human existence as "uniting with God" or, in another vocabulary, "becoming like God." This may be what the LDS Church wants members and non-members to believe that they teach. If so, they should at least admit that this is not what they have taught for over a century. To quote Joseph Smith in the "King Follett Sermon": "you have got to learn how to become Gods" yourselves.[5] There is no hint here that humans only become "like God." The LDS telos is to become a god. Just as all gods have done.

For our purposes, a useful description of deification is given by Orthodox priest and scholar John McGukin: "The concept of deification is the process of the sanctification of Christians, whereby they become progressively conformed to God; a conformation that is ultimately demonstrated in the glorious transfiguration of the just in the heavenly kingdom, when immortality and a more perfect vision (knowledge and experience) of God are clearly manifested in the glorification of the faithful."[6]

The LDS essay is admirably brief in its discussion of biblical sources for any concept of deification. Here we shall only examine those passages the essay cites.

The foundational passage is Genesis 1:26–27, where God is said to create man "in his own image." The LDS interpretation of this passage is grounded in the deep preference of Mormons for a univocal understanding of language used to describe God and humanity. Some in the Christian tradition have preferred an equivocal use of language in these cases, such that when we

---

5. Ibid., 2.

6. John McGukin, "Partakers of the Divine Nature," www.Sgtt.Org/writings/patristics/deification.

refer to God's qualities, these cannot be anything like qualities we understand in the temporal world. God's goodness, for example, cannot be anything like any goodness we recognize in this world.

Many in the Christian tradition, especially St. Thomas Aquinas, have argued that at least some of our language about God must be analogical. We use analogies regularly. When we refer to a boss as a tyrant, we analogize the behavior of the boss to that of real tyrants, for example, Hitler or Stalin. When we refer to someone's "river of tears," we analogize their crying to that of an actual river. In a specific Christian example, when Luther writes of "The Babylonian Captivity of the Church," he is analogizing the state of the Catholic Church in his era to the actual Babylonian captivity of Israel in the sixth century BCE. For Aquinas, a focus on equivocal language goes too far. If granted, as it is in purely negative religious thinkers like Maimonides, then we can say nothing meaningful about God.[7]

The difficulty of using analogical reasoning with respect to God is seen at this very point. We have a reasonably clear understanding of the Babylonian captivity of Israel in the sixth century BCE. As such, we can have reasonably clear understanding of the analogy Luther is making. However, God is not like any object or event that we have any substantial understanding of apart from revelation. How, then, can we have an analogy between two entities A and B when A is not anything like B. Indeed, if A is uncreated and any and all Bs are created, then there is a disconnection that makes any analogy difficult.

On the other hand, a univocal use of language brings God down to our level.

On this view, the language means the same when applied to God as it means when applied to human beings. In Isaiah 66:2 we read from the Lord "my hand made all these things." Then God must have a hand. In Isaiah 6 we read of Isaiah's vision of the Lord "sitting on a throne." Does this mean God sits on a real throne like an actual king? When the Psalmist writes, "When I consider Thy heavens, the work of Thy fingers" (Ps. 6), does this mean that God

---

7. Thomas Aquinas, *Summa Theologica*, 1:1 q. 13, par. 5–6. Ralph Mcinerny, Aquinas on Analogy. (Washington: Catholic Unversity of America Press, 1996)

has fingers? Finally, in Exodus 33:11 we are told that "the lord would speak to Moses face to face as a man speaks to his friend." On a univocal understanding of language, this must mean that God has a face, just as Joseph Smith said when he told of his 1820 visionary experience.

Mormonism is deeply invested in the univocal use of language about God. Thus, when God says that he will create man "in his own image," it means an image just like yours or mine, with face, hands, eyes, and ears.

The issues surrounding the use of univocal, analogical, and equivocal language in talking about God are too complicated to examine with any precision in this essay. Medieval thinkers such as Aquinas and Henry of Ghent focused much of their analysis on the necessity of analogy.[8] Others, especially Duns Scotus, thought they pushed analogy too far. Scotus held that at least some simple terms must be understood as univocal or analogy collapses to equivocation. What we can confidently say is that Mormonism over-emphasizes the univocal use of language. They do so not only with the fundamental simple terms about which Scotus was concerned but with complex terms which Aquinas and even Scotus thought required an analogical understanding unless we are willing to bring God down to our level.[9]

Aside from Genesis, the only other Old Testament passage discussed in the Gospel Topics essay is Psalm 82, which reads in verse 6: "I have said, you are Gods, sons of the most high." Unfortunately, the rest of the passage casts doubt on the literal idea that human beings are gods. In the following verse 7, we read, "But you will die like mere men, you will fall like every other ruler." A true

---

8. In the Fourth Lateran Council (1215), the Catholic Church declared that anyone using an analogy in relating God and man must recognize that the analogy will always be more misleading than correct.

9. Allan Wolter, *The Transcendentals and their Function in the Metaphysics of Duns Scotus* (St. Bonaventure, New York: Franciscan Institute Press, 1946); Stephen Dumont, "The Univocal Concept of Being in the 14th Century," *Medieval Studies* 49 (1987): 1–75; Richard Cross, *Duns Scotus.* (London: Oxford University Press, 1999); Roland Teske, S.J., *Essays on the Philosophy of Henry of Ghent.* (Milwaukee: Marquette University Press, 2012); G. A. Wilson, ed., *A Companion to Henry of Ghent.* (Leiden: E. J. Brill, 2011); and J. Decorte, "Henry of Ghent on Analogy" in *Henry of Ghent: Proceedings of an International Colloquium* (Leuven: Leuven University Press, 1996): 71–105.

God does not "die like mere men" for this God is not a "mere man" just as Christ was not a mere man.

In the New Testament the Gospel Topics essay refers to five passages, some of which only tangentially touch on this topic. Of course, they refer to Jesus' command to "be perfect" in Matthew 5:48. But they correctly note that the word "perfect" can be perhaps better translated as "whole" or "complete."[10] Also noted is John 10 where Jesus cites Psalm 82 but not actually to support the LDS reading and Revelation 3:21 where those who "overcome" sit with Christ "on my throne." No mention here of the LDS belief that the obedient get their own throne. The essay also refers to Romans 8:16–17 where Christians are said to be "joint heirs with Christ" who "share in his glory" and 2 Peter 1:4 where Christians are said to "participate in the divine nature." Neither of these passages teaches that man will become a separate God, only that man will unite with God's glory.

One is struck by the univocal use of language implicit in understanding all of these passages. It then seems to follow that when Revelation 3:21 reads, "He who overcomes I will grant him to sit down with me on my throne," Christ should have a throne to sit on. If not, then we are involved in an analogical use of language, as St. Thomas says.

After this brief consideration of available biblical texts, the Gospel Topics essay turns to an analysis of patristic texts that seem to speak of man becoming god, that is, the process of deification.

At the outset the essay admits that "what exactly the early Church fathers meant when they spoke of becoming God is open to interpretation."[11] This, of course, implies that the interpretation given in this essay is not the only plausible interpretation.

The essay refers to two widely known patristic writers who appear to state a view that is at least verbally similar to what the LDS Church teaches.[12]

First, the essay cites an often-quoted passage from St. Irenaeus

---

10. "Becoming Like God," 2.

11. Ibid., 3.

12. The essential text is Norman Russell, *The Doctrine of Deification in the Greek Patristic Tradition* (London: Oxford University Press, 2004).

who died about the beginning of the third century of the Christian era (200). In his work *Adversus Haereses* (*Against Heresies*), he writes that Christ "did, through his transcendent love, become what we are that he might bring us to what he is himself." Of course, this passage does not actually support the traditional LDS claim that the goal of human existence is to become a god on our own. It supports the human telos as being union with God. This view can and has been understood as deification in a broad sense.[13]

"He caused man to cleave to and become one with God. For unless man had overcome the enemy of man, the enemy would not have been legitimately vanquished. And again, unless it had been God who had freely given salvation, we could never have possessed it securely." Read in the context of Irenaeus' work as a whole, the LDS interpretation of man "becoming what he is" cannot ultimately be sustained. Irenaeus' work is directed against gnostic heretics of the second century who taught that only a "spiritual elite" could attain perfection because only this "in group" could fully understand the "special" or "secret" teaching required for perfection. Irenaeus argues that Christ's incarnation and the sacrament of baptism offer this eternal and incorruptible telos to everyone.[14]

The passage quoted is a classic statement of the patristic "exchange formula." In other words, he became what we are that we might become what he is. In the exchange formula, we are not Gods by nature. We are creatures. By baptism, we become adopted sons and daughters of God. One heresy in the early church, promoted especially by Paul of Samosata, held that Christ, too, was an adopted "son of God." Of course, the patristic church rejected this because it did not square with sacred scripture.[15]

Furthermore, Irenaeus' text should be read in the context of his developing Trinitarian theology. He is one of the first patristic

---

13. Iranaeus, *Adversus Haeresis*, Book 6, chap. 38.

14. Ibid., Book 3, chap. 6; also Denis Mins, O.P, *Iranaeus: An Introduction* (London: T. and T. Clark, 2010).

15. James Papandrea, *The Earliest Christologies*. (Chicago: IVP Academic, 2016); John Behr, *The Way to Nicea*. (New York: St. Vladimir's Seminary Press, 2001); and Richard Hanson, *The Search for the Christian Doctrine of God* (Edinburgh: T. and T. Clark, 1988).

thinkers to provide a rich Trinitarian understanding of God.[16] Understood in this framework, "becoming what he is" can only be understood as similar to the sort of unity the Son has with the Father. With, of course, the caveat that Christ is the eternal Son, co-existent with the Father, and we are adopted sons. So, the unity with the Father cannot be the same. (As a side note, I call attention to the clear statement that salvation is God's gift, not, as the LDS have traditionally claimed, a result of our good works.)

The second well-known passage is from St. Clement of Alexandria, a slightly younger contemporary of Irenaeus. He is generally thought to have died in 215 CE. In his *Protrepticus* (*Critique of the Heathen*), he writes, "The word of God became man that you may learn from man how man may become God."[17]

Much like Irenaeus in the west, Clement's target is pagan religions that provide a "secret" or "mysterious" way for initiates to become "gods." Clement attacks the deeply immoral portraits these writers paint of their "gods" and the secrecy of their rituals that are only open to the elite. If this sounds familiar after reading Irenaeus, it should. Most scholars hold that Clement had read Irenaeus.[18]

Clement's passage above is another example of the patristic "exchange formula"—he became as we are that we might become as he is. Throughout the text used here, Clement argues that the Father deifies man by giving sight to the blind, offering his own light to light man's way. "Deifying man by heavenly teaching. Putting His laws into our minds and writing them on our hearts."[19]

In so doing, God has transplanted Earth to Heaven and raised mortality to immortality. But Clement's God is a transcendent creator, who offers every person salvation through the cross, "who makes his sun to rise on all men."

Like Irenaeus, as well as Tertullian at the same time, Clement was one the earliest clear trinitarians in the patristic period. He writes of the Son being "co-existent with the Father" and "the word itself, the Son of God, who , being by equality of substance,

---

16. Jackson Lasher, *Iranaeus on the Trinity* (Leiden: E. J. Brill, 2014).
17. Clement of Alexandria *Protrepticus* (Exhortation Against the Heathen), Chap. 1.
18. Russell, *Doctrine of Deification*, 123–25.
19. Clement of Alexandria, *Protrepticus*, Chap. 11.

one with the Father is eternal and uncreated." Christ, being of one substance with the Father, is the foundation of trinitarian theology, a unity that the Latter-day Saints explicitly deny. However, if our telos is seen in the Son, a point Clement makes clear, then our telos is union with God, not becoming a separate god.[20]

Clement's view of the coming together of Greek philosophy and the Christian faith is a position the Latter-day Saints strongly reject. The LDS Church specifically holds that this marriage of faith and philosophy was one of the primary reasons that the patristic church lost its way, what the Mormons refer to as "The Great Apostasy." The most recent and authoritative statement of this view comes from another one of these Gospel Topics essays entitled: "Are Mormons Christian?" Here we read: "Latter-day Saints believe the melding of early Christian theology and Greek philosophy was a grave error."[21]

Following this brief treatment of patristic authors, the main text commendably notes that "what exactly the early church fathers meant when they spoke of becoming God is open to interpretation." Of course, the patristic writers never spoke of "becoming God" in the sense of becoming another or separate "God the Father." In a footnote at this point, the LDS Church admits, "There are likely important differences as well as similarities between the thinking of the Church fathers and Latter-day Saint teaching." An honest treatment of patristic writers will note the similarities, mostly verbal, as well as the differences that are much more substantive. Though the conclusions of this essay are contestable, the willingness to discuss these issues and the admission of differences are much appreciated.[22]

---

20. Clement of Alexandria, *Fragments, Commentary on the First Letter of John*. We may also note that Clement was one of the strongest early exponents of bringing faith and reason together in the form of Greek, especially Platonic, philosophy. His student, Origen, was the greatest patristic Platonist before Augustine. Many subsequent writers have often judged that Origen brought too much Platonism into Christianity. I doubt that such a conclusion can be made successfully. Origen was often accused of holding heretical positions that were declared errors only after his death. See Henri Crouzel, *Origen: The Life and Thought of the First Great Theologian*, trans. A. S. Worrall (New York: Harper Collins, 1989). Clement, *Stromata*, Book I, chaps. 2–5. In this he borrows heavily from the great Jewish neo-platonist Philo of Alexandria.

21. "Are Mormons Christian?"

22. "Becoming Like God," 10n15.

III

The Gospel Topics essay spends a great deal of time on the "man becomes God" portion. When it comes to LDS President Lorenzo Snow's famous statement "as man is God once was, as God is man may become," the essay admits the first part—"God was once a man"—but says almost nothing about it or its implications. "Little has been revealed about the first half of this couplet," the essay states, "consequently little is taught."[23]

The essay follows this up with what I read as a misleading reference to LDS President Gordon B. Hinckley's treatment of the topic. The essay accurately quotes Hinckley's statement to a *San Francisco Chronicle* reporter: "that gets into some pretty deep theology that we don't know very much about."[24] But the essay does not refer to Hinckley's answer to talk show host Larry King in Hinckley's celebrated and much admired interview: "I don't know that we teach that"—meaning God's having once been a man. In the context of the LDS reverence for the "living prophet," Hinckley's dismissal strikes me as an astounding claim. For the Christian tradition as a whole, the idea that God was once a man is a claim for which there is not even a verbally similar set of sources. Christians reject this picture of God because this cannot be a god in which we can have absolute trust for our salvation.[25]

What this essay and Hinckley wanted to avoid, Joseph Smith was not so reticent. In the King Follett sermon, Smith states at the beginning that his purpose is "to find out the character of the only wise and true God." His announced purpose is to tell humanity about God. What comes next is right out of the univocalist's playbook: "if the veil were rent today and you were to see the great God ... you would see him in the image and very form of a man. For Adam was created in the very fashion and image of God. He received instruction from and walked, talked, and conversed with him as one man talks and communes with another." This, of course, brings God down to our level, rather than elevate human beings to the divine.

---

23. Ibid., 6.

24. Don Lattin, "Musings of the Main Mormon," *San Francisco Chronicle,* Apr. 13, 1997.

25. Gordon B. Hinckley, Interview with Larry King, Sept. 8, 1998, transcript at www.lds-mormon.com/lkl_00.shtml.

To further this move, Smith states plainly that the idea that God was God from eternity is wrong. This foundational conviction of all western monotheism, that God is the eternal creator of all that exists, is here cast aside. Because, as Smith states, "God himself, the father of us all, dwelt on an earth the same as Jesus Christ." If God dwelt on an earth, then he cannot be the creator of everything, including all "earths."[26]

This idea has been consistently taught by LDS prophets, leaders, and other official sources, including past president Brigham Young, Lorenzo Snow, and Joseph Fielding Smith, and apostles George Q. Cannon, Melvin J Ballard, and Bruce R. McConkie.

It may be that the LDS Church and its officials know little about how such a process happened. The church cannot, however, deny that it is taught.

Some quotations suffice to make this point. In a general conference address in April 1921 Ballard said: "It is a Mormon truism that is current among us and we all accept it, that as man is God once was, and as God is man may become."[27] Young was more expansive: "He is our father. The father of our spirits and was once a man in mortal flesh as we are."[28] Cannon was equally direct: "the Prophet Joseph teaches us that our Heavenly Father was once a man and dwelt on an earth like we do."[29] In 1945, LDS general authority Milton R. Hunter wrote, "Mormon prophets have continuously taught the sublime truth that God the Eternal Father was once a mortal man who passed through a school of earth."[30] McConkie, who was later called to the LDS Quorum of Twelve Apostles, noted in his encyclopedic compendium *Mormon Doctrine* that God is "a personal being, a holy and exalted man."[31] McConkie's father-in-law, Joseph Fielding Smith, wrote: "God is

---

26. "King Follett Sermon."

27. Melvin J. Ballard, *Conference Report* (Salt Lake City: Church of Jesus Christ of Latter-day Saints, 1881), 98–108.

28. *Journal of Discourses*, 26 vols. (Liverpool: 1854–86), 7: 333.

29. George Q. Cannon, *Gospel Truth*, ed. Jerrald Newquist (Salt Lake City: Deseret Book Co., 1987), 101.

30. Milton R. Hunter, *The Gospel Through the Ages* (Salt Lake City: Deseret Book Co., 1945), 104.

31. Bruce R. McConkie, *Mormon Doctrine*, 2nd ed. (Salt Lake City: Bookcraft, 1966), 250.

an exalted man. Some people are troubled over statements of the Prophet Joseph Smith ... that our Father in Heaven at one time passed through a life and death and is an exalted man."[32] Finally, in the LDS Church's official magazine, the *Ensign*, in July 1996, Robert Millet, a professor of religion at LDS Church-owned Brigham Young University, stated: "knowing what we know concerning our Father—that he is a personal being; that he has a body of flesh and bones as tangible as our own; that he is an exalted and glorified and exalted being; that he was once a man and dwelt on an earth—knowing that this knowledge was had by many of the ancients, should we be surprised to find legends and myths throughout the cultures of the earth concerning Gods who have divine power but human attributes and passions."[33]

The central biblical text used by the Latter-day Saints at this point is John 5:19 where Jesus states: "I tell you the truth, the Son can do nothing by himself; he can only do what he sees his Father doing because whatever the Father does, the Son does also." Reading this passage in the manner in which Joseph Smith does shows again the pervasive preference of Mormons for a univocal understanding of language. If I drive a car and my son drives a car, he is doing the same as I.

The concept here seems to be that since God the Son does what "he sees his father doing," the father must have done these things before. Since neither the Bible nor any passage of uniquely LDS scripture gives any hint that the pattern Christ is following was performed by the Father on this planet, the Father must have done these things on another "Earth." Yet the LDS reading cannot be squared with the grammar of the passage. The LDS reading seems to be that the Father did something the Son is now doing. But the verb is not the past tense "did," but in the present tense "doing."

---

32. Joseph Fielding Smith, *Doctrines of Salvation*, comp. by Bruce R. McConkie, 3 vols. (Salt Lake City: Deseret Book Co., 1954–56), 1:10.

33. Robert Millett, "The Eternal Gospel," *Ensign*, July 1996, 53. For two recent studies exploring the LDS concept of God, see Terryl L. Givens, *Wrestling the Angel: The Foundations of Mormon Thought: Cosmos, God, Humanity* (New York: Oxford University Press, 2015); and John G. Turner, *The Mormon Jesus: A Biography* (Cambridge, Massachusetts: Harvard University Press, 2016).

Of course, this means that what Christ refers to as his "father" cannot be the creator of everything. At most, he is an organizer of some world. Mormons deny that God creates; rather, he designs. Even in the Gospel Topics essay that is the focus of this chapter, the LDS Church states that Mormons deny the idea of creation ex-nihilo.

There are more substantive analyses of this passage that are not even considered by Mormons because of Joseph Smith's and his church's commitment to a univocal understanding of language. For example, suppose what the Father does is show complete love and compassion to human beings in spite of our sin. Since God the Son is of the same divine substance as God the Father, the Son will be doing exactly what the Father does. This understanding is consistent with the biblical understanding of God as pure and continuous love (see 1 John 4:8: "God is Love"). It also reflects the grammar: what God does, not merely did.

The results of this line of thinking were reinforced for me in a recent conversation with a thoughtful, devout Latter-day Saint who is bishop of his local congregation. In the conversation he willingly admitted that the Latter-day Saints believe in an infinite regress of gods. Christ followed the pattern laid down by his father, who followed his father, ad infinitum.

IV

The denial of the Christian doctrine of creation ex-nihilo is fundamental to Mormonism and is explicitly noted in the Gospel Topics essay. For Latter-day Saints, God is an "organizer," a craftsman, not a creator. Of course, this raises a problem posed by Aquinas and others. If God is an organizer of pre-existing "stuff" or, in LDS parlance, of "unorganized" matter, then God's power is limited by the properties of this "stuff" or "matter." Consider a temporal example of the sort Mormons are fond of. A sculptor working with marble is limited in what he can do by the physical properties of the marble.[34]

In support of their view on creation, some recent LDS writers, and the Gospel Topics essay in particular, assert that creation

---

34. Aquinas, *Summa Theologica* 1, 1:44–45.

ex-nihilo is a post-biblical belief that emerged in the second century of the Christian era. For support of this view, the essay and other LDS writers cite Gerhard May, *Creation Ex Nihilo: The Doctrine of Creation out of Nothing in Early Christian Thought.*[35] This work is the best summary of a view which several other scholars have advanced in recent decades. Of course Genesis 1:1–2 does not explicitly answer the question as any competent Hebraist knows. Neither, however, does it decisively teach the LDS view.

Later biblical texts point to creation ex nihilo (see Ps.104). An explicit text is from 2 Maccabees 7:28: "I beg you child, look at the sky and the earth; see all that is in them and realize that God made them out of nothing and that man comes into being in the same way." This text is dated ca. 160 BCE.

In the first century of the Common Era, the great rabbinic scholar Gamaliel taught ex nihilo creation and referred to Isaiah 45:7, Psalm 148: 4 ff, Amos 4:13, and Proverbs 8:24 for support.[36] These all show God as creator, not just organizer. The most powerful of these is Psalm 148. The first six verses read:

> Praise the Lord
> Praise the Lord from the heavens
> Praise him in the heavens above
> Praise him, all his angels
> Praise him all his heavenly hosts
> Praise him sun and moon
> Praise him all you shining stars
> Let them praise the name of the Lord
> For he commanded and they were created
> He set them in place for ever and ever
> He gave a decree that will never pass away

35. William Lane Craig and Paul Copan, "Craftsman or Creator: An Examination of the Mormon Doctrine of Creation and a Defense of Creation Ex-Nihilo," in Francis Beckwith and Carl Mosser, eds., *The New Mormon Challenge* (Grand Rapids: Zondervan Publishers, 2002), 95–152.

36. [35]Gerhard May, *Creatio Ex Nihilo: The Doctrine of Creation out of Nothing in Early Christian Thought,* trans. A.S. Worrall (London: T. and T. Clark, 1994). For criticism of this thesis, see Markus Bockmuehl, "Creatio ex Nihilo in Palestinian Judaism and Early Christianity," *Scottish Journal of Theology* 65 (Aug. 2012): 253–70; Menahem Kister, "Tohu wa-Bohu: Primordial Elements and Creatio ex-Nihilo," *Jewish Studies Quarterly* 14 (2007): 229–56; and Paul Copan, "Is Creatio ex-Nihilo a Post-Biblical Invention: An Examination of Gerhard May's Proposal," *Trinity Journal* 17 (1996): 77–93.

I also note that an extensive foundation for creation-ex-nihilo is laid in the Dead Sea Scrolls. In an important passage, we read: "By his knowledge everything shall come into being, and all that does exist he establishes with his calculations and nothing is done outside of him. ... for beyond you there is no perfect path, and without your will nothing comes to be. You have taught all knowledge and all that exists is so by your will."[37]

Also relevant is an ancient Jewish prayer contained in a fourth-century Christian text known as the *Apostolic Constitutions*. In a passage from this prayer in section VII, we read: "Thou gave direction to thy wisdom and formed a reasonable creature as a citizen of the world saying 'let us make after our image and after our likeness;' and has exhibited him as the ornament of the world and formed him a body out of the four elements, those primary bodies, but has prepared a soul out of nothing."[38] Finally, we note that the great Jewish neo-platonist of the beginning of the Common Era, Philo of Alexandria, taught creation ex nihilo.[39] While a more worked out understanding of creation ex nihilo was developed in the second century of the Common Era, the roots are found in pre-Christian Judaism.

V

On the topic of God having once been a man, the Gospel Topics essay, at least, does not deny that this is LDS doctrine. However, the essay seems not to want to treat it, not even to provide the kinds of sources I have given to show its currency. But the essay does not deny its status in LDS belief.

Where the essay is especially misleading, in my view, is with the belief that is at the core of the King Follett sermon: that humans, when they become gods, will get or even create worlds to govern. The Gospel Topics essay reads: "A cloud and a harp are hardly a satisfying image for eternal joy, although most Christians

---

37. 1QS 11.11, in Florentino Martinez and Eibert Tigchelaar, eds., *The Dead Sea Scrolls*, 2 vols. (Leiden: Brill, 1997–98).

38. George Foot Moore, *Judaism in the First Centuries of the Christian Era*, 3 vols. (Cambridge, Massachusetts: Harvard University Press, 1966), 1: 381ff.

39. Harry Austryn Wolfson, *Philo*, 2 vols. (Cambridge, Massachusetts: Harvard University Press, 1949).

would agree that inspired music can be a tiny foretaste of the joy of eternal salvation. Likewise, while few Latter-day Saints would identify with caricatures of having their own planet, most would agree that the awe inspired by creation hints at our creative potential in the eternities."[40]

It may be true, as LDS bloggers and apologists have noted, that "there is no Mormon doctrine that says we will become Gods of our own planets."[41] But this is merely a linguistic spin. Joseph Smith used the word "kingdom" and spoke explicitly of getting "my own kingdom."[42] In recent decades the idea of getting one's own "planet" has been taught by many LDS leaders. For example, at the church's October 1968 general conference, Apostle Spencer W. Kimball said, "We shall need all of the accumulated secular knowledge in order to create worlds and furnish them."[43]

In 1976, in an address to students at the LDS Institute at the University of Utah, now-President Kimball said, "Each one of you has within the realm of his possibility to develop a kingdom over which you will preside as its king and God."[44] In *The Teachings of Spencer W. Kimball*, we read, "We educate ourselves in the secular and spiritual field, so that we may one day create worlds, people and govern them."[45] Joseph Fielding Smith, tenth president of the LDS Church, talked about human beings "building worlds and peopling them." In another publication, he wrote that "we will become Gods and have jurisdiction over them (worlds)."[46] Brigham Young, second president, spoke of faithful Mormons being "prepared to frame worlds, like unto ours, people them in the same manner as we have been brought forth."[47]

Technically none of these and other passages uses the word "planet." The idea, however, is the same. "Worlds," "earths," and

---

40. "Becoming Like God," 7.

41. Joanna Brooks, *Religion Dispatches*, July 8, 2011.

42. "King Follett Sermon."

43. Spencer W. Kimball, *Conference Report* (Oct. 1968), 131.

44. Spencer W. Kimball, Address at the LDS Institute, University of Utah, Oct. 22, 1976, copy in my possession.

45. Spencer W. Kimball, in Edward L. Kimball, ed., *Teachings of Spencer W. Kimball* (Salt Lake City: Deseret Book Co., 1982), 386.

46. Smith, *Doctrines of Salvation*, 2:132.

47. *Journal of Discourses*, 17:143.

"kingdoms" are equivalent to the general idea of "planet." We also note that in none of these passages is the concept of "becoming like God" mentioned. The idea is much more expansive. We will become "gods."

Distinguished LDS historian Richard L. Bushman has said that the idea of a "planet" for each of us as gods is not "a core Mormon belief."[48] Whether this belief is a "core" belief is not for an outsider to determine. We might point out that plural marriage on this earth was once taught as a central tenet of Mormonism. If the LDS Church desires to shed this belief, as it did with plural marriage in this world, perhaps it should more directly say so. The church cannot deny that the belief in a human/god ruling a separate kingdom has been taught officially, not even recently.

Conclusion

I believe that the picture of God and humankind in the King Follett sermon and in the Gospel Topics essay is fundamentally flawed. If God is not a creator or a first cause then the rational arguments for the existence of God simply cannot be adopted by the LDS Church. For the most part, Mormons do not use these arguments. If so, then what arguments can they make for the existence of God? In reality, the argument the Latter-day Saints fundamentally make is from personal experience. "I know the gospel (i.e., the LDS Church) is true because the spirit has confirmed its truthfulness to me." Of course, no Christian is going to deny the importance of the witness of the Holy Spirit for one's faith. But if that is the only ground you have, then the inroads of secularism and relativism will continue largely unchallenged. So keeping your family away from the critical questions about faith and morals is your only option because you have abandoned the rational arguments for the Christian faith and for moral truth that have been part of Christian faith for two millennia.

Moreover, if God is limited to being the God of this world, he is not the God who is all-knowing, all-good, and all-powerful. How, then, I ask, can God be our ultimate security in the face of

---

48. Richard Bushman, CNN interview, Oct. 10, 2011, at www.cnn.com/videos/politics/2011/10/10/jk-bushman-mormons-jeffress-cult.cn.

horrendous evils if his power, knowledge, and goodness are limited? If the god of this earth has to answer to someone above him, how can we know that he is always correct in what he asks us to do? How can we be sure that his salvation of us is secure if, in principle, he cannot know for certain what the roadblocks might be because he cannot know the future perfectly and if his power is limited by the properties of the "unorganized matter" out of which he fashioned this world?

Latter-day Saints are to be commended for admitting that what the patristic writers referred to as deification is not exactly what Mormons assert. The gulf is actually wider, but, at least, they admit that the two are not the same.

It is also welcome that they do not deny the LDS belief that God was once a man on an earth like this one. They may not want to talk about it, but they do not deny it. Unfortunately, they treat the idea that LDS "gods" will get their own "kingdom" to govern as a caricature, without, at a minimum, acknowledging to the numerous times this belief has been taught by the church's highest leaders in recent decades.

Of course, the Gospel Topics essay was not written to answer any of the profound questions raised by these beliefs. The problems remain for those of us who are non-LDS, and especially for those like myself who are Catholic. Catholicism has never shied away from the tough questions. We appropriated Greek philosophy to articulate and defend our faith. Mormonism, by contrast, seems not to find it helpful to think about the tough questions, instead holding that the marriage of faith and reason in the patristic church was the prime cause of the breakdown of the early Christian church. In my view, this is a loss.

3. DNA AND THE BOOK OF MORMON
SCIENCE, SETTLERS, AND SCRIPTURE

Thomas W Murphy and Angelo Baca

On January 31, 2014, the Church of Jesus Christ of Latter-day Saints released the sixth in a series of essays on Gospel Topics. Titled "Book of Mormon and DNA Studies," the essay "affirms that the Book of Mormon is a volume of sacred scripture comparable to the Bible." The "primary purpose of the Book of Mormon," the essay notes, "is more spiritual than historical." The authors then tailor a response to people who "have wondered whether the migrations it [the Book of Mormon] describes are compatible with scientific studies of ancient America." The essay contains an important acknowledgment: "the evidence assembled to date suggest that the majority of Native Americans carry largely Asian DNA." The essay counters, though, that the conclusions of science are tentative and "there are sound scientific reasons" that DNA from the Near East representing Book of Mormon peoples "might remain undetected." The essay sanctions a limited geographic setting for Book of Mormon events in the New World and offers a lengthy summary of basic principles of population genetics (for example, founder effect, population bottleneck, genetic drift, etc.) that might result in the loss of DNA profiles. The essay concludes with the claim that the current scientific evidence is simply too inconclusive for use by either critics or defenders of the Book of Mormon.[1]

This essay helps the LDS Church to reduce the gulf that has emerged between its views of Native America and those coming from the scientific community. Its acknowledgment of the DNA

---

1. "Book of Mormon and DNA Studies," at www.lds.org/topics/book-of-mormon-and-dna-studies.

indicating an Asian origin of Native Americans is a positive step forward for the LDS Church. The emphasis on the importance of the spirituality of scripture over historicity is particularly noteworthy. The words of caution issued to both defenders and critics of the Book of Mormon are likewise praiseworthy. The essay struggles, though, to escape fully settler colonialist thinking and to bridge the gap between science and scripture. The essay fails to address adequately Indigenous perspectives on either the science or the scripture.

In our reflections on this essay, we employ a decolonizing methodology to help bring to the forefront Indigenous perspectives on DNA and the Book of Mormon.[2] We consider the LDS Church's essay, not just within the context of new scientific insights into Native American origins, but also within the context of what settler colonial Mormons and Native Americans say about each other. Raised in the LDS Church with Indigenous heritage, both of us learned from an early age that we should aspire to become "white and delightsome." Due to intermarriage over multiple generations, one of us—Murphy—may appear closer to that than the other. When we read the Book of Mormon, we encounter conflicting messages. On the one hand, the scripture teaches that "all are alike unto God," yet it also represents dark skin as a curse from God for the wickedness of our ancestors and promises a removal of the curse, and thereby whiteness, in return for righteous behavior.[3] This conflicting message has its roots in the colonial

---

2. Gina Colvin and Joanna Brooks, *Decolonizing Mormonism: Approaching a Post-Colonial Zion* (Salt Lake City: University of Utah Press, 2018); Susan A. Miller and James Riding In, *Native Historians Write Back: Decolonizing American Indian History* (Lubbock: Texas Tech University Press, 2011); Margaret E. Kovach, *Indigenous Methodologies: Characteristics, Conversations, and Contexts* (Toronto: University of Toronto Press, Scholarly Publishing Division, 2010); Angela Waziyatawin Wilson and Michael Yellow Bird, *For Indigenous Eyes Only: A Decolonization Handbook* (Santa Fe: School of American Research, 2005); Michael Yellow Bird and Angela Waziyatawin Wilson, *For Indigenous Minds Only: A Decolonization Handbook* (Santa Fe: School of American Research Press, 2012); P. Jane Hafen and Brenden W. Rensink, eds., *Essays on American Indian and Mormon History* (Salt Lake City: University of Utah Press, 2019).

3. 2 Ne 5: 21–24, 26:33; 30:6; Alma 3:6–10, 23:18; Elise Boxer, "The Book of Mormon as Mormon Settler Colonialism," in Hafen and Rensink, eds., *Essays on American Indian and Mormon History*, 3–22; Kimberly M. Berkey and Joseph M. Spencer, "'Great Cause to Mourn': The Complexity of The Book of Mormon's

ideology that attributed ancient American civilizations to white immigrants from Israel who had purportedly been destroyed by the ancestors of the American Indians. In the twenty-first century, despite abundant evidence refuting that view, it remains difficult for white audiences to hear Native voices even when speaking about the origins of our own ancestors. As we read the forthright acknowledgments coming from the church's DNA essay, we see an opportunity, yet to be fully realized, for Latter-day Saints to disrupt the older settler narratives that have privileged the authority of colonizers over the bodies and voices of the colonized.

Historical Context

When Joseph Smith published the Book of Mormon in upstate New York in 1830, the idea that American Indians had descended from the lost tribes of Israel was commonplace.[4] Similarly, settler colonial scholars frequently claimed that an ancient white nation of mound builders had been responsible for the abundant evidences of civilization scattered across the landscape recently taken in violent confrontations with the Haudenosaunee (Iroquois) and a coalition of western tribes under the leadership of Tecumseh.[5]

Presentation of Gender and Race," in Elizabaeth Fenton and Jared Hickman, eds., *Americanist Approaches to The Book of Mormon* (New York: Oxford University Press, 2019), 298–320.

4. James Adair, *Adair's History of the American Indians* (Johnson City, Tennessee: Watauga Press, 1930 [1775]); Elias Boudinot, *A Star in the West; or a Humble Attempt to Discover the Long Lost Ten Tribes of Israel, Preparatory to the Return to Their Beloved City, Jerusalem* (Trenton, New Jersey: D. Fenton and S. Hutchinson & J. Dunham, 1816); Ethan Smith, *View of the Hebrews: Or the Tribes of Israel in America*, 2nd ed. (Poultney, Vermont: Smith and Smith, 1825); Thomas W Murphy, "Imagining Lamanites: Native Americans and the Book of Mormon," PhD diss., University of Washington, Seattle, 2003); Dan Vogel, *Indian Origins and the Book of Mormon* (Salt Lake City: Signature Books, 1986); Lee Eldridge. Huddleston, *Origins of the American Indians, European Concepts, 1492–1729* (Austin: Institute for Latin American Studies, University of Texas Press, 1967): Elizabeth Fenton, "Nephites and Israelites: *The Book of Mormon* and Hebraic Indian Theory," in Fenton and Hickman, eds. *Americanist Approaches*, 277–97.

5. Robert Silverberg, *Mound Builders of Ancient America: The Archaeology of a Myth* (Greenwich: New York Graphic Society, 1968); Barbara Alice Mann, *Native Americans, Archaeologists, and the Mounds* (New York: Peter Lang, 2003); Robert Wauchope, *Lost Tribes and Sunken Continents: Myth and Method in the Study of American Indians* (Chicago: University of Chicago Press, 1962); Cyrus Thomas, *Report on the Mound Explorations of the Bureau of Ethnology* (Washington, DC: Smithsonian Institution Press, 1985 [1894]).

Racial prejudice, fostered by acrimonious portrayals of Indian opponents during the American Revolution and the War of 1812, led
popular American authors to assert that American Indians were a
savage, nomadic people incapable of creating civilization without
inspiration from the peoples of the Old World.[6] These purported
savages, settler colonists in America had begun to tell themselves,
had once committed the same types of atrocities against an ancient American civilization that armies of American patriots were
inflicting upon Indigenous nations.[7] These images of American
Indians helped white settlers to ease their own consciences as they
occupied land that had belonged to others and reap the benefits of
conquest and colonization.

The Book of Mormon entered this cultural dialogue with a
narrative supporting the assertion that the ancestors of American
Indians had come from Israel. These ancestors, the new scripture
claimed, had once been white, delightsome, and chosen people, but
had degenerated, darkened, and lost their covenant status. After
a thousand-year struggle between Nephites and Lamanites that
strikingly resembled settler perceptions of the tensions between
European colonists and the Indigenous people they colonized, the
Book of Mormon ends with a cataclysmic war in which dark-
skinned Lamanites destroy the nation of lighter-skinned Nephites.
The Book of Mormon thus gave the sanction of scriptural status
to the popular Euroamerican accusations that American Indians

---

6. Alan Taylor, *The Divided Ground: Indians, Settlers, and the Northern Borderlands
of the American Revolution* (New York: Knopf, 2006); *William Cooper's Town: Power
and Persuasion on the Frontier of the Early American Republic* (New York: Vintage
Books, 1995), 39; Mann, *Mounds*; Roxanne Dunbar-Ortiz, *An Indigenous People's History of the United States* (Boston: Beacon Press, 2014), 107; James Fenimore Cooper,
The Last of the Mohicans: A Narrative of 1757 (New York: Macmillan, 1921 [1826]).
Intriguingly, an advertisement for the Book of Mormon appeared on the following
page when we consulted it on February 3, 2016. "James Fenimore Cooper," www.
online-literature.com/cooperj.

7. Mann, *Mounds*; George E. Tinker, *Missionary Conquest: The Gospel and Native American Cultural Genocide* (Minneapolis: Fortress Press, 1993); Vine Deloria
Jr., *Custer Died for Your Sins: An Indian Manifesto* (Norman: University of Oklahoma
Press, 1988); Robert Allen Warrior, "Canaanites, Cowboys, and Indians: Deliverance,
Conquest, and Liberation Theology Today," in *Native and Christian: Indigenous Voices
on Religious Identity in the United States and Canada*, ed. James Treat (New York: Routledge, 1996); Dunbar-Ortiz, *Indigenous People's History*.

were only recent immigrants themselves who had once destroyed an ancient white nation of mound builders.[8]

By the last decades of the nineteenth century, LDS views of ancient America and those emerging from the nascent field of anthropology had diverged in significant ways. The gradual acceptance of Darwinian ideas of human evolution removed the need for scientists to turn to the Bible for explanations of global history and migrations.[9] Similarities between the biology of Asians and American Indians undermined claims of ancient migrations from Europe and the Near East.[10] The idea that an ancient white race was responsible for American civilization fell by the wayside as archaeologists established what several nations of American Indians had been saying all along, that their ancestors built the mounds and other spectacular earthworks.[11] The anthropological community jettisoned these old ideas on the basis of both the accumulation of contradictory evidence and a recognition of their racist underpinnings.[12]

Some Latter-day Saint scholars began questioning their own beliefs, with a few acknowledging Asian origins of most Indians and starting to suggest that Mormons look for Nephites and Lamanites, not across the North and South American continents, but in more limited geographic settings such as southern Mexico and Central America or the Northeast and Midwest United States.[13] By the mid-twentieth century, an insurmountable gulf

---

8. Jace Weaver, "Missions and Missionaries," in *Native America in the Twentieth Century: An Encyclopedia* (New York: Garland Publishing, 1994); Murphy, "Imagining Lamanites."

9. Murphy, "Imagining Lamanites"; Wauchope, *Lost Tribes*; Simon G. Southerton, *Losing a Lost Tribe: Native Americans, DNA, and the Mormon Church* (Salt Lake City: Signature Books, 2004).

10. Murphy, "Imagining Lamanites"; Michael Crawford, *The Origins of Native Americans: Evidence from Anthropological Genetics* (New York: Cambridge University Press, 1998).

11. Mann, *Mounds*; Silverberg, *Mound Builders*; Thomas, "Mound Exploration"; Murphy, "Imagining Lamanites."

12. Stephen Jay Gould, *The Mismeasure of Man* (New York: W.W. Norton, 1996); Silverberg, *Mound Builders*.

13. Louis E. Hills, *A Short Work on the Geography of Mexico and Central America from 2234 B.C. To 421 A.D.* (Independence, Missouri: Louis E. Hills, 1917); *Historical Data from Ancient Records and Ruins of Mexico and Central America* (Independence, Missouri: Louis E. Hills, 1919); John Sorenson, *The Geography of Book of Mormon*

had developed between traditional LDS views and those coming from the scientific community. Of central concern to LDS scholars were not just questions of origins but also the different flora, fauna, and technology described in the Book of Mormon versus that found in oral histories and the archaeological record.[14] As their own scholars were beginning to articulate the tenuousness of Mormon beliefs about Native Americans, the LDS Church leadership responded with a defensive posture, proclaiming in the new introduction to the 1981 edition of the Book of Mormon that the Lamanites "are the principal ancestors of the American Indians."[15] By the twenty-first century, it would become increasingly evident to church leadership that this defensive posture would need to bend to the overwhelming new evidence coming from DNA.

That realization, though, would follow an unsuccessful attempt to quiet voices coming from the scholarly community. In November 2002, the LDS Church began, but then aborted, disciplinary action against one of us (Murphy) for his essay "Lamanite Genesis, Genealogy, and Genetics," published in the anthology *American Apocrypha*. This article summarized new evidence from DNA and its implications for the Book of Mormon.[16] Murphy successfully contested the disciplinary action and then assisted

---

Events: A Source Book (Provo, Utah: Foundation for Ancient Research and Mormon Studies, 1992); *An Ancient American Setting for the Book of Mormon* (Salt Lake City: Deseret Book Co., 1996); Terryl L. Givens, *By the Hand of Mormon: The American Scripture that Launched a New World Religion* (New York: Oxford University Press, 2002).

14. Stan Larson, *Quest for the Gold Plates: Thomas Stuart Ferguson's Archaeological Search for the Book of Mormon* (Salt Lake City: Freethinker Press/Smith Research Associates, 1996); B. H. Roberts, *Studies of the Book of Mormon*, 2nd ed. (Salt Lake City: Signature Books, 1992); George D. Smith, "B. H. Roberts: Book of Mormon Apologist and Skeptic," in *American Apocrypha: Essays on the Book of Mormon*, ed. Dan Vogel and Brent Lee Metcalfe (Salt Lake City: Signature Books, 2002).

15. Book of Mormon (Salt Lake City: Church of Jesus Christ of Latter-day Saints, 1981); Robert J. Mathews, "The New Publications of Standard Works—1979, 1981," *BYU Studies* 22, no. 4 (1982).

16. Thomas W Murphy, "Lamanite Genesis, Genealogy, and Genetics," in *American Apocrypha: Essays on the Book of Mormon*, ed. Dan Vogel and Brent Lee Metcalfe (Salt Lake City: Signature Books, 2002); "Double Helix: Reading Scripture in a Genomic Age," www.academia.edu/10367204/2003; Philip Lindholm, *Latter-Day Dissent: At the Crossroads of Intellectual Inquiry and Ecclesiastical Authority* (Salt Lake City: Greg Kofford Books, 2011); William Lobdell and Larry B Stammer, "Mormon Scientist, Church Clash over DNA Test," *Los Angeles Times*, Dec. 8, 2002; M. L. Lyke, "Church Put to DNA Test," *Seattle Post-Intelligencer*, Jan. 12, 2003.

Baca with a documentary film, *In Laman's Terms: Looking at Lamanite Identity*, drawing from diverse Indigenous perspectives to examine and challenge changing images and origins of Lamanites in the LDS Church.[17] In 2006, as we were working on the film, the LDS Church began to make changes to the introduction to the Book of Mormon with an updated edition published nationally by Doubleday.[18] These changes removed the term "principal" and amended the claim to assert that Lamanites were only "among the ancestors of the American Indians." By 2013 the LDS Church incorporated this correction, along with others reflecting changing views on race and plural marriage, into its own editions of the Book of Mormon.[19] Yet, even with these changes, LDS historian Elise Boxer (Fort Peck Assiniboine and Sioux) notes, "The Introduction to the Book of Mormon and the history therein not only ignores the diversity of Indigenous Peoples completely, but ignores their unique history that intimately connects them to the land."[20]

The film *In Laman's Terms* exemplifies Native concerns about historic representations of American Indians in the Book of Mormon and LDS pageantry, now challenged by DNA evidence. The Hill Cumorah Pageant in Palmyra, New York, for example, has been a Mormon cultural mainstay of many LDS family visitors to the Smith farm and surrounding area since the early 1920s. Now slated to close in 2020, the pageant demonstrates overt racism by having LDS actors in redface perform staged battles of Book of

---

17. Angelo Baca, *In Laman's Terms: Looking at Lamanite Identity* (Seattle: Native Voices, 2008); "Porter Rockwell and Samuel the Lamanite Fistfight in Heaven: A Mormon Navajo Filmmaker's Perspective," in Colvin and Brooks, eds., *Decolonizing Mormonism*, 67–76.

18. Both authors also appeared in another film released in 2005, and Murphy appeared in one in 2003. Scott Johnson and Joel Kramer, *The Bible Vs. The Book of Mormon* (Brigham City, Utah: Living Hope Ministries, 2005); Joel Kramer and Jeremy Reyes, *DNA Vs. The Book of Mormon* (Brigham City, Utah: Living Hope Ministries, 2003). These films, produced by Living Hope Ministries, represented an evangelical Christian, not an Indigenous perspective, on these debates. For critiques, see Thomas W Murphy, "Inventing Galileo," *Sunstone* 131 (2004): 60; "Decolonization on the Salish Sea: A Tribal Journey Back to Mormon Studies," in Colvin and Brooks, eds., *Decolonizing Mormonism*, 47–66.

19. Peggy Fletcher Stack, "Single Word Change in Book of Mormon Speaks Volumes," *Salt Lake Tribune*, Nov. 8, 2007; "New Mormon Scriptures Tweak Race, Polygamy References," ibid., Mar. 19, 2013; "Book of Mormon and DNA Studies."

20. Boxer, "Mormon Settler Colonialism," 9.

Mormon lore simultaneously stripping Native American cultural identity and reinforcing imagined ones from scripture presented as history. Such epic mythical story telling in New York, like Pioneer Days in Utah, keeps the heritage tales about days of yore alive, yet are clearly in direct contradiction to Native histories and Indigenous voices presented in the film.[21] Forrest Cuch (Ute) told the audience, "We are not of Israelite" heritage and "certainly are not going to turn white someday."[22] G. Peter Jemison (Seneca) questioned the idea that his ancestors had contributed to an ancient destruction of a Nephite civilization: "We were never the kind that thought you had to really wipe out every last person."[23] Tim Roderick (Wampanoag) observed that stories of Lamanites served as a tool for white Latter-day Saints to "let themselves at ease" over their own complicity in atrocities against Native America.[24] For people of Native heritage, the DNA evidence substantiated claims to an occupation of the Americas since time immemorial, dispelled racist allegations that our ancestors were once white and that we should aspire to be so again, and corrected the historical record about who had actually engaged in wars of ethnic destruction.[25]

Content

The church's publication of "Book of Mormon and DNA Studies" on its website on the last day of 2014 is a watershed moment in LDS understandings of the Book of Mormon. In the long term, the most significant statement in the essay is likely to be the forthright acknowledgment in the second paragraph that "the primary purpose of the Book of Mormon is more spiritual than

---

21. Baca, *In Laman's Terms*; Angelo Baca and Erika Bsumek, "On Pioneer Day, Don't Forget the People Who Were Already Here," *Salt Lake Tribune*, July 20, 2019; Philip J. Deloria, *Playing Indian* (New Haven, Connecticut: Yale University Press, 1998); Gerald S. Argetsinger, "The Hill Cumorah Pageant: A Historical Perspective," *Journal of Book of Mormon Studies* 13, 1–2 (2004); Elise Boxer, "'This Is the Place! Disrupting Mormon Settler Colonialism," in Colvin and Brooks, *Decolonizing Mormonism*, 77–99.

22. Baca, *In Laman's Terms*.

23. Ibid.

24. Ibid.

25. Ibid.; Murphy, *Imagining Lamanites*; P. Jane Hafen, "Afterword" in Colvin and Brooks, eds., *Decolonizing Mormonism*, 263–73.

historical." This statement follows the opening sentence of the first paragraph affirming "that the Book of Mormon is a volume of sacred scripture comparable to the Bible."[26] It is particularly significant that the opening sentence does not affirm the Book of Mormon as an ancient history, but instead affirms its status as scripture like the Bible.[27]

After setting the stage with an umbrella large enough to include those who do not find the Book of Mormon's history compelling, the essay narrows its focus to those who "have wondered whether the migrations it describes are compatible with scientific studies of ancient America." The essay acknowledges the central problem: "Some have contended that the migrations mentioned in the Book of Mormon did not occur because the majority of DNA identified to date in modern native peoples most closely resembles that of eastern Asian populations." Yet it claims that the conclusions of genetics and science more generally "are tentative," that "much work remains to be done," and suggests "the need for a more careful approach to the data." In particular, the essay asserts that "nothing is known about the DNA of Book of Mormon peoples, and even if their genetic profile were known, there are sound scientific reasons it might remain undetected." For the "same reasons," the essay's authors contend "arguments that some defenders of the Book of Mormon make based on DNA studies are also speculative." The essay's introduction concludes with the thesis, "DNA studies cannot be used decisively to either affirm or reject the historical authenticity of the Book of Mormon."[28]

The body of the essay begins with a section entitled "The Ancestors of the American Indians." This section immediately concedes, "The evidence assembled to date suggests that the majority of Native Americans carry largely Asian DNA." It briefly summarizes the work of scientists who "theorize that in an era that predated

---

26. "Book of Mormon and DNA Studies."
27. The Bible also has its share of problematic associations with history. For a deeper discussion of those issues, see Israel Finkelstein and Neil Asher Silberman, *The Bible Unearthed: Archaeology's New Vision of Ancient Israel and the Origin of Its Sacred Texts* (New York: Free Press, 2001); John C. Laughlin, *Archaeology and the Bible* (London: Routledge, 2000); Murphy, "Imagining Lamanites"; "Lamanite Genetics."
28. "Book of Mormon and DNA Studies."

Book of Mormon accounts, a relatively small group of people migrated from northeast Asia to the Americas by way of a land bridge that connected Siberia to Alaska." This small group of people, "scientists say, spread rapidly to fill North and South America and were likely the primary ancestors of modern American Indians."[29] These statements provide the rationale behind the recent textual changes to the introduction of the Book of Mormon. Even though the essay frames the evidence as theoretical perspectives of scientists, it was compelling enough that the church changed the introduction to its central scripture.

The essay suggests that the Book of Mormon's lack of "direct information about cultural contact between the peoples it describes and others who may have lived nearby" as reasons for LDS assumptions that Book of Mormon characters "Jared, Lehi, Mulek, and their companions were the first or the largest or even the only groups to settle the Americas." The essay counters that assumption with the assertion that the Book of Mormon "does not claim that the peoples it describes were either the predominant or the exclusive inhabitants of the lands they occupied" and that "cultural and demographic clues in its text hint at the presence of other groups."[30]

The essay proceeds with the suggestion that Joseph Smith may have been open "to the idea of migrations other than those described in the Book of Mormon." It notes that "many Latter-day Saint leaders and scholars over the past century have found the Book of Mormon account to be fully consistent with the presence of other established populations." It concedes, though, that "nothing is known about the extent of intermarriage and genetic mixing between Book of Mormon peoples or their descendants and other inhabitants of the Americas." It concludes this section with the claim that "the DNA of Book of Mormon peoples likely represented only a fraction of all DNA in ancient America."[31]

The next section of the essay is entitled "Understanding the Genetic Evidence." This section includes a brief description of DNA, explaining differences between data coming from Y chromosomes

---

29. Ibid.
30. Ibid.
31. Ibid.

that can be used to chart a male's paternal lineage and that of mitochondrial DNA that can be used to trace the maternal lineage of males and females. The essay concedes, "At the present time, scientific consensus holds that the vast majority of Native Americans belong to sub-branches of the Y-chromosome haplogroups C and Q and the mitochondrial DNA haplogroups A, B, C, D, and X, all of which are predominantly East Asian," not Near Eastern, which the Book of Mormon contends. Following this admission, the essay complicates the situation by pointing to admixture between European, West Asian, and Native American ancestors prior to "the earliest migration to the Americas." It also claims that there are some "Near Eastern DNA markers ... in modern native populations" but that "it is difficult to determine whether they are the result of migrations that predated Columbus, such as those described in the Book of Mormon, or whether they stem from genetic mixing that occurred after the European conquest." This section of the essay concludes with the observation that "scientists do not rule out the possibility of additional, small-scale migrations to the Americas."[32]

The remainder of the essay is devoted to explanations for why the DNA of Book of Mormon populations may never be found in the Americas. Concerns raised include uncertainty about "the DNA that [Book of Mormon characters] Lehi, Sariah, Ishmael, and others brought to the Americas." If these founding populations were uncharacteristic of Near Eastern populations, this would make it more difficult to recognize their descendants. In addition to this "founder effect," the essay points to "population bottleneck" and "genetic drift" as other complicating factors. "Population bottleneck is the loss of genetic variation that occurs when a natural disaster, epidemic disease, massive war, or other calamity results in the death of a substantial part of a population." The essay claims that "the catastrophic war at the end of the Book of Mormon [and] the European conquest of the Americas in the 15th and 16th centuries touched off just such a cataclysmic chain of events." "Genetic drift" is defined as "the gradual loss of genetic

---

32. Ibid.

markers in small populations due to random events."[33] Founder effect, population bottlenecks, and genetic drift are offered as possible explanations for why DNA from Book of Mormon populations is not found among today's Native Americans.

The essay concludes with caution directed towards both critics and defenders of the Book of Mormon and a reminder of the primacy of religious truth. "Much as critics and defenders of the Book of Mormon would like to use DNA studies to support their views, the evidence is simply inconclusive." "Book of Mormon record keepers were primarily concerned with conveying religious truths and preserving the spiritual heritage of their people." It ends with a recommendation to seek religious truth from the Holy Ghost and a reminder that the Book of Mormon's mission is that of "a volume of sacred scripture with the power to bring" readers "closer to Jesus Christ."[34]

Strengths

The distinction the essay makes at its outset between history and scripture sets the LDS Church on a pathway, already forged by the Community of Christ (previously Reorganized Church of Jesus Christ of Latter Day Saints), towards the embrace of once controversial views of the Book of Mormon as scripture but not history.[35] This pathway has been paved in the LDS community by published scholarship, such as that contained in the anthologies *The Word of God*, *New Approaches to the Book of Mormon*, *American Apocrypha*, and *Americanist Approaches to The Book of Mormon* as well as the monographs *Digging in Cumorah* and *An Imperfect Book*.[36]

---

33. Ibid.

34. Ibid.

35. William D. Russell, "Understanding Multiple Mormonisms," in *The Oxford Handbook of Mormonism*, ed. Terryl L. Givens and Philip L. Barlow (New York: Oxford University Press, 2015); Richard P. Howard, "Latter Day Saint Scriptures and the Doctrine of Propositional Revelation," in *The Word of God*, ed. Dan Vogel (Salt Lake City: Signature Books, 1990); Geoffrey F. Spencer, "A Reinterpretation of Inspiration, Revelation, and Scripture," ibid. (1990).

36. Dan Vogel, ed., *The Word of God: Essays on Mormon Scripture* (Salt Lake City: Signature Books, 1990); Brent Lee Metcalfe, ed., *New Approaches to the Book of Mormon: Explorations in Critical Methodology* (Salt Lake City: Signature Books, 1993); Dan Vogel and Brent Lee Metcalfe, *American Apocrypha: Essays on the Book of Mormon* (Salt Lake City: Signature Books, 2002); Fenton and Hickman, eds., *Americanist*

The essay's distinction between history and scripture expands the acceptability of approaches to the Book of Mormon to now include statements such as the following from scholar Anthony Hutchinson: "The Book of Mormon should be seen as authoritative scripture, part of a larger canon, ... as not containing the real history of the ancient Americas but an account of the origins of the American Indians and their relation to ancient biblical stories as conceived by its nineteenth-century author, Joseph Smith."[37] By placing a priority on the book's status as scripture over its historicity, the essay offers an inclusive embrace of even those who may not find its discussion of genetics convincing but are willing to accept the Book of Mormon's sacred status.

The essay brings the LDS Church into alignment with most of its apologists and many of its critics. There is significant common ground between the perspectives of most critics and apologists that is effectively captured in the essay. LDS scientists generally concede that DNA from Native America provides no affirmative support for Book of Mormon narratives. The previously predominant interpretation that the Book of Mormon described the founding of American Indian populations across both western hemispheres is clearly refuted by the evidence and now repudiated by this essay. Critics and apologists agree that scenarios can be imagined whereby a small population in the distant past interbred on a small scale with a much larger population and left few genetic traces in modern populations. Processes such as founder effect, population bottleneck, and genetic drift would be necessary for such a scenario to be plausible.[38] The essay puts church leadership

---

Approaches; Mark D. Thomas, *Digging in Cumorah: Reclaiming Book of Mormon Narratives* (Salt Lake City: Signature Books, 1999); Earl M. Wunderli, *An Imperfect Book: What the Book of Mormon Tells Us About Itself* (Salt Lake City: Signature Books, 2013).

37. Anthony Hutchinson, "The Word of God Is Enough: The Book of Mormon as Nineteenth-Century Scripture," in *New Approaches to the Book of Mormon*, ed. Brent L. Metcalfe (Salt Lake City: Signature Books, 1993), 1.

38. Terryl L. Givens, Thomas W Murphy, and Scott Woodward, Interview with Doug Fabrizio, Dec. 19, 2002; Michael F. Whiting, "Does DNA Evidence Refute the Authenticity of the Book of Mormon?" at www.publications.mi.byu.edu/video/does-dna-evidence-refute-the-authenticity-of-the-book-of-mormon/; Thomas W Murphy, "Sin, Skin, and Seed: Mistakes of Men in the Book of Mormon," *Journal of the John Whitmer Historical Association* 25 (2004); "Simply Implausible: DNA and a Mesoamerican Setting for the Book of Mormon," *Dialogue: A Journal of Mormon*

in agreement with this growing consensus from its scholarly community and provides context for the recent changes to the Book of Mormon's introduction.

The church's essay offers an important caution to defenders of Book of Mormon historicity who would use DNA to support historical claims. This warning appears to be directed towards church members who advocate that the presence of the X lineage of mtDNA in some North American Indian populations provides support for the Heartland geography that places the events of the Book of Mormon among the mound building populations of Midwest and Eastern North America.[39] Geneticists have undermined this Heartland hypothesis by demonstrating that the X2a variant found in North America "is not found in the Middle East." In fact, "none of the X2 lineages found in the Middle East are immediately ancestral to X2a" and the Indigenous American branch separated from the others more than 10,000 years prior to the events in the Book of Mormon.[40] Furthermore, the propensity of Heartland advocates to label the broader X lineage as European or Middle Eastern, when its various branches are also found in Africa, Asia, and North America, misrepresents the scientific data and undermines the LDS Church's efforts to eradicate racism.[41]

The essay's acknowledgment of existing scientific data and its caution directed at defenders of the Book of Mormon helps to

---

Thought (2003); D. Jeffrey Meldrum and Trent D. Stephens, "Who Are the Children of Lehi?" *Journal of Book of Mormon Studies* 12, 1 (2003); *Who Are the Children of Lehi? DNA and the Book of Mormon* (Salt Lake City: Greg Kofford Books, 2007); Dean H. Leavitt, Jonathan C. Marshall, and Keith A. Crandall, "How Defining Alternative Models Helps in the Interpretation of Genetic Data," *Dialogue: A Journal of Mormon Thought* 36, 4 (2003); Ugo A. Perego, "The Book of Mormon and the Origin of Native Americans from a Maternally Inherited DNA Standpoint," *FARMS Review* 22, 1 (2010); John Charles Duffy, "The Use of 'Lamanite' in Official LDS Discourse," *Journal of Mormon History* 34, 1 (2008).

39. See, for example, Rod L. Meldrum, *Rediscovering the Book of Mormon Remnant through DNA* (Mendon, New York: Digital Legend, 2009).

40. Jennifer A. Raff and Deborah A. Bolnick, "Does Mitochondrial Haplogroup X Indicate Ancient Trans-Atlantic Migration to the Americas? A Critical Re-Evaluation," *PaleoAmerica* 1, 4 (2015): 298–99; Ugo Perego, et al., "Distinctive Paleo-Indian Migration Routes from Beringia marked by two rare mtDNA haplogroups," *Current Biology* 19 (2009).

41. Thomas W Murphy and Angelo Baca, "Rejecting Racism in Any Form: Latter-Day Saint Rhetoric, Religion, and Repatriation," *Open Theology* 2 (2016).

distance the LDS Church from the lack of compassion and under-standing of Native perspectives demonstrated by some Latter-day Saints in discussions of the case of Kennewick Man. Also called The Ancient One, these skeletal remains found along the Colum-bia River in July 1996 date to approximately 9,000 years ago. At least one prominent LDS writer expressed excitement at the dis-covery of the Ancient One and took a hostile rhetorical position towards the Umatilla, who, he feared, "may succeed in hiding away this skeleton that could never have belonged to a member of their or any living tribe." This same writer accused Native Americans of displacing an ancient white civilization and expressed "plea-sure" at the report of a skeleton of presumed "Caucasoid physical structure" from ancient America and its implications for "Book of Mormon culture and archaeology."[42] The church's more cautious approach in its essay on DNA proved judicious when genetic tests subsequently demonstrated The Ancient One's common ancestry with and close ties to contemporary American Indians.[43]

While LDS scholars tend to focus on the validity of histori-cal claims of the Book of Mormon, Native American scholars are more concerned about the usurpation of power by the coloniz-ers over indigenous bodies. Tribal religions, as described by Vine Deloria Jr. (Standing Rock Sioux), do not require that a partic-ular event took place in the past. No nation asserts "its history as having primacy over the accounts of any other tribe." Sharing stories is a "social event embodying civility" and differing accounts receive credence because it is "not a matter of trying to establish power over others to claim absolute truth."[44] Anthropologist Kim Tallbear (Dakota) notes, "Native American origin narratives are generally missing the will to convert and so are without inherent intolerance for other ontologies." The most important issue for Native American concerns about genetic research "always focuses

---

42. Orson Scott Card, "Reopening the Question of the Origin of Pre-Columbian People," *Nauvoo: A Gathering Place for Latter-day Saints,* June 12, 1997, at www.nauvoo.com/library/card-lostman.html.

43. Morten Rasmussen et al., "The Ancestry and Affiliations of Kennewick Man," *Nature* 523, 7561 (2015), at www.nature.com/articles/nature14625.

44. Vine Deloria Jr., *God Is Red: A Native View of Religion, The Classic Work Updated* (Golden Colorado: Fulcrum Publishing, 1994), 98–100.

on who has the power to research whom and how, and who has the power to make policy that affects Native American lives."[45] Latter-day Saint scholar P. Jane Hafen (Taos Pueblo) explains, "Recognizing that more than one origin story can co-exist with another does not require the dismissal of either."[46] By opening itself to non-historical interpretations of the Book of Mormon, the LDS Church is creating space not just for its scientists and scholars but also for those who approach the Book of Mormon from an Indigenous perspective.

Shortcomings

The authors of the church's essay appear mostly to avoid racialized interpretations of genetic data, but they do not go far enough, in our opinion, to repudiate the racism coming from the Book of Mormon. The essay does not offer an approach that would realize the laudable expressions in the Gospel Topics parallel essay on "Race and the Priesthood," unequivocally condemning "all racism, past and present, in all its forms."[47] While it is an improvement over church-sponsored pageants and the writings of some Heartland geography proponents, the church essay perpetuates racial thinking when it slips from otherwise careful language to use the phrase "Asian DNA" or "Near Eastern DNA" rather than DNA markers found in Asia or the Near East. The essay authors are in a difficult situation as they aspire to move beyond a colonial legacy of racism. The Book of Mormon itself projects a nineteenth-century, settler colonial, stereotypical, racialized, social organization of civilized (Nephite) and savage (Lamanite) peoples back into the past. This representation of ancient social groups demarcated by skin color served important social and political functions in antebellum settler colonialism, but these types of racial divisions of society never existed in the pre-Columbian Americas.[48]

45. Kim Tallbear, *Native American DNA* (Minneapolis: University of Minnesota Press, 2013), 116.

46. Hafen, "Afterword."

47. "Race and the Priesthood," at www.lds.org/topics/race-and-the-priesthood.

48. Murphy, "Imagining Lamanites"; Mann, *Mounds*; Taylor, *Divided Ground*; Curtis M. Hinsley, "Digging for Identity: Reflections on the Cultural Background of Collecting," in *Repatriation Reader: Who Owns American Indian Remains?* ed. Devon

By trying to preserve room for reading the Book of Mormon as history, the essay perpetuates the idea that American Indians could not have developed civilization without inspiration from the Old World and negates the diverse origin stories told in Indigenous communities. Nineteenth-century settler colonists had disassociated the American Indians they were displacing from the abundant evidence of sophistication in the mounds dotting the landscape of New York and Ohio. They presumed that Haudenosaunee (Iroquois) and other Indigenous peoples were incapable of the arts of civilization, and developed elaborate myths about ancient white mound builders to deflect guilt over the atrocity in which they were participating. "Settlers," the Seneca descendant Barbara Alice Mann observed, "had an enormous stake in denying any cultural credit to Native Americans, inspiring Euroamericans to dream up a doomed, and by the time the myth was done, *white* race of Mound Builders in ancient America." "The myth," she continues, "was the only way, psychologically, to reconcile their ongoing genocide and land seizure—openly justified by the 'savage' state of Native America—with the undeniable evidence of 'civilization' presented by the math, astronomy, and artistry of the mounds."[49] The essay's attempt to use some uncertainty in scientific data to protect historical interpretations of the Book of Mormon serves the social function of perpetuating racist portrayals of the ancestors of the American Indians and displacing Indigenous histories that connect people to land.

In order to advance the idea that Native American populations experienced genetic bottlenecks, the essay points to "the catastrophic war at the end of the Book of Mormon" and European conquest as "a cataclysmic chain of events." In the first of these claims, the essay perpetuates the unsubstantiated settler colonial myth that American Indians destroyed an ancient white civilization. Settler colonial attributions of mound building to an ancient white race destroyed by American Indians were thoroughly

---

A. Mihesuah (Lincoln: University of Nebraska Press, 2000); Silverberg, *Mound Builders*; Murphy and Baca, "Rejecting Racism"; Baca, *In Laman's Terms*; Tallbear, *Native American DNA*.

49. Mann, *Mounds*, 53.

discredited in archaeological circles by the end of the nineteenth century.[50] In fact, there was ample evidence available in Joseph Smith's life time that the Haudenosaunee, Shawnee, Lenâpé, and Cherokee were responsible for the earthworks and burial mounds sometimes credited instead to immigrants from the Old World.[51] This evidence, however, did not serve as a salve for subconscious angst over the treatment of Native America and, thus, was ignored in favor of a legend with more social appeal to settler colonists. The DNA evidence presents the LDS Church with a chance to repudiate these racist portrayals of the American past and embrace Indigenous People's own histories, an opportunity missed by the current version of the church's essay.

In its reference to another bottleneck coinciding with the conquest and colonization "of the fifteenth and sixteenth centuries," the essay deflects responsibility for violence against American Indians from the United States. By implying that this destruction only took place in the fifteenth and sixteenth centuries, the essay implicitly places blame for atrocities on the Spanish, Portuguese, and French while ignoring the role of the Dutch, English, and American patriots in the seventeenth through nineteenth centuries. The violence, disease, and corresponding decline of Indigenous populations continued up through the end of the nineteenth century.[52] Mormons, themselves, would play a role in the violent colonization of the Great Basin as aptly demonstrated by the Western Shoshone historian Ned Blackhawk.[53] The essay's misrepresentation of this history is particularly problematic for those of us whose ancestors experienced abuse at the hands of settler colonists from the United States.

It is important to note that Joseph Smith was not the originator of the myth of ancient white mound builders that appears in the Book of Mormon. Instead, this was part of the cultural context

---

50. Silverberg, *Mound Builders*; Thomas, "Mound Exploration"; Murphy, "Inventing Galileo."

51. Mann, *Mounds*.

52. Catherine M. Cameron, Paul Kelton, and Alan C. Swedlund, *Beyond Germs: Native Depopulation in North America* (Tucson: University of Arizona Press, 2015).

53. Ned Blackhawk, *Violence over the Land: Indians and Empire in the Early American West* (Cambridge, Massachusetts: Harvard University Press, 2006).

that Smith brought to his mystical experiences. Ethan Smith, a Congregationalist minister in Poultney, Vermont, and no known relation to Joseph Smith, combined this popular legend with the widespread and long-standing belief that American Indians were the lost tribes of Israel in his book, *View of the Hebrews*, published in 1823 and 1825.[54] The Mormon prophet would give this racist ideology of settler colonialism the veneer of scripture and buttress it with the cultural and ecological portrayals of the Nephites in the Book of Mormon. Seeming to ignore the concerns of local Native Americans, the LDS Church continues to promote these racial mythologies indirectly in this essay and, until 2020, explicitly in its annual Hill Cumorah pageant.[55] The scripture and pageant portray Nephites as a civilized, white, Christian, agrarian nation using the domesticated plants, animals, and technology of European society and besieged by filthy, idolatrous, wandering Lamanites.

The DNA essay disappointingly avoids discussion of the anachronistic portrayal of European plants, animals, and technology in the Book of Mormon. LDS scholars have sought to explain away these mistakes by suggesting that Israelite immigrants had applied familiar names of plants and animals from the Old World to the unfamiliar flora and fauna they encountered in the New World.[56] One does not need to imagine such bizarre things as a tapir pulling a chariot or a deer yoked to a plow to explain these anomalies. Smith would likely have encountered ample evidence of horses, cattle, oxen, sheep, goats, wheat, barley, steel, plows, wagons, glass, ̓etc., in the burial mounds and ruins of the Haudenosaunee he explored as a treasure hunter. By the 1820s, Haudenosaunee had been trading with Europeans for these items for nearly two centuries and had incorporated them into their everyday lives. In fact, they even preferentially buried the dead with items recently obtained through trade with Europeans because these items were

---

54. Smith, *View of the Hebrews*; Vogel, *Indian Origins* ; Gershon Greenberg, *The Holy Land in American Religious Thought, 1620–1948* (Lanham, Maryland: University Press of America, 1994); Robert N. Hullinger, *Joseph Smith's Response to Skepticism* (Salt Lake City: Signature Books, 1992); Adair, *Adair's History of the American Indians*.

55. Baca, *In Laman's Terms*.

56. Sorenson, *An Ancient American Setting for the Book of Mormon*, 293–98.

novel and not readily available in the world of the dead.[57] These anachronisms cannot be explained away by genetic drift, founder effects, or misnomers.[58] A more forthright portrayal would consider these problems alongside the lack of evidence from DNA.

The essay does not fully realize the scripture's seemingly inspired message that the Creator "speaketh unto men according to their own language, unto their understanding" (2 Ne. 31:3). Whatever the nature of Joseph Smith's contact with divinity, his understanding of the experience was necessarily framed and articulated through his own language and cultural experiences.[59] Smith's historical setting was that of a colonizing society struggling to come to spiritual terms with the horrific violence it was unleashing upon Native America. If Mormons could find ways to read the Book of Mormon as a product of Smith's struggle with God in a settler colonial society, necessarily littered with nineteenth-century "mistakes of men," then its inclusive theology could be brought to the forefront and an ecumenical place could be created wherein Latter-day Saints might recognize the divinity of other sacred narratives from various times and places.[60] In particular, LDS could acknowledge that people of Indigenous heritage have sacred stories and histories of our own, akin to the Bible and the latter-day canon.

Besides the Book of Mormon's evident racism, the primary disagreement between apologists and critics debating DNA and the Book of Mormon is not over the genes of Native Americans. Rather, the issue is that the Book of Mormon narrative does not describe the types of possible scenarios that would lead to a loss

---

57. Dean R. Snow, *The Iroquois* (Cambridge, Massachusetts: Blackwell, 1996), 90; Taylor, *Cooper's Town*, 62; Barbara Graymont, *The Iroquois in the American Revolution* (Syracuse, New York: Syracuse University Press, 1972), 147, 219; Murphy and Baca, "Rejecting Racism"; Thomas W Murphy, "All the Wrong Plants and Animals: Grave-Robbery and the Book of Mormon," in *Northwest Anthropology Conference* (Tacoma, Washington, 2016); "Lee Yost to Diedrich Willers, Jr., 18 May 1897," in *Early Mormon Documents*, ed. Dan Vogel (Salt Lake City: Signature Books, 2003).

58. "Simply Implausible."

59. Murphy, "Imagining Lamanites"; "Lamanite Genetics"; Thomas W Murphy, "Other Scriptures: Restoring Voices of the Gantowisas to an Open Canon," in Hafen and Rensink, eds., *Essays on American Indian and Mormon History*, 23–40.

60. "Sin, Skin, and Seed"; "Decolonization"; "Other Scriptures"; Murphy and Baca, "Rejecting Racism."

of genetic heritage in modern populations. One must sacrifice the scripture's prophecies of Lehite descendants surviving into the last days and disregard its descriptions, some attributed to Jesus, of populations of hundreds of thousands, and in the case of the Jaredites millions, of descendants of immigrants from the Near East.[61] The plausible scenarios that might have diluted DNA of a Near Eastern origin do not coincide with the Book of Mormon narrative. While there are a few passages in the scripture that can be stretched to seem to refer to some unnamed social groups that could have been of Asian origin, the Book of Mormon clearly lacks the level of cultural diversity evident in other ancient narratives such as the Bible and the Popol Vuh.[62] The stated purpose of the scripture to restore Lamanites to a knowledge of their forefathers, its lineage histories that all tie its population back to the Near East, and its prophecies of the continuation of these lineages into the last days collectively undermine efforts to remake the Book of Mormon societies into the types of settler communities that might have lost their distinct genetic signatures.

To give the impression that these new views of the Book of Mormon might be compatible with the text of the book itself, the essay advances some rather incredulous interpretations. Particularly problematic is the assertion that the Book of Mormon "does not claim that the peoples it describes were either the predominant or the exclusive inhabitants of the lands they occupied."[63] This declaration ignores the Lord's commandment to the party of Jared to gather "thy flocks, both male and female, of every kind; and also of the seed of the earth of every kind" and "go forth into

---

61. For prophecies, see 1 Ne. 13:30–31, 15:14; 2 Ne. 4:3–7; Eth. 13:5–8; Morm. 7:1–5. For numerous Israelite populations, see 1 Ne. 12:1–20, 13: 10: Mos. 11:19, 12:34; Alma 56:3; 3 Ne. 15–17; Eth. 15:2. For dozens more similar passages cited in the scripture and a more extended version of this argument, see Murphy, "Simply Implausible"; Duffy, "Lamanite"; Brent Lee Metcalfe, "Reinventing Lamanite Identity," *Sunstone* 131 (2004); Meldrum, *Rediscovering the Book of Mormon*; Southerton, *Losing a Lost Tribe*.

62. Johnson and Kramer, "The Bible Vs. The Book of Mormon"; Finkelstein and Silberman, *Bible Unearthed*; Richard Elliot Friedman, *Who Wrote the Bible?* (New York: Summit Books, 1987); Laughlin, *Archaeology and the Bible*; Dennis Tedlock, *Popol Vuh: The Definitive Edition of the Mayan Book of the Dawn of Life and the Glories of Gods and Kings*, trans. Dennis Tedlock, revised and expanded (New York: Touchstone, 1996).

63. "Book of Mormon and DNA Studies."

the wilderness, yea, into that quarter where never had man been."[64] It also neglects Lehi's prophetic claim "that this land should be kept as yet from the knowledge of other nations" or that as long as "they shall keep his commandments" there "shall be none to molest them."[65] The essay offers no alternative explanation for these passages from the Book of Mormon that obviously contradict the interpretations it advances.

The essay exaggerates the likelihood that the Book of Mormon migrations would leave no genetic traces. In the scientific literature, there are ample examples of small migrations entering larger populations and leaving their signature behind in modern populations. Genetic evidence indicative of pre-Columbian Native American migrations to Iceland and Easter Island have been documented.[66] Similarly, evidence of Polynesian connections to the Americas has been found in Brazil.[67] Genetic traces of Hebrew migrations into southern African has been found in the Bantu-speaking Lemba population.[68] Additionally, distinctions between pre- and post-Columbian admixture appear to be easier to identify than implied by the essay authors.[69] The essay thus

---

64. Eth. 1:41, 2:5; Murphy, "Simply Implausible," 126.

65. 2 Ne. 1:8–9; Metcalfe, "Lamanite Identity."

66. Sigríður Sunna Ebenesersdóttir et al., "A New Subclade of mtDNA Haplogroup C1 Found in Icelanders: Evidence of Pre-Columbian Contact?" *American Journal of Physical Anthropology* 144, 1 (2011); J. Víctor Moreno-Mayar et al., "Genome-Wide Ancestry Patterns in Rapanui Suggest Pre-European Admixture with Native Americans," *Current Biology* 24, 21; Erik Thorsby, "The Polynesian Gene Pool: An Early Contribution by Amerindians to Easter Island," *Philosophical Transactions of the Royal Society of London B: Biological Sciences* 367, 1590 (2012).

67. Vanessa Faria Gonçalves et al., "Identification of Polynesian mtDNA Haplogroups in Remains of Botocudo Amerindians from Brazil," *Proceedings of the National Academy of Sciences* 110, 16 (2013).

68. Neil Bradman and Mark Thomas, "Why Y? The Y Chromosomes Traveling South: The Cohen Modal Haplotype and the Origins of the Lemba, the 'Black Jews of South Africa,'" *American Journal of Human Genetics* 66 (Feb. 2000); Murphy, "Lamanite Genetics."

69. Sriram Sankararaman et al., "Estimating Local Ancestry in Admixed Populations," *American Journal of Human Genetics* 82, 2 (2008); Yael Baran et al., "Fast and Accurate Inference of Local Ancestry in Latino Populations," *Bioinformatics* 28, 10 (2012); Garrett Hellenthal et al., "A Genetic Atlas of Human Admixture History," *Science* 343, 6172 (2014); Juan-Camilo Chacón-Duque et al., "Americans Show Wide-Spread Converso Ancestry and Imprint of Local Native Ancestry on Physical Appearance" *Nature Communications* 9, 5398 (2018).

misleads when it claims, "Finding and clearly identifying ... DNA [of Book of Mormon peoples] today may be asking more of the science of population genetics than it is capable of providing."[70] The scientific literature provides multiple examples in similar situations of the type of evidence missing from purported Book of Mormon populations.

While scientists acknowledge that it is possible for genetic signatures to be lost over time, the Book of Mormon narrative requires that such an unlikely event must occur repeatedly. Three different migration events in the Book of Mormon would each need to result in the loss of all of each migrating population's genetic markers. It would not be just descendants of one person from each migration but all of the descendants of each individual migrant would have to have lost completely their numerous genetic markers indicative of Near Eastern ancestry. Their modern descendants would need to have lost all traces of their origins in the maternal mitochondrial DNA, on the paternal Y chromosome, and across hundreds of markers on the nuclear genome as well. Genetic drift and founder effects are random events. They do not occur again and again in the same way, to the same lineages, always resulting in the same pattern of genetic extinction. Because the Jaredites also brought plants and animals with them, the same unlikely scenarios would need to have been repeated for every individual of every species they brought with them. As Murphy has argued previously, the implausibility of this "model escalates exponentially with each additional genetic marker examined."[71] The Book of Mormon narrative is fundamentally incompatible with the types of scenarios that would have resulted in the loss of the genetic heritage of its peoples. To make the story plausible, one would need to presume that the Creator is playing malevolent tricks on human subjects just to test their faith.

DNA is problematic for Latter-day Saints because it calls into question a presumed authority to tell Native American stories. It challenges a claim to be the latter-day arbiters of Native histories. For many Mormons, it has taken genetic science to begin to

---

70. "Book of Mormon and DNA Studies."
71. Murphy, "Simply Implausible," 120.

dislodge this colonial mindset. There is a spark of a changing approach in the essay with the acknowledgement that "the primary purpose of the Book of Mormon is more spiritual than historical."[72] What if the essay writers had explored that concept at length rather than offer a primer on population genetics? Discussing the lack of an historical foundation is the more difficult conversation. Rather than let the Book of Mormon stand as scripture, not history, the essay uses uncertainty inherent in the scientific process to try to create wiggle room. The fact of the matter remains that science provides no affirmative support from DNA for the migration of any of the Book of Mormon peoples, plants, or animals.[73] The essay writers do not come to terms with the sheer absence of evidence and, instead, try to salvage a sliver of authority to continue speaking authoritatively about Native America.

American Indians have not been sitting idly by (Lamanite-style) while some Mormons attempt to mold them into something more compatible with the newest science and current politics. Indigenous concerns about LDS portrayals and uses of our bodies and those of our ancestors have appeared in prominent newspapers including *Financial Times, L.A. Times, Salt Lake Tribune, New Zealand Herald, New York Times*, and *Indian Country Today*; in the documentary film *In Laman's Terms*; in the books *Native Americans, Archaeologists, and the Mounds, Native American DNA, Decolonizing Mormonism, Essays in American Indian and Mormon History*, and summarized in doctoral dissertations.[74]

---

72. "Book of Mormon and DNA Studies."

73. Thomas W Murphy and Simon G. Southerton, "Genetic Research a 'Galileo Event' for Mormons," *Anthropology News*, Feb. 2003; Southerton, *Losing a Lost Tribe*; Murphy, "Simply Implausible"; John Dehlin et al., "Three Geneticists Respond to the LDS Essay on DNA and the Book of Mormon, and to Apologist Michael Ash," podcast, *Mormon Stories*, 2015; Raff and Bolnick, "Haplogroup X."

74. William Lobdell, "Bedrock of a Faith Is Jolted," *Los Angeles Times*, Feb. 16, 2006; Suzan Mazur, "Mormons in the Olympic Spotlight: Polygamy and Scripture Threaten to Steal Some of the Thunder from Winter Games in Utah," *Financial Times*, Feb. 9 2002; ICTMN Staff, "Fraud? Mormon Prez Summoned to Defend Church Teachings on Natives," *Indian Country Today*, Feb. 5, 2014; Jon Antelope, "Living Cheap among Mormons Who Think Whites Are Natives," ibid., Nov. 17, 2015; ICTMN Staff, "Mormons Apologize for Postumous Baptism of Holocaust Survivor Wiesenthal's Parents," ibid., Feb. 15, 2012; Baca, *In Laman's Terms*; Colvin and Brooks, eds., *Decolonizing Mormonism*; Hafen and Rensink, eds., *Essays in*

Meanwhile Latter-day Saints have demonstrated disregard for Indigenous sovereignty in research programs emanating from BYU that include genetic sampling at LDS chapels without sufficient ethical review by Indigenous nations and foreign governments.[75] While largely ignored and overlooked, people of Native heritage have not been silent on these and similar important issues.

Conclusion

LDS fascination with Native American bodies originates in settler colonial society. Surrounded by colonial violence, the LDS prophet Joseph Smith offered his followers a sacred narrative claiming that American Indians, too, were recent immigrants from the Old World and that the losses they were experiencing were divine punishment for the sins of their fathers. He attributed dark skin to a curse from God for wickedness and linked skin color to purported moral failings, idleness, idolatry, and hunting in the wilderness. This new American Bible would credit civilization in the New World to an ancient white nation of Christian mound builders who looked, lived, and behaved much like European colonists. Smith gave these misinformed traditions the stamp of scripture. When archaeological, linguistic, and genetic evidence failed to support racist myths

---

American Indian and Mormon History; Murphy, "Imagining Lamanites"; Lori Elaine Taylor, "Telling Stories About Mormons and Indians," PhD diss., State University of New York, Buffalo, 2000; Tallbear, *Native American DNA*; Mann, *Mounds*; Suzan Mazur, "Mormon Scriptures on Indians Show Objectionable Side of Olympic Hosts," *Indian Country Today*, Feb. 9, 2002; Martin Johnston, "Mormons Trigger NZ Ethical Concerns over DNA," *New Zealand Herald*, May 17, 2001; ICTMN Staff, "Mormon Writer in Hot Water over Native DNA," *Indian Country Today*, Dec. 17, 2002; Roberta Jestes, "Is History Repeating Itself at Ancestry?" www.dna-explained. com/2012/08/30/is-history-repeating-itself-at-ancestry/; Peggy Fletcher Stack, "Book of Mormon Change Prompts Reflection among Native American Members," *Salt Lake Tribune*, Nov. 17, 2007; Angelo Baca, "Bears Ears Is Here to Stay," *New York Times*, Dec. 8, 2017; Baca and Bsumek, "On Pioneer Day"; Farina King, "Indigenizing Mormonisms," *Mormon Studies Review* 6 (2019).

75. Johnston, "Ethical Concerns over DNA"; Kent Larsen, "BYU Molecular Genealogy Research Project Accused of Ethical Lapse in New Zealand," *Mormon News*, May 18, 2001; Murphy, "Lamanite Genetics," 66–67; Murphy and Baca, "Rejecting Racism." Additional concerns have been raised about the Sorenson Molecular Research Group, its affiliations with Sorenson Genomics, GeneTree, and Ancestry where appropriate permissions may not have been obtained prior to the transfer of genetic information between these entities. Jestes, "History Repeating Itself"; Tallbear, *Native American DNA*, 79–82, 116; Murphy and Baca, "Rejecting Racism."

of white mound builders, Mormons would continue to hang tenaciously to these narratives to try to make them fit the latest political expediencies and newest scientific evidence.

Rather than offering a truth-telling confession of "mistakes of men," the LDS Church's Gospel Topics essay on "Book of Mormon and DNA Studies" minimizes the significance of findings from DNA by using a primer on population genetics to divert attention away from a lack of evidence and to give the impression that everything is okay. The essay continues the long-standing tradition of marginalizing the voices of American Indians, a pervasive practice in LDS discourse, public policy, and the academic field of Mormon Studies.[76] The failure of archaeology, linguistics, and textual analyses to support historical claims had already resulted in a paring down of Book of Mormon geography from a hemispheric to a limited setting, although disputes have arisen over whether those events might have been located in North or Mesoamerica. The essay puts the church on the side of a limited geography without explicitly endorsing a particular setting. It legitimately critiques those who would use the X lineage to support a North American setting. Yet the church's essay continues the longstanding silencing of Native voices. Our hope here is to have brought Indigenous scholarship to the forefront of the debate where it belongs.

The LDS Church has come a long way from its effort to excommunicate Thomas Murphy for the first peer-reviewed assessment of the implications of new DNA research for LDS understandings of American Indians. In his 2002 contribution to *American Apocrypha*, Murphy advocated discontinuing the view that Lamanites were the principal ancestors of American Indians and disavowing "the offensive teaching that a dark skin is a physical trait of God's

---

76. Thomas W Murphy, Review of Terryl L. Givens, *By the Hand of Mormon: The American Scripture that Launched a New World Religion*, *Journal of Mormon History* 28, 2 (2002); Review of Paul Gutjahr, *The Book of Mormon: A Biography*, *Nova Religio* 17, 3 (2014); Review of *The Oxford Handbook of Mormonism*, *Nova Religio* 20, 3 (2017); Teresa Montoya, "Where Is Rural? #WeNeedANewCounty: Enduring Division and Conquest in the Indigenous Southwest," *Journal for the Anthropology of North America* 22, 2 (2019); John Dougherty, "How Trump's Dismemberment of Bears Ears Was Driven by Racism, Grave Robbery and Mormon Beliefs," *The Revelator*, Dec. 6, 2017, at www.therevelator.org/trump-bears-ears-indigenous-scholars.

malediction."[77] Angelo Baca offered similar perspectives in his 2008 film, *In Laman's Terms*.[78] The 2006 and 2013 changes to the introduction and chapter headings of the Book of Mormon and recent essays on DNA and race have mostly realized the first request and put the church on the path towards the second. Murphy also encouraged an acknowledgment that "the Book of Mormon's origin is best situated in early nineteenth-century America, and ... emerged from an antebellum perspective, out of frontier people's struggle with their god, and not from an authentic American Indian perspective."[79] Baca similarly drew attention to the ongoing and offensive misrepresentations of American Indians in the Book of Mormon and the Hill Cumorah Pageant.[80] A more forthright confession of a nineteenth-century origin of the Book of Mormon and a more explicit repudiation of its racism are still needed if church leaders hope to rebuild trust with skeptical members and to establish more diplomatic and equitable relationships with American Indians.

The Latter-day Saints have lost any right to speak on behalf of Native American history, a settler colonial privilege that was assumed but never granted in the first place. While the Book of Mormon does not contain history, it does present its readers with a spiritual challenge to realize that all humans are fundamentally alike before their Creator and that we necessarily experience the sacred through the lens of our own language and understanding. The church's new essay moves members in the direction of favoring a spiritual over an historical reading of the Book of Mormon and cautions against defenders who misuse DNA to perpetuate racist readings. These are positive developments worthy of praise, but much work remains undone. We recommend the diplomatic embrace of a diversity of sacred narratives, untethered by assertions of cultural superiority and factual history, as an alternative model for reading LDS scripture in a genomic age.

---

77. Murphy, "Lamanite Genetics," 68.

78. Baca, *In Laman's Terms*.

79. Murphy, "Lamanite Genetics."

80. Baca, *In Laman's Terms*.

4. THE "BOOK OF MORMON TRANSLATION" ESSAY IN HISTORICAL CONTEXT

John-Charles Duffy

At the end of 2013, the LDS Church released a Gospel Topics essay on the translation of the Book of Mormon.[1] The claim that Joseph Smith Jr. miraculously translated the Book of Mormon from an ancient record inscribed on golden plates had been a foundation of the Mormon movement from its inception in 1830. Nearly two centuries later, the Gospel Topics essay reaffirmed that claim in the face of challenges posited both by skeptics outside the LDS Church and by theological liberals within it. The essay retold the conventional Mormon narrative for Smith's production of the Book of Mormon, from his vision of the angel Moroni in 1823 to the preparation of the manuscripts containing the English translation. The essay presented selected statements from Smith and his scribes about the translation process, attesting that the golden plates were a real, tangible artifact and that Smith had translated them by reading English words that appeared on a miraculous interpretive instrument. To corroborate these nineteenth-century claims, the essay drew on work done in the late twentieth and early twenty-first centuries by LDS scholars associated with the Foundation for Ancient Research and Mormon Studies (FARMS), housed at Brigham Young University, who argued that the earliest Book of Mormon manuscripts display grammatical features

---

1. "Book of Mormon Translation," Dec. 30, 2013, at www.lds.org/topics/book-of-mormon-translation (accessed Nov. 5, 2016). For the dating of the essay, see "Church Provides Context for Recent Media Coverage on Gospel Topics Pages," *Mormon Newsroom*, Nov. 11, 2014, at www.mormonnewsroom.org/article/church-provides-context-gospel-topics-pages (accessed Nov. 5, 2016).

"characteristic of Near Eastern languages"—evidence that the Book of Mormon really is a translation of an ancient text.[2]

Many observers were surprised by the essay's acknowledgment that Smith used two different instruments to translate the Book of Mormon: (1) a spectacles-like pair of stones called the Urim and Thummim, which was buried with the golden plates, and (2) an oval-shaped seer stone, which Smith had discovered and used, prior to translating the Book of Mormon, "to look for lost objects and buried treasure." The Urim and Thummim would already have been familiar to LDS readers of the Gospel Topics essay, since it is discussed in the canonical account of the Book of Mormon's translation, found in the Pearl of Great Price, one of the LDS volumes of scripture (see JS-H 1:35, 42, 52, 59, 62). The seer stone, by contrast, was a potentially controversial subject. Although attested in nineteenth-century sources, the seer stone's role in producing the Book of Mormon faded from LDS narrations during the twentieth century until it was re-publicized in the 1980s as a result of controversies that forced LDS to confront evidence of their founder's involvement in folk magical practices.[3] The seer stone gained publicity in popular culture via a 2003 episode of the satirical animated series *South Park*, which depicted Smith dictating the Book of Mormon while looking into a hat containing

---

2. FARMS became part of the Neal A. Maxwell Institute for Religious Scholarship at Brigham Young University in 2013. Some FARMS supporters, who did not share the Maxwell Institute's Mormon studies emphasis, founded the Interpreter Foundation in 2012.

3. In the early 1980s, documents dealer Mark Hofmann forged what was supposed to be an 1830 letter in which Martin Harris described Joseph Smith discovering the golden plates not, as in the canonical account, through an angelic vision but by use of a seer stone. Although the forgery was later exposed, in the interim LDS historians, struggling to make sense of the letter, revisited the bona fide historical evidence of Smith's involvement in folk magic (which had inspired Hofmann's forgery). The result was that even once the forgery had been recognized as such, LDS scholars were left with a greater consciousness than before of Smith's magical activities. Prior to the forgery's exposure, BYU religion professor Richard Anderson, who reappears later in my history of debates about Book of Mormon translation, developed an apologetic according to which Smith had practiced magic until he was visited by the angel, in 1827, but not afterward. Richard Lloyd Anderson, "The Mature Joseph Smith and Treasure Searching," *BYU Studies* 24, 4 (Fall 1984, publication delayed until 1986): 489–560. This argument of Anderson's is cited in the Gospel Topics essay on Book of Mormon translation (n19).

the stone, as described by nineteenth-century Mormon sources.[4] The Gospel Topics essay helps LDS readers make sense of this potentially startling information by asserting that "as Joseph grew to understand his prophetic calling, he learned that he could use this stone" not only to search for buried treasure, but also "for the higher purpose of translating scripture."[5]

For forthrightly addressing problematic historical information that might instead have been swept under the rug, the Gospel Topics essay may seem progressive. In a larger picture, however, the essay is significant not because it is progressive but because it is markedly conservative even by LDS standards. Although it is certainly unsurprising that the Gospel Topics essay reaffirms the LDS Church's long-standing position that the Book of Mormon was miraculously translated from golden plates, it was not inevitable that the Gospel Topics essay would assert the particular scenario it did for *how* the Book of Mormon was translated—namely, that Smith *read* the English translation from the interpretive instruments. By the time the Gospel Topics essay was written, LDS intellectuals who still believed that the Book of Mormon was an ancient record[6] had developed at least three different scenarios for how the English text might have been produced. The Gospel Topics essay adopts the most conservative of those scenarios—"conservative" both in the sense that this scenario corresponds to how Smith's earliest followers understood the Book of Mormon's production and in terms of the authority that this scenario attributes to the English text produced by Smith. Through the Gospel Topics essay, some especially conservative (and anonymous) LDS intellectuals have marshaled the authority of an official church publication to

---

4. *South Park*, "All About the Mormons?" episode 712 (originally aired Nov. 19, 2003). The episode presented Smith's claims about the plates and the translation as demonstrably fraudulent and contemporary LDS as credulous for believing them.

5. A footnote adds that the angel Moroni ordered Joseph to abandon his treasure-seeking. "Book of Mormon Translation," n19. Another footnote preempts allegations that the church had formerly attempted to cover up the seer stone by listing articles published in the official church periodical the *Ensign* during the 1970s-90s that referred to the seer stone. Ibid., n26.

6. I set aside LDS thinkers of more liberal stripes, who regarded the Book of Mormon as a purely nineteenth-century creation, not an ancient work. I discuss such thinkers later in this essay.

promote a very strong conception of the Book of Mormon's authority, akin to the way Protestant evangelicals view the Bible: as inerrant. In promoting this view, the Gospel Topics essay sidelines more liberal alternatives that had been championed earlier in the twentieth century, and at times in other official church publications.

This theological coup may be more easily recognized as such when the Gospel Topics essay is placed in a longer intellectual history. The story begins in the first decade of the twentieth century, when LDS Church general authority B. H. Roberts introduced what I will call a "composed-translation" scenario as rival to a traditional "read-translation" scenario. Over the course of the twentieth century, the composed-translation scenario was advocated in church publications and enjoyed widespread support among LDS intellectuals, even intellectuals who could be classed as theologically conservative given their belief in the Book of Mormon's antiquity. The intellectual landscape shifted dramatically, however, in the 1980s-90s, when a wave of challenges to Book of Mormon historicity within the LDS intellectual community prompted both a conservative backlash and the appearance of a new, more liberal translation theory—the "expansion" scenario—as an attempt at a mediating position. On the conservative side, some LDS scholars associated with FARMS revived a read-translation scenario, which they maintained was superior not only to the new, fiercely contested expansion scenario but also to the by then time-honored composed-translation scenario. Their position won out in the Gospel Topics essay.

The "Manual Theory" Controversy, 1903–1906:
A Composed Translation vs. a Read Translation

As the twentieth century opened, the LDS community was being transformed. The LDS were transitioning out of the polygamous period of their history into a phase of selective assimilation into the American cultural mainstream. Teachings and practices of the nineteenth century were being reassessed and in some cases revised or abandoned, as when church leaders quietly retreated from Brigham Young's Adam-God doctrine or when they revised temple endowment ceremonies during the 1920s. A small but growing number of LDS young people were traveling outside the Mormon cultural region to receive college educations and were bringing modern ideas back with them—for instance, about organic evolution and biblical criticism.[7] It was in this context that the church's governing First Presidency authorized publication of a then-innovative—and, as it proved, controversial—theory about the Book of Mormon's translation, quite different from the scenario espoused in the Gospel Topics essay a century later.

The theory in question was dubbed "the Manual theory" because it appeared in a lesson manual distributed by the LDS Church's young men's organization for the year 1903–1904.[8] The manual's author was B. H. Roberts, a mid-ranking general authority (one of the seven presidents of Seventy) and Assistant Church Historian. Much like the Gospel Topics essay, Roberts drew on nineteenth-century witnesses to affirm that Smith had translated the Book of Mormon with the aid of two different interpretive instruments: the Urim and Thummim and a seer stone. But that was not the innovative or controversial part of Roberts's theory; in 1903, the seer stone was still familiar to LDS readers. What was innovative was that Roberts rejected what he called "the popular understanding among the Latter-day Saints" of *how* Smith had used the interpretive instruments.[9] The popular understanding was that Smith looked into the Urim and Thummim or the seer stone and saw an English translation, which he then dictated word for word to his scribe. As Roberts described—pejoratively—this scenario: "the instruments did all, while he who used them did nothing but look and repeat mechanically what he saw there

---

7. Thomas G. Alexander, *Mormonism in Transition: A History of the Latter-Day Saints, 1890–1930* (Urbana: University of Illinois Press, 1986); David John Buerger, "The Adam-God Doctrine," *Dialogue: A Journal of Mormon Thought* 15, 1 (Spring 1982): 14–58; David John Buerger, *The Mysteries of Godliness: A History of Mormon Temple Worship* (San Francisco: Smith Research Associates), 1994; Thomas W. Simpson, *American Universities and the Birth of Modern Mormonism, 1867–1940* (Chapel Hill: University of North Carolina Press, 2016).

8. [B. H. Roberts,] *Young Men's Mutual Improvement Associations Manual, 1903–1904* ([Salt Lake City]: Deseret News, 1903), 66–72.

9. B. H. Roberts, *Defense of the Faith and the Saints*, 2 vols. ([Salt Lake City]: Deseret News, 1907), 1:253.

reflected."[10] Instead, Roberts argued for a scenario in which Smith looked at the ancient characters through the instruments, "bending every power of his mind to know the meaning thereof," and then received mental impressions, which he had to render into "such language as [he] could command, in such phraseology as he was master of."[11]

In the popular scenario, Smith *read* an English translation that appeared to him in the interpreters; in Roberts's new scenario, Smith *composed* the translation based on mental impressions he received from God. In Roberts's scenario, the language of the English translation originated with Smith, not with the interpreters. That distinction was crucial for Roberts because it explained "the faulty English" that peppered the original edition of the Book of Mormon. It also accounted, Roberts argued, "for the sameness of phraseology and literary style which runs through the whole volume" even though the Book of Mormon supposedly contains writings by multiple ancient authors.[12] In other words, Roberts's aim was apologetic: he urged the LDS to abandon the idea of a read translation in favor of a composed translation in order to answer challenges to the Book of Mormon's authenticity. Why would a revealed text contain faulty grammar? Why does the supposedly multi-authored book have only one authorial voice? Roberts's answer: Because the language of the translation was Smith's own, not a divine dictation.

Roberts's composed-translation scenario "gave rise to considerable discussion within the Church," as Roberts described the controversy later.[13] Concerned readers of the manual wrote letters to the young men's organization and to the church-run *Deseret News*. The *Deseret News* published an editorial supporting Roberts's scenario, while Roberts himself responded to critics in a series of articles published in three issues of the church magazine *Improvement Era* in 1906.[14] The main challenge to Roberts's scenario was

---

10. Roberts, *Manual, 1903–1904*, 68.

11. Ibid., 70–71

12. Ibid., 71.

13. B. H. Roberts, *New Witnesses for God II: The Book of Mormon*, vol. 2 of 3 ([Salt Lake City]: Deseret News, 1909), 121, note u.

14. Roberts recycled all this material defending the Manual theory in his 1907 book *Defense of the Faith and the Saints*, published by the Deseret News and thus

that it contradicted accounts of the translation process left by nine-teenth-century witnesses, especially David Whitmer and Martin Harris (familiar to LDS readers as two of the Three Witnesses who attested that an angel had shown them the golden plates).[15] According to those accounts, when Smith looked into the interpreters, he saw an English translation, which would disappear once Smith had read the translation aloud and the scribe attested that it had been correctly recorded. Whitmer's account claimed, even more specifically, that the English translation of each character appeared to Smith directly beneath that character, one character at a time.

Roberts countered that the process described by Whitmer simply did not make sense: a character-by-character translation would have sounded garbled, given inevitable differences of syntax between one language and another.[16] Furthermore, Roberts argued, a read-translation scenario would force the conclusion that "errors in grammar and diction" in the Book of Mormon manuscript must have been copied from the translation that God had given Smith to read via the interpreters. In short, the grammatical errors must be God's errors—a conclusion that Roberts called "unthinkable, not to say blasphemous."[17] To reduce the authority of the nineteenth-century witnesses, Roberts emphasized that their accounts were not based on first-hand experience with the interpreters and had been written fifty years after the Book of Mormon's production; ergo, the witnesses may have misunderstood or misremembered what Smith had told them about the translation process. The account attributed to Martin Harris was yet more problematic because it was actually someone else's recollection of what Harris had told him.[18]

Over against these problematic, fallible witnesses, Roberts took his stand on the unimpeachable authority of scripture. "I care very

---

under church auspices. The Deseret News republished Roberts's YMMIA manual in 1909 as *New Witnesses for God.*

15. B. H. Roberts, "Translation of the Book of Mormon," *Improvement Era,* Apr. 1906, 426.

16. B. H. Roberts, "Translation of the Book of Mormon (Concluded)," *Improvement Era,* May 1906, 544–47.

17. Roberts, "Translation," Apr. 1906, 428.

18. Ibid., 427, 432–33.

little, comparatively, for what Messrs. Whitmer and Harris have said about the subject," Roberts harrumphed. "I care everything for what the Lord has said about it."[19] Roberts was referring to a description of the translation process provided in one of Smith's early revelations, canonized in the church's own Doctrine and Covenants. In this revelation, the Lord explains to Oliver Cowdery why he, Cowdery, was unable to translate a portion of the golden plates when allowed the opportunity to do so. According to the revelation (frequently quoted among LDS as a model for obtaining personal inspiration), "you must study it [the translation] out in your mind." God will then either confirm that what you are thinking is right, by causing "your bosom to burn within you," or send a "stupor of thought, that shall cause you to forget the thing which is wrong" (D&C 9:7–9). From this passage, Roberts concluded that Smith could not have translated the Book of Mormon by reading an English translation provided by the interpretive instruments, since that process would not have required Smith to study anything out in his mind.

But why, then, were interpretive instruments needed? If Smith was not reading an English translation from the interpreters, why was he looking into them? This was a problem for Roberts's composed-translation scenario. His response was to theorize that the interpreters were "an aid … to concentration of mind," focusing Smith's attention on the particular set of characters to be interpreted. Roberts went so far as to speculate that after Smith had composed an English translation in his mind, the interpreters might have displayed that translation to help him remember it until it had been recorded by the scribe—a supposition that would reconcile Roberts's scenario with the witnesses' accounts.[20]

One LDS correspondent proposed to Roberts an alternative way of reconciling the witnesses' accounts with D&C 9 and with the problem of bad grammar. The correspondent theorized that when Smith looked into the interpreters, he saw a literal rendering into English of each character's meaning, as described by Whitmer. As Roberts had pointed out, such a translation would

19. Ibid., 432.
20. Ibid., 430.

be garbled—so Smith's task was to study out in his mind (per D&C 9) how to render those literal translations into intelligible English.[21] Roberts judged this theory "cumbersome." If God could give Smith an instrument capable of providing a literal translation of the characters, why could not God just as well give him an instrument capable of providing a polished, intelligible translation?[22] More importantly, Roberts spurned what he saw as his correspondent's attempt to "compromise" with an "untenable theory" that could only bring down on the LDS "ridicule" and "contempt" from "intelligent and educated people."[23] "It is no use resisting the matter," Roberts declared in an open letter; "the old theory must be abandoned. It could only come into existence and remain so long and now be clung to by some so tenaciously because our fathers and our people in the past and now were and are uncritical."[24] Mormonism had a "crying need," Roberts wrote, for innovative disciples who would "force it beyond its earlier and cruder stages of development."[25] At a time in American history when Christians were coming to be divided between theological liberals and conservatives—then called "modernists" and "fundamentalists"—over questions of scriptural historicity and authority, Roberts saw himself standing on the side of liberals, the side of reason and progress. The composed-translation scenario for Book of Mormon

---

21. B. H. Roberts, "Book of Mormon Translation—Correspondence," *Improvement Era*, July 1906, 706–707.

22. Ibid., 709. A similar challenge may be raised against Roberts's proposal that the interpreters displayed a translation Smith had composed in his mind: If the interpreters could do *that*, why could they not just translate the text for Smith to begin with?

23. Ibid., 710. To support this point, Roberts quoted correspondence from an LDS student at the University of Michigan, who recounted using the Manual theory to show classmates and a professor that the translation of the Book of Mormon was not as "incredulous" as they had first thought. Ibid., 710–11.

24. Ibid., 711.

25. Ibid., 712–713. In its original context, this statement is less blunt than it may sound as excerpted here. The line about "forc[ing]" a religion "beyond its earlier and cruder stages of development" comes from a lengthy passage Roberts quoted from John Fiske, a liberal Christian philosopher of the late nineteenth century. Fiske had said that there are two kinds of religious disciples: hidebound partisans versus innovators who "help to lead the thought that they accept to a truer expression. They force it beyond its earlier and cruder stages of development." Upon finishing the Fiske quotation, Roberts remarked that the LDS Church had a "crying need" for disciples of the second sort.

translation represented the LDS Church's way forward to greater light and truth, as well as to greater cultural respectability. The read-translation scenario, Roberts was convinced, would keep the LDS trapped in the past and on the cultural margins.

The Composed-Translation Scenario Reiterated, 1940s–90s

Church leaders stopped short of officially endorsing Roberts's composed-translation scenario. Nevertheless, the fact that the First Presidency authorized its publication, a fact Roberts underlined for his critics, lent it legitimacy.[26] The composed-translation scenario enjoyed a high profile among LDS intellectuals through the rest of the twentieth century. Between the 1940s and the 1990s, landmark publications promoting a composed-translation scenario were produced by LDS apostle John A. Widtsoe; by Richard Anderson, a BYU religion professor writing for the church's main English-language periodical; and (less prominently but noteworthy for other reasons) by Stephen Ricks, a scholar writing for FARMS.

A university president prior to his calling to the Quorum of Twelve Apostles, Widtsoe was one of the church's most prominent mid-century apologists. He championed a composed-translation scenario across the 1940s, 1950s, and 1960s.[27] Unlike Roberts, Widtsoe did not directly take issue with witnesses like Whitmer or Harris. Like Roberts, however, Widtsoe rejected the idea that the interpretive instruments provided Smith with a ready-made translation he could simply read. (When Widtsoe spoke of interpretive instruments, he spoke of the Urim and Thummim; he said nothing of the seer stone, which was fading from LDS collective memory.)

---

26. Roberts informed critics that his chapter on Book of Mormon translation had been reviewed by the First Presidency and several of the Twelve, who authorized its publication—although Roberts immediately backpedaled to acknowledge that this did not mean church leaders officially adopted the Manual theory. Roberts, "Translation," May 1906, 552.

27. John A. Widtsoe, "Why Did Joseph Smith, the Prophet, Need the Help of the Urim and Thummim?" *Improvement Era*, Jan. 1940, 33, 37; John A. Widtsoe, "What Was the Vocabulary of Joseph Smith?" *Improvement Era*, June 1951, 399, 476–477; John A. Widtsoe, *Joseph Smith—Seeker after Truth* (Salt Lake City: Bookcraft, 1951), 37–43; John A. Widtsoe, *Evidences and Reconciliations* (Salt Lake City: Bookcraft, 1960), 89–91.

Widtsoe envisioned that "the *ideas* set forth by the characters were revealed to the Prophet," who then "expressed the ideas in English as best he could." This explained for Widtsoe why the Book of Mormon was written in the "language of the Prophet as used in his every day conversation"[28]—the language of "a person of little education."[29] Like Roberts, Widtsoe grappled with the problem, inherent to the composed-translation scenario, of explaining why the interpretive instruments were needed if the translation was a process of revealing ideas to Smith's mind. Widtsoe theorized that the interpreters served as a kind of radio receiver for revelation until Smith's "body and spirit became spiritually 'tuned,'" at which point he could receive revelation without the interpreters' aid.[30] Again like Roberts, Widtsoe quoted D&C 9 as a description of this instrument-less revelation process. Widtsoe recognized a further problem, though, for the composed-translation scenario: it seemed to render superfluous not only the interpreters but also the golden plates. If God was going to reveal the contents of the Book of Mormon directly to Smith's mind, why did Smith need to possess a physical copy on plates? Widtsoe had no answer to this challenge except to fault those who would raise it: "the ways of the Lord are not the ways of man. Those who want the Lord to do things their way are usually frigid believers in divinity."[31]

Roberts's views on Book of Mormon translation were explicitly cited by Richard Anderson, a professor in BYU's religion department, in a 1977 article for the LDS Church's English-language periodical, the *Ensign*—a venue that lent authoritative weight to Anderson's argument, albeit short of an official church position.[32] Like Roberts (but unlike Widtsoe), Anderson directly challenged the reliability of statements by witnesses Whitmer and Harris that supported a read-translation scenario: Whitmer might have misunderstood what Smith had told him about how the interpreters worked, and Harris's account was secondhand. For an authoritative

---

28. Widtsoe, *Joseph Smith*, 42. My emphasis.

29. Widtsoe, "Vocabulary of Joseph Smith," 477.

30. Widtsoe, "Why Did Joseph Smith," 33; see also Widtsoe, *Joseph Smith*, 40–41.

31. Widtsoe, *Joseph Smith*, 43.

32. Richard Lloyd Anderson, "By the Gift and Power of God," *Ensign*, Sept. 1977, accessed online at www.lds.org (Nov. 5, 2016).

description of the translation process, Anderson turned to D&C 9, from which he argued that Smith's task had been, first, "to understand the ideas of the ancient language" with the "assistance of the Spirit," and then to "place [those ideas], with all their nuances, in coherent English," a task requiring Smith's own "creative activity." Anderson presented the composed-translation scenario as the solution to the problem of why a revealed translation would contain bad grammar. He also used the composed-translation scenario to account for lengthy parallels between the Book of Mormon and the King James Version of the Bible (which invited the skeptical question: How did Smith's translation happen to correspond so closely to the choices of the King James translators?). Anderson quoted another LDS religion professor, Daniel Ludlow, to assert that "there appears to be only one answer to explain the word-for-word similarities between the verses of Isaiah in the Bible and the same verses in the Book of Mormon"—namely, "that Joseph Smith must have opened Isaiah and tested each mentioned verse by the Spirit." This, Anderson said, was the consensus "view taken by Latter-day Saint scholars on this point."

Fifteen years after Anderson's article appeared in the *Ensign*, another defense of the composed-translation scenario appeared in the *Journal of Book of Mormon Studies*, a FARMS publication. The article's author, Stephen Ricks, was *JBMS*'s editor and a professor of Hebrew at BYU. Ricks's argument followed lines already worked out by Roberts and Anderson. He challenged the evidentiary value of statements by the nineteenth-century witnesses. He invoked D&C 9 to argue that Smith must have done more than simply read an English translation that "automatically appeared" in the interpreters.[33] He echoed Roberts in arguing that the character-by-character translation described by Whitmer would have "resulted in a syntactic and semantic puree."[34] He theorized—again, like Roberts—that if English words had appeared in the interpreters, they likely did so "*after* Joseph had formulated in his

---

33. Stephen D. Ricks, "Translation of the Book of Mormon: Interpreting the Evidence," *Journal of Book of Mormon Studies* 2, 2 (1993): 204.
34. Ibid., 203.

mind a translation that represented with sufficient accuracy the ideas found on the original."[35]

Ricks's article is noteworthy precisely because it did not add anything substantial to the arguments already made for the composed-translation scenario—thereby raising the question: Why did he feel the need to reassert these arguments? The closest Ricks came to answering that question was when he cautioned that "while it would be incorrect to minimize the divine element in the process of translation of the Book of Mormon, it would also be misleading and potentially hazardous to deny the human factor."[36] Who did Ricks worry, in 1993, was denying the human factor in the Book of Mormon's translation? The answer may be other FARMS scholars, who by the early 1990s were developing new arguments in favor of a *read* translation. Before that turn of events, though, a third competing scenario for Book of Mormon translation appeared on the scene.

The Expansion Scenario and Its Critics, 1980s-90s

The 1980s saw the emergence of sharp debates among LDS intellectuals over the antiquity of the Book of Mormon and traditional claims about how Joseph Smith produced the book; one observer dubbed these debates "the Book of Mormon wars."[37] LDS had long been accustomed to seeing the Book of Mormon's authenticity challenged by *outsiders*. But now, as the twentieth century ended, it appeared that a growing number of *insiders* was becoming persuaded that the Book of Mormon was not an ancient record and that Smith had not translated it in the way he claimed. During the 1980s-2000s, LDS or ex-LDS writers published studies asserting that the Book of Mormon's narratives were implausible given what scholars now knew about Native American cultures, demography, and genetics; that the book's narratives and teachings displayed parallels to Smith's nineteenth-century milieu, demonstrating the book's modern origin; that evidence for Smith's

---

35. Ibid., 205. My emphasis.
36. Ibid., 206.
37. Massimo Introvigne, "The Book of Mormon Wars: A Non-Mormon Perspective," in *Mormon Identities in Transition*, ed. Douglas J. Davies (London, England: Cassell, 1996), 25–34.

possession of golden plates was unreliable; and that Smith's claims about the discovery and translation of the golden plates arose from a folk magical world view (a world view that would be incredible to late twentieth-century LDS in the global West, even those prepared to believe in angels and the Urim and Thummim). Some LDS scholars who came to regard the Book of Mormon as a nineteenth-century creation argued that the book could still be regarded as scripture, based on liberalized conceptions of revelation and scriptural authority, such as reading the book as "inspired fiction." These revisions of LDS thought were opposed by apologists and church leaders who maintained that belief in the Book of Mormon as a miraculous translation of an ancient text was a *sin qua non* of LDS faith.[38]

In 1987, lawyer and philosopher Blake Ostler published an essay in the independent LDS-oriented journal *Dialogue* that opened a mediating position in the Book of Mormon wars. Ostler's theory of the Book of Mormon accepted certain arguments for the book's being a modern creation, most notably the anachronistic appearance of Christian teachings and practices in settings before the time of Jesus. But Ostler's theory also accepted certain arguments that apologists had advanced for the book's being ancient—namely, that the book's contents and structure were consistent with characteristics of ancient Near Eastern culture and literature that Smith would be unlikely to have known about. To account for the existence of both genuinely ancient and anachronistically modern characteristics, Ostler theorized that the English text of the Book of Mormon was an "expansion," by Smith, of the ancient text contained on the golden plates. Through a process of "human and divine interaction," God provided Smith with knowledge of the plates' contents, but the nature of the process was such that Smith interpreted—or, as Ostler preferred to say, "experienced"—the revelation "within his own conceptual paradigms."[39] The resulting text

---

38. For a more extensive overview of these disputes, see John-Charles Duffy, "Mapping Book of Mormon Historicity Debates—Part I," *Sunstone*, Oct. 2008, 36–62.

39. Blake T. Ostler, "The Book of Mormon as a Modern Expansion of an Ancient Source," *Dialogue: A Journal of Mormon Thought* 20, 1 (Spring 1987): 105, 111.

therefore mingled elements of the ancient text with elements of Smith's own nineteenth-century Christian world view.

One of Ostler's examples of this process was the Book of Mormon's account of a sermon delivered by the prophet-king Benjamin during the second century BCE. Scholarship produced at FARMS had persuaded Ostler that Benjamin's address was structured like an ancient Israelite "covenant renewal festival." But Ostler was also persuaded that the Christian content of Benjamin's sermon and the camp meeting-like response of his audience were anachronisms. Ostler theorized that the anachronisms resulted from Smith (mis)interpreting the ancient Israelite liturgy recorded on the golden plates "as a Christian confession" and rendering it in a form "familiar to him from revivals." The anachronisms thus constituted a Christian expansion by Smith of the plates' pre-Christian contents.[40] Ostler did not speculate as to *why* God was willing to let the plates' contents be misconstrued in this way, beyond implying that this was simply how divine revelation to a human mind worked.

Viewed from one angle, the expansion scenario was a third way, a via media, in the LDS debates over the Book of Mormon's antiquity. But viewed from another angle, Ostler's scenario stood on the liberal side of the conservative-liberal binary that Roberts had used to frame his own views on Book of Mormon translation. Like Roberts, whom Ostler cited as a precedent for his view, Ostler rejected a read-translation scenario as "merely mechanical or 'automatic'" and therefore incompatible with the revelatory process described in D&C 9.[41] Like Roberts, Ostler displayed a modernist impulse: Ostler insisted on "a need to continually render the divine word relevant to modern culture." Bound up in Ostler's expansion scenario was the premise that we cannot assume that "any particular statement of revelation is the final and complete word on any subject."[42] The expansion scenario, Ostler wrote, "logically preclude[s] taking scripture as a source-book of axiomatic truths which can be wielded as a sword ... to exclude all who disagree on

40. Ibid., 87–93, esp. 92.
41. Ibid., 104, 106.
42. Ibid., 113.

religious issues with *the* true understanding"—a critique aimed at LDS of more dogmatic temperaments.[43]

Given the "via media" quality of the expansion scenario, it was predictable that Ostler would be criticized from both sides. Anthony Hutchinson, a doctoral student in biblical studies who had come to regard the Book of Mormon as scripture (therefore "inspired") but nineteenth-century fiction, found Ostler's scenario unnecessarily complicated. Why, Hutchinson wondered, would God go to the trouble of preserving, across centuries, an ancient record whose message would be rendered unrecognizable by modern expansions?[44] But the strongest criticisms of the expansion scenario came from theological conservatives, notably BYU religion professors Stephen Robinson and Robert Millet. Both had trained in biblical studies at eastern universities, where they had been dismayed by the concessions they saw religiously liberal colleagues make to secular scholarship.[45] Robinson and Millet decried Ostler's expansion scenario for seeming to capitulate on fundamentals of LDS faith. The presence of Christian teaching in settings before the Christian era was not anachronism, they asserted; it was a witness that God had revealed the gospel even before Jesus' birth.[46]

Millet countered the mediating appeal of the expansion theory by championing a different mediating position: yes, the Book of

---

43. Ibid., 115.

44. Anthony A. Hutchinson, "The Word of God Is Enough: The Book of Mormon as Nineteenth-Century Scripture," in Brent Lee Metcalfe, ed., *New Approaches to the Book of Mormon* (Salt Lake City: Signature Books, 1993), 12.

45. Robinson recounted asking "a liberal Protestant colleague of mine at Duke University what elements of Christianity, as he understood it, were non-negotiable, which propositions must be believed in order for one to be Christian. His answer was that there were no such propositions. Everything was negotiable ..." Stephen E. Robinson, "The Expanded Book of Mormon?" in Monte S. Nyman and Charles D. Tate Jr., eds., *Second Nephi: The Doctrinal Structure* (Provo, Utah: Religious Studies Center, Brigham Young University, 1989), 400. Millet recounted, unhappily, sitting in two courses during his doctoral program in which the professors espoused the position that "it doesn't really matter" whether Moses parted the Red Sea or whether Jesus "literally rose from the dead"; what matters is that these stories "became a foundation for a people's faith for centuries." Robert L. Millet, "The Book of Mormon, Historicity, and Faith," *Journal of Book of Mormon Studies* 2, 2 (1993): 1–13.

46. Robinson, "Expanded Book of Mormon," 402–403; Millet, "Book of Mormon," 6, 11. Millet, unlike Robinson, did not name Ostler but was clearly shadowboxing with him.

Mormon was to some extent shaped by Smith himself, but not to the extent that the expansion scenario supposed. Millet readily granted, for example, that in translating "the Isaiah sections or the Savior's sermon in 3 Nephi," Smith had "use[d] the English language with which he and the people of his day were familiar in recording the translation"—meaning that Smith had borrowed from the King James Version in producing those portions of the Book of Mormon translation. In other words, Millet was espousing a composed-translation scenario, a position he characterized as standing between two "interpretive extremes," one of those extremes being the expansion scenario and the other, by implication, a scenario in which Smith merely dictated words fed to him by God.[47] Although Millet defended what he understood to be the fundamentals of LDS faith, he was nevertheless prepared to accept a via media in the Book of Mormon wars. But for Millet, the acceptable via media was the composed-translation scenario, not Ostler's expansion scenario.

The Read-Translation Scenario Reasserted: 1990s–2000s

Around the same time Millet championed a composed translation in opposition to the new expansion theory, other conservative LDS scholars were reviving support for the earliest scenario—a read translation. One line of argument advanced by conservatives during the Book of Mormon wars was that the English text contained linguistic features that supported its being a bona fide translation of an ancient document of Near Eastern cultural provenance. These features included Hebraisms, grammatical constructions that are nonstandard in English but correspond to Hebrew grammar, as well as numerous examples of chiasmus, a poetic structure common in the Hebrew Bible, and other ancient works, in which parallel elements are repeated in inverse order (a, b, b, a). In a 1990 book published by the LDS Church's commercial press, BYU law professor and FARMS founder John Welch pointed out that in order for Hebraisms and chiasms to be carried over from the original text into the English translation, Smith's

---

47. Millet, "Book of Mormon," 5.

translation must have corresponded very closely, "point-by-point, with the ancient writing." This would rule out a scenario in which "the English translation has only ... casual verbal connections ... with the underlying record"; it would also rule out a scenario in which the English text has "only ... infrequent thematic intersections" with the original.[48] The first of those scenarios appears to describe the kind of composed-translation scenario espoused by B. H. Roberts; the second looks like a reference to Ostler's expansion theory. Neither of those scenarios could be relied on to produce an English translation that resembled the original closely enough to preserve Hebraisms or chiasms—which Welch believed were, in fact, present in Smith's English translation.

What scenario was left? Welch did not assert that Smith must have *read* the translation from the interpreters. But he rejected the particular composed-translation scenario that Richard Anderson had characterized as the consensus view of late-twentieth-century LDS scholars: the scenario in which Smith copied chapters from the King James Version when he realized that the golden plates contained the same material. Citing nineteenth-century witnesses' accounts of Smith reading from the interpreters, Welch insisted that "none of their statements mentions anything about the use of a Bible or allows room for it." Welch theorized instead that as Smith studied the translation out in his mind—per D&C 9—God had by some means "projected a text similar to the biblical text through Joseph Smith."[49] Welch thus retreated from the scenario that LDS apologists had used for most of a century, starting with Roberts, to account for poor grammar and parallels to the King James Version. Where advocates of a composed translation had denied that God revealed to Smith the specific wording of the English text, Welch favored a scenario in which God did. Where advocates of a composed translation had questioned the reliability of nineteenth-century witnesses' descriptions of the translation process, Welch took them as authoritative. Welch stopped short of espousing a read-translation scenario, but he appeared to be leaning in that direction.

---

48. John W. Welch, *The Sermon at the Temple and the Sermon on the Mount* (Salt Lake City: Deseret Book Co./ Provo, Utah: FARMS, 1990), 140.

49. Ibid., 135–36.

Where John Welch leaned, another FARMS scholar landed. Royal Skousen was a linguistics professor at BYU who spent two decades creating a critical edition of the original English text of the Book of Mormon, working with what remained of the manuscripts penned by Smith's scribes. Skousen's edition was published in 2009 by Yale University Press. But by 1990, just two years after beginning the critical text project, Skousen had already drawn conclusions about the process by which the Book of Mormon had been translated. He repeated these conclusions for LDS readers over the course of the 1990s.[50]

Skousen identified three kinds of theories for how Smith had translated the Book of Mormon: "loose control," "tight control," and "iron-clad control." "Loose control" corresponded to the composed-translation scenario: in Skousen's words, "ideas were revealed to Joseph Smith, and he put the ideas into his own language." Skousen noted that this theory had been "advocated by many Book of Mormon scholars over the years."[51] Skousen's categories did not include the expansion scenario unless he considered that a kind of "loose control" theory. "Tight control" and "iron-clad control" were different variations on a read-translation scenario. "Iron-clad control" referred to nineteenth-century witnesses' claims that when Smith looked into the interpreters he saw an English translation, which remained on display *until the scribe verified that the translation had been correctly recorded.* Those claims, Skousen asserted, were "definitely false," as evidenced by the presence, in the original manuscript, of errors that were not corrected until later, whereas if control were iron-clad then Smith should have prompted the scribe to correct the error immediately.[52] Skousen did believe, however, that the witnesses were correct in reporting that Smith read an English translation from the interpreters—just not that the translation remained on display until

---

50. Royal Skousen, "Towards a Critical Edition of the Book of Mormon," *BYU Studies* 30, 1 (Winter 1990): 41–69; Royal Skousen, "Translating the Book of Mormon: Evidence from the Original Manuscript," in Noel B. Reynolds, ed., *Book of Mormon Authorship Revisited: The Evidence for Ancient Origins* (Provo, Utah: FARMS, 1997), 61–93.

51. Skousen, "Translating the Book of Mormon," 64.

52. Ibid., 65–66.

it was correctly recorded. Thus control of the translation was not iron-clad, but it was tight—"tight" in the sense that the interpreters provided Smith with "specific words written out in English" to read aloud to his scribes, as contrasted to a "loose control," or composed-translation, scenario in which Smith had to come up with the English on his own.[53]

Skousen's textual evidence for a tightly controlled read translation included instances where Smith apparently spelled a name for the scribe; a word-for-word quotation from 1 Nephi 1:8 preserved in Alma 36:22 (an observation Skousen borrowed from Welch); and nearly fifteen occurrences of a Hebraism called the "*if-and* conditional," as in, "*If* you come *and* I will come." The fact that Smith or his scribes subsequently edited out all *if-and* constructions indicated to Skousen that Smith understood the construction as ungrammatical and therefore would not have employed it unless it had appeared in the English translation he was reading from the interpreters.[54] (Why the interpreters would have preserved the Hebraism in English, instead of translating the *if-and* construction as a conventional English *if-then* construction, Skousen did not speculate.) Skousen went so far as to make a case for how many English words Smith could see in the interpreters at a time: twenty to thirty. Skousen based this claim on an instance when Smith briefly took over from Cowdery as scribe to record twenty-eight words. Skousen speculated that Cowdery had had to step away suddenly from the translation and that Smith needed to finish recording the text he was seeing in the interpreters before it disappeared.[55]

In advancing a read-translation scenario, Skousen was aware of the long-standing argument that a composed-translation scenario was needed to avoid the conclusion that God was responsible for grammatical errors in the English: Skousen quoted both B. H. Roberts and Richard Anderson as iterations of that argument.[56] Skousen deflected the argument by challenging the premise that

---

53. Ibid., 64–65.
54. Ibid., 75–84, 87–90.
55. Ibid., 71–75.
56. Skousen, "Towards a Critical Edition," 55.

it would be absurd to attribute ungrammatical English to God. Extrapolating from a statement in D&C 1:24, that God gives revelations to his servants "after the manner of their language," Skousen concluded that it would be perfectly plausible for God to provide Smith with a translation of the Book of Mormon written in Smith's dialectal English. God, Skousen remarked, "apparently does not share our insistence on 'proper English.'"[57] (This line of argument would not account for linguistic patterns that are non-standard even in dialectical English, like the *if-and* construction, since those would not be cases of God speaking to Smith after the manner of Smith's language.)

Advocates of the composed-translation scenario from Roberts forward had cited D&C 9 as a key prooftext. Skousen addressed that text only glancingly, asserting that "the phrases 'study it out in your mind' and 'you shall feel that it is right' do not necessarily imply a loose control over the text. Joseph Smith had to study it out in his mind till he got it right!"[58] It is unclear from this brief statement what Skousen imagined that Smith would need to study out in his mind "till he got it right" if he were reading a translation provided by the interpreters. Skousen also addressed briefly the theory advanced by composed-translation advocates that Smith had used the King James Version to render biblical quotations. Skousen's argument on this point echoed Welch's: statements from nineteenth-century witnesses ruled out Smith's having consulted a Bible, and it therefore "seems more reasonable that it was the Lord himself who chose to quote from the King James Version."[59]

Skousen's years of work with the Book of Mormon manuscripts lent considerable authority to his arguments for a read translation. Furthermore, a tightly controlled read translation had the appeal of providing the close correspondence between ancient original and English translation that Welch had observed was necessary to sustain popular apologetic arguments about Hebraisms and chiasmus. Skousen's read-translation scenario would also sustain another, less prominent apologetic tack of this period: wordprint

---

57. Ibid., 54–55; Skousen, "Translating the Book of Mormon," 90.
58. Skousen, "Towards a Critical Edition," 55.
59. Ibid.

studies professing to confirm that the Book of Mormon contained multiple authorial voices, distinct from Smith's own voice. Earlier in the twentieth century, B. H. Roberts had favored a composed-translation scenario to explain what he perceived as the Book of Mormon's "sameness of phraseology and literary style," and Widtsoe had appealed to a composed translation to explain why the Book of Mormon's language matched Smith's.[60] By the late twentieth century, LDS apologists were more confident that the book's language could be shown *not* to be Smith's; such apologists would therefore feel less need than Roberts and Widtsoe to resort to a composed-translation scenario.

Three books published by LDS scholars through non-LDS presses at the beginning of the twenty-first century betokened a growing, though still cautious, willingness to reassert a read-translation scenario after a century's preference for a composed translation. Two of these authors, history professor Grant Hardy and English professor Terryl Givens (neither at BYU), characterized arguments for a tightly controlled read translation as suggestive but not decisive. Both Hardy and Givens cited nineteenth-century witnesses' reports that Smith had dictated the translation while looking into interpreters; indeed, both authors reported Smith's use of a seer stone, a controversial subject among LDS laity but one that scholars had been digesting, by then, for two decades. Both authors pointed to the kinds of textual evidence that supported or were supported by Skousen's read-translation scenario: Hebraisms, chiasmus, and signs of tight control of the manuscript.[61] However, neither Hardy nor Givens was willing to dismiss D&C 9's support for a composed translation as easily as Skousen had. As composed-translation advocates since Roberts had done, Hardy appealed to D&C 9 to call the witnesses' understanding of the translation process into question: "using the seer stone or the interpreters apparently involved more than simply reading off what [Smith] saw in vision, though some of his

---

60. Roberts, *Manual, 1903–1904,* 71; Widtsoe, "Vocabulary of Joseph Smith."

61. Grant Hardy, ed., *The Book of Mormon: A Reader's Edition* (Urbana: University of Illinois Press, 2003), x–xiii; Terryl L. Givens, *By the Hand of Mormon* (New York: Oxford University Press, 2002), 30–33, 125, 133–35.

early associates assumed this was exactly what he did." Hardy concluded that "Mormons have yet to work out a fully satisfying theory of inspired translation" that would account for both evidence of ancient origins and Smith's own linguistic fingerprints.[62] Givens, similarly, took an undecided stance toward the mode of translation. In support of a read translation, he pointed readers to Skousen's work; also, he followed Skousen and Welch in citing the nineteenth-century witnesses to dispute that Smith had consulted a King James Bible to compose his translation of biblical quotations. "On the other hand"—to quote his own transition—Givens underscored that Smith "clearly understood his role to be that of an imperfect medium," and Givens invoked the authority of D&C 9 to assert that "clearly something more than visual observation was involved."[63]

A third LDS scholar, noted historian Richard Bushman, came down firmly in support of a read translation. In his influential 2005 biography, *Joseph Smith: Rough Stone Rolling*, Bushman lumped theories of Book of Mormon translation into two categories: "composition" and "transcription." "Composition" theories held that Smith "composed [the Book of Mormon] out of knowledge and imaginings collected in his own mind, perhaps aided by inspiration." Despite acknowledging that some composition theories involved divine inspiration, Bushman ultimately characterized composition, pejoratively, as "the naturalistic explanation" for the Book of Mormon. Composition was further damned because "it is at odds with … the historical record," which "has Joseph Smith 'seeing' the *Book of Mormon* text in the seerstone or the Urim and Thummim"—hence the Book of Mormon translation was a "transcription." In support of this assertion, Bushman cited the nineteenth-century witnesses, plus Skousen's work with the Book of Mormon manuscript.[64] A little later in his narrative, Bushman quoted D&C 9 while telling the story of Cowdery's failed effort to

62. Hardy, *Reader's Edition*, xv–xvi.

63. Givens, *By the Hand of Mormon*, 32, 255–256n97.

64. Richard Lyman Bushman, *Joseph Smith: Rough Stone Rolling* (New York: Knopf, 2005), 71–73.

translate, but Bushman did not address the potential challenge that D&C 9 posed to a "transcription," or read-translation, scenario.[65]

It should be noted that Bushman's category of "composition" theories of the Book of Mormon's production is different from the "composed-translation" scenario. When Bushman spoke of "composition," he meant theories that had Smith inventing the book's contents, "the way books are always written," maybe with some kind of divine inspiration involved. That would describe Anthony Hutchinson's idea of the Book of Mormon as inspired nineteenth-century fiction; it would not describe Blake Ostler's idea that Smith expanded the plates' ancient original contents, nor B. H. Roberts's idea that God revealed the meaning of the ancient text to Smith's mind and left him to render those ideas into words ("composed-translation"). This is to say that Bushman framed the debate over Book of Mormon translation in simplified terms, as a two-way contest between, on the one hand, naturalistic accounts, with "inspired fiction" lumped into those ("composition"), and, on the other hand, a read translation ("transcription"). In Bushman's dualistic framing, the composed-translation scenario that had attracted LDS intellectuals across the twentieth century simply disappeared.

Church Leaders Support a Read Translation: Russell M. Nelson and Neal A. Maxwell

During the 1990s, as Skousen was arguing for a tightly controlled read translation, two LDS apostles threw the weight of their office onto the question: Russell M. Nelson and Neal A. Maxwell. In 1992, Nelson, a former heart surgeon, gave a sermon at the church's Missionary Training Center, subsequently published in the *Ensign*, in which he quoted nineteenth-century witnesses to paint a picture of what Skousen would call iron-clad control of the Book of Mormon translation: looking into the interpreters, Smith saw an English translation, one character at a time, which remained on display until the scribe verified that the translation was correctly recorded. This was the translation scenario that Skousen proclaimed to be "definitely false" and that FARMS's Stephen

---

65. Ibid., 73.

Ricks had insisted would produce gibberish. In other words, Nelson was promoting an understanding of the translation process more fundamentalistic than some-to-many conservative LDS scholars were apparently prepared to accept. At the same time, Nelson lent support to the work of FARMS scholars by pointing to Hebraisms and chiasmus in the Book of Mormon as evidence of the book's antiquity.[66]

Maxwell held degrees in political science and had been a university administrator prior to his call to the Twelve. As an apostle, Maxwell was an important supporter of FARMS, which, readers may recall, became part of a center at BYU named for Maxwell after the apostle's death. Maxwell was more aware than Nelson of problems with the witnesses' accounts of the translation process, as evident in an essay Maxwell published in the *Ensign* in 1997.[67]

Maxwell's essay attempted to reconcile arguments for the read-translation and composed-translation scenarios. In support of a read translation, Maxwell quoted from the Three Witnesses to establish that Smith had read the English translation as it appeared in the interpreters. Maxwell did not, however, quote the portions of these witnesses' statements that asserted what Skousen called "iron-clad control"; that is, Maxwell did not quote the witnesses' claims that the translation remained on display until correctly recorded. Furthermore, Maxwell hedged on the reliability of the witnesses' claims by noting that two of the witnesses never used the interpreters themselves and by twice prefacing his conclusions with a qualifying "if," as in this example: "If these reports are accurate, they suggest a process indicative of God's having given Joseph 'sight and power to translate' (D&C 3:12)." Despite the cautionary "if," the thrust of Maxwell's statement was to affirm that the witnesses' descriptions are consistent with a scriptural statement about the Book of Mormon translation, thereby lending credence to the witnesses' read-translation claims.

But Maxwell also nodded to the composed-translation scenario,

---

66. Russell M. Nelson, "A Treasured Testament," *Ensign*, July 1993, accessed online at www.lds.org (Nov. 5, 2016).

67. Neal A. Maxwell, "By the Gift and Power of God," *Ensign*, Jan. 1997, accessed online at www.lds.org (Nov. 5, 2016).

conceding that "the Prophet sometimes may have used a less mechanical procedure. We simply do not know the details." Maxwell immediately followed that statement with a reference to D&C 9, from which he concluded that "whatever the details of the process, it required Joseph's intense, personal efforts along with the aid of the revelatory instruments." Rather than painting the read-translation/composed-translation question as either/or, Maxwell suggested it could be both/and: both scenarios could have been involved at different points of the translation process. "The process may have varied as Joseph's capabilities grew," Maxwell speculated, "involving the Urim and Thummim but perhaps with less reliance upon such instrumentalities in the Prophet's later work of translation." In other words: Early in the process, the translation might have been read; later it might have been composed.

Although Maxwell was willing to accommodate both a read-translation and a composed-translation scenario, he warned that "there is need for caution in assuming or suggesting that the Prophet had great flexibility as to doctrine and as to the substance of the language he used." Maxwell did not provide any examples of this dangerous assumption in practice, but he shortly afterward asserted that "the Prophet was not shaping the doctrine." This phrasing suggests that Maxwell had the expansion scenario in mind. *That* was not to be accommodated.

Notwithstanding the both/and nature of Maxwell's proposal, when contextualized in the longer history of LDS thinking about Book of Mormon translation, the essay stands out for providing a high-profile revival of the read-translation scenario. Maxwell's 1997 *Ensign* article, offering arguments for *both* a read translation and a composed translation, stands in contrast, for example, to Richard Anderson's *Ensign* article of twenty years earlier, which had championed a composed translation *instead of* a read translation. Significantly, where Roberts and Anderson had used the composed-translation scenario to account for errors in the Book of Mormon's English text, Maxwell's apologetic aim tended in the opposite direction. The Book of Mormon, Maxwell asserted, contains "no error." "There is no error in the revelations which I have taught," Maxwell quoted Smith as saying; to emphasize that assertion further, the quotation served as the heading of the final section of Maxwell's essay. Maxwell's affirmation of the reliability—literally, the inerrancy—of the Book of Mormon's teachings betokened a conservative theological impulse pulling against the liberal impulses displayed by Roberts or Ostler. Maxwell was not calling the LDS to "force [Mormonism] beyond its earlier and cruder stages of development" (Roberts) or to be skeptical that "any particular statement of revelation is the final and complete word on any subject" (Ostler).[68]

The Gospel Topics Essay: Read-Translation Scenario Triumphs

If we read the LDS Church's Gospel Topics essay as an intervention in this century-long LDS dispute over how the Book of Mormon was translated, on which side does the essay come down? Answer: The essay squarely endorses a tightly controlled read translation, without even acknowledging the existence of other scenarios.

According to "virtually all of the accounts of the translation process" left by witnesses, the Gospel Topics essay declares, "Joseph ... read aloud the English words that appeared on the instrument." One of the historical texts the essay quotes to support this assertion is an account attributed to Martin Harris. As recently as Stephen Ricks in 1993, advocates of the composed-translation scenario had contended that this particular account was problematic because (1) Harris was describing something he had not seen for himself, (2) he was describing events fifty years after the fact, and (3) his words had been preserved in a secondhand report. Without acknowledging these problems or earlier LDS scholars' reservations, the authors of the Gospel Topics essay accept the Harris account as support for their read-translation scenario. However, the essay ends its quotation from Harris literally just before the point at which that source claimed that the interpreters left an English translation on display until accurately recorded. That is to say, the authors of

---

68. Roberts, "Correspondence," July 1906, 713; Ostler, "Book of Mormon," 113.

the Gospel Topic essay present the Harris statement as reliable insofar as the statement supports the contention that Smith read an English translation, but they omit the statement's claim in support of what Skousen called an "iron-clad control" theory of translation. Neal A. Maxwell, in 1997, had selectively quoted the Harris statement to the same effect.

At another point, the essay cites Emma Smith, Joseph's wife, as having "flatly denied" the possibility that "Joseph had dictated from the Bible." The essay thus echoes Welch and Skousen's argument against the once—and still?—widely embraced scenario in which Smith used the King James Version to compose his translation of biblical quotations. The essay does not, however, explicitly rebut that scenario. That is, while the essay presents (in emphatic terms) the statement from Emma that Welch and Skousen used to argue against Joseph's having consulted the King James Version, the essay does not spell out the conclusion from the evidence. Does this subtlety indicate that the essay authors were not in agreement about Welch and Skousen's argument? Or perhaps they decided it would be impolitic to directly challenge, in this venue, what might still be a widely held contrary view?

The Gospel Topics essay notably omits two sources that had figured prominently in earlier debates about Book of Mormon translation.[69] One is a statement from David Whitmer, which had been quoted, whether favorably or skeptically, by B. H. Roberts, Richard Anderson, Stephen Ricks, Royal Skousen, Russell M. Nelson, and Neal A. Maxwell. Much like the Harris statement,

---

69. There is a third notable omission, in the Gospel Topics essay, of a historical source that LDS have long cited to authenticate the Book of Mormon translation; however, that source did not figure in the read-translation/composed-translation/expansion debate, and therefore I have not discussed it in the main text of this article. That source is Martin Harris's account in which Columbia professor Charles Anthon certified that Smith had correctly translated characters copied from the golden plates. It is puzzling that the Gospel Topics essay does not cite Harris's account (canonized as JS-H 1:63–65) to support the assertion that the Book of Mormon was a translation of an authentic ancient record. Possibly the essay authors shied away from the Anthon story because it is problematic: Anthon disputed Harris's account of what happened. However, conservative LDS scholars such as Terryl Givens and Richard Bushman have offered arguments that undermine Anthon's version of events; the Gospel Topics essay could have done the same. Givens, *By the Hand of Mormon*, 29–30; Bushman, *Rough Stone Rolling*, 64–65. The omission of the Anthon story remains a puzzle.

Whitmer claimed that Smith had seen an English translation when he looked into the interpreters. Why would the Gospel Topic essay writers not include, to their advantage, this quite famous statement from one of the Three Witnesses? One reason might be that Whitmer made claims beyond what the essay writers were willing to accept—namely, that an English translation had appeared directly beneath each character, and that the translation remained on display until accurately recorded ("iron-clad" control). But the essay writers could easily have circumvented that problem through selective quotation, as they did with the Harris statement. Another possible explanation is that the writers omitted Whitmer because they decided to spotlight only quotations from Book of Mormon *scribes*, thinking that those would be the strongest witnesses. Emma Smith and Martin Harris served as scribes; David Whitmer did not.[70]

The second notable source omitted by the Gospel Topics essay is D&C 9. The reason for that omission is easy to guess at: that passage had always served as a daunting prooftext for the composed-translation scenario. Still, it is surprising that the essay makes no attempt to address what may be among LDS readers the most well-known description of the translation process—a description, indeed, with the status of scripture. Welch, Skousen, and Maxwell had all engaged with the problem posed by D&C 9 in their contributions to reviving the read-translation scenario; Skousen even claimed to harness D&C 9 to the read-translation scenario, although how he thought he had done that was unclear. The Gospel Topics essay, by contrast, does not mention the famous passage. Did the essay writers lack confidence that they could persuasively reconcile D&C 9 with their read-translation scenario, especially after a century's worth of contrary arguments from composed-translation advocates?

In addition to using witnesses' statements to directly support a read-translation scenario, the Gospel Topics essay indirectly supports that scenario by citing FARMS scholars on the presence of

---

70. Whitmer does receive a nod in footnote 32 of the Gospel Topics essay: For additional accounts of translation by one of the Three Witnesses, see *David Whitmer Interviews: A Restoration Witness* ...

Hebraisms in the original manuscripts. This was the same kind of evidence that Skousen had cited to support his "tight control" theory. Although the Gospel Topics essay draws heavily on Skousen's work, citing six of his publications, the essay does not repeat Skousen's claim that Smith could see twenty-to-thirty English words at a time in the interpreters—perhaps because the essay writers were not entirely persuaded? Nor do the essay writers employ Skousen's argument that God does not care about proper grammar, an argument one might expect to have appealed to the writers given that it neutralizes one of the primary arguments for a composed-translation scenario. But then, the Gospel Topics essay does not directly tackle *any* arguments for the composed-translation scenario. The essay acts, rather, as if the composed-translation scenario, the scenario that Richard Anderson had once characterized as the consensus view among LDS scholars, simply does not exist.

Implications of the Gospel Topics Essay

The Gospel Topics essay could have been written very differently. The writers could have done what Grant Hardy or Terryl Givens did: characterize the topic as not yet settled and catalogue evidence in support of different theories. It was probably unrealistic to expect the essay to acknowledge the expansion scenario, given how emphatically conservatives like Stephen Robinson and Robert Millet opposed Ostler's work. It is more surprising that the essay offered no concession to the composed-translation scenario, given how widely held that scenario has been among LDS intellectuals, including some general authorities (B. H. Roberts and John A. Widtsoe). Conceivably, the Gospel Topics essay could have followed the lead of Maxwell, offering a both/and scenario in which Smith produced a read translation during one phase of the process and a composed translation in another. Instead, the essay writers chose sides. And the side they chose was the most fundamentalistic of the scenarios that LDS scholars were advocating at the beginning of the twenty-first century: a tightly controlled read translation. The Gospel Topics essay is more fundamentalistic, even, than Millet, when he advanced a composed-translation scenario to ward off the modernist threat posed by Ostler. The only position more fundamentalistic than the one adopted by the Gospel Topics essay would have been an iron-clad read translation, such as that promoted by Apostle Russell M. Nelson; but I have not seen any twentieth- or twenty-first-century LDS scholar advocate that position. Royal Skousen carried the day.

In 1903, Roberts persuaded church leaders to let him publish a manual that defended the Book of Mormon's divinity by advocating a composed-translation scenario in place of the more widely held read-translation scenario. One hundred-plus years later, anonymous writers persuaded church leaders to let them publish a Gospel Topics essay that defended the Book of Mormon's divinity by advocating a read-translation scenario in place of the more widely held composed-translation scenario. Why this reversal? Roberts, as champion of the composed-translation scenario, and the writers of the Gospel Topics essay, as champions of the read-translation scenario, shared an apologetic goal: to defend the claim that the Book of Mormon was a translation of an ancient text produced by Smith through revelation. But Roberts and the Gospel Topics essay writers were defending the Book of Mormon against different challenges. In 1903, Roberts was responding to critics who pointed to the Book of Mormon's poor English as evidence against its being revealed. By 2013, LDS apologists no longer regarded that as a pressing criticism. The Book of Mormon wars of the 1980s-2000s had generated a whole new set of arguments against the Book of Mormon's antiquity, to which apologists had developed new counter-arguments, including claims about Hebraisms and wordprint analyses ruling out Smith's authorship. The revived read-translation scenario both sustained and was sustained by these new apologetic lines. Roberts, at the beginning of the twentieth century, had regarded the read-translation scenario as a liability, an opening for the church's critics. Apologists at the beginning of the twenty-first century regarded the read-translation scenario not as a liability but as a complement to other lines of argument supporting the Book of Mormon's authenticity. In 1903, Roberts had tried to persuade church leaders that the composed-translation scenario was an indispensable apologetic line for the church. He lost that argument in 2013.

That loss was a loss for theological liberalism among the LDS. Roberts had championed the composed-translation scenario in order to cultivate a less dogmatic, more innovative Mormonism. By the end of the twentieth century, new generations of LDS intellectuals were advocating views of the Book of Mormon considerably more liberalized than Roberts's own, from the expansion scenario to views of the Book of Mormon as inspired nineteenth-century fiction. The Gospel Topics essay retreated not only from those views; it pulled back to a position even more conservative than Roberts's.

By comparison to the expansion scenario or the composed-translation scenario, the read-translation scenario confers greater authority on the Book of Mormon's English text. Ostler's expansion scenario was predicated on a conception of revelation as "continuing, dynamic, and incomplete," always occurring within the recipient's "own conceptual paradigms." This conception "preclude[s] taking scripture as a source-book of axiomatic truths" or as "*the* true understanding."[71] This approach limits the authority that the Book of Mormon can claim, which is why fundamentalists like Robinson and Millet rejected Ostler's scenario. Although not nearly to the same extent as Ostler, Roberts's composed-translation scenario also limits the authority of the Book of Mormon's English text, since it is the *ideas,* not the words, that are revealed. Roberts was therefore open to revising the text bequeathed by Smith, "since it is the thought, the facts of the book, that one should be concerned in preserving, not the forms in which they happen to be cast."[72] Roberts was dismayed that the read-translation scenario led "some" LDS to conclude "that we have no right ... to change a single word of the translation."[73]

The read-translation scenario advocated in the Gospel Topics essay does not lend so much authority to the received English text as to preclude the possibility of making relatively small revisions (which the church has done since Smith's death). However, a read-translation scenario lends greater authority to the words dictated by Smith

---

71. Ostler, "Book of Mormon," 109, 111, 115.
72. Roberts, "Translation (Concluded)," May 1906, 553.
73. Roberts, "Translation," Apr. 1906, 434.

than a composed-translation scenario does. God displayed these very words to Smith on the interpreters, the LDS are asked to believe. The read-translation scenario thus carries the potential for an LDS analogue to the evangelical Protestant doctrine of biblical inerrancy (that the Bible contains no error). Recall Maxwell's insistence that "there is no error" in the Book of Mormon.[74] In a similar vein, the Gospel Topics essay opens with a familiar quotation in which Smith pronounced the Book of Mormon "the most correct of any Book on earth."[75] During the 1990s—the same period when Robinson and Millett were denouncing the expansion scenario, when Welch and Sorenson were reviving the read-translation scenario, and when Maxwell preached that the Book of Mormon contains "no error"—church leaders officially discountenanced editions of the Book of Mormon in modernized or simplified English. The theological underpinning for their disapproval was that Smith had translated the Book of Mormon "by the gift and power of God" and that it was (again) "the most correct of any book on earth," implying that it was presumptuous for someone to try to improve on the words Smith had handed down.[76] Viewed in that context, the Gospel Topics essay's advocacy of a read-translation scenario can be interpreted as one more instance of the church reinforcing the authority of the Book of Mormon text to the point of tilting toward a doctrine of inerrancy—by strengthening the authority of the *words* Smith dictated.[77]

What does the Gospel Topics essay portend for the future? At the beginning of the twenty-first century, Richard Bushman (who, as we saw, favored a read translation) reported his impression that the expansion scenario was "attracting more and more fairly faithful church members."[78] Will the Gospel Topics essay lead such members to feel alienated from the church? What

---

74. Maxwell, "By the Gift and Power."

75. "Book of Mormon Translation," capitalization as in the original.

76. "Modern-Language Editions of the Book of Mormon Discouraged," *Ensign*, Apr. 1993, accessed online at ww.lds.org (Nov. 5, 2016).

77. Exactly what it would mean to say that the Book of Mormon is inerrant—in Maxwell's words, that it contains "no error"—is a question to which LDS thinkers could develop various answers, just as evangelical theologians have developed various understandings of what it means to call the Bible inerrant.

78. Quoted in Givens, *By the Hand of Mormon*, 173–74.

about LDS who subscribe to a composed-translation scenario such as that promoted in the *Ensign* as recently as the 1970s? The fact that the Gospel Topics essay came down on the side of the read-translation scenario does not rule out the possibility that the composed-translation scenario will continue to thrive among LDS intellectuals. It's even possible that the composed-translation scenario will continue to find its way into church publications. The Gospel Topics essay intervenes in the century-long dispute over Book of Mormon translation on behalf of the read-translation scenario, but that does not mean that LDS at large will grasp that this is what the essay has done nor that they will follow. Nevertheless, the Gospel Topics essay represents an institutional victory for theological conservatives who see the expansion scenario, and even the composed-translation scenario, as insufficiently faithful to the testimony of the miraculous left by Smith and his associates.

5. THE CULTURAL WORK OF THE "FIRST VISION ACCOUNTS" ESSAY[1]

David J. Howlett

In his last conference talk before his 2008 death, LDS Church President Gordon B. Hinckley returned to a subject of which he often spoke—Joseph Smith's 1820 theophany near Palmyra, New York, widely known by Mormons as the "First Vision." To his LDS audience, Hinckley exhorted, "You and I are faced with the stark question of accepting the truth of the First Vision and that which followed it. On the question of its reality lies the very validity of this Church."[2] Only two years before this talk, Hinckley had written, "This grand theophany is, in my judgment, the greatest such event since the birth, life, death, and Resurrection of our Lord in the meridian of time."[3] And, a decade before his final talk, Hinckley had written, "Our entire case as members of The Church of Jesus Christ of Latter-day Saints rests on the validity of this glorious First Vision. ... it stands as an absolute fundamental in the Church and its history and its well-being."[4] Again and again, Hinckley referred to the First Vision as a foundational part of the LDS mythos that had to have happened as a historical event or else, he suggested, the LDS Church itself was a sham. While there

---

1. Steven C. Harper generously read a draft of this essay. Any mistakes of fact or interpretation remain my own.

2. Gordon B. Hinckley, "The Stone Cut out of the Mountain," Oct. 2007, accessed Oct. 7, 2016, www.lds.org/general-conference/2007/10/the-stone-cut-out-of-the-mountain?lang=eng.

3. Gordon B. Hinckley, "The Great Things Which God Has Revealed," Apr. 2005, accessed Oct. 7, 2016, www.lds.org/general-conference/2005/04/the-great-things-which-god-has-revealed?lang=eng&clang=ase.

4. Gordon B. Hinckley, "What Are People Asking about Us?," Oct. 1998, accessed Oct. 7, 2016, www.lds.org/general-conference/1998/10/what-are-people-asking-about-us?lang=eng.

is a long history in this framing of Smith's theophany, dating, as we will see, to the early twentieth century, Hinckley surely raised the stakes held by LDS members vis-à-vis the First Vision.

As Hinckley knew when he made his remarks, Smith's First Vision had been the subject of simmering controversies, within and outside the LDS Church, since the mid-1960s. Until the mid-twentieth century, LDS Church officials by and large acknowledged only one First Vision account authored by Smith.[5] The officially recognized account, written in 1838 and later published in the LDS Church's newspaper in 1842, had been canonized in 1880 and became a foundational narrative for the church by the early twentieth century. Then, in the mid-1960s, an LDS graduate student in his master's thesis included the text of an even earlier account of Smith's First Vision, an account eventually dated to 1832. Found in a then-restricted manuscript in the LDS Church Historian's Office (later Archives), the 1832 account had been penned by Smith himself, unlike any other known account.[6] Beyond minor differences of date and provenance, the textual differences between the earlier and later accounts mattered. Unlike the canonized 1838 version, the 1832 version seemed to include a vision of only one divine, not two embodied divine beings. By the twentieth century, LDS members regularly used the 1838 account as a prooftext about the nature of gods, including the claim that "Heavenly Father" had a body of flesh and bone.[7] The earlier account did not seem to support this assertion. Additionally, the 1832 account read more like an evangelical conversion narrative than the calling of a prophet, and it was less detailed than the

---

5. Steven Harper notes that B. H. Roberts wrote about two First Vision accounts as early as 1909. Harper, *First Vision: Memory and Mormon Origins* (New York: Oxford University Press, 2019), 153. Nonetheless, widespread knowledge of multiple accounts, whether by scholars, general authorities, or members, appears to have begun only in the 1960s.

6. James B. Allen, "The Significance of Joseph Smith's First Vision in 'Mormon Thought'," *Dialogue: A Journal of Mormon Thought* 1, 3 (1966): 35; Karen Lynn Davidson, David J. Whittaker, Mark Ashcraft-McGee, and Richard L. Jensen, et al., eds., *The Joseph Smith Papers: Histories, Joseph Smith Histories, 1832–1844*, 23 vols. to date (Salt Lake City: Church Historian's Press, 2008–), 1:4.

7. Allen, "The Significance of the First Vision," 30.

1838 version.[8] In short, the 1960s LDS Church faced doctrinal questions, not simply historical questions, with the publication of a new, earlier First Vision account.

Over the next few decades, LDS historians made detailed studies of the early and later accounts of Smith's First Vision, expanding the number of accounts to include more first- and second-hand recollections, all having slightly different details. These LDS historians published their interpretations in official LDS publications, both scholarly (*BYU Studies*) and popular (*Improvement Era* and *Ensign*), as well as an independent Mormon journal (*Dialogue: A Journal of Mormon Thought*).[9] Evangelical counter-cult ministries offered counternarratives to these explanations and questioned the validity of what had become the founding narrative of the LDS Church. While evangelicals mainly published their findings in exposé-style books and ministry newsletters, one evangelical apologist presented his arguments about the First Vision in an issue of *Dialogue* that included a response by no less than Bancroft Prize-winning LDS historian Richard Bushman.[10] Rather than being submerged by other concerns, controversy over the multiple First Vision accounts has surfaced again and again in the last fifty years, forming a discursive tradition that functions as an index for how individuals and groups use the Mormon past.

Perhaps out of a desire not to create problems in the minds of LDS members unaware of Smith's multiple accounts, LDS Church officials provided little fanfare for their release of a 2013 essay at lds.org titled "First Vision Accounts." Part of the ongoing series of "Gospel Topics" essays, the "First Visions Accounts" essay offered

---

8. D. Michael Quinn, *The Mormon Hierarchy: Origins of Power* (Salt Lake City: Signature Books, 1994), 3.

9. Allen, "The Significance of the Joseph Smith's First Vision"; Dean C. Jesse, "The Early Accounts of Joseph Smith's First Vision," *BYU Studies* 9, 3 (1969): 275–94; James B. Allen, "Eight Contemporary Accounts of Joseph Smith's First Vision: What Do We Learn from Them?" *Improvement Era* 73, 4 (Apr. 1970): 4–15; Milton Backman, "Joseph Smith's Recitals of the First Vision," *Ensign*, Jan. 1985, accessed Oct. 13, 2016 at www.lds.org/ensign/1985/01/joseph-smiths-recitals-of-the-first-vision?lang=eng.

10. Wesley P. Walters, "New Light on Mormon Origins from the Palmyra Revival," *Dialogue: A Journal of Mormon Thought* 4, 1 (Spring 1969): 59–81; Richard L. Bushman, "The First Vision Story Revived," *Dialogue: A Journal of Mormon Thought* 4, 1 (Spring 1969): 82–93.

yet another official explanation for the differences found in the multiple accounts of Smith's First Vision. The "First Vision Accounts" essay bore no name for its author, though it acknowledged "the contribution of scholars to the historical content presented in this article."[11] In only 1,800-words, the essay's anonymous writers succinctly addressed various accounts authored by Smith or his contemporaries detailing the Palmyra prophet's earliest theophany. Then, they addressed two problems raised by "critics": Smith's memory of revivals in his area in 1820 and Smith's alleged "embellishments" to his later accounts of the First Vision. In an argument that echoed the language and ethos of the late President Hinckley, they concluded that "Knowing the truth of Joseph Smith's testimony requires each earnest seeker of truth to study the record and then exercise sufficient faith in Christ to ask God in sincere, humble prayer whether the record is true."[12]

Yet, despite this concluding devotional assertion, the writers of the "First Vision Accounts" essay revealed in their text multiple (sometimes conflicting) approaches to historical questions. As such, the essay reveals something about the present intellectual currents that shape the LDS Church as a whole. More specifically, the First Vision essay, along with the other Gospel Topics essays, testifies to the emergence of what I have previously called a "Post-Correlation LDS Church" and the growing influence of a "progressive orthodox" movement within the church.[13] As I argue, a close reading of the First Vision essay gestures toward such conclusions.

In a broader context, I propose that we may read the First Vision Accounts essay as an artefact of a particular cultural moment in the United States. As noted, the authors of the First Vision essay address issues of memory and embellishment related to Smith's theophany. By doing so, the essay performs a specific kind of "cultural

---

11. "First Vision Accounts," 2013, accessed Oct. 13, 2016, at www.lds.org/topics/first-vision-accounts?lang=eng.

12. Ibid.

13. David J. Howlett, "A Post-Correlation Church?" *John Whitmer Historical Association Journal* 35 (2014): 112–16. The idea of "progressive orthodoxy" in the LDS Church is taken from John-Charles Duffy, "Conservative Pluralists: The Cultural Politics of Mormon-Evangelical Dialogue in the United States at the Turn of the Twentieth-first Century," PhD diss., University of North Carolina-Chapel Hill, 2011, 131–207.

work" for the LDS members who read it: it frames a problem and answers questions more widely present in contemporary LDS culture (and thus does "work"). In its very material embodiment online as well as in its narrative effects, the essay renders another form of cultural work addressed to people who store memory in ephemeral electronic clouds and/or worry about dementia. In other words, the "First Vision Accounts" essay reveals an American culture beset with anxieties about memory loss and the concomitant effects of that on collective and individual identity.

Before addressing these larger arguments, I narrate a brief history of the publication of various accounts of Smith's First Vision and how this has been used in LDS doctrine and practice—a necessarily fragmentary excursus into the cultural life of the First Vision. Then, I provide a close reading of the Gospel Topics essay itself and offer observations about its inclusions, omissions, and general arguments. Finally, I turn to some of the larger conclusions that I have delineated in this introduction, including both the cultural work of the essay and what this signals for the LDS Church in the near future.

The Cultural Life of the First Vision

As the Gospel Topics essay notes, Smith's theophany appeared in several forms in the 1830s and 1840s. The first recorded narrative was written by the Mormon prophet himself in the summer of 1832 as part of an intended history of the church. While the narratives told by early Mormons about their church previously had started with the story of the Book of Mormon plates, Smith started his 1832 salvation history with a theophany in which "the Lord" appeared to him in a grove of trees near his upstate New York home and forgave his sins.[14] Smith never published this 1832 account, and it was unknown to the general public until 1965 when it was "discovered" anew in the Church Historian's Office.[15]

---

14. Davidson et. al., eds., *Joseph Smith Histories, 1832–1844*, 1:4–5.

15. Overseen by Church Historian and Recorder Joseph Fielding Smith and other officials suspicious of what they saw as secular pursuits, the mid-twentieth century LDS Church Historians Office (CHO) offered scholars limited access to its documents. Additionally, the CHO's archives functioned mainly as a depository for materials that were sometimes haphazardly cataloged. With a change in personnel

The first publication of any version of Smith's vision occurred in 1840 when LDS Apostle Orson Pratt on mission to the British Isles published the tract *A[n] Interesting Account of Several Remarkable Visions.*[16] However, the most iconic and influential account of Smith's vision appeared two years later in the *Times and Seasons*, the official Mormon organ published in Nauvoo, Illinois. In it, Smith and his editors narrated a detailed vision in which two personages appeared to Smith in answer to his prayer of which church he should join. One of the personages, identified by the other as "my beloved Son," told Smith to join none of the existing churches. Other variations of this vision were also produced and printed in this same time period, but the *Times and Seasons* account (originally composed in 1838 and hereafter cited as the "1838 account") became the text that most late-nineteenth and twentieth-century Mormons of all groups read.[17]

Despite its publication during Smith's lifetime, the First Vision did not become Mormon scripture for another forty years. In 1880, the LDS Church canonized *The Pearl of Great Price*, a collection of writings that had originally appeared as a missionary tract in England in 1851. This missionary tract included the *Times and Seasons*'s First Vision account, and LDS officials kept it in their newly canonized fourth book of scripture (see JS-H 1:1–20, in PGP). Canonization of the 1838 account, of course, did not automatically instantiate it as a source for a particular doctrinal point. That would come decades later, though LDS historian James B. Allen has pointed out that LDS Apostle George Q. Cannon was precisely using it in this way in a general conference talk in 1883.[18] As an upshot of canonization, late-nineteenth-century LDS leaders had created a singular authorized account of Smith's

---

and a move to professionalize the archives beginning in the mid- to late 1960s, new material, including the early unpublished First Vision account, became more generally available. See Gregory A. Prince, *Leonard Arrington and the Writing of Mormon History* (Salt Lake City: University of Utah Press, 2016), 79–81.

16. Davidson et. al., *Joseph Smith Histories, 1832–1844*, 1:517–46.

17. Ibid., 1:xvii, 208–18.

18. Allen, "The Significance of Joseph Smith's First Vision," 38. Cannon used the First Vision in earlier articles that he wrote as well. In an 1880 editorial, he used the an 1842 published letter from Smith to John Wentworth to assert, "We are told by the Prophet Joseph Smith, who saw the Father and the Son, that they were personages

vision that would become normative within the LDS Church in their era until the present.

However important canonization might have been, the crucial period in the transformation of the First Vision into a foundational narrative for the LDS Church occurred in the early twentieth century. Religious studies scholar Kathleen Flake has convincingly argued that the early-twentieth-century demise of church-sanctioned plural marriage/polygamy created something of an identity crisis for the church. Without polygamy, church leaders needed new ways to position their members as distinctive from other American Christians. As Flake argues, they found these identity markers through, among other things, a new emphasis on the importance of the First Vision. Specifically, the 1838 account of the theophany "was first used [by the LDS Church] in Sunday school texts in 1905, in priesthood instructional manuals in 1909, as a separate missionary tract in 1910, and in the histories of the church in 1912."[19] With the purchase of the Joseph Smith Sr. family farm by the LDS Church in 1907 and the concomitant rise of Mormon travel to "sacred sites" in the eastern United States, the 1838 First Vision account became a text that anchored a Mormon pilgrimage site, too.[20] Flake notes that these uses of the First Vision signaled a seismic shift in how the LDS Church would contest difference in the early twentieth century. She argues that "the First Vision changed the arena of confrontation over difference from social action to theological belief."[21] That is, LDS would be distinct not because of their marriage practices and theocracy (social actions), but because of their theological beliefs

---

alike in form, substance and glory." George Q. Cannon, "Editorial Thoughts," *Juvenile Instructor* 15, 14 (July 15, 1880): 162.

19. Kathleen Flake, *The Politics of American Religious Identity: The Seating of Senator Reed Smoot, Mormon Apostle* (Chapel Hill: University of North Carolina Press, 2004), 118. Flake's dating of the First Vision's appearance in church history is off by a decade. In B. H. Roberts's 1902 first edition of *History of the Church,* the 1838 First Vision began the very narrative of the modern restored church. B. H. Roberts, *History of the Church of Jesus Christ of Latter-day Saints,* 7 vols. (Salt Lake City: Deseret Book Co., 1902), 1:1–8. However, Flake's larger point still remains valid.

20. Kathleen Flake, "Re-placing Memory: Latter-day Saint Use of Historical Monuments and Memory in the Early Twentieth Century," *Religion and American Culture: A Journal of Interpretation* 13, 1 (2003): 83.

21. Flake, *The Politics of American Religious Identity,* 120.

extrapolated, in part, from the 1838 First Vision account. These beliefs included a non-Trinitarian doctrine about gods and claims about the exclusive sacerdotal and sacramental authority of the LDS Church. Just as important, Flake notes that Smith's 1838 narrative "emerged not just as a source of doctrine but also the modern church's master narrative."[22]

With the development of the modern LDS missionary program after the World War II, the LDS Church continued its expansion of the First Vision as a foundational narrative. Starting in the 1950s, a young Gordon B. Hinckley helped write various talks and educational materials that elders shared with "investigators," those whom LDS evangelized. As religious studies scholar John-Charles Duffy has shown, "all standardized [missionary] discussions" published from 1952 to 2004 "have introduced the First Vision as part of the first discussion." The explicit use of the First Vision varied, as Duffy notes: "in 1952, [the First Vision was used to introduce] the restoration of a knowledge of the true nature of God; in 1961 and 1973, the restoration of the true church."[23] These works both reflected popular approaches to the First Vision and further systemized how Mormons, both converts and "cradle-born," used the First Vision.

By the mid-1960s, historian James B. Allen could note that the 1838 account of the First Vision was "used by church leaders and teachers to demonstrate for believers many other aspects of the Mormon faith [other than what Joseph Smith apparently

22. Flake, "Re-placing Memory," 85. While my essay in the present volume was in the editorial process, Steven Harper published *First Vision: Memory and Mormon Origins*. Among other things, Harper argues that Smith's "First Vision" was better known in the latter part of Smith's lifetime than previous historians, like Flake, have assumed. Harper and Elise Peterson also point out in a 2015 essay that LDS artists had created images of the First Vision in prints and stained glass by the 1870s, signaling how the vision had become a consolidated collective memory by that era. However, like Flake, Harper sees the early twentieth-century as a crucial era for the repositioning of the First Vision within LDS beliefs. Harper, *First Vision: Memory and Mormon Origins*; Steven C. Harper, "Using Art and Film to Form and Reform a Collective Memory of the First Vision," in *An Eye of Faith: Essays in Honor of Richard O. Cowan*, ed. Kenneth L. Alford and Richard E. Bennett (Provo, UT: Religious Studies Center; Salt Lake City, 2015), 257–75.

23. John-Charles Duffy, "The New Missionary Discussions and the Future of Correlation," *Sunstone*, Sept. 2005, 32.

first intended]: the idea that God actually hears and answers prayers; the concept that there is a personal devil who tries to stop the progress of truth; and, perhaps most fundamental of all, the Mormon doctrine that the divine Godhead are actually separate, distinct, physical personages, as opposed to the Trinitarian concept of traditional Christianity."[24] In other words, the canonized First Vision had become, among other things, a series of foundational LDS scriptural "prooftexts" to support various formal and informal church doctrines.

By the late 1960s, two new movements would further transform the cultural life of the First Vision: the New Mormon History and the evangelical counter-cult movement. The New Mormon History, a movement among both professional and amateur historians, asked new sets of questions of old materials and narratives and hoped to more deeply contextualize Mormonism within its American context.[25] Indeed, Allen's 1966 article, quoted above, and the debate about what to do with multiple accounts of Smith's First Vision became a touchstone for historical investigations into the wider context of early Mormonism. Such research provoked responses from the then-nascent evangelical counter-cult movement. Most notably, evangelical Presbyterian minister Wesley P. Walters and, later, evangelical fundamentalists Jerald and Sandra Tanner seriously questioned details that Smith related in these various accounts: Smith's age at the time of the vision; the existence of revivals in the Palmyra area at the time; and the discrepancies in the various accounts of whom Smith saw in his vision (Jesus alone, an angel, a host of angels, or Jesus and Heavenly Father).[26] In the light of emerging historical research, counter-cult ministries questioned whether Mormons or any others could embrace the historical veracity of foundational Mormon stories.

LDS historians and researchers, many of them professionally

24. Allen, "The Significance of the Joseph Smith's First Vision," 30.

25. Newell G. Bringhurst, Introduction, in Newell G. Bringhurst and Lavina Fielding Anderson, eds., *Excavating Mormon Pasts: The New Historiography of the Last Half Century* (Salt Lake City: Kofford Books, 2004), x –xi.

26. Walters, "New Light on Mormon Origins from the Palmyra Revival"; Jerald Tanner and Sandra Tanner, *The Changing World of Mormonism: A Behind the Scenes Look at Changes in Mormon Doctrine and Practice* (Chicago: Moody Press, 1979), 148–71.

trained and teaching at universities, responded to these various criticisms. In 1967–68, for instance, more than forty LDS researchers and historians, organized by BYU professor Truman G. Madsen, combed New York archives to refute Walters's claims about the lack of a Palmyra revival. Historians not directly connected to this research foray, such as Richard Bushman and Leonard Arrington, lent their skills as well to the questions raised by the counter-cult evangelicals.[27] Even as LDS historians seriously engaged these questions, they found themselves occasionally attacked by various officials within the LDS Church who thought that their work overly secularized LDS salvation history and used sources that should be kept confidential, even sacred. For instance, a supervisor in the Church Historian's Office berated Dean C. Jesse, another employee, for writing an article in 1969 about various First Vision accounts. He told Jesse, "You have had published photographs of manuscripts which I have been instructed not to talk about," and the supervisor demanded a written apology by Jesse to be placed in the LDS First Presidency's files. Jesse obliged, but continued publishing.[28] As will be seen, the questions raised by counter-cult ministers, the answers posed by LDS historians, and the fears of certain LDS Church leaders about even engaging in discourse on the multiple accounts would shape the content of the Gospel Topics essay almost fifty years later.

By the 1970s, the First Vision had found material form as an antebellum evangelical conversion narrative, as a missionary tract, as a series of prooftexts about God's nature, as a text that anchored the geography of a pilgrimage site, as a story in Mormon salvation history, as a text whose analysis helped underwrite the emergence of the New Mormon history, and as a story used by countercult ministries to illustrate religious error and deception. If space provided, I could include discussions in this chapter about other appearances of the First Vision, both before and after the 1970s, in even more mediums: children's books, stained glass windows,

---

27. Samuel Alonzo Dodge, "Joseph Smith's First Vision: Insights and Interpretations in Mormon Historiography," in Samuel Alonzo Dodge and Steven C. Harper, eds., *Exploring the First Vision* (Provo, Utah: BYU Religious Studies Center, 2012), www.rsc.byu.edu/archived/exploring-first-vision/front-matter.

28. As quoted in Prince, *Leonard Arrington and the Writing of Mormon History*, 80–81.

hymns and popular LDS songs, animated stories and faith-pro-moting films, parodies on Broadway and cable television, and "gospel art" that hangs in the homes of LDS members. In short, the material apparitions of "the First Vision," even within the discourses of active LDS members, are multivocal and multivalenced. Given this, we might argue that the First Vision has what philosopher Paul Ricoeur called "semantic autonomy," that is, "the text's career has escaped the finite horizon lived by its author. What the text means now matters more than what the author meant when he wrote it."[29]

In a related vein, we might observe that the First Vision is what Robert Orsi provocatively has called an "abundant event." In his study of apparitions of the Virgin Mary, Orsi defines an abundant event, in part, as "not exhausted at its source. Presence radiates out from the [abundant] event along a network of routes, a kind of capillary of presence, filling water, relics, images, things, and memories ... The routes are formed and shaped by the abundant event: they develop through successive transactions among people wanting to share their experience of presence, and in this way, the routes of presence become media of abundance."[30] Conceived in this way, abundant events have "agency" in the sense that they help define the world in which people act.

However, lest I ascribe too much "agency" to the First Vision, I should observe that the various First Vision texts have life and force because the LDS Church has continued to promote one of them as part of the canon of Mormonism. Without this, there would be no "presence [that] radiates out from the event along a network of routes" and spills out into tracts, missionary talks, pilgrimage sites, or for that matter, scenes from the Broadway musical *The Book of Mormon*. As religious studies scholar Stephen Taysom argues (drawing from philosopher William James), an event has to be a "live option" within a believer's world for it to have power

---

29. Paul Ricoeur, *Interpretation Theory: Discourse and the Surplus of Meaning* (Fort Worth: Texas Christian University Press, 1976), 30.

30. Robert Orsi, "Abundant History: Marian Apparitions as Alternative Modernity," *Historically Speaking* 9, 7 (2008): 15. Orsi has extended these arguments in Robert A. Orsi, *History and Presence* (Cambridge, Massachusetts: Harvard University Press, 2016), 48–71.

and effects in the world. Osiris, Taysom notes, has limited "agency" in our world because few, if any, worship Osiris today.[31] Taysom has helpfully modified Orsi's concept of "abundant events" to think instead how narratives about events, not events *qua* events, have "narrative abundance." As Taysom persuasively argues, "none of these abundant events that Orsi describes … can exert influence on the real world without being inscribed within narratives."[32] Taysom himself speculates upon how the narratives of the "gold plates" have such narrative abundance, and, as they are a "live option" in the worlds of millions of Mormons, their narrative abundance has helped define the world in which those Mormons act.[33]

The 2013 "First Visions Accounts" essay, then, stands in a long line of material manifestations evidencing the "narrative abundance" of the First Vision. As such, it is part of the deep and deepening cultural history of the First Vision and itself gives the vision a "realness." As Taysom argues, "The gold plates are real precisely because they spill out of the narrative intended for them and move through history in unpredictable ways."[34] We could insert the words "First Vision" into Taysom's sentence and also have a valid point. We might also add that the First Vision becomes real in more predictable ways: by being contained, controlled, and reformatted by the LDS Church's leadership. To better understand this last point, I turn to the "First Vision Accounts" essay itself to observe how LDS officials have tried to further the life and realness of the First Vision.

Inclusions and Exclusions

In this section, I address three of the "First Vision Accounts" essay's sections: "memory," "embellishments," and the essay's faith-promoting conclusion. While it may be a bit tedious, I want to highlight both what the writers include in their arguments and exclude. Thus, we will have a firmer grasp of what the essay signals

31. Stephen Taysom, "Abundant Events or Narrative Abundance?: Robert Orsi and the Academic Study of Mormonism," *Dialogue: A Journal of Mormon Thought* 45, 4 (2012): 13.

32. Ibid., 9.

33. Ibid., 13.

34. Ibid., 21.

for the current culture of the LDS Church and the cultural work that the essay itself performs. More immediately, this section reveals that what may appear at first glance to be new arguments about the First Vision accounts actually parallel arguments by historians and apologists from the 1960s to the 1980s, or the formative period of the New Mormon History and the LDS response to the first-wave of the evangelical countercult.

Memory

In the section titled "Memory," the essay authors note that some claim "that historical evidence does not support Joseph Smith's description of religious revival in Palmyra, New York, and its vicinity in 1820." Such critics argue "that this undermines both Joseph's claim of unusual religious fervor and the account of the vision itself."[35] The authors do not name the critics who hold this view, but they probably refer to the late Wesley P. Walters who first made this claim in 1967 and whose argument entered into the realms of academic debate and religious polemic.[36] Against the argument of a revival's absence, the authors claim Methodist revival activity occurred in the vicinity of Palmyra between 1818 and 1820, and they cite the diary of a Methodist itinerant as evidence of this. Neither the late historian Milton Backman, the first to seriously challenge Walters, nor the historian D. Michael Quinn, the author of a 110-page treatment of the question, are cited by the essayists to address this question.[37] However, we can reasonably speculate that the essayists were conversant with the larger secondary literature. Notably, Steven Harper, a professor of church history and doctrine at BYU and collaborator on the essay, has engaged Walters and offered an argument that parallels the essay's arguments.[38]

---

35. "First Vision Accounts."

36. W. P. Walters, *New Light on Mormon Origins from the Palmyra Revival* (La Mesa, California: Utah Christian Tract Society, 1967).

37. Milton Vaughn Backman Jr., "Awakenings in the Burned-over District: New Light on the Historical Setting of the First Vision," *BYU Studies* 9, 3 (1969): 301–20; D. Michael Quinn, "Joseph Smith's Experience of a Methodist 'Camp Meeting' in 1820," *Dialogue Paperless,* Dec. 20, 2006, accessed Oct. 18, 2016 at www.dialoguejournal.com/wp-content/uploads/2010/04/QuinnPaperless.pdf.

38. Harper, "Evaluating Three Arguments against Joseph Smith's First Vision," in Dodge and Harper, eds., *Exploring the First Vision*, 307–23.

Nevertheless, after dispatching Walters's forty-five-year-old claim about the lack of a Palmyra-area revival, at least to their satisfaction, the authors do not address how Smith's vision fits into the antebellum American revival culture where participants had visions in abundance. As non-LDS historian Leigh Schmidt has noted, the era of the early American republic cannot be accurately characterized as an age of supernatural absence; instead, "God had more prophets, tongues, and oracles than before; thus, the modern predicament actually became as much one of God's loquacity as God's hush."[39] Whether intended or not, the essay's silence on this latter point preserves popular LDS notions of Smith's First Vision as an experience without parallel in antebellum America.

To address the varying details in Smith's accounts of his theophany, the essay authors note that "each account of the First Vision by Joseph Smith and his contemporaries has its own history and context that influenced how the event was recalled, communicated, and recorded."[40] This thought mirrors what Steven Harper and Anne Taves have called a "reframing event," a term they developed for a dialog on Smith's First Vision.[41] The argument also parallels a consideration raised by James Allen who, writing for LDS members in the official LDS Church magazine in 1970, posited that the reader should pay attention to "the circumstances under which he [Joseph] gave each account, including any special purposes he may have had in mind."[42] Thus, the essay authors draw upon arguments that seek to historicize the vision accounts themselves rather than simply concern themselves with what does or does not stand behind those accounts.

The First Vision Accounts essayists then use examples from the Bible that illustrate differing accounts of a single event, such as Paul's "Road to Damascus" vision or the apostles' experience "on the Mount of Transfiguration," and they draw parallels between the biblical retellings of these events and Smith's retelling of his

---

39. Leigh Eric Schmidt, *Hearing Things: Religion, Illusion, and the American Enlightenment* (Cambridge, Massachusetts: Harvard University Press, 2002), 11.

40. "First Vision Accounts."

41. Ann Taves and Steven C. Harper, "Joseph Smith's First Vision: New Methods for the Analysis of Experience-Related Texts," *Mormon Studies Review* 3 (2016): 55.

42. Allen, "Eight Contemporary Accounts of Joseph Smith's First Vision," 6.

vision. In 1985, Milton Backman published a similar argument for a popular LDS audience, stating, "Accounts of the Savior's appearance to Paul on the road to Damascus, related to us in Acts by Luke and by Paul in his letters, also vary."[43] Here, Backman, as well as the authors of the 2013 Gospel Topics essay, used an example easily understood by an LDS audience who largely assumed that scripture was written by eye-witnesses or relied on eye witnesses. Most evangelicals engaged in counter-cult ministries, then and now, make similar traditionalist assumptions about the authorship of biblical texts. Thus the First Vision Accounts authors appeal to common assumptions that most LDS and evangelicals share and thereby blunt some of the possible evangelical criticisms of the varying First Visions accounts. In other words, the essay authors imply that, if evangelical counter-cult ministers wish to criticize the varying accounts of the First Vision, they must also question the varying accounts of Paul's conversion experience in the Bible, texts that counter-cult evangelicals regard as doctrinally inerrant and historically factual.

However, there is something to be said about how these selected analogies (Paul's "Road to Damascus" vision and Jesus' Mount of Transfiguration experience) work in the light of academic scholarship on the same stories. For example, no mainstream biblical studies scholar would argue that Matthew's Mount of Transfiguration scene is based upon an eye-witness account from Peter and heard by a real-life Matthew. Rather, it is an account likely written by a Jewish-Christian community decades later.[44] One prominent interpreter sees the transfiguration story itself as largely illustrative of Jesus' power and how he stands in prophetic continuity with "Israel's lawgiver [Moses] and the prophetic precursor to the messiah [Elijah]."[45] As such, many mainstream interpreters

---

43. Backman, "Joseph Smith's Recitals of the First Vision." Backman preceded this statement with a discussion of various accounts in the New Testament of Jesus' resurrection.

44. J. Andrew Overman, *Matthew's Gospel and Formative Judaism: The Social World of the Matthean Community* (Minneapolis: Fortress Press, 1991).

45. J. Andrew Overman, *The New Oxford Annotated Bible with Apocrypha*, ed. by Michael D. Coogan et. al. (New York: Oxford University Press, 2001), New Testament, 33.

assume that the historicity of the Mount of Transfiguration account was not as important to the original authors as the message they were trying to convey with the story. Drawing on a wealth of mainstream scholarship, biblical studies scholar Bart Ehrman, for example, posits that gospel narratives fit comfortably within authorial conventions for ancient Greco-Roman biographies in which writers often invented stories about an exemplary figure to illustrate a larger truth about that same exemplary individual.[46] All of this is to say that if Smith's First Vision is read like biblical studies scholars read the Road to Damascus experience or the Mount of Transfiguration narrative, then LDS readers must stop reading Smith's First Vision accounts as history in any modern sense of that term and read them instead as narratives illustrating the prophet's various teachings, a reading practice much closer to what modern individuals do when they read for meaning within a poem or a novel. While most LDS readers may never read this intention into the text of the First Vision Accounts essay, I later present evidence that some of the essay writers might have intended this very thought in their section on narrative "embellishments."

Finally, the First Vision Accounts authors leave aside several glaring questions in their section on "memory." Most obviously, the essayists omit any questions about the 1820 date for Smith's First Vision. In the past forty years, this has been a frequently debated subject among historians and countercult critics. In his 1970 *Improvement Era* article, for instance, James Allen went to great lengths to harmonize Smith's varying accounts of his age at the time of the vision.[47] Additionally, while the essayists think about how individuals may narrate an event differently over time, they do not follow this with any comments on the biological dimensions of how memory is produced or how "false memories" are created. That may be asking too much of an 1,800-word essay. Still, such omissions, whether intended or not, function to

---

46. Bart D. Ehrman, *The New Testament: A Historical Introduction to the Early Christian Writings*, 5th ed. (New York: Oxford University Press, 2012), 83–86. For a recent study that expands upon this point, see Michael R. Licona, *Why Are There Differences in the Gospels? What We Can Learn from Ancient Biography* (New York: Oxford University Press, 2016).

47. Allen, "Eight Contemporary Accounts of Joseph Smith's First Vision," 7.

preserve the primacy and reliability of the canonized 1838 account for Mormons.

Embellishment

In the section titled "embellishments," the essay authors attempt to explain what some have suggested are Smith's embellishments to the canonized version of his theophany. Namely, the authors address how Smith discusses what seems to be one personage only appearing to him in the 1832 account (the personage is identified as "the Lord" who forgives his sins) and then details in the 1838 account that two personages appeared to him (one personage introduces the other as "my beloved son"). Given the long LDS use of the 1838 account as a scriptural prooftext about the embodiment of gods, average LDS members could have serious questions about the discrepancy between the two accounts. To explain the seeming inconsistencies between the early and later accounts, the writers use three arguments: one personage might actually equal two if the earliest account is read in a certain way; Smith's accounts reflect his growing spiritual insights over time; and Smith felt far more confined and restricted in writing than in speaking, and, thus, the 1832 handwritten account cannot be seen as his preferred text for self-revelation. These three arguments, tersely summarized here, deserve a closer analysis as they reveal varying understandings of how one can responsibly read a historical document.

In the first argument, the authors hypothesize how the number of divine persons in the 1832 vision could be consistent with the later accounts. They argue that Smith's term "the Lord" could actually be referring to two different individuals, one who "opens the heavens" and one who forgives Joseph his sins. Thus, "the Lord [the first person] opened the heavens upon me and I saw the Lord [a second person]." Milton Backman first made the argument in 1985, and then James B. Allen and John W. Welch revised it in 2005 and 2012.[48] However, the Gospel Topics authors make this point with far less polemical certainty than Welch and Allen did in 2012. And, unlike Welch and Allen, the authors allow for several

---

48. James B. Allen and John W. Welch, "The Appearance of the Father and the Son to Joseph Smith in 1820," in Dodge and Harper, eds., *Exploring the First Vision*, 41–89.

possible ways of reading the 1832 vision, of which the "one equals two" formula is just one possibility. Thus the authors advance an exploratory thesis rather than a fundamentalist axiom.

After discussing the possible number of divine persons in Smith's accounts, the essay authors insert a line that seems disconnected to arguments immediately before it. They write, "Joseph's increasingly specific descriptions can thus be compellingly read as evidence of increasing insight, accumulating over time, based on experience." This statement seems to suggest that the authors see Smith's divergent accounts of his theophany as his way of expressing increasing insights into the nature of God as his understanding evolved over time with more spiritual experiences. Thus the 1832 account rendered a theology that did not seriously challenge Trinitarian theology (there is one embodied being, presumably Jesus). However, the 1838 account speaks of an embodied, separate Heavenly Father, the understanding that Smith held by that later date. Smith's 1838 account is then a theological account expressing what Smith knew about God's nature then, but not what Smith knew as a youth in 1820.

If the authors intend what I suggest here, they do so with little explanation. Perhaps the line that I quoted above is simply evidence of multiple authors and editing, and, thus, there are thoughts lost in the editing that would provide further clarification about its intent. Whatever the authorial intent, the essay may be reasonably read as providing two divergent approaches to Smith's vision. One approach treats the vision as a tangible appearance of gods, captured by words that can be harmonized in all their essential details. This is not unlike a conservative evangelical approach to the synoptic gospels (Matthew, Mark, and Luke) that attempts to reconcile conflicting details into one harmonized story. The second, less conservative approach, treats the First Vision accounts much as mainstream biblical studies scholars understand the redacted gospel accounts in the New Testament. That is, such gospel accounts partially referred to past events, at times invented details, and consistently reflected the understandings and concerns of their writers at a much later date. So, too, Smith created details for his vision later to illustrate a truth he believed about gods at a later date.

Even so, the essay still does not go as far as other interpretations which suggest that Smith himself sought again and again to understand his experience by telling it in various ways. The official Church Historian for the Midwestern-based Reorganized Church of Jesus Christ of Latter Day Saints (later Community of Christ), Richard P. Howard, advanced such an idea in the 1980s and 1990s. As one of the founding members of the Mormon History Association and a practitioner of the New Mormon History, Howard served as an intermediary between what was published in the scholarly world and what was discussed in RLDS Sunday schools. As such, he offered a pastorally-minded account of Smith's First Vision in his 1992 official RLDS church history. In it, he argued, "The event [the First Vision] was of such vast importance to him [Joseph Smith] that he could not reduce it to so many words on paper. The event continued to challenge the interpretive powers of its one human participant to convey to others its deepest meanings. We today simply accept our distance from the reality of Joseph Smith's boyhood vision. We truthfully affirm that it happened, but we openly confess the mystery of its specific content."[49] Here, Howard focused on the mystery of Smith's experience, almost in the Ottoian sense of the vision as a manifestation of the "holy," a numinous other sensed but essentially ineffable.[50] All of this mitigated against using the First Vision as the doctrinal basis of anything other than an affirmation of mystical experience. In this way, Howard's account was well-suited to a Mormon denomination that had taken a progressive turn in the 1960s and was attempting to reconcile itself, in part, with mainline Protestant Christianity.[51]

The LDS authors of the First Vision Accounts essay agree with Howard that Smith found it hard to convey his vision, but

---

49. Richard P. Howard, *The Church Through the Years: RLDS Beginnings to 1860,* 2 vols. (Independence, Missouri: Herald Publishing House, 1992–93), 1:100–101.

50. Rudolph Otto's early-twentieth-century notion that realness of religion can be intuited by our experience of the "holy," the "wholly other" that is beyond the rationale and beyond words, exerted considerable influence on the emerging field of religious studies at mid-century. For instance, see Mircea Eliade, *The Sacred and the Profane: The Nature of Religion,* trans. by William R. Trask (New York: Harcourt, 1959), 8–10.

51. For a brief account of the progressive turn of the RLDS Church in the 1960s and beyond, see David J. Howlett and John-Charles Duffy, *Mormonism: The Basics* (New York: Routledge, 2016), 22–26.

they suggest that the different accounts may be best explained by Smith's use of different means to produce the earliest and later accounts, rather than Smith's mystification with how to convey his numinous experience. They suggest that Smith's handwritten account is an inadequate expression of his vision because he wrote it, whereas his 1838 account was dictated to a scribe, a medium that they claim allowed Smith freer expression. They cite Smith who wrote in an 1832 letter to W. W. Phelps about his frustration with "paper pen and Ink and a crooked broken scattered and imperfect Language" and the written word as a "little narrow prison."[52] The full context of the letter actually does not indicate that Smith preferred speaking to writing. Instead, it shows his frustration more generally with the imperfection of human reading and writing and how he looked forward to a day in which Phelps and he could "stand together and gaze upon eternal wisdom engraven upon the heavens" and "read the reccord [sic] of eternity to the fulness [sic] of our immortal souls."[53] In other words, Smith believed that there would be a perfected form of reading and writing in the coming millennial kingdom, even while mortals had to struggle with the imperfections of media in his present age. Even if the Smith-Phelps letter does not directly support the essay authors' claims, other evidence suggests Smith's preference for dictation over handwriting. For instance, Smith more often than not had scribes to record his words and rarely wrote letters or revelations in his own hand. Still, Smith's practical preference for one medium of communication over another does not logically lead to the conclusion that the "expansiveness of the later accounts is more easily understood and even expected," as the essay authors claim.[54] The "expansiveness" is understood and expected only if one has already prioritized the later 1838 account as the normative account that must be defended.

---

52. "First Vision Accounts." The authors cite Joseph Smith, Letter to William W. Phelps, Nov. 27, 1832, Joseph Smith Collection, Church History Library, Church of Jesus Christ of Latter-day Saints, Salt Lake City, Utah, accessed on Oct. 17, 2016, at www.josephsmithpapers.org/paper-summary/letter-to-william-w-phelps-27-november-1832/1.

53. Smith to Phelps, Nov. 27, 1832.

54. "First Vision Accounts."

Even if the LDS essayists believe that the specific content of Smith's canonized 1838 First Vision account matters, they advance arguments in the "embellishments" section that quietly undercut an interpretative strategy utilized by many LDS for getting at that meaning. Namely, they subtly destabilize the use of the canonized First Vision account as a doctrinal prooftext. As several scholars have shown, LDS members and many LDS general authorities across the twentieth century increasingly adopted textual approaches to scripture akin to the biblical literalism of evangelicals.[55] By doing this, LDS leaders and members utilized a hermeneutic that assumed that scriptural texts ostensibly corresponded in a one-to-one way with external realities; scriptural texts could be clearly understood (or misunderstood) by a reader with little reference to the texts' cultural contexts; and scriptural texts therefore could be atomized from their contexts and made into specific faith-serving propositional truths. Such an approach to a text echoes eighteenth-century Baconian rationalism, the intellectual framework that produced and helped to perpetuate nineteenth-century evangelical prooftexting and twentieth-century Protestant fundamentalism.[56] However, the authors of the First Vision accounts essay seem to find such reading habits as naïve. They suggest that the various First Vision accounts may be read reasonably in multiple ways; that the various accounts are grounded in their own historical horizons; and, thus, that the accounts do not necessarily offer unmediated, direct access to Smith's experience in the grove. With these moves, the authors shrewdly challenge the framework that supports proof-texting as a reliable interpretive practice.

---

55. Armand Mauss, *The Angel and the Beehive: The Mormon Struggle with Assimilation* (Urbana: University of Illinois Press, 1994), 179–80; O. Kendall White, *Mormon Neo-Orthodoxy: A Crisis of Theology* (Salt Lake City: Signature Books, 1987). White's use of "neo-orthodoxy" should not be confused with the liberal Protestant project of "neo-orthodoxy" initiated by Karl Barth. White's "neo-orthodoxy" is closer to what most regard as Protestant fundamentalism, but to avoid confusion with Mormon Fundamentalism (contemporary non-LDS Mormon groups who practice polygamy), White opted for "neo-orthodoxy."

56. George M. Marsden, *Fundamentalism and American Culture*, 2nd ed. (New York: Oxford University Press, 2006), 55–62.

Ways of Knowing

After refuting various criticisms of the First Vision accounts, the authors conclude with a series of assertions that recall the conclusion of an LDS general authority's conference talk—assertions that are devotional, faith-affirming, and require orthodoxy and orthopraxy on the part of the hearer. The authors declare: "Neither the truth of the First Vision nor the arguments against it can be proven by historical research alone. Knowing the truth of Joseph Smith's testimony requires each earnest seeker of truth to study the record and then exercise sufficient faith in Christ to ask God in sincere, humble prayer whether the record is true. If the seeker asks with the real intent to act upon the answer revealed by the Holy Ghost, the truthfulness of Joseph Smith's vision will be manifest."[57] This statement stands in continuity and contrast with a similar argument by James Allen in 1970. He wrote, "In the last analysis, the First Vision becomes truly meaningful in a personal way only when one seeks as Joseph Smith sought, to reach God through private, earnest supplication."[58] However, Allen did not imply that one would know the "truthfulness" of the vision in a historical sense, as the 2013 essay seems to imply; rather, one would simply know the "meaningfulness" of the vision. Furthermore, the final paragraph in the First Vision Accounts essay jarringly—to my ears—refers to "the record" of Smith's vision in a singular sense, rather than refer to the "records" or "accounts." Thus, read one way, the primacy of the 1838 account is again subtly reinforced, and (LDS orthodox) spiritual truth and testimony trump rather than augment the historical arguments previously advanced in the essay. Read another way, the historical method and revelation are presented as different and complementary ways of knowing.

While the presence of this explicitly devotional paragraph in a largely historical essay could simply indicate multiple authorship of the essay, I believe that it evidences something more. Namely, it manifests the influence of a "progressive orthodox" movement within the LDS Church, a movement that I define in the next section. For now, I simply note that the contemporary LDS

57. "First Vision Accounts."
58. Allen, "Eight Contemporary Accounts of Joseph Smith's First Vision," 12.

progressive orthodox, some of whom I suggest wrote, or significantly contributed to, the essay, exist alongside majoritarian LDS members who inhabit what Armand Mauss terms "folk fundamentalism."[59] With the final set of devotional assertions in the essay, the authors reassure the majoritarian LDS reader that they are on their side, speak their language, and affirm the same spiritual truths. On the other hand, if the final paragraph is simply indicative of multiple authorship (and not actually written by a member of the progressive orthodox), the explicit need to include the final paragraph highlights how majoritarian LDS leaders and laity are still trying to adjust to new ways of knowing the past. Read either one way or the other, the First Vision Accounts essay reveals how multiple strains of LDS religiosity are being allowed to coexist officially in the contemporary church.

In a section that follows, I argue how the First Vision Accounts essay indicates the aforementioned changes in LDS culture and the culture of contemporary America. Yet, in my reading of the essay in this section, I have persistently noted that most of the arguments that are advanced in the First Vision Accounts essay were made decades ago in official LDS publications intended for a general church audience or in articles by scholars of the New Mormon History movement. These arguments include the assertion that revivals happened near Palmyra in 1820, that circumstances shape what is recorded in any narrative of a past event, and that the two divine persons versus one divine person in Smith's vision accounts may be harmonized. What then do we make of this? Do we simply conclude that Mormons and countercult evangelicals have contested the same basic arguments for the last fifty years?

Perhaps predictably, I answer this question with a qualified "no." Apologetical or critical arguments, even if they are reiterations of past arguments, are always "new" in the sense that the context in which they are articulated always changes. When we apply this thought to the First Vision Accounts essay, we observe that the controversies about Smith's narrative within the 1960s LDS Church are both new and familiar: how does the LDS

---

59. Mauss, *Angel and the Beehive*, 177–92.

Church deal with outside criticism? How does the LDS Church disseminate its response through various media? How does the LDS Church incorporate secular historical ways of knowing with traditional salvation histories? How does a scriptural text remain a fundamentalist prooftext after rigorous scholarly examination? These questions were live questions in the LDS Church when James Allen first wrote about multiple accounts of Joseph Smith's First Vision. Since then, their urgency has only intensified within a new context: a church set within the digital age, beset by the push-pulls of globalization's cultural, economic, and political forces of homogenization and diversification. It is a church that may be best typified as the Post-Correlation LDS Church.

The Post-Correlation LDS Church and Progressive Orthodoxy

What is the Post-Correlation Church? By this, I do not mean to announce the collapse of "correlation" as a formal bureaucratic program of ecclesiastical standardization. Instead, I suggest that the LDS Church is moving out of an era of relative homogeneity among its members. Elsewhere, I have argued that the LDS Church is becoming more like the American Catholic Church after the 1960s, with conservative leaders and a culture war division between progressive and conservative members.[60] Below, I nuance this with a third category, but, for now, I simply note that the culture war divisions within the American LDS Church have necessitated leaders' pluriform responses to various issues. For instance, conservative leaders have sided with conservative members by denying women ordination, going so far as to excommunicate some pro-ordination activists. However, they have also sided with members advocating for modest reforms and allowed LDS women more power at the local and general church level where women now serve alongside priesthood-holding men on various councils. Furthermore, LDS leaders have allowed much more official latitude on various controversial questions compared to what they allowed in the early 1990s, an era in which leaders

---

60. David J. Howlett, "A Post-Correlation Church?" *John Whitmer Historical Association Journal* 34, 2 (2014): 112–16.

retreated from embracing the diversity found within the church.[61] The Gospel Topics essays, as well as the multiple viewpoints found within each one, are products of a new church in a new era. In this sense, the LDS Church is now a Post-Correlation Church, even as the formal program of correlation, with all of its mechanisms for ecclesiastical standardization, has endured.

My characterization of a conservative versus liberal divide in the Post-Correlation Church lacks some subtlety for the internal divisions within the LDS Church. Religious studies scholar John-Charles Duffy provides a helpful corrective to the commonplace culture wars dichotomy by suggesting that a third movement has also emerged in the last thirty years, what Duffy calls "progressive orthodoxy." Duffy sees progressive orthodoxy as an intellectual movement characterized by "the effort to mitigate Mormon sectarianism, the rejection of Mormon liberalism, and the desire to make Mormon supernaturalism more intellectually credible."[62] Expanding upon his last point, Duffy argues that, by defending Mormon supernaturalism, progressive orthodox have actually revised "traditional LDS claims in ways intended to make Mormonism more credible to Mormons socialized into late twentieth-century academia."[63] People do not formally identify as "progressive orthodox" LDS members, of course. The term is simply Duffy's way of grouping together people and projects that follow a similar pattern. Duffy offers a genealogy for the movement that shows the utility of his term to explain the rationale and production of Mormon-Evangelical dialogue. I see his history of the emergence of progressive orthodoxy as a useful way of situating the emergence of the "First Vision Accounts" essay, as well. For

---

61. Joanna Brooks, Rachel Hunt Steenblik, and Hannah Wheelwright, eds., *Mormon Feminism: Essential Writings* (New York: Oxford University Press, 2016), 18–20; Jonathan Stapley, *The Power of Godliness: Mormon Liturgy and Cosmology* (New York: Oxford University Press, 2018), 26–32.. Women who occupy the roles of the General Young Women's Presidency, the Relief Society General President, and the General Primary President also now serve on the formerly all-male Missionary Executive, the Priesthood and Family Executive Council, and the Temple and Family History Executive Council. See Tad Walch, "In Historic Move, Women to Join Key, Leading LDS Church Councils," *Deseret News*, Aug. 18, 2015.

62. Duffy, "Conservative Pluralists," 133.

63. Ibid.

example, the First Vision Accounts essay defends certain Mormon supernatural truth claims, but, in several sections, it does so with a tone and argumentative strategy culled from academic writing, as well as engages secular historical methods to present its case. It furthermore revises how LDS might use the First Vision, subtly undercutting its use as a fundamentalist-like scriptural prooftext and suggesting new historicized narrative approaches.

While few LDS members may be classified as part of progressive orthodoxy, this does not mean that the movement has been without influence in places like BYU, the Maxwell Institute, some independent LDS-oriented presses, and even some academic presses.[64] The Gospel Topics essays may be usefully seen as one of a host of progressive orthodox movement projects. And even though the original Gospel Topics essays emerged on the LDS Church's website without the same trumpeting from general authorities as, say, the release of "The Family: A Proclamation to the World" in 1995, the LDS Church has begun to promote the essays in select ways. For example, in April 2016, the "First Vision Accounts" essay was singled out by Seventy Richard J. Maynes as essential reading for all LDS members. Maynes did so in a talk to LDS young adults that was live-streamed to gatherings across the world.[65] Even if general authorities or members may not hold the general goals of progressive orthodoxy, they are being urged to read materials influenced by the movement.

The Cultural Work of the First Vision Essay

Finally, I now turn my attention to the wider cultural effects and cultural traces that the "First Visions Accounts" essay reveals as a material artefact of a particular time and place. In doing so, I

64. For sampling of publications that fit within the rubric of "progressive orthodoxy," see the works of Terryl Givens, such as *Wrestling the Angel*, vol. 1, *The Foundations of Mormon Thought: Cosmos, God, and Humanity* (New York: Oxford University Press, 2014); Grant Hardy, ed., *The Book of Mormon: A Reader's Edition* (Urbana: University of Illinois Press, 2005); the Maxwell Institute's *Journal of Book of Mormon Studies*; Neylane McBane, *Women at Church: Magnifying LDS Women's Local Impact* (Salt Lake City: Kofford Books, 2014).

65. Peggy Fletcher Stack, "Mormon Leader: Differing Versions of Joseph Smith's 'First Vision' Make it the Best Documented in History," *Salt Lake Tribune*, May 1, 2016.

note that the essay itself does not simply answer critical queries. It poses the very questions to which it provides answers. Thus, the essay signals to LDS readers what questions are important in the first place. Framed in a different way, we can see the essay as doing "cultural work." Literary studies scholar Jane Tompkins famously argued that "novels and stories should be studied not because they manage to escape the limitations of their particular time and place, but because they offer powerful examples of the way a culture thinks about itself, articulating and proposing solutions for the problems that shape a particular historical moment."[66] Tompkins called this last part the "cultural work" of novels. When we apply Tompkins's concept of cultural work to the First Vision essay, we observe that the essay raises and articulates questions relevant in contemporary LDS culture and beyond.

First, critics and the essayists alike have framed the various First Vision accounts as Smith's perceived embellishment of his story rather than, say, Smith's narrative creativity. Underlying the problem of embellishment is a cultural anxiety over trust in authority figures, and, more broadly, of faith in institutions in general. Of course, questioning authority figures has had a long history in America, and Smith's own accounts of his First Vision reflected an antebellum culture rife with populist, anti-clerical, anti-elite sentiment.[67] Still, trust and participation in institutions, whether it be government and the PTA or churches and church attendance, is in modest decline in the contemporary US and in sharp decline among several demographic groups, including millennials. Even institutions that give members great incentives for conformity to institutional demands (incentives such as social networks, elevated

---

66. Jane Tompkins, *Sensational Designs: The Cultural Work of American Fiction, 1790–1860* (New York: Oxford University Press, 1986), xi.

67. Nathan O. Hatch, *The Democratization of American Christianity* (New Haven, Connecticut: Yale University Press, 1988), 17–46. Hatch's thesis has been challenged and nuanced, but his general point about currents of anti-clericism and anti-elitism in antebellum American society seems, in my mind, to still be valid. For challengers to specific arguments made by Hatch, see Amanda Porterfield, *Conceived in Doubt: Religion and Politics in the New American Nation* (Chicago: University of Chicago Press, 2012); and Kathleen Flake, "Ordering Antinomy: An Analysis of Early Mormonism's Priestly Offices, Councils, and Kinship," *Religion and American Culture: A Journal of Interpretation* 26, 2 (2016): 139–83.

personal status, ritual access, etc.) are losing participants.[68] The Gospel Topics essays are, in part, a direct response to the declining activity and declining retention of LDS members—especially young members—in the North Atlantic world.

Second, as noted in a previous section, the authors of the essay claim that critics question the accuracy of Smith's memory, as well as point to alleged embellishments by Smith. What might these problems posed as problems be doing? I argue that we see within these two categories, memory and embellishment, culture-wide fears and hopes that transcend the LDS Church and their evangelical counter-cult critics. For example, contemporary middle-class Americans are preoccupied with brain health and memory, as attested by the rise of dementia and Alzheimer's disease in the population, as well as the amount of media coverage for these and similar problems.[69] In elite culture, the 2014 Nobel Prize committee awarded a French author its highest accolades for books that focused upon characters with amnesia and perpetually unstable identities.[70] In popular culture, movies like *The Eternal Sunshine of the Spotless Mind* (2004) or even action movies like the Jason Bourne franchise (2002, 2004, 2007, and 2016) and the Disney blockbuster *Finding Dory* (2016) address the existential problems of forgetting. Contemporary middle-class Americans live in a metaphorical atmosphere filled with "data clouds" and are offered a myriad of ways to back-up their most personal and most public information. Yet ever new technological platforms and new software increasingly makes what was once saved obsolescent and practically irretrievable. Taking this cultural trend to its logical extreme, Google, that corporate behemoth that indexes the web

---

68. Jean M. Twenge, W. Keith Campbell, and Nathan T. Carter, "Declines in Trust in Others and Confidence in Institutions Among American Adults and Late Adolescents, 1972–2012," *Psychological Science* 25, 10 (2014): 1914–23; "U.S. Becoming Less Religious," *Pew Research Center,* Nov. 3, 2015, accessed Oct. 18, 2016, at www.pewforum.org/2015/11/03/u-s-public-becoming-less-religious; Mark Chaves, *American Religion: Contemporary Trends* (Princeton, New Jersey: Princeton University Press, 2013), 42–54.

69. "2016 Alzheimer's Disease Facts and Figures," *Alzheimer's Association,* accessed Oct. 18, 2016 at www.alz.org/facts/#quickFacts.

70. "The Nobel Prize in Literature 2014," *Nobel Foundation,* accessed Oct. 18, 2016, at www.nobelprize.org/nobel_prizes/literature/laureates/2014.

and backs up so much of our data, infamously founded a company in 2013 whose aim was nothing less than to "solve death."[71] Middle-class Americans inhabit a culture saturated with warnings about forgetting and herculean attempts to overcome loss.

To create Joseph Smith's memory as a problem to be solved is not simply a product of the LDS Church's attempt to legitimize itself against counter-cult critics. It is not simply an outgrowth of Mormonism's obsession with lost books, ancient records, and quite literally "Books of Remembrance" in which an individual LDS member records her genealogy. And it is not simply a psychological projection stemming from the Mormon intellectual community's worries about the LDS Church hierarchy as a gerontocracy, susceptible to dementia.[72] Surely the focus on Smith's memory is caused in part by these particular Mormon factors. Yet it also reflects a much wider American cultural obsession with replicable and stable memories, as well as a cultural anxiety around the loss of memory as a fundamental loss to one's identity. This, then, is the most far-reaching act of cultural work performed by the "First Vision Accounts" essay: it articulates, refracts, and frames cultural problems and anxieties far beyond the concerns of the "Mormon curtain."

Conclusion: Reading Between and Beyond the Lines

I have offered an account of the cultural life and work of the "First Vision Accounts" essay published on lds.org in 2013. First, to situate the essay, I offered a select history of the cultural life of Joseph Smith's First Vision narratives. After reviewing this history, I argued that the "narrative abundance" of the various First Vision accounts has given them a realness in the lives of millions of Mormons, spilling over into the many twenty-first-century material artefacts of print, art, film, song, and digital media. Then, in a close reading of "The First Vision Accounts" essay, I analyzed the arguments advanced by the essay authors about revivals near Palmyra,

---

71. John Durham Peters, *The Marvelous Clouds: Toward a Philosophy of Elemental Media* (Chicago: University of Chicago Press, 2015), 376.

72. Lester E. Bush, Gregory A. Prince, and Brent N. Rushforth, "Gerontocracy and the Future of the LDS Church," *Dialogue: A Journal of Mormon Thought* 49, 3 (2016): 89–108.

the number of divine persons in Smith's vision, and possible ways to reconcile Smith's varying accounts of his vision. While many of the 2013 essay's arguments seem to reproduce earlier apologetic answers advanced by LDS scholars during the formative era of the New Mormon History and the rise of the evangelical counter-cult (the 1960s to the 1980s), I have argued that the essay's twenty-first century American cultural context produces new functions and frameworks for its content.

Reading between the lines, I noted that the essay authors proposed multiple ways that the various accounts may be plausibly read. From this observation, I inferred that the authors were attempting to subtly undercut use of the First Vision for uncomplicated doctrinal prooftexts. Still, the weight of their arguments sustain the primacy and reliability of the canonized 1838 First Vision account over all others, even if the authors did not intend this effect. Finally, the authors ended their essay by bearing their "testimony" that the reader can know the truthfulness of "the record" of the Vision by spiritual means. Taken together, these arguments signaled the orthodoxy of the essay authors as well as their discomfort with LDS "folk fundamentalism."

Reading beyond the lines, I argued that the "First Vision Accounts" essay may be interpreted as an artefact of a particular cultural moment in which LDS members inhabit a less homogenous and more fragmented church, at least as compared to the church of the 1960s. In this new church, some members have been deemed beyond the pale of membership, but other reformers, such as the authors of the "First Vision Accounts" essay, have been given a secure place and voice within a "progressive orthodox" movement, even while many LDS members inhabit a world of folk fundamentalism akin to evangelical fundamentalism. This is all part of what I call the era of a Post-Correlation LDS Church, noting that I mean to denominate a new era in history and rather than to announce the end of a bureaucratic program.

Finally, I have argued that the "First Vision Accounts" essay itself performs cultural work. That is, it raises and addresses questions generated from an early-twenty-first-century American cultural matrix marked by anxiety about memory loss and its concomitant effects on individual and collective identity. By observing this, we see that what may at first glance seem like an "insider" LDS conversation about harmonizing Smith's varying First Vision accounts actually presupposes and participates in cultural trends far beyond itself. In sum, the "First Vision Accounts" essay points to how the LDS Church bureaucracy in a Post-Correlation era is attempting to hold together a church in the process of being rent by larger cultural forces not entirely of its own making.

6. "THINGS ARE SO DARK AND MYSTERIOUS"
THE THOMAS LEWIS CASE AND VIOLENCE IN EARLY LDS UTAH

John G. Turner

It is well known that members of the Church of Jesus Christ of
Latter-day Saints repeatedly suffered from violent persecution
during their church's first quarter-century. Mormon collective
identity was forged, in part, through the church's expulsions from
Missouri and Illinois, and through the deaths and hardships endured by church members during their exodus to the Great Basin.
At the same time, the church has been dogged by accusations that
during the mid-to-late nineteenth century it sanctioned vigilante
reprisals against both dissenters and non-Mormons. In 1838, for
instance, a number of Latter-day Saints organized "Danites" to
threaten Mormon dissenters and defend church members against
anti-Mormon mobs. In his 1842 exposé, Latter-day Saint lead-
er-turned-apostate John C. Bennett maintained that thousands
of Mormon Danites swore an oath to "Joe Smith," promising to
commit acts of murder and treason if so ordered.[1] Allegations
about church-sponsored violence became most intense in the
decades following the 1857 Mountain Meadows Massacre, in
which members of a southern Utah militia slaughtered nearly 120
non-Mormon emigrants. In 1889, the church's First Presidency
denounced "as entirely untrue the allegation ... that our Church
favors or believes in the killing of persons who leave the Church or
apostatize from its doctrines."[2] The statement came in the midst
of the US government's political and judicial campaign against
Mormon polygamy. Apparently, some federal judges pointed to

---

1. John C. Bennett, *History of the Saints...* (Boston: Leland and Whiting, 1842),
esp. 267–68.
2. "Official Declaration," Dec. 12, 1889, *Deseret Weekly*, Dec. 21, 1889, 809–10.

the church's sanctioning of violence as an additional reason to refuse naturalization to Mormon immigrants.

Debates about the complicity of the LDS Church hierarchy in nineteenth-century acts of violence have not disappeared. In the early twenty-first century, Will Bagley and Sally Denton published books accusing Brigham Young of having ordered the Mountain Meadows Massacre.[3] Also, in his *Under the Banner of Heaven: A Story of Violent Faith*, Jon Krakauer drew a straight line from the church's nineteenth-century roots to a 1980s double murder committed by two Mormon fundamentalists.[4] Like Bagley and Denton, Krakauer asserted that Brigham Young explicitly ordered the massacre at Mountain Meadows. Krakauer's book reached a wide audience. Richard E. Turley, managing director of the church's Family and Church History Department, wrote an extended response in which he refuted Krakauer's account of the massacre and concluded that the "vast majority of Latter-day Saints in the nineteenth century, like today's Saints, were peace-loving people who wished to practice their religion in a spirit of nonviolence."[5]

In the minds of church members and outsiders alike, books such as those authored by Krakauer, Denton, and Bagley raised questions about the authority of past and present church leaders. "Peace and Violence among 19th-century Latter-day Saints" is the church's most recent response to such concerns. This Gospel Topics essay addresses the fraught relations between Mormons and other Americans in the quarter-century that began with Mormon settlement of Jackson County, Missouri, and ended with the 1857 Mountain Meadows Massacre.[6] "Peace and Violence" reassures readers that "throughout the Church's history, Church

---

3. Bagley, *Blood of the Prophets: Brigham Young and the Massacre at Mountain Meadows* (Norman: University of Oklahoma Press, 2002); Denton, *American Massacre: The Tragedy at Mountain Meadows* (New York: Knopf, 2003).

4. Krakauer, *Under the Banner of Heaven: A Story of Violent Faith* (New York: Doubleday, 2004).

5. See www.mormonnewsroom.org/article/church-response-to-jon-krakauers-under-the-banner-of-heaven, accessed Dec. 20, 2016.

6. "Peace and Violence among Nineteenth-Century Latter-day Saints," at www.lds.org/topics/peace-and-violence-among-19th-century-latter-day-saints?lang=eng; accessed June 3, 2016.

leaders have taught that the way of Christian discipleship is a path of peace." The essay asserts that "the vast majority of Latter-day Saints ... lived in peace with their neighbors and families, and sought peace in their communities." At the same time, early Mormons suffered intense persecution from their opponents, and the essay allows that the actions of a few Latter-day Saints "caused death and injury, frayed community relationships, and damaged the perception of Mormons as a peaceful people." In short, nineteenth-century Mormons were a persecuted people, and a small number of church members ignored their savior's peaceful teachings and responded in kind toward their enemies.

"Peace and Violence" reaches plausible if not definitive conclusions about the Danites and the Mountain Meadows Massacre. The essay states that "Joseph Smith approved of the Danites but that he was probably not briefed on all their plans and likely did not sanction the full range of their activities." In its discussion of the September 1857 Mountain Meadows Massacre, the essay summarizes the conclusions of LDS historians Ronald W. Walker, Richard E. Turley, and Glen M. Leonard that while fiery preaching "contributed to a climate of hostility," Brigham Young "did not order the massacre." Local church leaders planned and executed the mass murder. More broadly, the essay correctly asserts that at least the heart of Mormondom was anything but a hotbed of violence. Partly because the Latter-day Saints had quickly established the forms of civilized morality ostensibly lacking in many frontier communities, there were few popular demands for extralegal violence. According to Richard Maxwell Brown, in comparison to other western states and territories Utah was remarkable for its lack of organized vigilante activity.[7]

"Peace and Violence" includes within its purview violence between early Mormon settlers and the native peoples onto whose lands they encroached. The essay observes that "the Saints had more amicable relations with Indians than did settlers in other areas of the American West." For some of the Great Basin's native peoples, that is true. Much depended on local circumstances

---

7. See Richard Maxwell Brown, *Strain of Violence: Historical Studies of American Violence and Vigilantism* (New York: Oxford University Press, 1975), chap. 4, esp. 101–104.

and leadership. Still, if Mormon colonists of the Great Basin had distinctive objectives, the results for the region's native peoples were familiar, including reservations, poverty, and political marginalization. The Mormon settlement of the Great Basin is part of, not separate from, the white American conquest and colonization of the American West.[8] The church might well have published a Gospel Topics essay on LDS-Indian relations, one that might also have addressed the LDS purchase of Indian slaves as children or servants and the twentieth-century placement of Indian children with white LDS families.

It is also important to note that "Peace and Violence" could not possibly discuss everything pertinent to its subject. Notable omissions include the 1834 Zion's Camp march in response to the expulsion of Mormons from Jackson County; the allegation that Orrin Porter Rockwell—with Joseph Smith's encouragement or approval—attempted to assassinate former Missouri governor Lilburn Boggs; Sidney Rigdon's "Salt Sermon," in which he called for Mormon reprisals against both mobs and dissenters; instances of violence in Nauvoo, Illinois, in the wake of Joseph Smith's 1844 murder, including the existence of "whistling and whittling brigades" to threaten church enemies; and controversy surrounding the temple endowment ceremony, in which initiates promised to pray that God would avenge the deaths of Joseph and Hyrum Smith upon the United States.

In the following response, I focus on the observation made by "Peace and Violence" that "a few Latter-day Saints committed other violent acts against a small number of dissenters and outsiders." The essay explains that "the heated rhetoric of Church leaders directed toward dissenters may have led these Mormons to believe that such actions were justified," and continues that "perpetrators of these crimes were generally not punished." Still, the essay cautions that "many allegations of such violence are unfounded" and asserts that anti-Mormon writers unfairly "blamed Church leaders for many

---

8. Among many valuable studies, see Jared Farmer, *On Zion's Mount: Mormons, Indians, and the American Landscape* (Cambridge, Massachusetts: Harvard University Press, 2008); Ned Blackhawk, *Violence Over the Land: Indians and Empires in the Early American West* (Cambridge, Massachusetts: Harvard University Press, 2006).

unsolved crimes or suspicious deaths." While the essay's observation about anti-Mormon literature is true in many instances, "Peace and Violence" fails to recognize the extent to which church leaders explicitly sanctioned and condoned extra-legal violence. In order to support this point, I reconstruct one episode of violence in its gruesome detail. It took place at the height of the 1856–57 Reformation, one of the darkest and most troubling times in the history of Mormonism. I conclude that "Peace and Violence" does not provide contemporary church members or outsiders with sufficient theological resources to understand the actions of nineteenth-century Mormon leaders. What is needed is more than just accurate history. Latter-day Saints, like members of other religious traditions, need a realistic ecclesiology to make sense of their past and present.

———

The victim was Thomas Lewis, a Welsh immigrant and church member in his early twenties who lived in central Utah's San Pete Valley. In the 1870s, two prominent former church members published accounts of the misfortune that befell Lewis in the fall of 1856.

In the process of divorcing her husband and church president Brigham Young, Ann Eliza Young (née Webb) published *Wife No. 19*, a portrait of her "life in bondage" and a broad indictment of her church and its leaders. As part of a broader discussion of church-sanctioned violence, she introduced Thomas Lewis as "a very quiet, inoffensive fellow" who lived "with his widowed mother" in Manti, Utah, and avoided "gay society." Per Ann Eliza Young, Lewis and his local ward bishop wanted to marry the same young woman. Lewis was unmarried at the time; Bishop Warren Snow already had several wives. Young explained that "Lewis's doom was sealed at once; the bewitched Bishop was mad with jealous rage, and he had only to give a hint of his feelings to some of his chosen followers." After keeping Lewis under surveillance, Snow's "band of ruffians ... inflict[ed] on the boy an injury so brutal and barbarous that no woman's pen may write the words that describe it." Lewis survived the attack but lived a much diminished life. Young added, with outrage, that her husband, Brigham Young, "knew all about" the affair but sustained Snow, sent him on missions, and sealed him to additional wives. At the time of the incident, Ann Eliza Webb was twelve years of age and lived with her parents in Salt Lake City.[9]

Two years later after the publication of *Wife No. 19*, John D. Lee's *Mormonism Unveiled* appeared, shortly after the author's execution for his role in the Mountain Meadows Massacre. While based in part on Lee's recollections and diaries, the book also reflects the editorial hand of Lee's attorney, William W. Bishop. As of late 1856, Lee lived in southern Utah and was not an eyewitness to the events in central Utah. Just two weeks before Lee's death, Bishop begged his client to chronicle the Utah portion of his life. In particular, Bishop wanted an account of "the *Reformation* and the massacre." Given the complexity of the book's authorship, it is impossible to determine exactly how the passage about the Lewis incident found its way into *Mormonism Unveiled*.[10]

According to *Mormonism Unveiled*, castration had a long history as a favored extralegal tool of church leaders. "In Nauvoo," Lee (or Bishop) wrote, "it was the orders from Joseph Smith and his apostles to beat, wound and castrate all Gentiles [non-Mormons] that the police could take in the act of entering or leaving a Mormon household under circumstances that led to the belief that they had been there for immoral purposes." In Utah, Lee continued, "it was the favorite revenge of old, worn-out members of the Priesthood, who wanted young women sealed to them, and found that the girl preferred some handsome young man." Lee alleged that "many a young man was unsexed for refusing to give up his sweetheart."

Despite all inducements and threats, Lewis (unnamed in *Mormonism Unveiled*) refused to relinquish his bride-to-be. Thereupon Snow called faithful members of the community to a meeting in Manti's schoolhouse. Given a final chance, Lewis rebuffed Snow's demand: "The lights were then put out. An attack was made on the young man. He was severely beaten, and then tied with his

9. Ann Eliza Young, *Wife No. 19, or the Story of a Life in Bondage* (Hartford, Connecticut: Dustin, Gilman & Co., 1875), 280–81.

10. Richard E. Turley Jr., "Problems with Mountain Meadows Massacre Sources," *BYU Studies* 47, 3 (2008): 143–58.

back down on a bench, when Bishop Snow took a bowie-knife, and performed the operation in a most brutal manner, and then took the portion severed from his victim and hung it up in the school-house on a nail, so that it could be seen by all who visited the house afterwards." At another meeting at the same school-house, Snow "publicly called attention to the mangled parts of the young man ... and stated that the deed had been done to teach the people that the counsel of the Priesthood must be obeyed." *Mormonism Unveiled* diverged somewhat from *Wife No. 19* by reporting that Brigham Young "was very mad" when he got wind of Lewis's treatment, but Lee observed that the church president nonetheless retained Snow as Manti's bishop and "ordered the matter hushed up." Despite some differences in detail, then, both Ann Eliza Young and John D. Lee told a similar story. A bishop ordered the emasculation of an innocent young man, and Brigham Young imposed no ecclesiastical penalties for this brutal crime.[11]

The Lewis case has remained obscure to most historians of mid-nineteenth-century Utah. In his biography of Warren Snow, John A. Peterson provided a detailed account of the incident; his analysis does much to explain the mutual loyalty between Snow and Brigham Young. Mostly relying on Peterson's findings, D. Michael Quinn also briefly discusses the castration in the context of church-sanctioned violence.[12] The historical record is still fragmentary, but new evidence brings us closer to understanding both the specific circumstances of the Lewis incident and the context in which it took place. Not entirely the "innocent" youth as portrayed by Ann Eliza Young, Lewis suffered his misfortune after two criminal convictions in the fall of 1856 (assault and threatened assault). Young privately sustained Snow after the crime, though he refused to publicly support the bishop's actions.

---

11. John D. Lee, *Mormonism Unveiled; or The Life and Confessions of the Late Mormon Bishop, John D. Lee* (St. Louis: Bryan, Brand & Co., 1877), 284–86.

12. Peterson, "Warren Stone Snow, a Man in Between: The Biography of a Mormon Defender," MA thesis, Brigham Young University, 1985), 109–22, also 203–204n17; D. Michael Quinn, *The Mormon Hierarchy: Extensions of Power* (Salt Lake City: Signature Books, 1997), 250–51, 534–35n170.

Born in 1833 in southwestern Wales, Thomas Lewis was the first child of David Thomas Lewis and his wife Elizabeth Jones. Over the next dozen years, the couple brought an additional five children into the world.

In 1845, Dan Jones arrived in his native Wales as a Mormon missionary. After immigrating to the Mississippi River Valley, Jones had converted to Mormonism, become friends with Joseph Smith, and operated a steamship (for which he earned the enduring title of "Captain Dan Jones"). Jones proved a tireless and effective missionary. In 1848, the last full year of his mission, 1,700 persons joined the church in Wales.[13]

The Lewis family was among those many converts, and they answered the call to flee Babylon for an American Zion. In 1849, Elizabeth Lewis and her children boarded the *Buena Vista* in Liverpool, bound for New Orleans under Jones's leadership. It is unclear why David Lewis was not on the *Buena Vista*. David and Elizabeth Lewis possessed a large amount of property, some of which she had evidently brought to the marriage and wanted to sell in order to help impoverished converts emigrate. John E. Davis, a Welsh Mormon who emigrated and then left the church in great bitterness, later asserted that Dan Jones persuaded David Lewis to remain behind to handle a lawsuit pertaining to some of the couple's property. Davis added that Jones wanted "a clear stage and fair play to pursue his designs on Mrs. Lewis." According to Isaac Nash, another Welsh emigrant, Jones tricked David Lewis into selling a large amount of property, whereupon he and Elizabeth Lewis absconded with the proceeds. Whatever the exact circumstances, Elizabeth Lewis apparently expected her husband to emigrate the following year and join the family in America.[14]

After the *Buena Vista* reached New Orleans, Elizabeth Lewis and her children began their long journey west, heading by boat to

---

13. See Ronald D. Dennis, *The Call of Zion: The Story of the First Welsh Mormon Emigration* (Provo, Utah: Brigham Young University Religious Studies Center, 1987).

14. See John E. Davis, *Mormonism Unveiled; or, a Peep into the Principles & Practices of the Latter-day Saints* (Bristol: C.T. Jefferies, 1856), 33–34; Isaac Nash, Autobiography, ca. late 1880s, typescript at www.welshmormon.byu.edu/Resource_Info.aspx?id=202, accessed June 3, 2016; Elizabeth Lewis, Letter to J. Davis, Apr. 10, 1850, in Dennis, *Call of Zion*, 195.

Kanesville, Iowa (present-day Council Bluffs). Shortly after Jones and Elizabeth Lewis had departed for Liverpool in February, Jane Melling Jones (Dan Jones's wife) gave birth to a daughter. Jane Jones had planned to wait until the next year to emigrate. Instead, she sailed from Liverpool in March and caught up to her husband at Council Bluffs. Collectively, around 400 Welsh emigrants traveled overland in a company led by Apostle George A. Smith. Evidently, the joint presence of Jane Jones and Elizabeth Lewis generated considerable friction on the trail west. "Jones wanted his wife to ride with Mrs. Lewis," Nash later recorded, "but she would not do it. She said she would rather walk than ride with Mrs. Lewis."[15]

The trail west also brought about moments that transcended such discord. In early September 1849, just past Scott's Bluffs in what is now western Nebraska, Elizabeth Lewis, Thomas Lewis, and Jane Jones were among nearly twenty persons who were rebaptized after George A. Smith called on members of the company to confess their sins and renew their dedication to the church. On September 21, when teams sent by Brigham Young provided them with needed supplies, the emigrants "Dance[d] before the Lord" with great joy, and some of the Welsh entertained the company with songs in their native tongue.[16] After they entered the Salt Lake Valley, many of the Welsh emigrants settled on land situated on the banks of the Jordan River. Within a month of her arrival, Elizabeth Lewis had received a farm there, and she also possessed—according to Dan Jones—"a paradise-like lot near the temple [block]" with a house nearing completion. Because of her wealth and prominence within this immigrant Mormon community, Elizabeth Lewis Jones became known as the "Welsh Queen."[17]

Rumor now became reality. After reaching Salt Lake City, Elizabeth Lewis became the plural wife of Dan Jones. In the fall of 1850 and the winter of 1851, Jones, his two wives, and their

---

15. Nash, Autobiography.

16. Isaac Clark Emigrating Company, Journal, Sept. 21, 1849, at www.history.lds.org/overlandtravels/sources/5994/isaac-clark-emigrating-company-journal-1849-july-oct, accessed June 3, 2016.

17. "paradise-like lot" in Dan Jones, Letter to W. Phillips, Nov. 20, 1849, in Dennis, Call of Zion, 190; "Welsh Queen" in Elizabeth Jones, Letter to J. Davis, Apr. 10, 1850, in Dennis, Call of Zion, 196.

children gradually moved to Manti, a recently established settlement in the San Pete Valley. On the 1851 census, Jones identified himself as a farmer. With $1,075 in property, he was very prosperous by early Utah standards.[18] The expansion of the family led to nearly constant tension, much of it hinging on Jones's division of his resources between his two wives, a situation complicated by the wealth that Elizabeth had brought into her second marriage. Meanwhile, about the time of Elizabeth Lewis Jones's relocation to Manti, her first husband arrived in Salt Lake City. According to John E. Davis, David Lewis complained to Brigham Young about the loss of his wife and their money, which Elizabeth had controlled since her emigration.[19]

In 1852, Dan Jones returned to Wales on what would become a four-year mission. In his absence, Elizabeth Jones convinced Brigham Young that she deserved a divorce from her second husband, alleging that he allocated a greater share of the family's resources to his first wife. The church president persuaded Elizabeth to defer informing her husband until his return from Wales. With her husband en route for Utah in 1856, she wrote to Young, asking if she could obtain the divorce without having to meet with her husband, requesting the church president to forbid Jones to make any attempt to contact or see her. It is unclear if Young required her to meet in person with her husband, but in any event, Elizabeth Jones journeyed to Salt Lake City at the end of October. Dan Jones paid the standard divorce fee of $10 and signed his name to a bill. Either Elizabeth Jones or a clerk marked an "X" in the place of her signature.[20]

As of the fall of 1856, there were around 500 people living in Manti itself, and LDS settlers recently had formed a nearby

---

18. 1850 [1851] Census, State of Deseret, San Pete County, 114, accessed via ancestry.com.

19. Davis, *Mormonism Unveiled*, 34–35.

20. Elizabeth Jones, Letter to Brigham Young, Aug. 14, 1856, Box 66, Folder 16, Brigham Young Papers (hereafter BYP), CR 1234, Church History Library, Church of Jesus Christ of Latter-day Saints (hereafter CHL); divorce certificate, Box 67, Folder 11, BYP.

community they named Ephraim. Even in sparsely populated central Utah, layers of ecclesiastical and political authority were complex. Dan Jones had served as Manti's mayor until his departure from Wales, whereupon Jezreel Shoemaker and then Albert Petty assumed the office. Welcome Chapman was president of the local stake, a regional division of the church that encompassed both Manti and Ephraim. The most authoritative figure in the San Pete Valley, however, was Warren Stone Snow, who was Manti's bishop, the region's presiding bishop, and a representative in the territorial legislature. Snow's responsibilities included spiritual leadership, Indian affairs, economic policies, and the difficult task of maintaining harmony among the San Pete Valley's settlers. As John A. Peterson explains, just as Brigham Young united a variety of ecclesiastical, civil, and military functions within his single person, "Warren [Snow] had become his counterpart on the local level."[21]

In Nauvoo, Snow had served as a bodyguard for both Joseph Smith and Brigham Young. During the intervening months between Smith's June 1844 murder and the early 1846 exodus of the Latter-day Saints from Nauvoo, Young lived in nearly constant fear of arrest or assassination. Persecution had also left a deep imprint on Snow's personality. An anti-Mormon mob had killed his infant brother in Missouri, and vigilantes burned Snow's home in 1845. Perhaps because of such traumas, Snow brooked no challenges to Young's authority or his own. Other Saints sometimes commented on Snow's complete dedication to the church president. "[H]e would come as near cutting his throat as any man if Brigham Young told him to," commented a Manti resident in 1861. Young repaid Snow's dedication with his own displays of loyalty.[22]

Outside of his parents' marital strife, very little is known about Thomas Lewis's early years in Utah. Then in 1856, Lewis became involved in a series of altercations. That September, the twenty-two-year-old Lewis nearly killed fellow Manti resident John Price by striking him on the back of the head with a shovel. The pair had

---

21. Peterson, "Warren Stone Snow," 74–75, 77.

22. "throat" comment by Jezreel Shoemaker, minutes of Apr. 15, 1861, Box 70, Folder 20, BYP. For the contours of Stone's pre-Manti life, I rely on Peterson, "Warren Stone Snow."

quarreled about a sawing mill. Probate judge George Peacock wrote to Young about the matter. When he received Peacock's letter, Young immediately advised him to let the law take its course. He added that "such men as Bro Lewis are too dangerous to be tolerated in civilized society, and should at least be confined." Price recovered. Not everyone in Manti blamed Lewis alone. Welcome Chapman, one of the Manti colony's earliest leaders and now the region's stake president, commented "in reference to a recent quarrel and fight between J Price & T Lewis [and] said if person wish to fight let them fight but he felt like disfellowshiping those that set them to it."[23]

Whether or not others had instigated the quarrel, Lewis was arrested, convicted of assaulting Price, and fined $100. Young later remitted the fine, and Lewis remained a free man. Despite Chapman's earlier opinion, the Manti branch of the church voted unanimously that Lewis "be cut off from the Church" or excommunicated. Lewis apparently regained his standing in the church soon afterwards, but his trouble was just beginning.[24]

That fall, church leaders across the territory were preaching sermons calling for reformation, demanding confession, repentance, and stricter obedience to ecclesiastical superiors. Nearly a decade after the first arrival of LDS pioneers in the Salt Lake Valley, the church had enjoyed years of steady growth and relative freedom from both internal dissent and external threats. According to historian Steven C. Taysom, the Mormon Reformation was "the *intentional* creation of a crisis by church leaders in an attempt to reinvigorate Mormon communal and religious identity" during an absence of external persecution.[25] By the mid-1850s, though, pressure from non-Mormon politicians was mounting, and for unclear

---

23. George Peacock, Letter to Brigham Young, Sept. 14, 1856, Box 25, Folder 4, BYP; Brigham Young, Letter to George Peacock, Sept. 18, 1856, Letterpress Copybook 3, BYP, p. 79; Chapman in minutes of Sept. 14, 1856, Manti Ward General Minutes, vol. 2, LR 5253 11, CHL.

24. Minutes of Sanpete County Court, Sept. 23, 1856, microfilm at Harold B. Lee Library, Brigham Young University, Provo, Utah; remission of fine in Elizabeth Jones, Letter to Brigham Young, Nov. 2, 1856, Box 69, Folder 7, BYP; minutes of Oct. 5, 1856, Manti Ward General Minutes.

25. Stephen C. Taysom, *Shakers, Mormons, and Religious Worlds: Conflicting Visions, Contested Boundaries* (Bloomington: Indiana University Press, 2011), 171; emphasis in original.

reasons Young had apparently concluded that his people had lost their earlier ardor. Concerns about declension, coupled with calls for reformation and sometimes rebaptism, were not unusual for Young. Never before, however, did he and other leaders preach such messages with such fervor and persistence.

In the spring of 1856, Young announced that it was time for the elders "to put away their velvet lips and smooth things and preach sermons like pitch forks tines downwards that the people might wake up." Young and his counselor Jedediah Grant soon began hurling those rhetorical pitchforks. In a sermon that September, Young condemned a multitude of sins, ranging from adultery to dishonesty to a failure to tithe. Mincing no words, he complained that some Saints kept their "brains … below their waistbands." He warned that the "whole people will be corrupted if we do not lop off those rotten branches." Grant and other LDS leaders traveled to communities across the territory, insisting that church members confess their sins, seek rebaptism, and demonstrate a higher level of commitment and obedience. As part of that obedience, Young encouraged hesitant Latter-day Saints to enter into or expand their practice of plural marriage, reminding them of their sacred duty to prepare tabernacles (bodies) for spirit children ready to assume their time on earth.[26]

During this season of reformation, Young and other church leaders preached that some men would have to atone for their sins with their own blood. The death of Jesus did not make satisfaction for all human sins. "[T]here are transgressors," Young explained, "who, if they knew themselves, and the only condition upon which they can obtain forgiveness, would beg of their brethren to shed their blood, that the smoke thereof might ascend to God as an offering to appease the wrath that is kindled against them." Young explained that to kill such sinners was a form of spiritual charity. When facing individuals whose sins could not "be atoned for without the shedding of their blood," Young asked, "Will you love that man or woman well enough to shed their blood? That is what

---

26. "velvet lips" in Wilford Woodruff, Journal, Mar. 2, 1856, in Ronald W. Walker, "Raining Pitchforks: Brigham Young as Preacher," *Sunstone* 8 (May-June 1983): 5–9; "waistbands" in discourse of Sept. 14, 1856, Box 3, Folder 17, CR 100 317, CHL.

Jesus Christ meant." In a reinterpretation of the golden rule, Young suggested that killing people before they had the opportunity to forsake their salvation "is loving our neighbor as ourselves." In the late-1840s and early-1850s, Young and several other high-ranking church leaders had occasionally hinted at this teaching, but during the reformation they preached it openly and repeatedly.[27]

Church leaders preached sermons designed to convict the Saints of their guilt, but they also promised forgiveness to those who confessed. As did American evangelicals, many Latter-day Saints hungered for the assurance that God would forgive their sins and that their transgressions would not nullify their salvation. During the reformation, church leaders promised that Christ's sacrifice would cleanse them of their sins. "The Presidency," announced James C. Snow, Warren Snow's brother and stake president in Provo, "requires of the saints to turn unto the Lord & be baptized for the remission of your sins & be faithful in keeping your covenants. They have promis'd that the atonement of our Lord Jesus Christ shall wash away your sins for you have gone estray but now there is a chance for you to turn unto the Lord." In this sense, the Mormon Reformation mirrored a protracted evangelical revival, with fire-and-brimstone sermons designed to help church members progress from conviction to repentance to an assurance of forgiveness. On an individual basis, Young assured several Latter-day Saints that God had absolved them even of grievous sins, such as past adultery. For example, in December 1856 a man informed Young in a letter that he had suffered "in *hell* for the last *Eight* years" because of "unlawful communication with the other sex." He was prepared to atone for his sin. "I want salvation and if it Costs the penalty of [the] transgressor so mote it be." Young wrote back a consoling note. "I have only to say be faithful and sin no more," he counseled. "Sin always carries with it its own condemnation."[28]

---

27. "transgressors" in discourse of Sept. 21, 1856, in *Journal of Discourses by Brigham Young, His Two Counsellors, the Twelve Apostles and others...* 26 vols. (Liverpool and London: various publishers, 1854–1886) [hereafter abbreviated JD], 4:53; other quotes in discourse of Feb. 8, 1857, JD, 4:219–20.

28. Minutes of Oct. 12, 1856, Provo Central Utah Stake, LR 9629 11, CHL; William H. Bishop, Letter to BY, Dec. 10, 1856, Box 69, Folder 7, BYP.

In outlying settlements, bishops and others repeated the themes articulated by Young and Grant.[29] In Provo, for example, local leaders warned thieves, adulterers, and apostates that they faced severe penalties should they not repent. "This is the Last time that they can be Baptized for the remission of their sins," warned Dominicus Carter, "& if a man steals he is to be stoned to death in the streets." Carter had stern words for those who questioned the teaching of church leaders on the issue of plural marriage. "If any man comes here & finds fau[l]t with the plurality of Wives or speaks against the authorities," he instructed, "Whang away at them." While church leaders in Provo warned unrepentant sinners that they had best leave town, they added that apostates were not simply free to flee. "[Y]ou may share the same fate," preached James Snow, "that some have started back & were met by some of the Remnants of Jacob [Indians] who laid them out!" In particular, the disaffected would not be permitted to carry Deseret's (the Saints' term for Utah) wealth with them. "I have word," informed Lewis Zabriskie, "from Brigham & John Young to not let any More Devils leave here with the Honey of the Bee Hive."[30]

Provo leaders preached the doctrine of blood atonement as well. "I will prophecy in the name of the Lord," James Snow asserted, "that whosever does have unlawful intercourse with his neighbours wife his Blood shall Atone for it." Thieves, also, should not simply be shot. Instead, they should have their "damnd throats cut." "The time will come," said Snow, "when such thieves will be taken out & their blood spilt to pay the debt for the terror of the Law must be magnified & will be."[31]

The extant minutes of Manti branch meetings are much less extensive, but what records exist suggest that local preachers delivered reformation sermons with at least as much fervor as their

---

29. See, for example, the discussion in Polly Aird, *Mormon Convert, Mormon Defector: A Scottish Immigrant in the American West, 1848–1861* (Norman, Oklahoma: Arthur H. Clark, 2009), 168–69.

30. "last time" in minutes of Sept. 28, 1856; "any man" in minutes of Oct. 26, 1856; "laid them out" in minutes of Oct. 12, 1856; "have word" in minutes of Nov. 2, 1856, all in Provo Central Utah Stake Record.

31. "prophecy" in minutes of Nov. 2, 1856; "damnd throats cut" in minutes of Nov. 9, 1856; "blood spilt" in minutes of Nov. 6, 1856, all in Provo Central Utah Stake.

counterparts in Provo. On October 19, Stake President Chapman warned that "half way Saints would not do," and another speaker explained that the reformation was a "necessity" because the people "needed the rust rubbing off." Warren Snow regularly preached in Provo during visits to that community. Of sisters who would ask Gentiles to sleep with them during their husbands' absence, the bishop suggested, "a dagger should be put through both their hearts." Snow predicted that some church members would embrace the doctrine of blood atonement: "there is others here that will go yet to the Prophet [Brigham Young] & desire that they would take their lives that they might have Salvation for themselves & their families." It is reasonable to presume that Snow preached similar messages in Manti.[32]

Historians have disagreed about how to assess the violent rhetoric employed by Young and other church leaders during the reformation. In one of the few extended studies of the reformation, Paul Peterson argues that Young spoke of blood atonement to prod his wavering flock toward repentance. The church president wanted confession and rededication, not actual throat-slittings. Moreover, while Peterson allows that "some Mormons, possibly taking their cue from the inflammatory remarks of Church leaders, engaged in abusive and uncharitable and, perhaps, even violent acts," he asserts that such actions "had little connection to the doctrine of blood atonement."[33] By contrast, other historians have linked the reformation sermons, particularly those calling for blood atonement, with a number of violent incidents. Will Bagley suggests that the "sermons of Brigham Young and Jedediah Grant helped to inspire their followers to acts of irrational violence."[34] Polly Aird notes that Peter McLausen blamed "reformation excitement" for the deaths of William Parrish, his son Beason, and Duff Potter in Springville.[35] More broadly, Michael Quinn contends that the

---

32. "half way" and "rust" in minutes of Oct. 19, 1856, Manti Ward Record, LR 5253 11, CHL; "dagger" in minutes of Nov. 16, 1856, Provo Central Utah Stake Record.

33. Paul H. Peterson, "The Mormon Reformation," PhD diss., Brigham Young University, 1981, 199.

34. Bagley, *Blood of the Prophets*, 52.

35. Aird, *Mormon Convert, Mormon Defector*, chap. 12, quote on 176.

establishment of an LDS theocracy in the Great Basin fostered a "culture of violence," and he argues that "the Mormon hierarchy bore full responsibility for the violent acts of zealous Mormons who accepted their instructions literally and carried out various forms of blood atonement."[36] More judiciously, in their chronicle of the *Massacre at Mountain Meadows*, Walker, Turley, and Leonard state that "the tough talk about blood atonement about blood atonement and dissenters must have helped create a climate of violence in the territory."[37]

"Peace and Violence" notes that church "leaders taught that some sins were so serious that the perpetrator's blood would have to be shed in order to receive forgiveness." In a footnote, the essay allows "it is likely that in at least one instance, a few Latter-day Saints acted on this rhetoric." However, in that same footnote the essay quotes Paul Peterson's conclusion that the blood atonement sermons were "hyperbole or incendiary talk … likely designed to frighten church members into conforming with Latter-day Saint principles." More broadly, "Peace and Violence" allows that incendiary preaching "led to increased strain between the Latter-day Saints and the relatively few non-Mormons in Utah." As noted above, the essay also suggests that "the heated rhetoric of Church leaders toward dissenters" may have led the perpetrators of extra-legal punishments "to believe that such actions were justified."

Regardless of Jedediah Grant and Brigham Young's exact intentions, in Manti the reformation produced both spiritual exhilaration and fomented fear and violence. At the San Pete Valley's stake conference in December 1856, reported a clerk, the "Fire of the <u>Reformation</u> glowed with great intensity." Church members confessed their sins, then received forgiveness and "testimonies to the Gospel's power." Those present reported the "presence of the Holy Spirit, Angels, and the Spirit of Joseph Smith." Some at the conference spoke in tongues. "I saw the faces of angels singing with the Choir," said Warren Snow ten days later. "[T]he people saw Joseph & Hiram Stand by my side while speaking." By the

---

36. Quinn, *Mormon Hierarchy: Extensions,* chap. 7, quote on 256.

37. Walker, Turley, and Leonard, *Massacre at Mountain Meadows: An American Tragedy* (New York: Oxford University Press, 2008), 25.

end of the year and especially by the spring, those who had embraced the reformation and demonstrated their obedience often found their faith strengthened. The next February, Apostle Orson Hyde heralded Manti as "Number one in the Reformation."[38]

———

In the midst of this spiritual maelstrom, the excommunicated Thomas Lewis once again found himself in trouble. According to his mother Elizabeth Jones's secondhand account (she was in Salt Lake City at the time), Lewis spent two days working for Isaac Voorhees, the husband of Lewis's sister Eliza and also brother-in-law to Warren Snow. Voorhees had agreed to pay Lewis by repairing an ox yoke, but Voorhees did not complete the task by the agreed-upon time. The two men began quarreling. Voorhees ordered Lewis to leave his property. When the latter refused, Voorhees "started into the house for his gun to shoot him, which so terrified Thomas that he jerked up a rock, but did not throw at him." Eventually, Lewis left. He was arrested later that night but apparently escaped. When he arrived at an aunt's home the next evening, she brought him back to Manti, where he stood trial. George Peacock sentenced Lewis to five years' imprisonment for the threatened assault. According to Elizabeth Jones's account, her son's conviction rested on the testimony of Eliza Lewis Voorhees, who "said that Thomas threatened to knock Isaac's brains out." A few days later, he was again "cut of[f]" from the church. According to Elizabeth Jones, a group of men attacked him on his way home and stuffed his mouth "full of filthy rags till he was near choacked."[39]

On October 29, the day after Dan Jones signed the bill that granted Elizabeth Lewis her divorce, Thomas Lewis was handcuffed and placed in a wagon driven by George Snow (another brother of Warren Snow), ostensibly bound for the Salt Lake City penitentiary. Lewis never reached the jail. At William Creek, to

---

38. "Fire" and "presence" in minutes of Dec. 25–28, 1856, Manti Ward Record; "saw the faces" in minutes of Jan. 10, 1857, Provo Central Utah Stake Record; "number one" in minutes of Feb. 19, 1857, Manti Ward Record, LR 5253 11; emphasis in original.

39. Account of the incident in Elizabeth Jones, Letter to Brigham Young, Nov. 8, 1856; "cut of[f]" and "full of filthy rags" in Elizabeth Jones, Letter to Brigham Young, Nov. 2, 1856.

the south of Ephraim, he was—according to Elizabeth Jones—"taken out of the wagon a blanket put round his head & actulay alter him like a pig by taking his Testicles clean out & he laid at this place in a dangerous state he was out two nights & part of two days before he was found." Three Indians sent to search for him tracked his blood for seven miles. Lewis, who crawled on his hands and knees due to the loss of so much blood, was eventually found in the "Stock Yard."[40]

A few days after the attack, during her return from Salt Lake City, Elizabeth Jones met Warren Snow at Nephi. At that point, the bishop "seemed to doubt whether he [Thomas Lewis] would be found or not." Snow told her that he did "not know" who had attacked Lewis, "no more than if they came from the moon." Warren Snow and George Peacock informed Jones that they had ridden up to the spot of the attack and had been fired upon by "Ruffains [ruffians]." The attackers had allegedly dragged George Snow out of the wagon before assaulting Lewis. Even while disclaiming any responsibility for the attack, Bishop Snow told Jones that her son Thomas was "full of the devil," just like his father and her former husband David Lewis.[41]

Within another week, Lewis's mother somehow learned that several Manti leaders (including Warren Snow, George Snow, and George Peacock) had planned and carried out the attack. She lamented that her son was now a "bloodless breathing tabernacle." Jones, who placed great emphasis on money matters and apparently did not have a close relationship with her son, complained to Young that she would have "the grief, trouble, and expense of having him on my hands." "If such a deed was right," she asked Brigham Young in a November 8 letter, "why not have it done decently in a private room and not leave him so low and helpless that he cannot turn himself or help himself any more than a new born babe?" "[T]hings are so dark and mysterious," she added.[42]

Indeed, despite Elizabeth Lewis's detailed letters to Young and scattered references to Thomas Lewis in local Manti records,

---

40. Elizabeth Jones, Letters to Brigham Young, Nov. 2 and Nov. 8, 1856.
41. Ibid.
42. Ibid., Nov. 8, 1856.

several aspects of the incident remain mysterious. Who ordered and carried out the attack? Why was Lewis castrated?

From the above evidence, Warren Snow, George Snow, and George Peacock were at the scene of the crime. Nephi resident Samuel Pitchforth asserted the next spring that John Lowry was also "one that helped to cut Lewis."[43] Thomas Lewis, as will become clear below, blamed Warren Snow for his misfortune.

It is unclear what exactly prompted the castration, long used as a legal or extralegal punishment for the alleged sexual crimes of black men against white women. In 1855, for example, the pro-slavery legislature in the Kansas Territory introduced castration as the judicial punishment for "Negroes" and "mulattoes" who raped or attempted to rape white women.[44] In later decades, whites often castrated African Americans—and sometimes Chinese Americans—as part of the torture that preceded many lynchings. Indeed, in 1866 assailants castrated and murdered Thomas Coleman, a black resident of Salt Lake City, either because of an alleged relationship with a white woman or because Coleman possessed knowledge of extralegal acts of violence.[45] Castration as a vigilante punishment against white men, however, was extremely uncommon. Jilted husbands revenging themselves upon their wives' seducers typically shot them, a form of "mountain common law" endorsed by George A. Smith in 1851.[46] As referenced below, though, community leaders in Payson, Utah, castrated a man accused of committing adultery.

Why did Thomas Lewis endure this unusual punishment? In explaining Thomas Lewis's emasculation, authors have offered two competing explanations. As noted above, John D. Lee alleged that Snow ordered the castration after Lewis refused to abandon his interest in a young woman Snow wanted to marry. Ann Eliza Young

---

43. Pitchforth Journal, typescript, May 31, 1857, MS 1739, CHL.

44. W. Haywood Burns, "Race Discrimination: Law and Race in America," in David Kairys, ed., *The Politics of Law: A Progressive Critique* (New York: Pantheon Books, 1982), 89.

45. See Connell O'Donovan, "'Let This Be a Warning to All Niggers': The Life and Murder of Thomas Coleman in Theocratic Utah," unpublished essay, www.connellodonovan.com/coleman_bio.pdf.

46. Kenneth L. Cannon II, "'Mountain Common Law': The Extralegal Punishment of Seducers in Early Utah," *Utah Historical Quarterly* 51 (Fall 1983): 310–17.

asserts that Lewis's mere attentions to the young woman led to the punishment. Not long after Lewis's emasculation, Snow did marry a sixteen-year-old woman, Maria Baum. The records of the Salt Lake City Endowment House record that Snow and Baum were sealed in Provo on December 2. Snow married two more women the following April.[47] Had Lewis and Snow clashed over a woman, however, Elizabeth Lewis would probably have discussed it in her letters to Young rather than concentrating on her son's dispute with Isaac Voorhees. Moreover, Lewis's five-year term in the penitentiary would have removed him as a viable suitor.

Dismissing the explanations of *Mormonism Unveiled* and Ann Eliza Young, John Peterson concludes that the "[s]ermons delivered in the Manti Ward, the spirit of the times, the form of punishment itself and the record of Brigham's reaction to it, make it clear that Lewis had committed a sexual crime."[48] Elizabeth Jones may have had this rationale for castration in mind. "I never knew him to tell a lie or do any thing mean," she wrote to Young, "to try to injure a female or any kind of guilt."[49] However, there is no record of Lewis having committed a sexual crime or indiscretion in the ward minutes or court records in September or October of 1856. Lewis assaulted and nearly killed John Price, and he was convicted of threatening Isaac Voorhees. It seems unlikely that Lewis committed a sexual crime immediately after the latter incident.

There were several other alleged castrations in early Utah. In February 1858, attorney and territorial politician Hosea Stout wrote in his diary that a group of men "disguised as Indians" dragged Payson resident Henry Jones "out of bed with a whore and castrated him by a square & close amputation."[50] Jones was subsequently murdered, along with his mother. In March 1859, two young men fled the San Pete Valley and took refuge in the US Army's Camp Floyd. Soldier John W. Phelps reported that one

47. Snow Family Record Group, in Warren S. Snow Papers, Box 1, Folder 1, MSS SC 376, L. Tom Perry, Special Collections, Harold B. Lee Library.

48. Peterson, "Warren Stone Snow," 205.

49. Elizabeth Jones, Letter to Brigham Young, Nov. 8, 1856.

50. Hosea Stout Journal, Feb. 27, 1858, in Juanita Brooks, ed., *On the Mormon Frontier: The Diary of Hosea Stout, 1844–1889* (Salt Lake City: University of Utah Press, 1964), 653.

of the men, a "handsome young Dane," wanted "to marry a Danish girl. But the Bishop of the town wanted her for himself." The men claimed that the bishop "got up the story that his rival had committed bestiality and had him castrated."[51] The next month, the *St. Louis Republican* published a letter from an army "officer" repeating the same story: "some hoary-headed old scoundrel of a bishop, or other official, wanted the girl for *his* harem, and jealous of the handsome youth, had him tied, and thus mutilated him, first giving him a chance between that and death!"[52] On New Year's Eve in 1861, short-tenured Utah Governor John Dawson, who had been accused of making advances toward a Mormon widow in Salt Lake City, was attacked while fleeing the territory. Later rumors suggested that the governor had received "almost emasculating injuries" or been "half emasculated."[53] Especially in the latter two instances, it is impossible to distinguish between rumor and fact.

In the absence of further evidence, it is not possible to conclude with certainty why Snow and other Manti leaders orchestrated the castration of Lewis. Given the 1858 castration of Henry Jones and the alleged castration reported by John Phelps in 1859, one cannot definitively link the violent rhetoric of the reformation to the Lewis incident. Still, Snow and others attacked Lewis during a crescendo of reformation sermons threatening violence against sinners, apostates, and trouble-makers. The most likely conclusion is that, in this context, Manti's leaders made an example of a truculent and repeatedly violent young man.

"I beg and implore you," Elizabeth Jones wrote to Brigham Young, "to drop me a line to let me know if it is right and righteous?"[54] Two weeks after the incident, Young responded to Jones's several letters. He simultaneously consoled Elizabeth in her anxiety and offered a theological justification for her son's emasculation:

---

51. John W. Phelps Journal, Mar. 28, 1859, typescript in John Wolcott Phelps Papers, MSS B-120, Box 1, Folder 9, Utah State Historical Society, Salt Lake City. I am grateful to Will Bagley for pointing me to this source.

52. "Mormon Civilization," *The Missouri Republican* [St. Louis], Apr. 29, 1859.

53. See the discussion in Will Bagley, "Conan Doyle Was Right: Danites, Avenging Angels, and Holy Murder in the American West," in Leslei S. Klinger, ed., *A Tangled Skein: A Companion Volume to The Baker Street Irregulars' Expedition to The Country of the Saints* (New York: The Baker Street Irregulars, 2008), 7–8.

54. Elizabeth Jones, Letter to Brigham Young, Nov. 8, 1856.

I can feel and appreciate a parents anxiety in behalf of their offspring, still I would prefer that any child of mine should lose his life in atonement for his sins than lose eternal salvation in the Kingdom of our God. I am not intimately acquainted with the personal character of your son, but he has been represented to me as a wilful wicked and ungovernable disposition that neither you, himself, nor any one else could control, be this as it may Sister Lewis the deed is done, and if he lives which I sincerely hope he may, we can only make the best of it and time will develope whether it is not only for his but your best interests, as it cannot be helped. Sister Lewis it appears to me to be wisdom to be resigned and comfort yourself in doing what you can to save his life, and he may yet prove a comfort and support to you, in your declining years; It is far better for him to be saved as he is in the kingdom of our God then to turn away from the truth or by committing some overt act be finally damned.

Young's words alluded to a passage that appears in the Gospels of Matthew (5:29–30) and Mark (9:43, 45, 47): "for it is profitable for thee that one of thy members should perish, and not that thy whole body should be cast into hell." His reasoning ("I should prefer that any child of mind should lose his life in atonement for his sins") also reflects his belief that some grievous sins would require the sacrifice of the transgressor's own blood.[55]

Jones was not the only resident of Manti horrified by Lewis's emasculation. Stake President Welcome Chapman wrote to Brigham Young to ask if "thomas Lewises fine" should be remitted, referring to the court costs associated with Lewis's September conviction. In his response to Jones, Young added a postscript warning to "brother Chapman and others who are talking and acting so violently about the deed that has been committed." They had, Young cautioned, "far better keep quiet and act wisely, if they wish to find out, who committed it." Despite the cryptic nature of the warning, the message was clear. Chapman would face consequences if he continued to talk about the crime. Chapman stopped talking. At a Manti ward meeting later that month, he and two others "made acknowledgements of having made us of improper

---

55. Brigham Young, Letter to Elizabeth Jones, Nov. 13, 1856, Letterpress Copybook 3, 186a.

sayings in regard to T Lewis." "[N]ot a word came from my mouth after I got a hint," he assured Young in a letter the next month.[56]

In his letter to Jones, Young expressed no disapproval of Lewis's emasculation, and he made it clear to Chapman that he intended to use his power to protect the perpetrators. It is unclear whether or not Young authorized the crime in advance. In her first letter to Young, Jones observed that George Snow was bringing her son "hancuffed in a wagon to Salt Lake to put him in the Penitentiary according to your advise." George Peacock had sought Young's counsel after Lewis's fight with John Price. Thus, it seems reasonable to conclude that Peacock and other local leaders sought Young's advice in this instance as well. However, the existing evidence does not reveal whether or not Warren Snow and Peacock sought Young's approval for the castration itself.[57]

Young further signaled his support for Warren Snow the following spring. Although open opposition to the bishop ceased in Manti, word of the crime slowly made its way out of the San Pete Valley. Samuel Pitchforth predicted that "Bro W Snow will loose some influence through that affair." Pitchforth, and presumably many others, knew the gory details. Lewis's attackers had taken "him into the willows and took from him his stones in a b[r]utal manner Tearing the chords right out." In May, when Young's brother Joseph and Albert P. Rockwood visited Nephi, Pitchforth recorded that they "entirely disapproved of the cutting of young Lewis at Fort Ephraim." Evidently, Joseph Young had sought to exclude John Lowry (one of those involved) from a position of leadership at Manti because "he did not want a man who would shed blood before he was duly commanded."[58]

Joseph Young also complained about the course of Bishop Elias Blackburn and Stake President James C. Snow in Provo. According to a later source, the Provo leaders were threatening rebellious young men with Lewis's fate. In 1873, former LDS editor Thomas

---

56. "gang" and "got a hint" in Chapman, Letter to Brigham Young, Dec. 22, 1856, Box 69, Folder 7, BYP; "Lewises fine" in Chapman, Letter to Brigham Young, Nov. 9, 1856, Box 24, Folder 16, BYP; Brigham Young, Letter to Elizabeth Jones, Nov. 13, 1856; minutes of Nov. 30, 1856, Manti Ward Record.

57. Elizabeth Jones, Letter to Brigham Young, Nov. 2, 1856.

58. Pitchforth Journal, May 31, 1857.

Stenhouse published an anonymous letter discussing the Mormon Reformation in Provo and the San Pete Valley:

> I was at a Sunday meeting in the spring of 1857, in Provo, when the news of the San Pete castration was referred to by the presiding bishop—[Elias] Blackburn. Some men in Provo had rebelled against authority in some trivial matter, and Blackburn shouted in his Sunday meeting—a mixed congregation of all ages and both sexes—"I want the people of Provo to understand that the boys in Provo can use the knife as well as the boys in San Pete." ... The result of this was that two citizens, named Hooper and Beauvere, both having families at Provo, left the following night for Fort Bridger.[59]

The letter contains at least some accurate information. In early June 1857, Apostle Wilford Woodruff referenced in his diary "some persons leaving Provo who had Apostitized" and that "[s]ome thought that Bishop Blackburn & President Snow was to blame."[60]

In relation to the leaders at both Provo and Manti, Brigham Young disagreed with his brother's objections, predicting that "the day would Come when thousands will be made Eunochs in order for them to be saved in the kingdom of God." Even if Warren Snow had prematurely implemented this principle, Young sympathized with the bishop's intentions. "I will tell you," Young insisted, "that when a man is trying to do right & do[es] some thing that is not exactly in order I feel to sustain him." Aware of the discontent his actions had generated, Warren Snow wrote to the church president and requested a public epistle to counter grumbling against his leadership. "[I]t would be like pissing upon a hot iron," Young explained, "only make the more smoke." "Just let the matter drop," he advised Warren Snow.[61]

––––––––––

The matter dropped. There is no evidence that any of Lewis's

59. Stenhouse, *The Rocky Mountain Saints* (New York: D. Appleton and Co., 1873), 302.

60. Wilford Woodruff Journal, June 2, 1858, in Scott G. Kenney, ed., *Wilford Woodruff's Journal, 1833–1898: Typescript* (Midvale, Utah: Signature Books, 1984), 5:54–55.

61. Woodruff Journal, June 2, 1857, 5:55; Brigham Young, Letter to Warren Snow, July 7, 1857, Letterpress Copybook 3, 707–08.

relatives contravened Young's warning via Chapman to keep quiet about the case. Others matters soon dominated Utah affairs. Shortly after Young's conversation with his brother Joseph about the Lewis incident, Utahns learned that an American army was escorting a new, non-Mormon governor to the territory. Young mobilized Utah's militia, the Nauvoo Legion, and prepared to resist the army's approach. Warren Snow was appointed the commander of the militia's San Pete Military District, and in late-October he led a contingent of cavalry to Fort Bridger and reinforced a campaign of harassment against the approaching army. In this context, the Lewis incident quickly disappeared as an item of public discussion.

Elizabeth Lewis Jones, for her part, worried more about financial struggles than gaining justice on her son's behalf. She hardly lost her faith in the church president. After a third unhappy marriage (to John Tuttle), she wrote to Young to request her addition to his family. "I belong to you," she wrote the church president in June 1858, adding that Young had caused her to marry two men against her wishes. Had Young given Jones "her rights," she would have been "comfortably off" and "another woman." Young apparently ignored her letter, so she wrote him again in April 1859: "You know as well as I know where my place is, and if it is not given to me you must take what follows ... Please to answer this note for I do not mean to stop here and suffer as I have suffered. I have been told to give you another trial for the last time."[62]

Jones's vague threats came at a fraught time for Young. In June 1858, he had accepted a presidential pardon, ended the Nauvoo Legion's military resistance, and permitted US Army troops to pass through Salt Lake City and garrison Utah. The end of the Utah War did not lead to reconciliation between Young and his church on the one hand and the US government and its territorial representatives on the other. In March 1859, Judge John Cradlebaugh, an Ohio native, traveled to Provo with a military escort, impaneled a grand jury, and proceeded to investigate unpunished crimes. At the top of Cradlebaugh's list was the September 1857

---

62. Elizabeth Jones, Letters to Brigham Young, June 5, 1858, and Apr. 21, 1859, Box 66, Folder 16.

Mountain Meadows Massacre, but he also fixed his eye on other incidents: the Parrish-Potter murders; the disappearance and presumed murder of Henry Fobbs, a non-Mormon who attempted to leave the territory during the Utah War; and the castration and murder of Henry Jones in Payson, Utah. "To allow these things to pass over," Cradlebaugh warned his jury, "gives a color as if they were done by authority."[63]

The castration of Thomas Lewis was not high on Cradlebaugh's list of crimes, but the judge intended to pursue that case as well. In early April 1859, soldiers attempted to arrest Warren Snow (along with George Peacock, Welcome Chapman, and "Father" Isaac Morley), but the bishop eluded his would-be captors and fled to a mountain retreat to the north of Manti, where a number of wanted Latter-day Saints took refuge from Cradlebaugh's warrants. The Utah legislature soon reassigned Cradlebaugh to a different judicial district, and federal authorities never revived an investigation of the Lewis case. Despite complaints against him, Snow remained Manti's bishop and stake president until 1861, and he played a significant role in the mid-1860s Blackhawk War.[64]

The story of the Lewis incident contains several codas. After she returned to Dan Jones's household in 1861, Elizabeth Jones inherited the erstwhile missionary's property in Provo, where she continued to live with several of her children. She also continued to desire Brigham Young for her husband. Seven years after Dan Jones's 1862 death, Young and Elizabeth Jones finally kneeled together at the Endowment House altar. Ann Eliza Webb later alleged that Young married Jones because her property in Provo interfered with his factory-building plans, an obstacle removed after Elizabeth's move to Young's 800-acre Forest Farm property east of Salt Lake City. Elizabeth Jones did own land north of the woolen factory, and she did leave Provo after her sealing to Young. She did not deed the land to Young until 1876, however. In any event, she—like several of Young's other wives who spent time there—did not find contentment at Forest Farm. Chores at the farm, including cooking for a large number of workers, were grueling. In 1875,

63. "Charge," *Valley Tan* [Salt Lake City], Mar. 15, 1859.
64. See Peterson, "Warren Stone Snow," chaps. 5 and 6.

Young instructed one of his workers to "say to Sister Jones unless she takes care of the farm I shall have to place some one in possession who will take care of it." Now sixty-one years of age, Elizabeth Jones Lewis Jones Tuttle Young probably found her marriage to Young more arduous than she had imagined.[65]

For his part, Thomas Lewis continued to live in misery. In April 1859, the non-Mormon *Valley Tan*, reported that he "live[d] in a hole in the ground near one of the settlements [in] San Pete Valley, and is perfectly crazy."[66] With only one exception, there is no mention of Lewis in any known historical record after the 1860 census. Then, in 1872, a group of men attempted to exact vengeance upon Warren Snow. According to a letter Snow wrote to one of his wives, the group included the brothers "Cana [Canaan] Lewis And Tom." They apprehended Snow with shot guns and revolvers. At one point, Snow lay on the ground with two revolvers pointed at his head. The attackers may have intended to inflict the same punishment on Snow that Snow had inflicted on Thomas Lewis. Remarkably, the fifty-three-year-old former bishop fought back, shot two of his attackers, and escaped intact. Snow intended to track down the surviving assailants "when they little think of it and make them bite the dust."[67]

The Lewis family made no second attempt to take revenge on Warren Snow, but Canaan Lewis never forgave the former bishop. In 1880, he wrote church president John Taylor. Canaan Lewis's wife had died recently. Shortly after his wife's funeral, Lewis received word that "Warren Snow was going to occupy the [Sunday] meeting" in the San Pete County town of Wales. "It seems this special visitation to Wales on this particular occasion in my saddest Moments," Lewis informed Taylor, "were Intentional on his behalf in recalling Vividly to my mind the brutality that he Exhibited to my brother Thomas 20 years ago." He added that despite the

---

65. Young, *Wife No. 19*, 280–86; record of deed in Brigham Young Real Estate Book A, 153, MS 10324, CHL; Brigham Young, Letter to Charles Crabtree, Jan. 3, 1875, Letterpress Telegram Book, 1873–75 Box 12, BYP. On Forest Farm, see Todd Compton, *In Sacred Loneliness: The Plural Wives of Joseph Smith* (Salt Lake City: Signature Books, 1997), 417–18.

66. *Valley Tan* [Salt Lake City], Apr. 26, 1859.

67. Snow, Letter to Sarah Whiting, Mar. 19, 1872, Box 1, Folder 2, Snow Papers.

appeals of "Government officers," he was not interested in helping obtain Snow's indictment. Instead, Lewis asked the church president for what amounted to an ecclesiastical restraining order against Snow. "I can forgive but never forget," Lewis stated.[68]

———

"Peace and Violence" asserts that "throughout the Church's history, Church leaders have taught that the way of Christian discipleship is a path of peace." While that is true of most church leaders, the above evidence demonstrates that in certain circumstances, it was not the case. Taking their cues from the highest-ranking leaders of the church, local leaders in Provo and Manti called for violence against criminals and dissenters. Indeed, they did more than call for violent reprisals. They mutilated a defenseless prisoner. It remains unclear why Warren Snow and other Manti leaders decided to inflict their chosen penalty upon him. There is not enough evidence to conclude that Brigham Young ordered or gave advance approval to Thomas Lewis's emasculation, but Young—then governor of the Utah Territory—obstructed justice by intimidating those in Manti who complained about the crime. Young privately condoned Snow's conduct, and the bishop evidently remained in Young's good graces. At the very least, Young's violent rhetoric and his upholding of local leaders who meted out extralegal punishments created an expectation among local LDS leaders that they would not be punished for taking the initiative to "cleanse the platter." Regardless of whether Young, Snow, and others taught that "the way of Christian discipleship is a path of peace," in their worst moments they traveled a very different path.

In recent years, historians have persuasively reconstructed several incidents, such as the February 1857 ambush in the Santa Clara Canyon and the March 1857 deaths of three men in Springville, Utah (known as the Parrish-Potter murders).[69]

———

68. Canaan Lewis, Letter to John Taylor, Feb. 7, 1880, typescript of John A. Peterson, copy in my possession.

69. On these incidents, see Ardis E. Parshall, "'Pursue, Retake & Punish': The 1857 Santa Clara Ambush," *Utah Historical Quarterly* 73 (Winter 2005): 64–86; Polly Aird, "'You Nasty Apostates, Clear Out': Reasons for Disaffection in the Late 1850s," *Journal of Mormon History* 30 (Fall 2004): 173–91.

Additional research will no doubt produce greater clarity on many cases, perhaps including the castration of Thomas Lewis, while some episodes will remain dark and mysterious. Other historians might determine with greater precision the rate of violence in Utah relative to that in other states and territories. "Peace and Violence" is no doubt correct that the vast majority of Latter-day Saints "lived in peace with their neighbors and families, and sought peace in their communities," but it may well be that certain Utah settlements were "enclaves of violence," as scholars have described certain gold camps, Chinatowns, and reservations.[70]

The most important questions facing readers of "Peace and Violence" do not, however, pertain to the details of individual instances of violence. They do not pertain to whether or not Brigham Young or other high-ranking church leaders ordered or condoned specific acts of violence. Instead, the most important questions pertain to matters of theology, specifically those pertaining to human nature and the church.

My Presbyterian Church (U.S.A.) has its own heritage of troublesome history and doctrine. For example, John Calvin, the single largest theological influence on early Presbyterianism, sanctioned the death of alleged heretic Michael Servetus at the stake. During the lifetimes of Joseph Smith and Brigham Young, moreover, southern Presbyterians such as James Henry Thornwell were among the most articulate theological defenders of slavery. Calvin also articulated doctrines abhorrent to both early Mormons and a broad range of antebellum Americans. He asserted that God predestined certain individuals to salvation and others to damnation. More specifically, following the lead of early Christian theologians such as Augustine of Hippo, Calvin believed that such divine predestination extended to children who die in infancy. "Even infants," Calvin wrote in his *Institutes of the Christian Religion*, "are guilty not of another's fault but of their own." Even if those infants had not yet sinned, "their nature is a seed of sin; hence it can be only hateful and abhorrent to

---

70. C. V. McKanna, "Enclaves of Violence in Nineteenth-Century California," *Pacific Historical Review* 73 (Aug. 2004): 391–424.

God."[71] For Calvin, this was not cruelty on God's part, but justice and equity. God treated perishing infants precisely as he treated all other human beings. Despite its theological consistency, the doctrine itself is abhorrent. How much more attractive are the words of Moroni 8:17 that God loves "little children with a perfect love; and they are all alike and partakers of salvation." The Book of Mormon defines a good number of Calvin's beliefs as abominable, sometimes for good reason.

Some of Calvin's theological disciples, however, have constructed theologies of the church that might help Latter-day Saints make sense of those times when their ancestors and past leaders uttered abhorrent words and engaged in immoral behavior. Church membership and the holding of ecclesiastical offices do not eliminate the frailties of human nature. Like all individuals, Dan Jones, Elizabeth Jones, Thomas Lewis, Warren Snow, and Brigham Young exhibited various forms of sometimes perplexing frailties. Why did Thomas Lewis hit John Price with a shovel? How did his emigration, his parents' divorce, and his mother's marriage to Dan Jones affect Lewis's psychology and emotional well-being? Why did Warren Snow choose to castrate Lewis? Why did Brigham Young condone some violent actions? How did the Missouri and Illinois persecutions affect Snow and Young's approaches to leadership? In their own ways, Lewis, Snow, and Young were all men of many sorrows.

Those frail human beings come together in churches, in congregations, and in geographically broader units. Even well-designed institutional procedures offer no perfect protection against those same human frailties, either on an individual or institutional level. As Reformed theologians such as Paul Tillich and Reinhold Niebuhr have articulated, human beings and their religious institutions always remain embedded in the "ambiguities of life … with all the disintegrating, destructive, and tragic-demonic elements which make historical life as ambiguous as all other life processes." From a strictly sociological point of view, we err and set ourselves up for grave disappointment when we expect our

---

71. Calvin, *Institutes of the Christian Religion*, trans. Ford Lewis Battles, ed. John T. McNeill (Philadelphia: Westminster, 1960), 1:251 (Book II, Chap. I, sec. 8).

religious institutions to even approximate the holiness and unity of their ideals. Tillich contends that a church's "holiness cannot be derived from the holiness of [its] institutions, doctrines, ritual and devotional activities, or ethical principles; all these are among the ambiguities of religion."[72] Instead, a church's holiness rests upon its foundation in Jesus Christ, who redeems it despite its lack of perfect holiness. Or, as Niebuhr once explained, the good news of the gospel is not that God enables human beings or institutions to live Christ's law of love. Instead, the good news is that even though we and our institutions remain "inevitably involved" in human sinfulness and injustice and therefore fail to live that law of love, "there is a resource of divine mercy which is able to overcome" this fundamental contradiction.[73]

Of course, Reformed ecclesiology is rather different than Mormon ecclesiology. Tillich, for instance, regarded the existence of ecclesiastical divisions as "unavoidable." Noting differences in ecclesiology, he observed that the Catholic Church was intensely averse to criticism. "Since the Roman Church identifies its historical existence with the [true] Spiritual Community," Tillich wrote, "every attack on it (often even on non-essentials) is felt as an attack on the Spiritual Community and consequently on the Spirit itself."[74] So it has largely been with the Church of Jesus Christ of Latter-day Saints, which far more closely resembles Catholic than Protestant ecclesiology. Latter-day Saints revere their leaders, past and present, and those leaders have asserted that God guides their actions. "The Lord will never," asserted Wilford Woodruff in 1890, "permit me or any other man who stands as President of this Church to lead you astray."[75]

Even so, I would suggest that these differences in ecclesiology do not preclude an acceptance of Tillich's basic point about the

72. Paul Tillich, *Systematic Theology, Volume III: Life and the Spirit, History and the Kingdom of God* (Chicago: University of Chicago Press, 1963), 162–72.

73. Niebuhr, "Why the Christian Church Is Not Pacifist," in Robert McAfee Brown, ed., *The Essential Reinhold Niebuhr* (New Haven, Connecticut: Yale University Press, 1986), 102–103. Niebuhr originally published his essay in 1940 in the emerging context of the Second World War.

74. Tillich, *Systematic Theology*, 3:167.

75. D&C Official Declaration 1, "Excerpts from Three Addresses by President Wilford Woodruff."

"ambiguities of religion." Indeed, Latter-day Saints have expected rather too much holiness from their ancestors, past leaders, and current leaders, and those expectations have impeded a straightforward and sober accounting with the frailties of the church's members and its institutional history.

At the same time, it is not LDS doctrine that those leaders are infallible. For example, the Gospel Topics essay on "Race and the Priesthood" suggests that the decision of Joseph Smith's successors to withhold the priesthood and temple blessings from black members rested on the sinful foundation of nineteenth-century American racism. Human beings, Latter-day Saints and otherwise, respond imperfectly to the circumstances in which they find themselves.

In the end, then, Latter-day Saints maintain that their leaders are both fallible (and therefore make mistakes) and that they will not lead the church astray. It is the basic paradox of the church as articulated by Tillich. It is a paradox that reminds all Christians to place their faith in Jesus Christ rather than in institutions and individuals. This paradox, moreover, might help church members make better sense of the "dark and mysterious" aspects of their nineteenth-century history.

7. "THROUGH A GLASS, DARKLY"
JOSEPH SMITH AND PLURAL MARRIAGE

Gary James Bergera

The LDS Church's release on October 22, 2014, of an unsigned scholarly oriented article on the beginnings of the church's past practice of plural marriage—part of its Gospel Topics series of essays—quickly attracted considerable public attention.[1] The essay admitted that the church's founding prophet, Joseph Smith (1805–44), had married some very young women, had married other men's wives, and had concealed many of these polygamous marriages from his first wife, Emma Hale Smith (1804–79). The essay represented an important departure from previous church efforts to minimize the controversial practice.[2] Clearly, LDS officials had decided that "hard truths" are the most effective palliative to faith-related obstacles resulting from the study of the church and plural marriage. The church's willingness to confront its controversial past invites us to evaluate the essay and to offer some observations regarding future discussion.

The essay begins with a word of caution:

> Many details about the early practice of plural marriage are unknown. Plural marriage was introduced among the early Saints incrementally, and participants were asked to keep their actions confidential. They

---

1. Available at www.lds.org/topics/plural-marriage-in-kirtland-and-nauvoo?lang=eng. All quotations are from the on-line version of the essay. See also George D. Smith, "Plural Marriage Among Early Latter-day Saints," *Sunstone*, Summer 2015, 12–13. An earlier brief essay on polygamy appeared on Dec. 17, 2013 (appreciation to Clair V. Barrus).

2. See the discussion in Newell G. Bringhurst, "Where Have All of Brigham Young's Wives Gone? Latter-day Saint Ambivalence over Its Polygamous Past," in Newell G. Bringhurst and Craig L. Foster, eds., *The Persistence of Polygamy: From Joseph Smith's Martyrdom to the First Manifesto, 1844–1890* (Independence, Missouri: John Whitmer Books, 2013), 87–112.

did not discuss their experiences publicly or in writing until after the Latter-day Saints had moved to Utah [from Illinois] and Church leaders had publicly acknowledged the practice [in 1852]. The historical record of early plural marriage is therefore thin: few records of the time provide details, and later reminiscences are not always reliable. Some ambiguity will always accompany our knowledge about this issue. Like the participants, we "see through a glass, darkly" and are asked to walk by faith.

All students of the history of LDS plural marriage would do well to take such advice to heart. The contemporary first-person sources for the beginnings of Mormon polygamy are almost non-existent. Our knowledge of the subject depends almost entirely upon later memory-based reminiscences, narratives both "subject to numerous influences" and "fragile." In recalling the past, we all "are motivated by a desire to be correct, to be observant, and to avoid looking foolish. [We] want to give an answer, to be helpful, and many will do this at the risk of being incorrect."[3] Such factors impact the accuracy of the sources regarding Smith and plural marriage and mean that any history of the beginnings of Mormon polygamy will be, at best, incomplete. This is not to suggest that all attempts at recreating that history are unavoidably flawed—some are more factually accurate than others—merely that scholars need to exercise special caution in excavating and interpreting the story of Mormon polygamy.[4]

Despite the initial caveat, the church's essay proposes a reconstruction that, in my opinion, too uncritically accepts the reliability of the primary sources and adopts a defensive reading of those sources that minimizes, if not misrepresents, the underpinnings of Smith's teaching. The essay paints a reverential portrait of Smith as a prophet of God that emphasizes his spiritual qualities and avoids serious consideration of erotic appeal and other factors in the implementation of plural marriage. It presents Smith as a very

---

3. Elizabeth Loftus, *Eyewitness Testimony* (1979; rpt., Cambridge, Massachusetts: Harvard University Press, 1996), 86–87, 109.

4. I specifically reference here to my own past dependence. Having reconsidered the sources underlying the traditional chronology, I have come to conclude that I and other historians have probably been too uncritical of the presumed accuracy of these early sources.

reluctant polygamist who only accepted the sexual component of plural marriage after an angel "with a drawn sword" visited him three times and "threaten[ed] [him] with destruction unless he went forward and obeyed the commandment fully" by consummating his marriages.

The essay posits that Smith's July 12, 1843, revelation on plural marriage (since canonized as section 132 in LDS editions of the Doctrine and Covenants, an official compilation of Smith's revelations) first emerged in proto-form twelve years earlier, in 1831, while Smith was revising the text of the Old Testament.[5] According to later reminiscences and hearsay testimony, Smith concluded that the Old Testament practice of polygamy was part of the "dispensation of the fullness of times" that God had commanded him to restore. (The essay does not point out that no where in the Hebrew Bible is polygamy specifically commanded for God's people generally. Nor does the essay explain why other ancient practices—circumcision, for example—were not so privileged in Smith's restoration program.) After a series of angelic visitations, again according to later accounts, Smith told a few close associates about the necessity of plural marriage and eventually acted

---

5. The first mentions of polygamy appeared in 1830 in Joseph Smith's Book of Mormon and almost entirely condemned the practice:

> And now it came to pass that the people of Nephi, under the reign of the second king, began to grow hard in their hearts, and indulge themselves somewhat in wicked practices, such as like unto David of old desiring many wives and concubines ... (Jacob 1:15)

> Behold, David and Solomon truly had many wives and concubines, which thing was abominable before me, saith the Lord. ...
> Wherefore, my brethren, hear me, and hearken to the word of the Lord: For there shall not any man among you have save it be one wife; and concubines he shall have none; ...
> For if I will, saith the Lord of Hosts, raise up seed unto me, I will command my people; otherwise they shall hearken unto these things. (Jacob 2:24, 27–28, 30)

> For behold, he did not keep the commandments of God, but ... had many wives and concubines. (Mosiah 11:2)

> Riplakish did not do that which was right in the sight of the Lord, for he did have many wives and concubines. (Ether 10:5)

Jacob 2:30 may be read as a possible exception to the rule against polygamy and may indicate that reproduction is the only justification for its practice.

to institute what he and others knew was an illegal practice that would undoubtedly "stir up public ire" (the essay's words) against him and his church. The essay speculates that Smith may have secretly taken a young, unmarried Smith family housekeeper, Fanny Alger (1816–89), as his first plural wife in the mid-1830s, an extra-legal marriage that ended in dissolution. Smith's next, and better documented, plural marriage took place half a decade later in Nauvoo, Illinois, to Louisa Beaman (1815–50). This union inaugurated the active period of Smith's plural marriage practice, by the end of which the Mormon prophet had married thirty-plus women (the precise number will probably never be known), including almost a dozen already married civilly to other men.

The essay further addresses a series of polygamy-related topics. It suggests a difference between plural marriage sealings that were said to be for time and eternity versus plural marriage sealings said to be for eternity only. ("Sealing" is the noun a marriage authorized by Smith was sometimes termed.) The former sealing, according to the essay, implies the possibility of sexual relations in this life (for time); the latter sealing implies marital relations in heaven after death only (for eternity). Such a difference functions to defend Smith against charges that he committed adultery when he married already civilly married women, since such plural marriages would have been for eternity only and would not have been consummated in this life. The essay also excuses Smith's marriages to teenagers—one of whom was fourteen at the time, but whose plural marriage the essay describes as having occurred "several months before her 15th birthday." It admits that such marriages are "inappropriate by today's standards," but asserts they were, in fact, "legal in that era" and hence not as unusual as we today may judge.[6]

The essay next speculates about Smith's plural marriages to already civilly married women—which the essay implies is the most problematic aspect of Smith's practice. Perhaps such marriages functioned to link entire families together in social chains

---

6. On this subject, see Todd M. Compton's insightful discussion, "Early Marriage in the New England and Northeastern States, and in Mormon Polygamy: What Was the Norm?" in Newell G. Bringhurst and Craig L. Foster, eds., *The Persistence of Polygamy: Joseph Smith and the Origins of Mormon Polygamy* (Independence, Missouri: John Whitmer Books, 2010), 184–232.

of eternal duration. Or possibly such marriages, if understood to be eternity-only sealings, were Smith's way of obeying the letter of the command that he practice plural marriage "without requiring him to have normal [i.e., sexual] marriage relationships," this, in turn, saving his own civil wife, Emma Smith, "the sorrow it would [otherwise] bring to" her. Or perhaps the marriages were sought after, if not actually instigated, by the already-married women themselves, who "may have believed [an eternal] sealing to Joseph Smith would give them blessings they might not otherwise receive in the next life," particularly those women in unhappy marriages and/or married to non-Mormons. Each of these explanations ostensibly dulls the sting of adultery and/or stresses that Smith tried hard not to practice plural marriage in its full (sexual) sense.

The essay adopts a much less judgmental tone towards Emma Smith than past discussions—especially those originating among nineteenth-century LDS Church members—that painted the Mormon leader's polygamy-loathing wife as a traitor to her husband's attempts to obey God's command. The essay admits that Smith deliberately kept the majority of his plural marriages secret from Emma, including his supposed eternity-only marriages. It further concedes that "many aspects of their story remain known only to the two of them." Importantly, however, the essay adds that Smith's 1843 revelation (referenced above) provided Smith a way out of having to inform Emma of his plural marriages, since once she rejected the teaching, he was thereafter "exempted" from having to "gain [her] consent," implying that Smith's clandestine behavior was heaven-approved.

The essay concludes with a brief discussion of the possible religious reasons for plural marriage. These include plural marriage as a means of "raising up seed [i.e., children]" unto God and as a "redemptive process of sacrifice and spiritual refinement." The latter encompasses such additional justifications as plural marriage as a test of one's and of one's spouse's faith in and obedience to God's prophet; as a means of securing a spiritual witness of God's wisdom and favor; and as a vehicle for progressing in one's faith. The essay stresses that for Smith and for his followers, the command to practice plural marriage was "wrenching" and the decision to accept it "usually came only after earnest prayer and intense soul-searching," followed by "struggle, resolution, and ultimately, light and peace." The essay ends with the admission that while the LDS Church no longer practices plural marriage, it permits eternity-only plural marriage sealings in its temples when one spouse is deceased. While "the precise nature of these [plural] relationships in the next life is not known," the essay's final sentence urges faith: "Latter-day Saints are encouraged to trust in our wise Heavenly Father, who loves His children and does all things for their growth and salvation."

———

Reconstructing an accurate historical narrative of Joseph Smith's practice of plural marriage, based on factually reliable contemporary sources, is a near-Sisyphean undertaking: The nearer we come to what we believe is a "true" understanding of the topic, the farther away that understanding seems to retreat. It is tempting to rely on the reminiscences of Smith's plural wives and reportedly knowledgeable insiders and to assume that their accounts are wholly trustworthy. After all, why would they misrepresent the facts of their experiences, when they have much to lose by admitting to illegal, transgressive behaviors? Unfortunately, the boundaries separating truths from untruths in the arena of memory—especially when so many years have elapsed between event and telling—are not clearly demarcated. "[E]very time we recall an event," researchers Elizabeth Loftus and Katherine Ketcham explain, "we must reconstruct the memory, and with each recollection the memory may be changed—colored by succeeding events, other people's recollections or suggestions, increased understanding, or a new context." Consequently, the remembered past "takes on a living, shifting reality … that changes shape, expands, shrinks, and expands again, an amoeblike creature with powers to make us laugh, and cry, and clench our fists." As memories form, evolve, and reform, "we become convinced that we saw or said or did what we remember. We perceive the blending of fact and fiction that constitutes a memory as completely and utterly truthful."[7]

___

7. Loftus and Ketcham, *Witness for the Defense: The Accused, the Eyewitness, and the Expert Who Puts Memory on Trial* (New York: St. Martin's Press, 1991), 20–21.

Daniel L. Schacter further notes that as we "rewrite"—intentionally or unconsciously—our past experiences, we produce "a skewed rendering of a specific incident, or even of an extended period in our lives."[8] When we talk about the past, especially to an audience—actual or implied—our objectives are more than truth-telling. We want to make sense, to explain, to justify our life; we want also to entertain and to arouse sympathy. Memory must be considered from within its "social context," because "a person's confident and vivid personal memories may not be accurate ones."[9] People's memories "can be distorted through the inclusion in those memories either of … information that has been fed to [them] subsequent to the event they are being asked to remember but prior to the moment when the testimony is delivered … or of ideas suggested in the course of questioning at the moment of delivery."[10] Not only does "talking about witnessed events [lead] to changes in memory," the "focus of retelling directs those changes."[11] Thus, whenever we recall, tell, and retell important events—especially emotion-laden events—"we risk error."[12]

When memory constitutes "a major source of self-justification"—in the present case, participation in a transgressive activity—it easily can become "warped." We tend to remember only "confirming examples" and to forget "dissonant instances." As our memories solidify, we find it increasingly "difficult to see the whole"—that is, "the mixture of good and bad, strengths and flaws, good intentions and unfortunate blunders."[13] When memory functions to legitimize past acts—especially controversial ones—"self-serving

---

8. Daniel L. Schacter, *The Seven Sins of Memory: How the Mind Forgets and Remembers* (New York: Houghton Mifflin, 2001), 5.

9. Elizabeth J. Marsh and Barbara Tversky, "Spinning the Stories of Our Lives," *Applied Cognitive Psychology* 13, 5 (June 2004): 500.

10. Geoffrey Cubitt, *History and Memory* (Manchester, England: Manchester University Press, 2007), 84.

11. Elizabeth J. Marsh, Barbara Tversky, and Michael Hutson, "How Eyewitnesses Talk About Events: Implications for Memory," *Applied Cognitive Psychology* 19, 5(July 2005): 542.

12. Barbara Tversky and Elizabeth J. Marsh, "Biased Retellings of Events Yield Biased Memories," *Cognitive Psychology* 40, 1 (Feb. 2000): 34.

13. Carol Travers and Elliot Aronson, *Mistakes Were Made (but Not by* Me*): Why We Justify Foolish Beliefs, Bad Decisions, and Hurtful Acts* (New York: Harcourt, Inc., 2007), 76–77.

distortion is even more likely."[14] Memory-dependent narratives are "notoriously subject to the aberrations of memory, the prejudices of the informant, the selective character of the reporting, and the subtle transformations that occur when a story is either resurrected from the depths of the past or recalled repeatedly over time."[15]

Any responsible attempt to recover the murky beginnings of LDS plural marriage practice must exhibit an awareness of the pitfalls of that reconstruction. The contemporary documentation—except, ironically, that denying that Joseph Smith and others practiced polygamy—is virtually absent. The later reminiscences come primarily from well-intended church members who affirmed their belief in Smith as a latter-day prophet of God and who embraced the controversial practice as revealed from heaven. Their personal identities were so tied to their belief in, defense of, and participation in Smith's transgressive teaching that it is difficult to know where factual truth ends and well-meaning, albeit confabulated, self-justification begins. I am not asserting that the women and men who created the documentation upon which the reconstruction of early Mormon polygamy depends knowingly misrepresented some or most of the specific details of the practice, including their involvement. There is, in fact, reason to assume that they believed genuinely in the historical accuracy of their record. But we today risk error to conclude, absent corroborative documentation, that their remembered narratives are, in every detail, entirely accurate and reliable.

Despite such potential problems, reminiscent accounts can provide insight into the narrators' own experiences, subjective and otherwise, with Smith's teaching, including some of the general and possibly generalizable reactions to the doctrine that the church's essay itself cites. Our primary concern should be the specific historical details the reminiscences contain, including, but not limited to, direct and indirect (as well as paraphrased and summarized) quotations attributed to Smith and others, precise dates for Smith's and others' plural marriages, and specific actions

---

14. Ibid., 79.
15. Douglas L. Wilson, *Honor's Voice: The Transformations of Abraham Lincoln* (New York: Alfred A. Knopf, 1998), 6; courtesy Ronald O. Barney.

and behaviors of Smith and others that more accurately reflect later historical contexts and later interpretations of Smith's doctrine. It is with these kinds of specific factual details that all must exercise special caution.

———

In reconstructing the early years of Joseph Smith's practice of plural marriage, the church's essay would enjoy greater credibility, I believe, if its author(s) had reflected more skepticism regarding the sources and arguments. The essay does not sufficiently take into account the weaknesses of the documentary evidence, but instead exhibits a disposition to accept as reliable statements supportive of Smith while rejecting sources critical—as the essay reads them—of the Mormon prophet. The essay privileges later recollections over earlier statements—again, when the later statements may be read more positively of Smith. For example, in positing that Smith told "associates that an angel appeared to him three times between 1834 and 1842 and commanded him to proceed with plural marriage when he hesitated to move forward," the essay relies on sources dating from 1853 to 1905 obtained from practicing LDS polygamists committed to the celestial principle and to the church.[16] The essay does not reflect an awareness of the reasons why such reminiscent testimony may be compromised and/or tainted but accepts the assertions as historical fact.[17]

The essay also privileges later, defensive sources in treating the Smith/Alger relationship. The essay cites sources for an early plural marriage that date from "decades later" (actually five to six decades later). In fact, the more contemporaneous the account of Smith and Alger, the more their relationship is described in the

---

16. The essay references Brian C. Hales, "Encouraging Joseph Smith to Practice Plural Marriage: The Accounts of the Angel with a Drawn Sword," *Mormon Historical Studies* 11, 2 (Fall 2010): 69–70.

17. Hales identifies eleven individuals as giving statements regarding Smith's mention of an angel with a drawn sword. Actually, only two people—Lorenzo Snow and Mary Elizabeth Rollins Lightner—left first-hand statements of such conversations with Smith. The remainder are second- or third-hand or hearsay statements. It is possible, of course, that Snow and Lightner may have influenced one another's recall of events.

sources as an extramarital affair.[18] The essay's dependence on later sources, which support the idea of a proto-plural marriage, speaks to an interpretive stance that minimizes evidence portraying the Smith-Alger relationship as extra-martial. (I am not suggesting that earlier sources are always more accurate, simply that one should not dismiss sources without sufficient reason.)

A third example of the essay's preference for later readings—one that functions to discount Smith's sexual relations with already civilly married plural wives—is the distinction it makes between eternity-only marriage sealings and time-and-eternity marriage sealings. In defining eternity-only sealings and time-and-eternity sealings as its does, the essay displays a presentist understanding of marriage sealings that may or may not accurately reflect Smith's own understanding of the terms. The scant contemporary lexical record is unclear if Smith and his associates so carefully differenti-ated between the two terms as the church's essay does. When Zina Diantha Huntington Jacobs Smith Young—married sequentially to both Smith and Brigham Young (1801–77)—was questioned in 1898 about her plural marriage to Smith, which had report-edly occurred almost sixty years earlier, she did not dispute the assertion that she had married Smith for "time and eternity."[19] In another autobiographical statement, Huntington implied a sexual component in her plural marriage to Smith: "I mad[e] a greater sacrifise than to give my li[f]e for I never anticipated a again to be looked uppon as an honerable woman by those I dearly loved."[20]

The essay's use of eternity-only sealings and time-and-eternity sealings is intentional: to defuse charges that Smith committed adultery when he married already civilly married women since such eternity-only plural marriages were intended to take effect

---

18. See the first four statements, dated 1838–42, in Brian C. Hales, *Joseph Smith's Polygamy, Volume 1: History* (Salt Lake City: Greg Kofford Books, 2013), 94, "Ta-ble 4.1. Historical Accounts Referring to a Relationship Between Joseph Smith and Fanny Alger."

19. See "Evidence from Zina D. Huntington-Young," in *Saints' Herald* 52, 2 (Jan. 11, 1905): 28–30. Of course, it is possible that Huntington, at the time in her late seventies, was confused and did not fully grasp any distinctions.

20. Zina D. H. Young, Autobiography, n.d., in Zina Card Brown Family Collec-tion, Church History Library, Church of Jesus Christ of Latter-day Saints, Salt Lake City; hereafter CHL.

only after death when, presumably, all civil marriages had been dissolved. (In Smith's theology, marriages survived death only if performed with his church's priesthood authority.) The essay relies on previously published arguments that the absence of any explicit documentary reference to Smith's having been sexually active with his already civilly married wives must be read to mean that such activity, in these cases, at least, did not occur.[21] Yet, given the general reticence in the nineteenth century to discuss sexual matters publicly,[22] it is not surprising that the documentary sources for such transgressive marital arrangements should be non-existent. There is, of course, another explanation for Smith's decision to marry already married women: to conceal the paternity of any children resulting from these polyandrous-type plural marriages.[23]

Another presentist reading of the sources concerns the essay's assertion that the Old Testament patriarch Elijah appeared to Smith and a colleague in 1836 and "restored [to Smith] the priesthood keys necessary to perform ordinances for the living and the dead, including sealing families together." Only marriages sealed by this restored priesthood authority were sanctioned by God and, the essay contends, "meant that the procreation of children and perpetuation of families would continue into the eternities." Yet the contemporary evidence linking Elijah's reported appearance to the restoration of special priesthood sealing authority is lacking. LDS scholars Gregory A. Prince and Charles R. Harrell have

---

21. This is Brian C. Hales's contention in his *Joseph Smith's Polygamy, Volume 1*, chaps. 11–16.

22. See Jan Marsh, "Sex & Sexuality in the 19th Century," Victoria and Albert Museum, ww.vam.ac.uk/content/articles/s/sex-and-sexuality-19th-century; accessed Feb. 6, 2016. Sexual conduct was not the only subject for which documentation is virtually absent. Consider other intimate matters—for instance, personal hygiene. Yet one would not conclude that such private activities never occurred.

23. It is especially telling that one of Smith's married wives apparently believed that Smith had fathered one of her children. Later DNA testing proved that the child had been fathered by the woman's civil husband. That the mother believed that Smith was the biological father would suggest that she had engaged in sexual relations with Smith while still married to her civil husband. For this particular case, see Todd Compton, *In Sacred Loneliness: The Plural Wives of Joseph Smith* (Salt Lake City: Signature Books, 1997), 183–84; and Ugo A. Perego et al., "Resolving a 150-Year-Old Paternity Case in Mormon History Using DTC Autosomal DNA Testing of Distant Relatives," *FSI Genetics* 42 (Sept. 2019): 1–7.

each independently documented that Smith's understanding of any relationship between Elijah and the performance of various priesthood ordinances, including sealings, evolved gradually ex post facto and never developed as clearly or as fulsomely as later LDS teaching suggests.[24] The essay thus presents an understanding of LDS doctrine that is absent in the earliest sources.

Finally, the essay does not reference some of the most important scholarship on the history of Mormon polygamy. Frankly, I find it difficult to read this omission as anything other than deliberate given that the essay refers explicitly to "the contributions of scholars to the historical content presented in this article." Not mentioned are Martha Bradley and Mary Woodward's *Four Zinas: A Story of Mothers and Daughters on the Mormon Frontier* (2000), an award-winning study of women and polygamy; Lawrence Foster's *Religion and Sexuality: The Shakers, the Mormons, and the Oneida Community* (1981), an early important work by an eminent non-LDS historian; and George D. Smith's *Nauvoo Polygamy: "... But We Called It Celestial Marriage"* (2008; 2nd ed. 2011), a work noteworthy for its statistical and genealogical data. Even Todd M. Compton's multiple award-winning study of the beginnings of LDS polygamy, *In Sacred Loneliness: The Plural Wives of Joseph Smith* (1997), merits only one mention.[25] (The omission of George Smith's book is particularly egregious since Smith was the first scholar to calculate the number of men and women involved in plural marriage by the time the church reached the Salt Lake Valley in mid-1847. Instead, the essay, at note 20, ignores Smith's pioneering study and instead cites a later author's work to document the number.)

By contrast, the essay most frequently cites researcher Brian C. Hales, who aided in the preparation of the essay and whose own

---

24. See Prince, *Power from On High: The Development of Mormon Priesthood* (Salt Lake City: Signature Books, 1995), 35–45; and Harrell, *"This Is My Doctrine": The Development of Mormon Theology* (Salt Lake City: Greg Kofford Books, 2011), 75–78. See also William Victor Smith, *Textual Studies of the Doctrine and Covenants: The Plural Marriage Revelation* (Salt Lake City: Greg Kofford Books, 2018), 44.

25. In the interests of full disclosure, Bradley/Woodward's, Compton's, and Smith's books were all published by Signature Books (Salt Lake City), where I was employed as managing director from 1985 to 2000.

work is referenced eight times. (The next most frequently cred-ited author is Assistant LDS Church Historian Andrew Jenson [1850–1941], cited four times.)[26] Hales is the author (assisted by Don Bradley) of an important three-volume study of the begin-nings of Mormon plural marriage, *Joseph Smith's Polygamy, Volume 1: History, Volume 2: History,* and *Volume 3: Theology,* published in 2013. Hales's study is informed by a commitment to scholarship as well as by a personal testimony of the divinity of Joseph Smith's prophethood.[27] Hales's faith-driven conclusions—especially re-garding an angel with a drawn sword, time-and-eternity versus eternity-only sealings, and Smith's sexless, eternity-only marriages to already civilly married women—bolster the essay's defense of Smith as a reluctant polygamist, which is also Hales's assertion. My concern here is not so much with Hales's work, however much one may agree or disagree with his interpretations,[28] as it is with the essay's tethering itself so tightly to the arguments and conclusions of only one scholar when the insightful work of other scholars is just as, if not more, persuasive. The essay, given its stated appeals to scholarship, owes readers a more grounded, catholic appreciation of the breadth of the relevant scholarship, or, at a minimum, a more honest explanation of its preferences.

The argument that Joseph Smith was a reluctant polygamist downplays Smith's *joie de vivre* and charismatic allure—he was, after all, thirty-five years old in 1841. It imposes on him a brand of morality that was foreign to him and ignores the ramifications of his own and others' perception of him as heaven's lawgiver. "That which is wrong under one circumstance, may be, and often is,

26. See Brian and Laura Hales, "005," interview by Brent Lee Metcalfe, www.mormonstudiespodcast.com; accessed Dec. 5, 2015. Hales briefly details his involve-ment in the essay beginning at about the six-minute mark.

27. In explaining his reasons for researching Smith and polygamy, Hales wrote in 2007 that he intended to "DEFEND THE PROPHET (WITH DOCUMENTATION)" ("Re-quest for Copying Services," signed by Hales and dated Nov. 12, 2007, emphasis in original, available at www.mormonpolygamydocuments.org; retrieved Dec. 6, 2014). See also Hales's statement of his personal witness of Smith at www.mormonscholars-testify.org/793/brian-c-hales.

28. See Bergera, Review of Brian C. Hales, *Joseph Smith's Polygamy, 3 Vols.,* in *John Whitmer Historical Association Journal* 33, 2 (Fall/Winter 2013): 188–97; and Hales's rejoinder, "Stretching to Find the Negative: Gary Bergera's Review of Joseph Smith's Polygamy: History and Theology," at www.mormoninterpreter.com.

right under another," Smith reportedly taught of plural marriage, and elsewhere elaborated that there are "many things in the Bible which do not, as they now stand, accord with the revelation of the Holy Ghost to me."[29] "When brother Joseph Smith lived," one of his followers stated, "he was our dictator in the things of God, and it was for us to listen to him, and do just as he told us."[30] "[I]f he [Smith] taught any thing[,] I believed it was the truth or he would not teach it," a second adherent said.[31] Smith was "too wise to err and too good to be unkind," a third commented.[32] "It was not my prerogative to call [Smith] in question," a fourth added, "with regard to any act of his life. He was God's servant, and not mine. He did not belong to the people but to the Lord, and was doing the work of the Lord, and if He should suffer him to lead the people astray, it would be because they ought to be led astray."[33] While such statements may be discomfitting to modern sensibilities, they evince a devotion that helps to explain Smith's power to persuade and convince.

Smith may have been a man possessed of intense spirituality and craving for contact with the divine. But he was also a man of singular intellect, passion, and appetite. Excitement powered his existence.[34] Friendship and family formed the bedrock of his idealized celestial social order. Love and sex, or, as he termed, "reproduction," occupied an integral place in his plural marriage teaching.[35] "[T]hat same sociality which exists among us here,"

29. Joseph Smith et al., *History of the Church of Jesus Christ of Latter-day Saints. Period I. History of Joseph Smith, the Prophet by Himself* (Salt Lake City: Deseret Book Co., 1980), 5:134; and Andrew F. Ehat and Lyndon W. Cooks, eds., *The Words of Joseph Smith: The Contemporary Accounts of the Nauvoo Discourses of the Prophet Joseph* (Provo, Utah: Brigham Young University Religious Studies Center, 1980), 211.

30. Heber C. Kimball, in *Journal of Discourses*, 26 vols. (Liverpool, England: Latter-day Saints Book Depot, 1855–86), 2:106.

31. Bathsheba W. Smith, in Temple Lot Case, Respondent's Testimony, page 320 Q-621, Library-Archives, Community of Christ, Independence, Missouri.

32. Mercy Fielding Thompson Smith, Untitled autobiographical sketch, Dec. 20, 1880, CHL.

33. Brigham Young, in *Journal of Discourses*, 4:297–98.

34. See Susan Staker, "Waiting for World's End: Wilford Woodruff and David Koresh," *Sunstone*, Dec. 1993, 12–13; reference courtesy of Joseph Geisner.

35. "It is naive to divorce Joseph Smith from physical desire," writes a recent historian of early Mormon polygamy (Smith, *Textual Studies of the Doctrine and Covenants*, 11n31).

Smith taught, "will exist among us there [i.e., in heaven], only it will be coupled with eternal glory, which glory we do not now enjoy" (D&C 130:2). His 1843 revelation stated explicitly that plural wives "are given unto him [i.e., the husband] to multiply and replenish the earth" (D&C 132:63). In fact, according to the brother of one of his plural wives, Smith believed that one's "Dominion & powr in the great Future would be Comensurate with the no [number] of 'Wives childin & Friends' that we inheret here."[36] As his male followers recalled, Smith taught that plural marriage "was a privilege with blessings."[37] It seems clear that Smith intended that plural marriage provide sexual intimacy and facilitate the production of offspring.[38] While there may be other aspects as well to Smith's teachings, the affectional/erotic component should not be minimized. To do so, I believe, misrepresents Smith's practice.

My unsolicited advice to the author(s) of the Gospel Topics essay on Joseph Smith and LDS plural marriage? Do not be afraid to acknowledge the problematic nature of the primary sources, especially when memory-dependent reminiscences form the foundation of your work. Be skeptical of the details such sources contain, including precise dates, direct and summarized quotations attributed to Smith and to others, interpretations of doctrine that cannot be supported by contemporary documents, recitals of events that sound too good and/or too convenient to be true, especially when they cannot be independently corroborated. Be aware of your own presentist and other biases—if you cannot set them aside, admit them to readers. Be cautious, avoid making definitive-sounding conclusions. Invite pre-publication comment from a variety of scholars, not simply those who share your own inclinations.

Finally, a positive note: The church is to be complimented for its willingness to tackle especially problematic aspects of its past, for its

---

36. In Dean R. Zimmerman, ed., *I Knew the Prophets: an Analysis of the Letter of Benjamin F. Johnson to George F. Gibbs, Reporting Doctrinal Views of Joseph Smith and Brigham Young* (Salt Lake City: Horizon, 1976), 47.

37. Sarah M. Kimball, qtd. in Augusta J. Crocheron, comp., *Representative Women of Deseret: A Book of Biographical Sketches, to Accompany the Picture Bearing the Same Title* (Salt Lake City: J. C. Graham & Co., 1884), 26. See also George A. Smith, Letter to Joseph Smith III, Oct. 9, 1869, copy in CHL; original in Archives, Community of Christ.

38. "Reproduction seems to be the primary purpose behind polygamy," agrees William Victor Smith (*Textual Studies of the Doctrine and Covenants*, 156).

support and encouragement of scholarship, for its engagement with the primary sources, and for making the results of its research widely available knowing the kinds of discussion and debate such research will generate. While much remains to do in narrating as accurately as possible the tortuous history of the beginnings of Mormon polygamy, the Gospel Topics essay represents a step forward.

8. REMEMBERING, FORGETTING, AND RE-REMEMBERING
NINETEENTH-CENTURY LDS PLURAL MARRIAGE

George D. Smith

"The past is never dead. It's not even past."
—William Faulkner, *Requiem for a Nun* (1951), Act 1, Scene 3.

On December 17, 2013, the LDS Church-produced essay "Plural Marriage and Families in Early Utah" appeared on-line as part of the church's new Gospel Topics outreach series.[1] According to this officially sanctioned anonymous essay: "The Bible and the Book of Mormon teach that the marriage of one man to one woman is God's standard, except at specific periods when He [God] has declared otherwise" to a living LDS Church prophet.[2]

The church posted its "Plural Marriage and Families in Early Utah" just days after a federal judge declared unconstitutional a key portion of Utah's long-standing anti-polygamy law. The original case was brought before U.S. District Court Judge Clark Waddoups by practicing polygamist Kody Brown, who along with his four wives had been featured on the television reality series *Sister Wives*. Waddoups threw out the law's section prohibiting "cohabitation," declaring that it violated constitutional guarantees of due process and religious freedom. The precise relationship between these two events is unclear. One news report characterized LDS Church reaction to the ruling as "muted." It further suggested a direct link between the court's ruling and the church's official

---

1. At www.lds.org/topics/plural-marriage-and-families-in-early-utah?lang=eng& old=true. Links to the church's other polygamy-related essays are at www.lds.org/topics/ plural-marriage-in-the-church-of-jesus-christ-of-latter-day-saints?lang=eng&old=true.

2. Published in 1830, the Book of Mormon prohibits polygamy unless "the Lord [to] raise up seed ... will command [his] people" presumably thru a prophet (Jacob 2:27, 30).

statement, albeit in a jocular fashion, stating: "the Church-owned *Deseret News* pointed readers to a new document which restated that while Mormon polygamy had been instituted for a time, it was now forbidden, so don't get any ideas."[3]

Following the posting of "Plural Marriage and Families in Early Utah," *New York Times* op-ed journalist Timothy Egan described once visiting nineteenth-century LDS leader Brigham Young's winter home in St. George, Utah, where he asked a docent the obvious question: "Where did the other women sleep?" Egan noted the tour guide's blush; it was obvious that the question embarrassed her. Many devout members of the LDS Church had not known that plural marriage was an important part of the church's history. The practice of plural marriage, if not hidden, had been in the shadows for many years. Egan explained that he was simply curious about the "conjugal timing of the man who was married to 55 women," and was not trying to probe into the "sexual acrobatics of the great pioneer." Considering it ironic that "it took the Mormon church more than a century to acknowledge what scholars have long known to be true," Egan concluded on a more positive note that "the Mormon Church has done a fine thing in opening up about its past."[4]

What did the church's 2013 announcement mean? Were official historians speaking on-line through the press to a community of followers unaware of their own past, oblivious to practices which had defined them and for which nineteenth century LDS pioneers had been branded as outlaws and deviants?

When the Latter-day Saints migrated westward from Nauvoo, Illinois, to the Great Salt Lake Valley, they collected polygamy-related primary documents intended to cement their communal memory. They also sought to counter allegations from the recently formed Reorganized Church of Jesus Christ of Latter Day Saints (now Community of Christ) that plural marriage did not originate

---

3. Jeremy Lott, "Will Mormons Bring Back Polygamy?" *Real Clear Religion*, Dec. 20, 2013, at www.realclearreligion.org/printpage/?url=http://www.realclearreligion.org/org.

4. At www.nytimes.com/2014/11/30/opinion/sunday/timothy-egan-sex-and-the-saints.html.

with founder Joseph Smith (1805–44) but was the innovation of Brigham Young (1801–77).

Yet, until the Saints were secure in their new home in the Mountain West, the marriage practice that had brought civil disruption in Nauvoo went largely unspoken.

———

Following at least a decade of polygamy practiced mostly in secret, the LDS Church in 1852 publicly announced the practice and in 1876 included the revelation as Doctrine and Covenants Section 132. But Mormon settlers also wanted to have Utah admitted to the United States. In 1856 Republican politicians linked polygamy and slavery in their platform as "twin relics of barbarism." Beginning in the late 1860s, both the US government and LDS leaders collected affidavits and other documentary materials concerning plural marriage, which had become the primary issue that caused the United States to be in opposition to the Mormons, and delayed Utah statehood. Meanwhile, California received statehood in 1850, Nevada in 1864, Colorado in 1876, Montana in 1889, Wyoming and Idaho in 1890. The territory of "Deseret" (to be renamed Utah and materially shrunk in size) had to wait until January 4, 1896, to become a state.

Pressure against plural marriage had increased when federal laws (initiated by the Morrill Anti-Bigamy Act of 1862) and the courts (notably in the *Reynolds v. United States* decision of 1878) lined up against the practice, and put the opposing parties on notice to reach a solution. LDS President Brigham Young married some fifty-eight women, supporting (more or less) twenty-seven families and participating in at least thirty-one afterlife sealings. Young reasoned that plural marriage was, in part, a moral alternative to prostitution.[5] He declared that plural marriage protected women who would otherwise be single and would have no proper means of financial support.

But the United States did not see it that way. In order to

---

5. See Brigham Young, *Journal of Discourses*, 26 vols. (London, England: Latter-day Saints' Book Depot, 1855–86), 11:128. See also John G. Turner, *Brigham Young: Pioneer Prophet* (Cambridge, Massachusetts: Harvard University Press, 2012).

settle the dispute, after Young's death his later successor as church president, prophet, apostle, and revelator, Wilford Woodruff (1807–98) traveled to San Francisco to negotiate a deal with the U.S. government. In 1889, Woodruff eventually agreed with Senator Leland Stanford and others to end the practice of plural marriage. For its part, the United States backed away from threats to disincorporate the church and seize its assets. Returning to Salt Lake City to announce the decision at the church's worldwide fall 1890 general conference, Woodruff formalized the decision by issuing a proclamation, or "manifesto," on September 24, 1890, to end Mormon polygamy.

The energy generated in ending plural marriage fueled some hundred years of institutional suppression of both the practice and its memory. This century of officially forgetting the church's history of plural marriage began in the late 1800s, as church officials pursued statehood established their "American" bona fides. Both processes—remembering their past with pride, then suppressing both the practice and memory of polygamy in the early LDS Church—took place simultaneously as the Saints attempted to accommodate and conform to the marriage laws considered moral by the rest of the country.[6] First-person accounts of plural marriage gradually diminished from common view. LDS manuals erased most mention of plural wives, and church colleges and universities discouraged research on the subject.[7]

The following table shows that in LDS semi-annual worldwide general conference addresses, mention of "plural marriage" and "polygamy" significantly decreased after the 1890s.

---

6. See Thomas G. Alexander, *Mormonism in Transition: A History of the Latter-day Saints, 1890–1930* (Urbana: University of Illinois Press, 1986).

7. In 1973, LDS Church Archivist Earl E. Olson specifically identified "plural marriage" as a topic to be restricted for research. Earl E. Olson, statement dated Jan. 30, 1973, photocopy in my possession. See also Newell G. Bringhurst, "Where Have All of Brigham Young's Wives Gone?: Latter-day Saint Ambivalence over Its Polygamous Past," in Newell G. Bringhurst and Craig L. Foster, eds., *The Persistence of Polygamy: From Joseph Smith's Martyrdom to the First Manifesto, 1844–1890* (Independence, Missouri: John Whitmer Books, 2013), 87–112; and Gary James Bergera and Ronald Priddis, *Brigham Young University: A House of Faith* (Salt Lake City: Signature Books, 1985), 72–74.

Mention of "Polygamy" and "Plural Marriage"
in LDS General Conference Talks, 1850s-2010s

Year	1850s–90	1900s–2010s
Occurrence	528	97

Decade of Most Frequent Occurrence: 1880s = 221 (35% of all occurrences).[8]

In the mid-twentieth century, however, three meticulous researchers with LDS backgrounds embarked upon a process of rediscovery: Stanley Snow Ivins (1891–1967), Dale Morgan (1914–71), and Fawn McKay Brodie (1915–81).[9] The niece of LDS Church President David O. McKay (1951–70), Fawn Brodie gained limited access to church archival records. Morgan, great grandson of LDS apostle Orson Pratt, in 1954 became a scholar at the Bancroft Library, University of California, Berkeley. Ivins, whose father had been a top-ranking LDS official, Apostle Anthony W. Ivins (who helped colonize New Mexico, Arizona, and developed Colonia Juarez, the first stake in Mexico), began his own archival quest in the 1930s.

Brodie published the results of her research in 1945 as the trail-blazing *No Man Knows My History: The Life of Joseph Smith*.[10] Ivins released his pioneering work on polygamy in 1956.[11] Morgan's efforts tended to center on western history more broadly, though his

---

8. Derived from *Corpus of LDS General Conference Talks, 1851–2010* (www.lds-general-conference.org).

9. In addition, in a church immersed in genealogy and family history, many LDS descendants even knew from which plural wives they descended. When church lesson manuals identified only the first wife, these edited portrayals were critiqued—albeit it quietly—by those familiar with their own family's history.

10. It was for this book that Brodie was awarded an Alfred A. Knopf Fellowship in Biography and which Bernard de Voto reviewed in the *New York Herald Tribune* as: "not only the first honest and intelligent biography of Joseph Smith, it is also the first history of the early Mormon church that, because of its general excellence can be held to rigorous standards throughout … in a class by itself" (*New York Herald Tribune*, Dec. 16, 1945). The *New York Times* echoed: "a master job of thorough research" (*New York Times Book Review*, Nov. 25, 1945). A second edition of Brodie's biography appeared in 1971.

11. See his "Notes on Mormon Polygamy," *Western Humanities Review* 10, 3 (Summer 1956): 229–39.

important contribution to LDS history appeared posthumously.[12] The work of each historian helped to break the wall of secrecy that had tended to separate most Mormons from their polygamous past.[13]

Other historians, offering a variety of interpretations, followed Brodie, Morgan, and Ivins. These included, in chronological order, Danel Bachman,[14] Lawrence Foster,[15] Linda King Newell and Valeen Tippets Avery,[16] D. Michael Quinn,[17] Richard S. Van Wagoner,[18] B. Carmon Hardy,[19] Todd Compton,[20] Martha Sonntag Bradley,[21] Kathryn M. Daynes,[22] Richard Lyman Bushman,[23] George D. Smith,[24] Brian C. Hales,[25] and Laurel Thatcher Ulrich,[26] among others.

---

12. See *Dale Morgan on Early Mormonism: Correspondence and a New History,* ed. John Phillip Walker (Salt Lake City: Signature Books, 1986).

13. Ivins was a first cousin once-removed of Heber J. Grant (1856–1945), the last LDS Church president to have practiced polygamy. Ironically, Grant's mother, Rachel Ridgway Ivins (1821–1909), had rebuffed Joseph Smith's plural marriage proposals, reportedly stating that she would "sooner go to hell as a virtuous woman than to heaven as a whore" (qtd. in Heber J. Grant, Letter to Ray O. Wyland, Dec. 12, 1936, Church History Library, Church of Jesus Christ of Latter-day Saints, Salt Lake City). A decade later, however, Rachel did marry the deceased Joseph Smith by proxy for "eternity" and at the same time became the seventh wife for "time only" of LDS official Jedediah Grant. Heber was Rachel's only child.

14. "A Study of the Mormon Practice of Plural Marriage before the Death of Joseph Smith," MA thesis, Purdue University, 1975.

15. *Religion and Sexuality: Three American Communal Experiments of the Nineteenth Century* (New York: Oxford University Press, 1981).

16. *Mormon Enigma: Emma Hale Smith, Prophet's Wife, "Elect Lady," Polygamy's Foe, 1804–1879* (Garden City, New York: Doubleday, 1984).

17. "LDS Church Authority and New Plural Marriages, 1890–1904," *Dialogue: A Journal of Mormon Thought* 18 (Spring 1985): 9–105.

18. *Mormon Polygamy: A History* (Salt Lake City: Signature Books, 1986).

19. *Solemn Covenant: The Mormon Polygamous Passage* (Urbana: University of Illinois Press, 1992).

20. *In Sacred Loneliness: The Plural Wives of Joseph Smith* (Salt Lake City: Signature Books, 1998).

21. *Four Zinas: A Story of Mothers and Daughters on the Mormon Frontier* (Salt Lake City: Signature Books/Smith Research Associates, 2000); with Mary Brown Firmage Woodward.

22. *More Wives Than One: Transformation of the Mormon Marriage System, 1840–1910* (Urbana: University of Illinois Press, 2001).

23. *Joseph Smith: Rough Stone Rolling* (New York: Alfred A. Knopf, 2005); assisted by Jed Woodworth.

24. *Nauvoo Polygamy: "… But We Called It Celestial Marriage"* (Salt Lake City: Signature Books, 2008; 2nd ed. 2011).

25. *Joseph Smith's Polygamy, Volume 1: History, Volume 2: History,* and *Volume 3: Theology* (Salt Lake City: Greg Kofford Books, 2013).

26. *A House Full of Females: Plural Marriage and Women's Rights in Early Mormonism,*

In later 2013, after more than a half-century of information about the church's practice of plural marriage had appeared in various academic publications, the LDS Church publicly acknowledged that plural marriage had been practiced beginning in the early 1840s (if not earlier), and that those marriages had been kept underground by multiple levels of subterfuge. Now, in the twenty-first century, the LDS Church brought its rich history of plural marriage out of the closet.[27]

The idea of plural marriage was introduced in 1830, practiced secretly in the early 1840s, and a decade later, in 1852, was publicly announced. Twenty-four years later, in 1876, plural marriage was canonized as LDS Doctrine and Covenants 132. Just fourteen years after that, in 1890, polygamy was ended by "manifesto." The historical reality was then suppressed for over a century, but was gradually re-introduced by dedicated historians. In December 2013 the practice of plural marriage was officially admitted in some detail by an LDS Gospel Topics on-line historical essay. Thus, from the perspective of 2013 the arc of documenting a memory, suppressing that memory, and collective rediscovery had come full circle.

The LDS Church's essay on "Plural Marriage and Families in Early Utah" walked a tightrope in reflecting, on the one hand, belief in the church's doctrines and prophetic reliability of its nineteenth-century officials—sustained by church members as living prophets—and, on the other hand, a commitment to scholarly-oriented analysis and discourse. In walking this tightrope, the essay articulated several statements that merit our attention.

The essay stated that LDS plural marriage "shaped 19th-century Mormon society in other ways: marriage became available to virtually all who desired it; per-capita inequality of wealth was

---

1835–1870 (New York: Alfred A. Knopf, 2017). Additional recent book-length studies of LDS plural marriage include Christine Talbot, *A Foreign Kingdom: Mormons and Polygamy in American Political Culture, 1852–1890* (Urbana: University of Illinois Press, 2013), and Paula Kelly Harline, *The Polygamous Wives Writing Club: From the Diaries of Mormon Pioneer Women* (New York: Oxford University Press, 2014).

27. Despite the historical progress, LDS President Gordon B. Hinckley (1910–2008) in 1998 seemingly dismissed plural marriage as "This is not us" (qtd. in "On the Record: 'We Stand for Something,'" *Sunstone,* Dec. 1998, 70–72). Sixteen years later, the 2013 Gospel Topics essay officially opened up community awareness of the history and extent of nineteenth-century plural marriage practices.

diminished as economically disadvantaged women married into more financially stable households; ethnic intermarriages were increased, which helped to unite a diverse immigrant population." While the essay provided notes in support of the latter two points (including one to an unpublished paper, making it difficult to evaluate the claim), it did not offer precise data, leaving readers to wonder about the actual significance of these assertions. Some readers may also wonder about the essay's unqualified use of the term "ethnic," which implied a broader diversity of church members and converts than was actually the case during the mid- and later decades of the nineteenth century.

The essay asserted that "there was much love, tenderness, and affection within many plural marriages," but, at the same time, alleged that "the practice was generally based more on religious belief than on romantic love." The essay provided, at this point, a reference to one plural couple's experiences, ostensibly implying that such an example might be generalized across other such marriages. Yet the essay also pointed out, correctly, I believe, that where plural families lived geographically—Nauvoo in the 1840s, then Salt Lake City—"made a difference in how plural marriage was experienced, publicly acknowledged vs. unannounced. It is therefore difficult to accurately generalize about the experience of all plural marriages." Despite this caution, the essay occasionally risked doing precisely what it sought to avoid; it cast plural marriage in a generally positive light, making its judgments about a practice in the early LDS Church that twenty-first-century members lacked evidence to understand or evaluate either positively or negatively.

The essay stressed that while "church leaders viewed plural marriage as a command to the church generally," they "recogniz[ed] that individuals who did not enter the practice could still stand approved of God." In this instance, the essay might be read as misstating, if not misrepresenting, the actual position of the nineteenth-century church and its leadership on the central place of plural marriage in its theology and practice. In fact, belief in and practice of plural marriage was, according to the highest-ranking LDS Church officials, the central, defining tenet of church doctrine. The practice of plural marriage was the *sine qua non* of full membership in the nineteenth-century LDS Church.

The following four representative statements from LDS officials made clear the status plural marriage occupied in the church during the years 1852 to 1890:

> Now if any of you will deny the plurality of wives, and continue to do so, I promise that you will be damned.
> —Brigham Young, 1855[28]

> Where did this commandment come from in relation to polygamy? It also came from God ... and was made binding upon His servants. When this system was first introduced among this people, it was one of the greatest crosses that ever was taken up by any set of men since the world stood. ... When this commandment was given, it was so far religious, and so far binding upon the Elders of this Church, that it was told them if they were not prepared to enter into it, and to stem the torrent of opposition that would come in consequence of it, the keys of the kingdom would be taken from them. When I see any of our people, men or women, opposing a principle of this kind, I have years ago set them down as on the high road to apostasy, and I do to-day; I consider them apostates, and not interested in this church and kingdom.
> —John Taylor (LDS apostle and later church president/prophet), 1866[29]

> The only men who become Gods, even the Sons of God, are those who enter into polygamy. Others attain unto a glory and may even be permitted to come into the presence of the Father and the Son; but they cannot reign as kings in glory, because they had blessings offered unto them, and they refused to accept them.
> —Brigham Young, 1866[30]

> Some people have supposed that the doctrine of plural marriage was a sort of superfluity, or non-essential, to the salvation or exaltation of mankind. ... I want here to enter my solemn protest against this idea, for I know it is false. ... The marriage of one woman to a man for time and eternity by the sealing power, according to the will of God, is a fulfillment of the celestial law of marriage in part—and is good so

---

28. *Journal of Discourses*, 3:266, July 14, 1855.
29. Ibid., 11:221, Apr.7, 1866.
30. Ibid., 11: 269, Aug. 19, 1866.

far as it goes—and so far as a man abides these conditions of the law, he will receive his reward therefore, and this reward, or blessing, he could not obtain on any other grounds or conditions. But this is only the beginning of the law, not the whole of it. Therefore, whoever has imagined that he could obtain the fullness of the blessings pertaining to this celestial law, by complying with only a portion of its conditions, has deceived himself.

> —Joseph F. Smith (LDS apostle, counselor to the president, and later church president), 1878[31]

While church members—adult men and women—were not required as a condition of continuing membership to contract plural marriages, they had every reason to understand that, from the church's perspective, couples who chose to remain in monogamous marriages were not only less than fully committed to the church, they would not attain in the hereafter the greatest reward awaiting only those most obedient to church teachings: reigning forever as gods and goddesses over an endless, eternal progeny.

More practically, polygamists, during the mid- to late 1800s, occupied positions of special status and privilege in LDS culture that rendered them more likely than monogamists to rise to higher levels of leadership, visibility, and prestige.[32] The church's essay, in attempting to soften or mitigate the church's hardline nineteenth-century position regarding the centrality of plural marriage, may have left some readers with a mistaken, if not erroneous, understanding of polygamy's importance to the historical church.

Where the church's essay summarized the demographic work of scholars of nineteenth-century polygamy practices, it provided a valuable service in helping to separate fact from folklore. For example, the essay explained that while "some leaders had large polygamous families, two-thirds of polygamist men had only two

---

31. Ibid., 20:28–29, July 7, 1878.

32. Historian D. Michael Quinn notes: "From 1845 to 1888 only fourteen (31.8 percent of 44 appointees during that period) were monogamists at the time of their advance [in the church hierarchy]. As long as polygamy was the norm in headquarters culture, there was an obvious preference for polygamist general authorities ... polygamists were far more likely to be advanced to leadership, both general and local" (*The Mormon Hierarchy: Extensions of Power* [Salt Lake City: Signature Books/Smith Research Associates, 1997], 180).

wives at a time," and notes that divorce was available, permitted, and sometimes even encouraged.

Regarding what may be one of the more problematic aspects of nineteenth-century LDS polygamy—wives' ages at marriage—the church's essay appealed to historical context in ways that could be read as apologetic excuse for whatever happened as an inspired practice, as much a caution against presentist interpretations:

> [w]omen did marry at fairly young ages in the first decade of Utah settlement (age 16 or 17 or, infrequently, younger), which was typical of women living in frontier areas at the time. As in other places, women married at older ages as the society matured. Almost all women married, and so did a large percentage of men. In fact, it appears that a larger percentage of men in Utah married than elsewhere in the United States at the time. Probably half of those living in Utah Territory in 1857 experienced life in a polygamous family as a husband, wife, or child at some time during their lives. By 1870, 25 to 30 percent of the population lived in polygamous households, and it appears that the percentage continued to decrease over the next 20 years.[33]

Thus, the church's Gospel Topics essay attempted to normalize, or, at least, downplay, the practice of polygamy in nineteenth-century Utah. It asserted that polygamy was not—despite strong theological advocacy—the dominant form of marriage among the Latter-day Saints; that polygamy encouraged marriage; that, due to easily obtainable divorces, unhappy or abusive marriages were minimized; and that marriage at young ages for LDS women was not unusual for the period of time but, in fact, mirrored marriage patterns among developing societies generally.

Several of the above assertions deserve additional consideration as the controversies they address are sometimes more complicated and nuanced than the 2013 essay implied. Following an exhaustive analysis of nineteenth-century marriage pattern across the United States, historian Todd Compton found that "in nineteenth-century Utah, early marriage, including very early marriage, marriage at age 14 or 15, was common. There were fewer early marriages in Utah as time went on, but they were

---

33. "Plural Marriage and Families in Early Utah."

always more frequent than in the eastern American states."[34] Anthropologist William Volf noted, based on his review of the relevant literature, that "females related to the [general authorities] of the Mormon Church were married four and a half years earlier tha[n] those who are not related (18.44 vs. 22.83 years)."[35] The young marriage age in LDS polygamy was, Compton continued, "an accepted part of Mormon culture, and polygamy was an important factor that contributed to marriage at lower ages."[36] In fact, in Utah during the years 1867 to 1886, girls as young as twelve, with parental permission, could marry.[37]

As an example of nineteenth-century-LDS attitudes towards marriage age, Compton cited the case of LDS Church apostle Charles C. Rich (1809–83), who, at age thirty-seven, married a fourteen-year-old girl in 1847. Compton quoted Rich's biographer who wrote in 1936 that the girl was "a beautiful young woman, fully matured," and was "much sought after, both by married and by single men."[38] Later, as a high-ranking apostle, Rich told church members in 1871 that "it is just as natural for a girl to marry an old man, as it is to marry a young one; provided both parties have their agency and choice; and the girls would do better in many instances, to marry good and tried men, [even] if they were old, than to marry young, and thoughtless, boys, who would get drunk [at] every opportunity."[39]

I do not necessarily suggest that the Gospel Topics essay

34. "Early Marriage in the New England and Northeastern States, and in Mormon Polygamy: What Was the Norm?" in Newell G. Bringhurst and Craig L. Foster, eds., *The Persistence of Polygamy: Joseph Smith and the Origins of Mormon Polygamy* (Independence, Missouri: John Whitmer Books, 2010), 225.

35. "Mormon Polygamy in the Nineteenth Century: The Practice of 'The Principle' in Reality," *Nebraska Anthropologist,* Paper 126, 43, at www.digitalcommons.unl.edu/cgi/viewcontent.cgi?article=1125&context=nebanthro.

36. Compton, "Early Marriage in the New England and Northeastern States, and in Mormon Polygamy," 229.

37. See "Table: Table of Marriage Ages by State," in "Marriage in 1890 Utah: Very Normal," at www.somemormonstuff.com/marriage-in-1890-utah-very-normal.

38. Compton, "Early Marriage in the New England and Northeastern States, and in Mormon Polygamy," 226 and n62. Whatever the intent of Rich's biographer, such Lolita-esque descriptions of a young adolescent girl would probably cause most readers today to cringe.

39. Qtd. in John R. Patrick, "The School of the Prophets: Its Development and Influence in Utah Territory," MA thesis, Brigham Young University, June 1970, 118.

misrepresents the sources it cites in contextualizing the prevalence and parameters of polygamy in nineteen-century LDS society. However, de-emphasizing or deflecting some of the practice's more problematic aspects—at least, for today's readers—again risks misrepresenting the historical reality of the practice that was extremely important to Latter-day Saints before they were forced to give it up.

As it draws to a conclusion, the 2013 LDS essay noted that after the US Supreme Court declared anti-polygamy laws to be constitutional, the church and its members responded by "continuing to practice plural marriage and by attempting to avoid arrest" as public and private acts of "civil disobedience." Offending church members paid fines and submitted to incarceration, as well as "separated into different households" and/or "went into hiding under assumed names, particularly when [plural wives were] pregnant or after giving birth."[40] The essay's strategic use of the term "civil disobedience" seems calculated to bestow greater nobility upon members' actions at willfully engaging in unlawful activities than non-Latter-day Saints may have been inclined to grant (or than the LDS Church today might be so willing to afford).

During the decade of the 1880s, at the high point of the federal campaign against polygamy, LDS leaders adopted a strident tone—one absent in today's more public relations-conscious church—in their rhetoric of civil resistance. Consider, for example, the following two statements—the first, presented as a revelation from God; the second, as an authoritative declaration from the church's highest governing council, the three-member First Presidency:

> And I say again, woe unto that nation or house or people who seek to hinder my people from obeying the Patriarchal law of Abraham [i.e., plural marriage], which leadeth to Celestial Glory, which has been revealed unto my Saints through the mouth of my servant ..., for whosoever doeth these things shall be damned, saith the Lord of Hosts, and shall be broken up and wasted away from under heaven by the judgments which I have sent forth, and which shall not return unto me void.

---

40. "Plural Marriage and Families in Early Utah."

And thus, with the sword and by bloodshed, and with famine and plagues and earthquakes and the thunder of heaven and the vivid lightenings shall this nation and the nations of the earth be made to feel the chastening hand of an Almighty God until they are broken up and destroyed and wasted away from under heaven, and no power can stay my hand. Therefore, let the wicked tremble; let them that blaspheme my name hold their lips, for destruction will swiftly overtake them.

—Revelation to Wilford Woodruff (LDS apostle and later president), 1880[41]

... according to the latest rulings, a promise to obey the law signifies an agreement to violate the most solemn covenants of marital fidelity that mortals can make with each other and their God. It means the utter repudiation of loving wives and the separation either of the father and some of his children or of the mother and her children. It is a promise not to visit, go to the same place of worship or amusement, or recognize, associate with, or even call on when sick or dying, or when her child is sick or dying, the plural wife who has been faithful in all things. It means dishonor, treachery, cruelty and cowardice. It places, not the law but a gross and wicked perversion of the law, above the revealed will of God and the noblest promptings of the human heart. It is a promise that no true Latter-day Saints can make and that no humane being would demand.

— LDS First Presidency, Epistle to the Latter-day Saints, 1886[42]

The 1880s also saw ranking church leaders perform a special cursing ordinance after compiling a thirteen-page list of nearly 400 names of the church's enemies, including past and sitting US presidents Martin Van Buren, Ulysses S. Grant, Rutherford B. Hayes, and James Buchanan.[43] Five years later, in 1885, Church President John Taylor (1808–87) had himself ritually anointed as "King [and] Priest and Ruler over Israel on the Earth, over

---

41. At www.historyofmormonism.com/2010/03/29/woodruff-revelation.

42. In James R. Clark, ed., *Messages of the First Presidency of the Church of Jesus Christ of Latter-day Saints, 1833–1964* (Salt Lake City: Bookcraft, Inc., 1966), 3:79–80.

43. See "Names of Persons, To be held in Remembrance before the Lord, For their Evil Deeds, and who have raised their hands against the Lord's Anointed" (Title Page), reproduced in unpaginated photographs section in David John Buerger, *The Mysteries of Godliness: A History of Mormon Temple Worship* (San Francisco: Smith Research Associates, 1994, 2002).

Zion & the Kingdom under Christ, our King of Kings."[44] While Taylor's anointing as ruler, both temporal and spiritual, over the world was entirely symbolic, it nonetheless spoke to the frustration and impotence LDS leaders experienced in confronting the civil opposition they believed was Satan-inspired to deprive them of their constitutionally guaranteed right to practice their religion (plural marriage).

Despite the Latter-day Saints' best—if ultimately ineffectual—efforts to continue plural marriage as both doctrine and practice, the federal government prevailed, and, according to the 2013 essay, the 1890 "manifesto" banning polygamy "lifted the command to practice plural marriage." By this time, however, the essay continues, the church had begun to encourage its members not to immigrate to Utah but to remain in their home countries where "monogamous families became central to religious worship and learning. As the church grew and spread beyond the American West, the monogamous nuclear family was well suited to an increasingly mobile and dispersed membership." In addition, LDS polygamy had provided a "lineage [through which] have come many Latter-day Saints who have been faithful to their gospel covenants as righteous mothers and fathers, loyal disciples of Jesus Christ, and devoted church members, leaders, and missionaries." "[M]odern Latter-day Saints," the essay concludes, "honor and respect these [polygamous nineteenth-century] pioneers who gave so much for their faith, families, and community."[45]

By 2013 the ability to control an "official" narrative of the past had long since given way to the realities of an uncensored, transparent, free-for-all worldwide web of shared information. LDS leaders acknowledged as much when Steven E. Snow, at the time official Church Historian and Recorder, explained why the church had decided to issue the Gospel Topics series of historical essays, including those on plural marriage. There is "so much out there on the Internet," Snow said, "we felt we owed our members a safe place to get reliable, faith-promoting information that was true

---

44. In Jedediah S. Rogers, ed., *The Council of Fifty: A Documentary History* (Salt Lake City: Signature Books, 2014), 352.

45. "Plural Marriage and Families in Early Utah."

about some of these more difficult aspects of our history. ... We need to be truthful, and we need to understand our history."[46] Earlier, Snow had stated: "We try to tell the story as accurately as possible, and then we hope there will be those of faith who will step forward and add other insights. ... I think we need to be very careful that we are accurate, because if we aren't, it can come back to really haunt us. It's good to tell the truth."[47]

With an appreciation of the benefits of more honest approaches to its past, the LDS Church is to be commended for its willingness to confront directly the many difficulties of its advocacy and practice of polygamy during the nineteenth century. The church's 2013 Gospel Topics essay "Plural Marriage and Families in Early Utah" is evidence of a laudable institutional willingness to begin to address the challenges of a past that is more controversial and more interesting than many earlier church officials had us believe.

Appendix: Brief Chronology of Mormon Plural Marriage

Nineteenth century: Formulated, practiced, outlawed

1830   The Book of Mormon introduced polygamy as a prohibited practice, except as required by revelation.

1831   Joseph Smith Jr. reportedly instructed missionaries to marry Native American wives (according to 1867 letter from W.W. Phelps to Brigham Young).

1832   Fanny Alger, a teenager, cared for infant Joseph Smith III in his Kirtland, Ohio, home; she is then romanically linked to Joseph Smith Jr.

1835   Revelation (D&C section 101) officially denied rumors of polygamy in Kirtland, Ohio.

---

46. Qtd. in Laurie Goodstein, "It's Official: Mormon Leader Had Up to 40 Wives," *New York Times*, Nov. 10, 2014, at www.nytimes.com/2014/11/11/us/its-official-mormon-founder-had-up-to-40-wives.html; see also George D. Smith, "Plural Marriage Among Early Latter-day Saints," *Sunstone*, Summer 2015, 12–13.

47. "Start with Faith: A Conversation with Elder Steven E. Snow," *Religious Educator* 14, 3 (2013): 1–11, at www.rsc.byu.edu/archived/volume-14-number-3-2013/start-faith-conversation-elder-steven-e-snow.

1841	Plural marriage began at Nauvoo, Illinois, the church's new headquarters, with Smith's April 5 marriage to Louisa Beaman.
1843	On July 12, Smith dictated a revelation authorizing polygamy.
1844	After opposing polygamy, the *Nauvoo Expositor* newspaper was destroyed, Smith was arrested and suffered a fatal gunshot wound in the Carthage, Illinois, jail.
1845	Illinois governor Thomas Ford advised Brigham Young and church members to head west to nominally Mexican territory.
1846	Young initiated a pioneer trek west; and also sent Samuel Brannan with a shipload of Mormon migrants from New York to San Francisco.
1852	Polygamy was publicly announced in Great Salt Lake City.
1856	A Republican Party platform formally opposed both polygamy and slavery as "twin relics of barbarism."
1862	The Morrill Anti-Bigamy Act banned polygamy in US territories.
1876	D&C 132 canonized polygamy in official LDS scripture.
1878–79	US Supreme Court ruled anti-polygamy law constitutional.
1882	Edmunds Act strengthened Morrill act.
1887	Edmunds–Tucker Act passed, further restricting LDS plural marriage.
1890	US Supreme Court upholds Edmunds–Tucker Act. LDS President Wilford Woodruff subsequently issued Manifesto to end polygamy (augmented in 1904 and 1910–12).
1896	Utah was granted statehood.

Twentieth century: Rediscovered

1900s   LDS tried to erase the memory of polygamy in teaching manuals.

1912   Some determined LDS groups began to organize as "Fundamentalists" and to practice their own forms of plural marriage in the rural west.

1855–1912 Polygamist colonies were established in Mexican high country.

1945   Independent scholarly research revisited the history of plural marriage.

1998   LDS leadership dismissed the importance of plural marriage to church doctrine.

2013   An LDS online historical essay officially confirmed the existence and place of plural marriage in Mormon history.

2014   The *Salt Lake Tribune* confirmed the historical reality of LDS polygamy.

9. PLURAL MARRIAGE AFTER 1890

Newell G. Bringhurst

On October 25, 2014, the Church of Jesus Christ posted on its official website lds.org the Gospel Topics essay entitled "The Manifesto and the End of Plural Marriage," which the church-owned *Deseret News* characterized as the church's "willingness to openly address difficult topics."[1] "The Manifesto and the End of Plural Marriage" is one of three Gospel Topics dealing with plural marriage. Ten months earlier LDS officials had posted "Plural Marriage and Families in Early Utah." A third essay, "Plural Marriage in Kirtland and Nauvoo," appeared in October 2014, concurrent with "The Manifesto and the End of Plural Marriage." Plural marriage stands out as the only LDS Gospel Topic examined in three separate essays.

This analysis of the "The Manifesto and the End of Plural Marriage" is divided into three sections. The first provides an overview of the contents of the Gospel Topics essay. The second highlights the essay's attributes and/or strengths. The third discusses the essay's weaknesses and/or shortcomings, in particular noting the information omitted and ideas/concepts not fully developed.

Overview

"The Manifesto and the End of Plural Marriage" provides a detailed overview consisting of six and half pages of text along with three and a half pages of footnotes—fifty-three in all, many of which are annotated. All of this makes the essay the longest of the three addressing plural marriage.[2]

---

1. Tad Walch, "Polygamy Essays Provide Information about Early LDS Church—and Current Leadership," *Deseret News*, Oct. 25, 2014.

2. "Plural Marriage and Families in Early Utah" released a year earlier, contains a mere two and half pages of text and twenty-five footnotes, whereas "Plural Marriage

The essay is divided into four sections: The first, "Anti-polygamy Laws and Civil Disobedience," describes the series of laws passed by the federal government to force the Latter-day Saints to "relinquish plural marriage" commencing with the 1862 Morrill Anti-Bigamy Act and culminating in the 1880s with enactment of the stringent 1882 Edmunds Act and 1887 Edmunds-Tucker Act. Church officials "maintained that plural marriage was a religious principle protected under the U.S. Constitution." Accordingly, LDS officials "mounted a vigorous legal defense all the way to the U.S. Supreme Court" resulting in the landmark *Reynolds v. United States* (1879) decision in which the high court ruled against the church. The LDS Church faced a dilemma. On the one hand, Latter-day Saints "sincerely desired to be loyal citizens of the United States" but also embraced plural marriage as "a commandment from God." Ultimately, "Church leaders encouraged members to obey God rather than man." Thus, the church embarked "on a course of civil disobedience ... continuing to live in plural marriage and [entering] into new plural marriages." The anti-polygamy campaign "strengthened the Saints' resolve to resist," the result of which was that "many Latter-day Saints were convinced that the anti-polygamy campaign was useful in accomplishing God's purposes" and believed that "God was humbling and purifying his covenant people."[3]

The second section, entitled "The Manifesto," focuses on the official 1890 directive leading "to the end of plural marriage in the Church." Of primary importance in prompting church leaders to issue this directive was the US Supreme Court's action in upholding the constitutionality of the Edmunds-Tucker Act, which allowed for the confiscation of church property. Alarmed, LDS Church President Wilford Woodruff (1807–1898) feared that "the Church's temples and its ordinances were now at risk." The 1890 Manifesto states that the church "was not teaching polygamy, or plural marriage, nor permitting any person to enter into

in Kirtland and Nauvoo," issued concurrently with"The Manifesto and the End of Plural Marriage" contains five and a half pages of text and fifty-five footnotes.

3. "The Manifesto and the End of Plural Marriage" (Oct. 25, 2014), at www.lds. org/topics/the-manifesto-and-the-end-of-plural-marriage. All quotations from the essay are from this on-line publication.

its practice," with Woodruff personally declaring his "intention to submit to those laws ... enacted ... by Congress forbidding plural marriage ... and to use my influence with the members of the Church over which I preside to do likewise."

A third section, entitled "After the Manifesto," discusses how LDS leaders and rank-and-file members dealt with issues ostensibly unresolved by the Manifesto. The essay asserts: "At first, many Church leaders believed the Manifesto merely 'suspended' plural marriage for an indefinite period"—carefully adding that for members of the church "having lived, taught, and suffered for plural marriage for so long, it was difficult to imagine a world without it." The Manifesto was "silent on what existing plural families should do." This, in turn, caused confusion, with some polygamous couples, acting on their own initiative, "separat[ing] or divorc[ing] as a result of the Manifesto," while other husbands ceased to cohabit with all but one of their wives but continue "to provide financial and emotional support to all dependents." At the same time, "many husbands, including Church leaders continued to cohabit with their plural wives and father children with them well into the 20th Century," despite the illegality of such actions.

The fourth section, entitled "The Second Manifesto," focuses continuing church efforts to deal with controversies over plural marriage as it persisted into the 1890s and early 1900s. The LDS Church found its "marital practices [subject] to renewed scrutiny" following the 1898 election of Brigham H. Roberts to the U.S. House of Representatives. That body barred Roberts, a member of the church's First Council of the Seventy and a practicing polygamist, from taking his seat. Concurrently, the church allowed "a small number of new plural marriages" to be performed into the early twentieth century, usually outside the boundaries of the United States. "The Church's role in these marriages became a subject of intense debate after Reed Smoot, an Apostle, was elected to the U.S. Senate in 1903." At issue was whether to seat the LDS apostle, who unlike Roberts was not a practicing polygamist. The ensuing controversy became the focus of the so-called Smoot Hearings, attracting national attention over the following several years. Among those who testified was church president Joseph F. Smith, himself a practicing polygamist. In the end, Smoot was allowed to take his senate seat, serving in that body over the next three decades.

All this and more prompted Joseph F. Smith to "publically ... clarify the Church's position about plural marriage" which he did through "a forceful statement known as the Second Manifesto" issued at the April 1904 general conference. This manifesto, characterized as "a watershed event," warned church members "that new plural marriages stood unapproved by God and the Church." It attached "penalties to entering into plural marriage," specifically formal expulsion from the church, or excommunication. The so-called Second Manifesto "expanded the scope and reach of the first. Whereas the 1890 edict "simply gave notice to the Saints that they need not enter plural marriage any longer," the second declaration "made that manifesto prohibitory."

In issuing the Second Manifesto, Smith was motivated by other important factors, the essay further asserts. Among these was the fact that "a majority of Mormon marriages had always been monogamous" combined with "a shift toward monogamy as the only approved form" of marriage which "had long been underway." This change affected the highest councils of the church, beginning with the calling of Anthon H. Lund to the Quorum of the Twelve Apostles in 1889. "After 1897, every new Apostle called into the Twelve, with one exception, was a monogamist at the time of his appointment." Also prompting the Second Manifesto was a directive by church leaders urging members living outside the Intermountain West "to remain in their native lands and 'build Zion'" in those places rather than to immigrate to Utah as had been church policy in previous years. Thus it became important for such church members "to abide the laws mandating monogamy."

Church leaders "acted to communicate the seriousness" of the Second Manifesto and to see that it was "strictly enforced." Wayward church apostles John W. Taylor and Matthias F. Cowley, both of whom "continued to perform and encourage new plural marriages," were summarily "dropped from" the Quorum of the Twelve. Joseph F. Smith subsequently ordered Taylor's excommunication. Rank-and-file church members "who rejected the Second Manifesto" were likewise disciplined.

The essay concludes by noting: "Marriage between one man and one woman is God's standard, unless He declares otherwise, which He did through his prophet, Joseph Smith. The Manifesto marked the beginning of the return to monogamy, which is the standard of the Church today."

Positive Features

There is much to praise in "The Manifesto and the End of Plural Marriage" essay. Most basic is its effort to deal openly and forthrightly with this controversial topic. The essay states: "Like the beginning of plural marriage in the Church, the end of the practice was a process rather than a single event. Revelation came 'line upon line, precept upon precept.'" Equally significant, it confesses that abandoning the practice "required great faith and sometimes complicated, painful—and intensely personal" decisions by leaders and rank-and-file members. This was because "Church members viewed plural marriage as a commandment from God, an imperative that helped 'raise up' a righteous posterity unto the Lord" combined with a firm belief that "they would be blessed for their participation."

The essay admits that the federal government's anti-polygamy campaign "created great disruption in Mormon communities." Polygamous husbands fleeing arrest compelled their wives and children to tend farms and businesses, which, in turn, caused "incomes to drop and economic recession to set in." The campaign also "strained families" with "new plural wives" forced to "live apart from their husbands," and pregnant women often chose to go into hiding to avoid the "risk of being subpoenaed to testify in court against their husbands. Children lived in fear that their families would be broken up or that they would be forced to testify against their parents."

Forthrightly acknowledged are the limits of the 1890 Manifesto, specifically that it was "carefully worded to address the immediate conflict with the U.S. government." "Rank-and-file Latter-day Saints," the essay concedes, "accepted the Manifesto with various degrees of reservation. Many were not ready for plural marriage to come to an end." It further admits that the 1890

Manifesto did not prohibit individual church members "from continuing to practice or perform plural marriage as a matter of religious conscience."

Also refreshing is the essay's frank acknowledgment of so-called Post-Manifesto polygamous marriages. Facilitating such marriages was that the Manifesto "said nothing about the laws of other nations." Thus, church leaders continued to perform marriages in Mexico and Canada—two nations where Latter-day Saints had established settlements prior to 1890. The essay states: "Latter-day Saint couples who lived far away from temples were permitted to be sealed in marriage outside them ... For a time, post-Manifesto plural marriages required the approval of a member of the First Presidency. There is no definitive evidence, however, that the decisions were made by the First Presidency as a whole ..."

The essay also broaches Joseph F. Smith's ambiguous, contradictory behavior. After becoming church president in 1901, Smith allowed a small number of new plural marriages "during the early years of his administration." Smith also defended his own polygamous "family relationships" during the Smoot Hearings, freely admitting that he had "cohabited with his wives and [had] fathered children with them since 1890." When questioned about new plural marriages, Smith "carefully distinguished between actions sanctioned by the Church and ratified in Church councils and conferences, and the actions undertaken by the Church," going so far to claim: "There never has been a plural marriage by the consent or sanction or knowledge or approval of the church since the [1890] manifesto."

Weaknesses and/or Exclusions

The Gospel Topics essay's positive attributes, notwithstanding, a number of important topics are not sufficiently explored and/ or are excluded from consideration. The essay neglects mention of the Mormon push for Utah statehood as a major factor propelling LDS Church leaders toward the 1890 Manifesto. LDS leaders "became almost obsessed" with the idea of Utah statehood, viewing it "as a way to obtain independence from federal control." As early as 1882, Wilford Woodruff, then an apostle, discussed the possibility "of yielding ... principal [i.e., plural marriage] for a state government."[4]

Misleading is the essay's statement "though not all Church members were expected to enter plural marriage, those who did so believed they would be blessed for their participation" along with its assertion that "Church members viewed plural marriage as a commandment from God, an imperative that helped 'raise up' a righteous posterity unto the Lord."[5] Both of these statements refer to the 1843 revelation to church founder Joseph Smith that ultimately was canonized as section 132 in the Doctrine and Covenants.

This all-important revelation is nowhere mentioned, let alone discussed, in the essay, which is mystifying given that the church utilized Section 132 as *the* primary scriptural proof text not only sanctifying plural marriage but *commanding* its practice. Joseph Smith brought forth this seminal revelation shortly before his death. Church officials ordered its initial publication in 1853 under the title "CELESTIAL MARRIAGE: A Revelation on the Patriarchal Order of Matrimony, or plurality of Wives."[6] In 1876, the revelation was elevated to the status of canonized scripture in with its inclusion in the Doctrine and Covenants. Two years later, church officials placed the revelation in a second scriptural work, The Pearl of Great Price, under the title "Revelation on the Eternity of the Marriage Covenant including the Plurality of Wives." In fact, the 1843 revelation is unique as the only revelation ever to have been published in two separate works of official scripture.[7]

---

4. This according to B. Carmon Hardy, in *Doing the Works of Abraham: Mormon Polygamy, Its Origin, Practice, and Demise* (Norman, Oklahoma: Arthur H. Clark, 2007), 326–30. For definitive discussions of LDS efforts to secure statehood, see E. Leo Lyman, *Political Deliverance: The Mormon Quest for Utah Statehood* (Urbana: University of Illinois Press, 1986), and *Finally Statehood! Utah Struggles, 1849–1896* (Salt Lake City: Signature Books, 2019).

5. "The Manifesto and the End of Plural Marriage" essay.

6. "CELESTIAL MARRIAGE: A Revelation on the Patriarchal Order of Matrimony, or Plurality of Wives," *The Seer*, Jan. 1853.

7. For two perspectives on this revelation, see Newell G. Bringhurst, "Section 132 of the LDS Doctrine and Covenants: Its Complex Contents and Controversial Legacy," and Craig L. Foster, "Doctrine and Covenants Section 132 and Joseph Smith's Expanding Concept of Family," both in Newell G. Bringhurst and Craig L. Foster, eds., *The Persistence of Polygamy: Joseph Smith and the Origins of Mormon Polygamy* (Independence, Missouri: John Whitmer Books, 2010), 59–98.

The revelation characterized adherence to plural marriage as essential for full salvation or "exaltation" in the hereafter, enabling male practitioners to achieve ultimate godhood in conjunction with their wives and rule over new worlds of their own creation (D&C 132:119–20).

Also ignored in the Gospel Topics essay is the declining importance that the church assigned to Doctrine and Covenants 132, in particular to those portions dealing with plural marriage, in the wake of the 1890 Manifesto. In 1891 church officials removed the entire revelation from the Pearl of Great Price (it retained its place in the Doctrine and Covenants). LDS leaders placed less emphasis on those parts of the revelation dealing with plural marriage—evident in the wording of the introduction from the original "Revelation on the Eternity of the Marriage Covenant, including Plurality of Wives" to "Revelation on the Eternity of the Marriage Covenant, as also Plurality of Wives." Over time church leaders mandated the inclusion of additional text to the introduction, dealing with other aspects of the revelation. Such additions focused on doctrinal issues such as "power of the Holy Priesthood, as being operative beyond the grave" (only marriages performed by proper authority survive death); "essentials for the attainment of the status of godhood"; and "the sin of adultery. The doctrinal status of polygamy was further downgraded with the addition of the following to the introduction: "Plurality of wives acceptable only when commanded by the Lord."[8] None of this change in status of the revelation is treated in the church's essay.

Also problematic is the essay's truncated discussion of a second important revelation affirming plural marriage: a September 1886 revelation received by church president John Taylor (1808–87), never canonized and only published years after Taylor's death. The revelation commanded Taylor to promote and perpetuate plural marriage, despite increasing pressure from federal authorities to abandon the practice. The essay's discussion of Taylor's so-called "purported revelation" is buried in a single footnote at the end (note 14). Moreover, the status of the revelation is discounted with the

---

8. See superscript to Section 132 as contained in editions of the Doctrine and Covenants that appeared beginning in the early twentieth century.

statement that the revelation was "never submitted to the councils of the Priesthood nor the church," and that, in any event, "the revelation had been superseded by the [1890] Manifesto ..." Omitted is any discussion of the contents of the revelation itself. The revelation's actual wording is significant. The revelation stated that the Lord's "covenants cannot be abrogated nor done away with; but they will stand forever," and then directed: "And have I not commanded men that if they were Abraham's seed and would enter into my glory they must do the works of Abraham. I have not revoked this law nor will I for it is everlasting and those who will enter into my glory must obey the conditions thereof, even so Amen."[9]

Also misleading is the essay's discussion of the church's so-called "shift to monogamy" in the wake of the 1890 Manifesto. On the one hand, the essay states that "every new Apostle called into the Twelve after 1897 (excepting one) was a monogamist." On the other, the essay declares that "8 of the 19 members of the Quorum of the Twelve who served between 1890 and 1904 married new plural wives during those years ..."[10] The essay does not mention that the three LDS presidents who directed church affairs during most of the first half of the twentieth century had been practicing polygamists. Included in that number are Lorenzo Snow, married to nine women; Joseph F. Smith, husband to six women; and Heber J. Grant, who had three wives.[11]

The essay misleads again when it states: "Since the administration of Joseph F. Smith, Church Presidents have repeatedly emphasized that the Church and its members are no longer

---

9. Although photographs of the revelation exist, indicating that it is written in the hand of John Taylor, the original document is not extant. For complete text of the revelation, see Fred C. Collier, ed., *Unpublished Revelations of the Prophets and Presidents of the Church of Jesus Christ of Latter-day Saints*, 2nd ed. (Salt Lake City: Colliers Publishing, 1981), 1:180–206. For a comprehensive discussion of 1886 revelation, see Brain C. Hales, "John Taylor's 1886 Revelation," in Newell G. Bringhurst and Craig L. Foster, eds., *The Persistence of Polygamy: Fundamentalist Mormon Polygamy from 1890 to the Present* (Independence, Missouri: John Whitmer Books, 2015), 58–111.

10. "The Manifesto and the End of Plural Marriage" essay.

11. For a comprehensive discussion of the wives of LDS Church Presidents, see Craig L. Foster, "The Wives of the Prophets: The Plural Wives of Brigham Young to Heber J. Grant," Newell G. Bringhurst and Craig L. Foster, eds., *The Persistence of Polygamy: From Joseph Smith's Martyrdom to the First Manifesto, 1844–1890* (Independence, Missouri: John Whitmer Books, 2013), 113–45.

authorized to enter into plural marriage and underscored the sincerity of their words by urging local leaders to bring noncompliant members before Church disciplinary councils."[12] In fact, plural marriage persisted within mainstream Mormonism throughout Smith's presidency (1901–18) and beyond. Perpetuating this situation was what one historian has characterized as "ambiguity and actual obfuscation concerning new plural marriages," with such "confusion and uncertainty" continuing even after the Second Manifesto.[13] George Q. Cannon, John W. Taylor, and Matthias F. Cowley were the most prominent church leaders promoting the practice. Following their example was a significant number of rank-and-file Mormons who embraced polygamy into the mid-twentieth century. Among these was Barr White Musser, a younger brother to Joseph White Musser—the latter a prominent Fundamentalist Mormon leader. The younger Musser lived with his two wives while continuing to be accepted in full fellowship in the mainstream church.[14] Heber Erastus Farr and Heber Bennion also entered into polygamous marriages while remaining loyal, practicing Latter-day Saints[15]

Two high profile Latter-day Saints, Alpha J. Higgs and Richard Lyman, embraced plural marriage well after the Second Manifesto. Higgs, general secretary of the LDS Church's Young Men's Mutual Improvement Association and assistant manager of *The Improvement Era*—the church's official publication for adults, entered into a polygamous marriage in 1909, albeit without proper authorization. When revealed, it created a public scandal resulting in Higgs's disfellowshipment. Eventually, he was restored to full fellowship and continued to live with both of his wives without ecclesiastical penalty.[16]

---

12. "The Manifesto and the End of Plural Marriage" essay.

13. Craig L. Foster has documented this situation in his "The Persistence of Plural Marriage within Mainstream Mormonism: The Example of the Barr and Mary Lance Musser Family," in Newell G. Bringhurst and John C. Hamer, eds., *Scattering of the Saints: Schism within Mormonism* (Independence, Missouri: John Whitmer Books, 2007), 297–98.

14. Ibid., 300–14.

15. Ibid. 298. See also John Bennion, "Mary Bennion Powell: Polygamy and Silence," *Journal of Mormon History* 24 (Fall 1998): 85–128.

16. Foster, "The Persistence of Plural Marriage within Mainstream Mormonism: The Example of the Barr and Mary Lance Musser Family."

Apostle Richard R. Lyman became involved with Anna S. Jacobson in what "he considered a plural marriage, entered into in 1925 by secretly exchanged vows in a mutual covenant."[17] In 1943 church leaders upon discovering Lyman's relationship immediately excommunicated the errant apostle (and later Jacobsen) for "violating the Christian Law of Chastity." As with Higgs, Lyman was rebaptized into church in 1954.[18] The marital situation of all of the above individuals dramatize the existence of a polygamous subculture within mainstream Mormonism that persisted well into the twentieth century.[19]

Largely ignored in the Gospel Topics essay is Fundamentalist Mormonism relative to its impact on the mainstream LDS Church. The essay simply states that "some [LDS Church members] who were excommunicated coalesced into independent movements and are sometimes called fundamentalists," then cryptically adds: "These groups are not affiliated with or supported by The Church of Jesus Christ of Latter-day Saints."[20]

In fact, LDS leaders considered the fledgling Fundamentalist movement an existential threat, and acted accordingly. By the 1920s, Heber J. Grant, who succeeded Joseph F. Smith as president, asserted himself as an intractable foe of fundamentalist plural marriage—despite himself having earlier taken plural wives.[21] Grant issued a series of stern warnings during the late 1920s and early 1930s condemning Mormon Fundamentalist teachings and practices as heretical.[22] In June 1933, Grant issued what became

---

17. D. Michael Quinn, *The Mormon Hierarchy: Extensions of Power* (Salt Lake City: Signature Books, 1997), 183, states that Lyman was "the only twentieth century apostle who definitely entered polygamy."

18. Hales, *Modern Polygamy and Mormon Fundamentalism*, 112–14; D. Michael Quinn, *The Mormon Hierarchy: Extensions of Power* (Salt Lake City: Signature Books, 1997), 669–70.

19. Foster "The Persistence of Plural Marriage within Mainstream Mormonism."

20. "The Manifesto and the End of Plural Marriage" essay.

21. Decades earlier, as a new polygamist, Grant had recorded : "My love for each of my wives is *unbounded* and it is perfect nonsense for anyone to tell me a man can't *sincerely* and *truly* love more than one wife" (Diary, May 27, 1888, Church History Library, Church of Jesus Christ of Latter-day Saints, Salt Lake City).

22. Grant's statements issued in 1925, 1926, and 1931 are reprinted in James R. Clark, ed., *Messages of the First Presidency of the Church of Jesus Christ of Latter-day Saints* (Salt Lake City: Bookcraft, 1965–71), 5:242, 249, 292–303.

known as the Third or Final Manifesto. This seminal directive, actually written by J. Reuben Clark, Grant's second councilor, denounced the "few misguided members of the church ... who had secretly associated themselves together for the avowed purpose of perpetuating the practice of polygamy or plural marriage ..." Such individuals lacked authority, making their actions both "illegal and void because the Lord has laid down without qualification the principle that 'there is never but one on the earth at a time on whom this power and the keys of the priesthood are conferred." The bottom line was that "polygamous or plural marriages are not and cannot be performed." Thus there was "no excuse for any church member to be mislead by the false representatives of the corrupt, adulterous practices of the members of this secret, and (by reputation) oath-bound organization." The statement also denied the existence of John Taylor's 1886 revelation, characterizing it a "pretended" and/or "spurious" document in an effort to undermine Fundamentalist claims to ecclesiastical legitimacy.[23]

Shortly after the Final Manifesto, the LDS Church issued an "ecclesiastical 'loyalty oath' that suspected fundamentalist sympathizers were required to sign." Those who refused faced excommunication. Individuals had to pledge that they were not themselves practicing or advocating polygamy, or spreading rumors that general authorities secretly condoned plural marriage in their private circles.[24]

Clearly, LDS officials wanted to stamp out Fundamentalist Mormonism. All such punitive measures, however, had the opposite effect, transforming "a rag-tag collection of polygamous sympathizers ... into a cohesive movement" by the early 1940s.[25] Fundamentalist Mormonism attracted an increasing number of adherents throughout the remainder of the twentieth century and

---

23. Clark, ed., *Messages of the First Presidency*, 5:317. For a discussion of the circumstances surrounding the crafting of the final manifesto, see D. Michael Quinn, *Elder Statesman: A Biography of J. Reuben Clark* (Salt Lake City: Signature Books, 2002), 240–50.

24. For a discussion of this development, see Ken Driggs, "Twentieth Century Polygamy and Fundamentalist Mormons in Southern Utah," *Dialogue: A Journal of Mormon Thought* 24, 4 (Winter 1991): 46–47.

25. As stated in Quinn, *Elder Statesman*, 246.

into the twenty-first. At present, the number of Fundamentalist Mormons is estimated to be 35,000 to 50, 000. Its adherents are scattered throughout the Intermountain West and beyond.[26]

Virtually all individuals embracing Fundamentalist Mormonism have roots in and/or are former members of the mainline LDS Church. Also, the vast majority claim early Mormon polygamous ancestry.[27] All of this underscores the fact that although the 1890 Manifesto facilitated the end of plural marriage within the LDS Church, the practice continues to flourish outside of mainstream Mormonism. Its adherents claim to be the truest, most orthodox of Latter-day Saints, embracing what they call "old fashioned Mormonism" or "the fullness of the Gospel" as taught by Joseph Smith, Brigham Young, and all other early LDS leaders.[28]

Another omission in the Gospel Topics essay is its failure to acknowledge a number of the significant scholars who have written on this topic. Most conspicuously absent is any mention of D. Michael Quinn, whose trail-blazing writings on post-Manifesto polygamy and Fundamentalist Mormonism go back to the 1980s.[29] Also completely ignored is Ken Driggs, whose extensive scholarship on Fundamentalist Mormonism dates from the early 1990s.[30] Although Martha Sontag Bradley's 1983 *Utah Historical*

---

26. According to figures compiled by Anne Wilde in "Fundamentalist Mormonism: Its History, Diversity, and Stereotypes, 1886–Present," in Bringhurst and Hamer, 'eds., *Scattering of the Saints*, 258–89. For a broader view of Fundamentalist Mormonism from two different perspectives, see Brian C. Hales, *Modern Polygamy and Mormon Fundamentalism: The Generations after the Manifesto* (Draper, Utah: Greg Kofford Books, 2006), and Bringhurst and Foster, *The Persistence of Polygamy: Fundamentalist Mormon Polygamy from 1890 to the Present.*

27. Marianne T. Watson, "Polygamous Ancestry of Contemporary Fundamentalist Mormons," in Bringhurst and Foster, eds., *The Persistence of Polygamy: Fundamentalist Mormon Polygamy from 1890 to the Present*, 434–71.

28. Anne Wilde, "Section 132 of the Doctrine and Covenants: A Fundamentalist Mormon Perspective," in ibid., 434–71.

29. See, in particular, Quinn's "LDS Authority and New Plural Marriages, 1890–1904," *Dialogue: A Journal of Mormon Thought* 18 (Spring 1985): 9–105; "Plural Marriage and Mormon Fundamentalism," *Dialogue: A Journal of Mormon Thought* 31 (Summer 1998): 1–68; and *Elder Statesman.*

30. Most noteworthy are Driggs's "After the Manifesto: Modern Polygamy and Fundamentalist Mormons," *Journal of Church and State* 32 (Spring 1990): 367–89; "Twentieth Century Polygamy and Fundamentalist Mormons and Southern Utah," *Dialogue: A Journal of Mormon Thought*, 24, 4 (Winter 1991): 44–58; "Who Shall Raise the Children? Vera Black and the Rights of Polygamous Utah Parents," *Utah Historical*

Quarterly article "Hide and Seek: Children on the Underground" is referenced in a note, any mention of her three more consequential books exploring plural marriage and Fundamentalist Mormonism is completely, inexplicably absent.[31]

Likewise overlooked are three recent book-length studies dealing with the 1890 Manifesto, its impact, and the emergence of Fundamentalist Mormonism. The first of these, by researcher Brian C. Hales, *Modern Polygamy and Mormon Fundamentalism: The Generations after the Manifesto* (2007), takes an apologetic position in discussing LDS Church reaction to developments relating and subsequent to the Manifesto.[32] The other two ignored studies are *The Persistence of Polygamy: From Joseph Smith's Martyrdom to the First Manifesto* (2013) and *The Persistence of Polygamy: From 1890 to the Present* (2015), edited by Craig L. Foster and myself. Each is an anthology containing original essays written by a variety of scholars on specific aspects of this topic.[33]

Conclusion

Such omissions notwithstanding, "The Manifesto and the End of Plural Marriage" essay provides a readable, carefully written overview of the topic at hand. As such, it deserves the attention of interested individuals both within and outside the LDS community. This essay along with the other two dealing with plural marriage—"Plural Marriage in Kirtland and Nauvoo" and "Polygamy and Marriage in Early Utah"—indicate a willingness on the

---

Quarterly 60 (Winter 1992): 27–46; "This Will Someday Be the Head and Not the Tail of the Church," *Journal of Church and State* 43 (Winter 2001): 49–80; and "Imprisonment, Defiance, and Division: A History of Mormon Fundamentalism in the 1940s and 1950s," *Dialogue: A Journal of Mormon Thought* 38 (Spring 2005): 65–95.

31. *Kidnapped from That Land: The Government Raids on the Short Creek Polygamists* (Salt Lake City: University of Utah Press, 1983); *Zinas: A Story of Mothers and Daughters on the Mormon Frontier* (Salt Lake City: Signature Books, 2001); and *Plural Wife: Mabel Finlayson Allred* (Logan: Utah State University Press, 2012). Also noteworthy is her "Changed Faces: The Official LDS Position on Polygamy, 1890–1990," *Sunstone* 14 (Feb. 1990): 26–34.

32. Brian C. Hales, *Modern Polygamy and Mormon Fundamentalism: The Generations after the Manifesto* (Salt Lake City: Greg Kofford Book, 2007).

33. Bringhurst and Foster, eds., *The Persistence of Polygamy: From Joseph Smith's Martyrdom to the First Manifesto, 1844–1890*; Bringhurst and Foster, eds., *The Persistence of Polygamy: Fundamentalist Mormon Polygamy from 1890 to the Present*.

part of LDS Church officials to acknowledge the church's past association with plural marriage. For their efforts, the LDS Church, its leaders, and media representatives deserve the praise they have received from those within and outside of the LDS community.

10. WHITENESS THEOLOGY AND THE EVOLUTION OF MORMON RACIAL TEACHINGS

Matthew L. Harris

On December 6, 2013, the Church of Jesus Christ of Latter-day Saints posted on its website a 2,000-word document entitled "Race and the Priesthood," which LDS Church-owned and -operated *Deseret News* modestly described as an "enhanced page" on this admittedly "hot topic."[1] Without question, the tersely written essay is the fullest, richest, and most authoritative expression to date of Mormonism's evolving racial teachings. It repudiates what were once settled Mormon doctrines by rejecting the "curse of Cain" designation and by disavowing the quintessential LDS teaching that black people were "less valiant" in a pre-earth life. Nevertheless, the essay stops short of full disclosure. It neither acknowledges past LDS racial teachings as essential doctrine nor addresses problematic issues of race in LDS scripture. Consequently, Mormon whiteness teachings continue to pose significant challenges for black Latter-day Saints, even as the church tries to distance itself from those teachings.

Overview

The "Race and Priesthood" essay opens by quoting 2 Nephi 26:33 affirming "that all are alike unto God." This popular Book of Mormon scripture sets the tone for the remainder of the document, for the essay's primary purpose is to remind readers that the church welcomes "all "races, colors and creeds.""[2]

---

1. Tad Walch, "LDS Church Enhances Web Pages on Its History, Doctrine," *Deseret News,* Dec. 10, 2013.
2. "Race and Priesthood" essay (Dec. 6, 2013): www.lds.org/topics/race-and-the-priesthood?lang=eng. All quotations from the essay are taken from his source.

The "Race and Priesthood" writers assert that the church emerged "amidst a highly contentious racial culture in which whites were afforded great privilege." The essay affirms that the church was "restored" in 1830 when slavery was legal and "racial discrimination" permeated American culture. This, in turn, influenced the formation of LDS racial policies wherein Brigham Young implemented the priesthood and temple ban aimed specifically at blacks of African heritage. Most significantly, the essay admits that the ban resulted from human error rather than divine will. It further explains that Young reflected the prejudices of his nineteenth-century environment when "many people of African descent lived in slavery and racial distinctions and prejudice were not just common but customary among white Americans." The essay candidly acknowledges that church leaders used the "curse of Cain ... as justification for the priesthood and temple restrictions," along with another essential LDS teaching: "blacks were [not] ... valiant in the premortal battle against Lucifer and, as a consequence, were restricted from priesthood and temple blessings."

In another important admission, the essay disavows past Mormon teachings about "mixed-race marriages" and the inferiority of "black skin." Specifically, it disavows "the theories advanced in the past that black skin is a sign of divine disfavor or curse" and declarers that "leaders today unequivocally condemn all racism, past and present, in any form." Furthermore, the essay acknowledges that "a few black men" had been ordained to the priesthood under the leadership of Joseph Smith and that "one of these men, Elijah Abel, also participated in temple ceremonies in Kirtland, Ohio, and was later baptized as a proxy for deceased relatives in Nauvoo, Illinois." Finally, the essay admits that "there is no evidence that any black men were denied the priesthood during Joseph Smith's lifetime."

In one of its more instructive sections, the essay explains that only persons of African descent were denied the priesthood. Following World War II as questions of race and ethnicity arose as the church proselytized in biracial nations, then-church president David O. McKay implemented a policy that limited the ban "only to men of black African descent." This new policy allowed black Fijians, Australian Aborigines, and other dark-skinned peoples to receive the priesthood and receive temple blessings. In another significant change, McKay "reversed a prior policy that required prospective priesthood holders to trace their lineage out of Africa," which created a less restrictive screening process in determining priesthood and temple eligibility.

The essay, moreover, acknowledges that the priesthood and temple ban made it difficult to fulfill the church's "overarching mission" to take the LDS gospel to "every nation, kindred, tongue, and people." The priesthood restriction was particularly challenging considering that people of African descent could not enjoy the full rituals of the temple or serve in key leadership positions in the church. Thus the ban "created significant barriers … as the Church spread in international locations and mixed racial heritages." This was especially acute in Brazil, in a country that "prided itself on its open, integrated, and mixed racial heritage."

Further complicating LDS expansion in Brazil were black Brazilian Mormons who donated their time and money to build the church's São Paulo temple in the early 1970s. Then church-president Spencer W. Kimball agonized over the stark reality that they could not attend the temple. The essay explains that this is one of many factors prompting Kimball to lift the ban, leading to the June 1978 priesthood revelation in the Salt Lake temple. Appropriately, the essay calls the event "a landmark revelation and a historic event" further explaining that after Kimball announced the revelation church leaders and members officially canonized it as "Official Declaration 2" in the Doctrine and Covenants.

The essay closes on an optimistic note, reminding readers that the LDS Church teaches that "all are alike unto God." It affirms "that God is 'no respecter of persons' and emphatically declares that anyone who is righteous—regardless of race—is favored of Him."

Weaknesses and/or Exclusions

The universalist message notwithstanding, the "Race and Priesthood" essay is problematic, both for what it says and for what it does not say. It offers neither an apology nor a recognition of pain caused by the ban, echoing a refrain from LDS Apostle Dallin H. Oaks who noted in 2015 that "the church doesn't 'seek apologies'

... and we don't give them."[3] The "Race and Priesthood" essay also fails to acknowledge LDS racial teachings as established doctrine, identifying them instead as "theories" and "opinions." To buttress this claim, the essay cites an unpublished, previously unknown 1907 letter from Joseph Fielding Smith, then Assistant Church Historian, explaining that the "curse" and "less valiant" positions were "not the official positions of the Church." They were "theories"—"the opinion[s]" of earlier leaders.[4] The essay also incorrectly implies that Smith was an apostle when he wrote the letter when, in fact, he was not ordained to the Council of the Twelve until 1910. Most problematic, the essay ignores Smith's later writings, both published and unpublished, in which he affirms LDS racial theories as essential doctrine. Indeed, for much of the twentieth century Smith was the chief purveyor of LDS racial teachings through authoritative books and articles.[5]

---

3. Oaks, as quoted in Peggy Fletcher Stack, "No Apology? Really? Mormons Question Leader Dallin H. Oaks' Stance," *Salt Lake Tribune*, Jan. 30, 2015. By contrast, First Presidency counselor Dieter Uchtdorf expressed a contrite tone, acknowledging that church leaders have made mistakes. See "Come, Join With Us," *Ensign*, Oct. 2013: www.lds.org/general-conference/2013/10/come-join-with-us?lang=eng; "President Uchtdorf: 'Come, Join with Us,'" *Deseret News*, Oct. 5, 2013; Laurie Goodstein, "A Top Mormon Leader Acknowledges the Church 'Made Mistakes,'" *New York Times*, Oct. 5, 2013.

4. Joseph Fielding Smith, Letter to Alfred M. Nelson, Jan. 31, 1907, Church History Library, Church of Jesus Christ of Latter-day Saints, Salt Lake City; hereafter CHL. Smith initially adopted his father's position stating that there was no doctrine of the church that the "negroes are those who were neutral in heaven at the time of the great conflict or war," in First Presidency (Joseph F. Smith, Anthon H. Lund, Charles W. Penrose), Letter to Milton H. Knudson, Jan. 13, 1912, in Lester E. Bush, ed., "Compilation on the Negro in Mormonism" (1972), privately circulated, 216–17, CHL.

5. See, for example, Joseph Fielding Smith, "The Negro and the Priesthood," *Improvement Era* 27 (Apr. 1924): 564–65; Smith, *The Way to Perfection: Short Discourses on Gospel Themes*, 5th ed. (orig. pub. 1931; Salt Lake City: Genealogical Society of Utah, 1945), chap. 7 ("Appointment of Lineage"), chap. 15 ("The Seed of Cain"), chap. 16 ("The Seed of Cain After the Flood"); Smith, *Answers to Gospel Questions*, 5 vols. (Salt Lake City: Deseret Book Co., 1957–66), 2:185–86, 4:169–72, 5:162–64, 168; Smith, *Doctrines of Salvation*, comp. Bruce R. McConkie, 3 vols. (Salt Lake City: Deseret Book Co., 1954–56), 1:61, 64–66, 2:55, 3:172. For Smith's ordination as an apostle, see Joseph Fielding Smith Jr. and John J. Stewart, *The Life of Joseph Fielding Smith* (Salt Lake City: Deseret Book Co., 1972), 174–75. In the Joseph Fielding Smith Papers, CHL, there are dozens of unpublished writings, mostly answers to theological questions, in which Smith characterizes the church's race teachings as doctrine. See, in particular, Box 23, Folder 8; Box 28, Folder 1; Box 38, Folder 9. Born into patrician LDS stock—Smith's father was an LDS Church president and his great

Smith's most influential book *The Way to Perfection* (1931) exerted a profound influence on Latter-day Saints. When inquisitive members queried him about "the Negro and the Priesthood," Smith recommended chapters 15 ("The Seed of Cain") and 16 ("The Seed of Cain After the Flood") of his book to answer their questions. The First Presidency and the Quorum of the Twelve Apostles also recommended these chapters when asked about the priesthood and temple ban.[6] In this controversial work, which spanned eighteen reprint editions from 1931 to 1986, Smith proclaimed that blacks bore the "mark of Cain" for their sinful behavior in a premortal spirit world. Even more controversial, he declared that Cain "became the father of an inferior race"—an assertion he would later deny—and characterized black skin as

---

grandfather was a brother to Joseph Smith, the LDS founder—the oft-quoted Joseph Fielding Smith was widely recognized as the faith's foremost "scriptorian." The LDS *Church News* remarked that it "would be difficult to find a subject of Church doctrine or history that President Smith has not written extensively upon in magazine articles, pamphlets and books" (*Church News*, in *Deseret News*, Nov. 26, 1966). Historian Matthew Bowman notes that Smith was one of "Mormonism's most respected religious thinker[s]" in the decades after World War II. In Bowman, *The Mormon People: The Making of An American Faith* (New York: Random House, 2012), 200. See also Terryl L. Givens, *Wrestling the Angel—The Foundations of Mormon Thought: Cosmos, God, Humanity* (New York: Oxford University Press, 2015), 15. For an affectionate perspective on Smith, see Frances M. Gibbons, *Joseph Fielding Smith: Gospel Scholar, Prophet of God* (Salt Lake City: Deseret Book Co., 1992).

6. Smith recommended these chapters in a number of letters. See, for example, letters to J. Reuben Clark, Apr. 3, 1939, Box 17, Folder 7, Joseph Fielding Smith Papers; to Ida E. Holmes, Feb. 9, 1949, Box 27, Folder 3, ibid.; letter to Eulis E. Hubbs, Mar. 5, 1958, Box 9, Folder 7, ibid.; letter to Joseph H. Henderson, Apr. 10, 1963, Matthew L. Harris files; Smith, *Answers to Gospel Questions*, 2:188. The First Presidency also referred to chapters 15 and 16 of Smith's work when asked about racial questions. See George Albert Smith, J. Reuben Clark Jr., and David O. McKay, Letter to Francis W. Brown, Jan. 13, 1947, in Bush, ed., "Compilation on the Negro in Mormonism," 246–47; and Box 78, Folder 7, George Albert Smith Papers, Special Collections, J. Willard Marriott Library, University of Utah, Salt Lake City. *The Way to Perfection* shaped perceptions about LDS racial doctrine among Smith's colleagues in church leadership. For this point, see Spencer W. Kimball's notes, Box 64, Folder 5, Spencer W. Kimball Papers, CHLibrary; J. Reuben Clark's "Negro and the Church" folder, Box 210, J. Reuben Clark Papers, L. Tom Perry Special Collections, Harold B. Lee Library, Brigham Young University, Provo, Utah; Boyd K. Packer, "The Curse Upon Cain and Descendants," Jan. 3, 1951, Box 63, Folder 11, Leonard J. Arrington Papers, Special Collections, Merrill-Cazier Library, Utah State University, Logan; Joseph F. Merrill, letter to J.W. Monroe, Jan. 26, 1951, Box 20, Folder 2, Joseph F. Merrill Papers, Perry Special Collections; and Bruce R. McConkie, *Mormon Doctrine* (Salt Lake City: Bookcraft, 1958), 477.

"emblematical of eternal darkness." Less dramatic but no less significant, Smith averred that the priesthood and temple restrictions "did not originate with President Brigham Young but was taught by the Prophet Joseph Smith."[7]

Smith's other authoritative works, *Doctrines of Salvation* (1954–56) and *Answers to Gospel Questions* (1957–66), also influenced the LDS community. His three volumes entitled *Doctrines of Salvation*, edited by son-in-law Bruce R. McConkie, contain his most important addresses and sermons. His *Answers to Gospel Questions*, by contrast, was the result of his monthly column called "Your Question," in which Latter-day Saints asked Smith difficult doctrinal questions. Smith published his answers in the *Improvement Era*, the official church magazine, and later republished them in a five-volume series over a nine-year span. In these influential volumes, Smith reaffirmed LDS racial teachings but tempered his rhetoric. "The Latter-day Saints ... have no animosity towards the Negro," he explained during the midst of the contentious civil rights era. "Neither have they described him as belonging to an 'inferior race.'"[8] Smith also advanced a conciliatory position on civil rights and optimistically explained that blacks could be baptized, receive their patriarchal blessings, and "enter the celestial kingdom" if they remained faithful in the church.[9]

The "Race and Priesthood" essay also distorts the work of Apostle Bruce R. McConkie, whose own statements on black priesthood denial are neither acknowledged nor explained in the Gospel Topics essay. In *Mormon Doctrine* (1958), among the most influential books ever published by an LDS leader (it sold hundreds of thousands of copies and went through forty printings

---

7. Smith, *Way to Perfection*, 101–102, 110; and the accompanying lesson manual outline based on Smith's work: "Topical Outlines to *The Way to Perfection*" (Salt Lake City: Genealogical Society of Utah, 1936), 15.

8. Smith, *Answers to Gospel Questions*, 4:170. Smith's monthly column "Your Question" was first published in the *Improvement Era* 56 (May 1953): 310, and ended thirteen years later in the *Improvement Era* 69 (Sept. 1966): 766–67.

9. Smith, *Answers to Gospel Questions*, 2:185; 4:170; Smith, *Doctrines of Salvation*, 2:55; 3:172. For an overview of Smith's published writings, see Reid L. Neilson and Scott D. Marianno, "True and Faithful: Joseph Fielding Smith as Mormon Historian and Theologian," *BYU Studies Quarterly* 57:1 (2018): 7–64.

from 1958–2010),[10] McConkie reflected the anti-black attitudes of his generation. The work bears a striking resemblance to the writings of southern Protestant clergymen, to say nothing of his father-in-law, who also declared segregation divinely inspired, interracial marriage a sin, and black people cursed.[11] McConkie asserted in *Mormon Doctrine* that Cain was "the father of the Negroes" and that "Cain, Ham, and the whole negro race have been cursed with a black skin ... so they can be identified as a caste apart" to keep blacks and whites from marrying. In another passage, McConkie averred that "negroes are not equal with other races where the receipt of certain spiritual blessings are concerned, particularly the priesthood and the temple blessings that flow therefrom." This "inequality is not of man's origin," he added, but "is the Lord's doing" and is "based on his eternal laws of justice."[12]

Rather than contextualize this highly influential, albeit controversial work, the essay focuses on an obscure McConkie statement published following the lifting of the priesthood and temple ban. The essay cites the apostle's sermon "All Are Alike Unto God," in which McConkie explained that church leaders spoke with a "limited understanding" during the 126-year-old ban. The essay further notes, quoting McConkie, that leaders offered "new 'light and knowledge'" on LDS racial teachings without explaining how he characterized the ban in his sermon ("the ancient curse") or how he *still* portrayed black people ("the seed of Cain").[13] More

10. Peggy Fletcher Stack, "Landmark 'Mormon Doctrine' Goes Out of Print," *Salt Lake Tribune*, May 21, 2010, at www.archive.sltrib.com/story.php?ref=/ci_15137409.

11. For a Protestant theology of race, particularly among southern clergymen, see David L. Chappell, *A Stone of Hope: Prophetic Religion and the Death of Jim Crow* (Chapel Hill: University of North Carolina Press, 2004), 109–10; Paul Harvey, *Freedom's Coming: Religious Culture and the Shaping of the South from the Civil War through the Civil Rights Era* (Chapel Hill: University of North Carolina Press, 2005), 230–41; Paul Harvey, *Christianity and Race in the American South: A History* (Chicago: University of Chicago Press, 2016), chap. 7; Mark A. Noll, *God and Race in American Politics* (Princeton, New Jersey: Princeton University Press, 2008), chap. 3; Fay Botham, *Almighty God Created the Races: Christianity, Interracial Marriage, and American Law* (Chapel Hill: University of North Carolina Press, 2009), chap. 4.

12. McConkie, *Mormon Doctrine*, 102, 107, 477.

13. Bruce R. McConkie, "All Are Alike unto God," CES Religious Educator's Symposium at Brigham Young University, Aug. 18, 1978, CHL. The sermon was republished as "The New Revelation on Priesthood," in [no editor] *Priesthood* (Salt Lake City: Deseret Book Co., 1981), 126–37 (quotes on 127–28).

troubling, the essay's selective reading of McConkie causes readers to assume, incorrectly, that he was progressive on racial matters when he was not. In published writings after the "All Are Alike Unto God" sermon, McConkie continued teaching about the hierarchy of lineages and the divine curse.[14]

Equally problematic is the essay's attempt to link the ban to the larger socio-racial context of nineteenth-century America. This obscures the particular uniqueness of LDS racial doctrine and exonerates LDS leadership from accountability over its teachings. A more forthright approach would have been to discuss what LDS scriptures teach about race, particularly the passages that recount dark skin as a sign of divine disfavor and white skin as something blessed and holy.[15] This is critical, for the Book of Mormon and especially the Pearl of Great Price account for much of the theological framework undergirding the priesthood and temple ban.[16]

The Book of Mormon recounts the story of the Lamanites, whom God cursed with a "dark skin" for their wickedness. In vivid detail, the Nephite prophets discuss how their rivals became "a dark, filthy and loathsome people"—"full of idleness and all manner of abominations." To maintain racial purity, the Book of

---

14. Armand Mauss, "Late But Welcome: 'Race and the Priesthood' Essay," *Sunstone* 178 (Summer 2015): 22. For McConkie's racial teachings in the post-ban era, see his updated version of *Mormon Doctrine* (Salt Lake City: Bookcraft, 1979), 109, 114, 526, 616; "New Revelation on Priesthood," *Priesthood*, 128; Joseph Fielding McConkie, *The Bruce McConkie Story: Reflections of a Son* (Salt Lake City: Deseret Book Co., 2003), 377; McConkie, *The Mortal Messiah* (Salt Lake City: Deseret Book Co., 1979), 23; McConkie, *The Millennial Messiah* (Salt Lake City: Deseret Book Co., 1982), 182–83, and chap. 16; and McConkie, *A New Witness for the Articles of Faith* (Salt Lake City: Deseret Book Co., 1985), 510–12, and chap. 4. See also Armand L. Mauss, *Shifting Borders and a Tattered Passport: Intellectual Journeys of a Mormon Academic* (Salt Lake City: University of Utah Press, 2012), 232–33n32.

15. Matthew L. Harris and Newell G. Bringhurst, eds., *The Mormon Church and Blacks: A Documentary History* (Urbana: University of Illinois, 2015), chap. 1; Newell G. Bringhurst, *Saints, Slaves, and Blacks: The Changing Place of Black People Within Mormonism* (Westport, Connecticut: Greenwood Press, 1981), 4–11; Armand L. Mauss, *All Abraham's Children: Changing Mormon Conceptions of Race and Lineage* (Urbana: University of Illinois Press, 2003), 116–18; Givens, *Wrestling with the Angel*, 173–74; and especially W. Paul Reeve, *Religion of a Different Color: Race and the Mormon Struggle for Whiteness* (New York: Oxford University Press, 2015), 205–07; and Max Perry Mueller, *Race and the Making of the Mormon People* (Chapel Hill: University of North Carolina Press, 2017), 38–59.

16. See note below.

Mormon prophets instructed the "white" and "delightsome" Nephites not to mix "seed" with the sinful Lamanites lest they "bring the same curse upon [their] seed" (2 Ne. 5:21; Morm. 5:15; 1 Ne. 12:23, Alma 3:9, 14). But at the same time when the wicked Lamanites repented of their sins and embraced Christ's redemption, the Book of Mormon prophets proclaimed they would lose "their scales of darkness" and became a "white and delightsome people."[17]

The Pearl of Great Price also posits a link between moral purity and skin color. In the Book of Moses, it teaches that the descendants of Cain and Ham had "black" skin because of their unrighteousness, prompting God to segregate them from the rest of the "seed of Adam." In like manner, the Book of Abraham states that God cursed Pharaoh—a descendant of Ham—and denied him the priesthood (Moses 7:22; Abr. 1:21–27). These racial teachings were further manifest in a passage discussing a "war in Heaven" between Jesus and Satan. In this premortal battle, Jesus' followers were loyal to "God's plan" and destined to become the favored lineage in mortality. Those Latter-day Saints blessed with white skin could hold the priesthood and perform sacred temple rituals while black people were barred from such privileges because of their "less valiance" in the preexistence.[18]

These unique LDS scriptures served as the basis for a theology of whiteness, enabling LDS leaders to justify their anti-black practices.[19] Some LDS leaders believed that the curse of blackness

---

17. 2 Ne. 30:6. Joseph Smith identified a "white Lamanite" named Zelph who experienced this racially cleansing process. See Richard Lyman Bushman, *Joseph Smith: Rough Stone Rolling* (New York: Alfred A. Knopf, 2005), 240–41; Kenneth W. Godfrey, "What Is the Significance of Zelph in the Study of Book of Mormon Geography?" *Journal of Book of Mormon Studies* 8 (1999): 70–79.

18. Abr. 3:22–28. The seminal LDS leaders on this point include Brigham H. Roberts, "To the Youth of Israel," *The Contributor* 6 (1885): 296–97; Smith, *Way to Perfection*, 43–44, 105–06; Smith, *Doctrines of Salvation*, 1:64–66; and McConkie, *Mormon Doctrine*, 476–77, 553–54. For a nuanced reading of Mormon teachings on the preexistence, see Boyd Jay Petersen, "'One Soul Shall Not Be Lost': The War in Heaven in Mormon Thought," *Journal of Mormon History* 38 (Winter 2012): 1–50; and Givens, *Wrestling with the Angel*, 170–75.

19. Historian Newell Bringhurst is the first scholar to write about LDS scriptures in relation to Mormon racial policy. See *Saints, Slaves, and Blacks*, chap. 3. For two other insightful accounts of the same topic, see Reeve, *Religion of a Different Color*, and Mueller, *Race and the Making of the Mormon People*. Reeve and Mueller focus almost exclusively on the nineteenth century. This essay extends the discussion into

would be lifted over time, gradually returning dark-skinned people to their pre-cursed state of whiteness after their LDS conversion. Others opined that they would return to their primitive state of whiteness in the resurrection.[20] For Latter-day Saints, then, whiteness theology was not solely a metaphorical, spiritual, or symbolic interpretation of skin color as apologists have argued. Rather, the evidence clearly suggests that Latter-day Saints believed in a tangible, literal transformation of flesh pigmentation when blacks and Native Americans converted to Mormonism.[21]

The most prominent LDS leader to teach such views was Apostle Spencer W. Kimball. In 1960, he delivered a landmark church general conference address declaring that when American Indians left the reservation after converting to Mormonism they became "as light as Anglos." Kimball theorized that Native Americans had "been growing delightsome and ... are now becoming white and delightsome as they were promised (2 Ne. 30:6)." To underscore the point, Kimball showed a "picture of ... twenty Lamanite missionaries," avowing that "fifteen of the twenty were as light as *Anglos*; five were darker but equally delightsome." Additionally, he claimed that the "children in the home placement

---

the twentieth century. I am indebted to these three scholars for their insights and observations about the development of LDS racial hierarchies.

20. See the discussion below.

21. For an apologetic reading of whiteness in Mormon scripture, see John A. Tvedtness, "The Charge of 'Racism' in the Book of Mormon," *FARMS Review* 15 (2003): 183–97; Brant A. Gardner, *Second Witness: Analytical and Contextual Commentary on the Book of Mormon*, 6 vols. (Sandy, Utah: Greg Kofford Books, 2007–2008), 2:114–22; Rodney Turner, "The Lamanite Mark," in Monte S. Nyman and Charles D. Tate Jr., eds., *Second Nephi: The Doctrinal Structure* (Provo, Utah: Religious Studies Center, Brigham Young University, 1989), 133–57; Ethan Sproat, "Skins as Garments in the Book of Mormon: A Textual Exegesis," *Journal of Book of Mormon Studies* 24 (2015): 138–65; Hugh W. Nibley, *Lehi in the Desert and the World of the Jaredites* (Salt Lake City: Bookcraft, 1952), 84–85; Sidney B. Sperry, *Book of Mormon Compendium* (Salt Lake City: Bookcraft, 1968), 154–55, 251; Daniel H. Ludlow, *A Companion To Your Study of the Book of Mormon* (Salt Lake City: Deseret Book Co., 1976), 132, 153; John L. Sorenson, *An Ancient America Setting for the Book of Mormon* (Salt Lake City: Deseret Book Co., 1985), 89–90. For a nuanced reading of the Book of Mormon and Lamanites, see Thomas W. Murphy, "From Racist Stereotype to Ethnic Identity: Instrument Uses of Mormon Racial Doctrine," *Ethnohistory* 46 (Summer 1999): 451–80; and Jared Hickman, "The Book of Mormon as Amerindian Apocalypse," *American Literature* 86 (Sept. 2014): 429–61.

program in Utah are often lighter than their brothers and sisters in the hogans on the reservation."[22]

Kimball was not the only apostle to teach a whiteness theology. Six years earlier in a private meeting, senior apostle Joseph Fielding Smith stated to LDS religious educators in the Salt Lake temple that "we know of cases" where the "dark skin [of negroes] really has disappeared."[23] Smith's assertion about black people was consistent with his teachings about Lamanites. In *Answers to Gospel Questions*, he stated that Lamanites were beginning to lose "their dark pigment." He further alleged that when "the Lamanites fully repent and sincerely receive the gospel, the Lord has promised to remove the dark skin." Apostles Harold B. Lee, Alvin R. Dyer, LeGrand Richards, and Bruce R. McConkie also linked white skin with righteousness and moral purity.[24]

22. Kimball, "The Day of the Lamanites," *Improvement Era* 63 (Dec. 1960): 922–25 (quotes at 923). See also Kimball, "The Lamanites: 'And They Shall Be Restored,'" *Improvement Era* 50 (Nov. 1947): 765. The Home Placement Program, also called the Lamanite Placement Program, operated from 1954 until the mid-1990s. LDS Native American students were placed in the homes of LDS Church members, where they could assimilate into Mormon culture by attending schools off the reservation. The best account of this program is Matthew Garrett, *Making Lamanites: Mormons, Native Americans, and the Indian Student Placement Program, 1947–2000* (Salt Lake City: University of Utah Press, 2016). For Kimball's lifelong fascination with Native Americans, see Edward L. Kimball, *Lengthen Your Stride: The Presidency of Spencer W. Kimball—Working Draft* (Salt Lake City: Benchmark Books, 2009), chap. 30; Edward L. Kimball, ed., *The Teachings of Spencer W. Kimball* (Salt Lake City: Bookcraft, 1982), chap. 22. Kimball's racialized general conference sermon elicited a flood of letters from concerned Latter-day Saints who queried the apostle about his teachings. Edward L. Kimball, his son and principal biographer, told me that his father responded to his interlocutors explaining that his sermon was a figurative expression and not a manifestation of changing skin color. As Kimball conveyed to Harris over dinner at the Kimball home, Nov. 26, 2013, Provo, Utah.

23. Joseph Fielding Smith and Mark E. Petersen, "Discussion after Talk on Racial Prejudice," Oct. 7, 1954, 22, in Box 4, Folder 7, William E. Berrett Papers, Perry Special Collections. The two apostles met with LDS religion instructors after Apostle Petersen gave a controversial talk at BYU. See "Race Problems—As They Affect the Church," address given at Brigham Young University, Aug. 27, 1954, CHL.

24. Smith, *Answers to Gospel Questions*, 3:123. Harold B. Lee, "Youth of a Noble Birthright" (1945), reprinted in Lee, *Youth and the Church* (Salt Lake City: Deseret Book Co., 1955), 170; Alvin R. Dyer, *The Meaning of Truth* (Salt Lake City: Deseret Book Co., 1961; rev. ed., 1970), 70; LeGrand Richards, *A Marvelous Work and a Wonder* (Salt Lake City: Deseret Book Co., 1950; rev. ed., 1976), 72–73; McConkie, *Mormon Doctrine*, 661. See also James E. Talmage, *Jesus the Christ* (Salt Lake City: Deseret News, 1915), 49.

Church-sponsored publications promoted a whiteness theology as well, particularly among Native Americans, whom the church targeted for "redemption and whiteness."[25] In the *Millennial Star*, for example, a periodical published by the LDS Church in England, a writer noted in 1917 that "the American Indians are becoming 'white' in their mode of living, their education, their occupation, their ideals and aspirations. There is no doubt that this radical change will ultimately affect their complexion and general appearance." The writer further explained that in "due time" Native Americans will "come under the influence of the gospel and become white and delightsome. All accidental and imaginary race boundaries must be eliminated through the gospel," he asserted, "before the coming of the day of the universal brotherhood of man, and that is the leveling work which is going on today in the United States, where the gospel was first proclaimed to the Indians." He concluded that it is "impossible to contemplate the great change that has come upon the red race in America, without feeling convinced that the prophecy in the Book of Mormon has begun to be fulfilled."[26]

25. Reeve, *Religion of a Different Color*, 56; Mauss, *All Abraham's Children*, 41–43, 79–96; Bruce A. Chadwick and Stan L. Albrecht, "Mormons and Indians: Beliefs, Policies, Programs, and Practices," in Marie Cornwall, Tim B. Heaton, and Lawrence A. Young, eds., *Contemporary Mormonism: Social Science Perspectives* (Urbana: University of Illinois Press, 1994), 287–90; and Elise Boxer, "'The Lamanites Shall Blossom as the Rose': The Indian Student Placement Program, Mormon Whiteness, and Indigenous Identity," *Journal of Mormon History* 41 (Oct. 2015): 132–76. For LDS efforts to convert Native Americans, see Max H. Parkin, "Lamanite Mission of 1830–1831," in Daniel H. Ludlow, et al., eds., *Encyclopedia of Mormonism*, 4 vols. (New York: Macmillan, 1992), 2: 802–04; Jared Farmer, *On Zion's Mount: Mormons, Indians, and the American Landscape* (Cambridge, Massachusetts: Harvard University Press, 2010); Leonard J. Arrington and Davis Bitton, *The Mormon Experience: A History of the Latter-day Saints* (New York: Alfred A. Knopf, 1979), chap. 8; Kimball, *Lengthen Your Stride* (Working Draft), chap. 30; Terryl L. Givens and Reid L. Neilson, eds., *The Columbia Sourcebook of Mormons in the United States* (New York City: Columbia University Press, 2014), 234–39. For LDS efforts to assimilate Native Americans into LDS culture, especially through an Indian Placement Program, see Boxer, "'The Lamanites Shall Blossom as the Rose': The Indian Student Placement Program, Mormon Whiteness, and Indigenous Identity"; Chadwick and Albrecht, "Mormons and Indians"; Jessie L. Embry, "Indian Placement Program Host Families: A Mission to the Lamanites," *Journal of Mormon History* 40 (Spring 2014): 235–76; and Garrett, *Making Lamanites*, chap. 4.

26. J. M. S., "Indians Becoming White and Delightsome," *Latter-day Saint Millennial Star* 79 (Feb. 1, 1917): 72–74.

Another LDS periodical, the *Improvement Era*, published a pair of stories in the 1920s illustrating the effect of conversion on native peoples. One focused on Louis Armell, a Winnebago Indian, who "is said to be the object of scientific observation because for many years his skin has gradually been turning white." "He is now 54 years old," the *Improvement Era* explained. "He still has 'copper patches' but physicians believe that if he lives a few more years he will become entirely white." Another story in the same publication explained that the "promise" of racial purity was not just reserved for "those living in the last days," but was also "partly fulfilled during the Nephite period when the persons with the dark skin repented and joined the Church."[27] In 1952 an LDS author observed that after the Catawba Indians in South Carolina embraced the church they became "white and delightsome, as white and fair as any group of citizens of our country. I know of no prophecy, ancient or modern, that has had a more literal fulfillment."[28]

Minority groups associated with Lamanites were no less immune to whiteness theology. Some LDS leaders taught that the Maori people in New Zealand—"a remnant of the Lamanites"— bore "the Lamanite mark of a dark skin, [which] could be removed through conversion."[29] Others taught that Hawaiians were cursed. In 1927 Eugene J. Neff, a former president of the church's Hawaii mission, recounted an experience in general conference when

---

27. [No author], "Passing Events," *Improvement Era* 31 (Apr. 1928): 537; Cecil McGavin, "The Lord's Promise to the Lamanites," *Improvement Era* 30 (Oct. 1927): 1095–96.

28. George Edward Clark, *Why I Believe: 54 Evidences of the Divine Mission of the Prophet Joseph Smith* (Salt Lake City: Bookcraft, 1952), 129. See also Melvin Brooks, *L.D.S. Reference Encyclopedia* (Salt Lake City: Bookcraft, 1960), 261–62; Smith, *Answers to Gospel Questions*, 3:123; Stanley Kimball, "Book of Mormon Promises to Indians Coming True, Says Chief," *Church News*, May 1, 1954; and Daniel Liestman, "'We Have Found What We Have Been Looking For!' The Creation of the Mormon Religious Enclave Among the Catawba, 1883–1920," *South Carolina Historical Magazine* 103 (July 2002): 243.

29. Nolan P. Olsen, "New Zealand—Our Maori Home," *Improvement Era* 35 (May 1932): 404; Hyrum G. Smith, "The Day of Ephraim," *Utah Genealogical and Historical Magazine* 20 (Apr. 1929): 125; Ian G. Barber, "Matakite, Mormon Conversions, and Maori-Israelite Identity Work in Colonial New Zealand," *Journal of Mormon History* 41 (July 2015): 176; Marjorie Newton, *Mormon and Maori* (Sandy, Utah: Greg Kofford Books, 2014), 34; "Hagoth's Children," *Time Magazine* 71 (May 26, 1958): 65, 67.

George Q. Cannon, a missionary (and later apostle), preached the gospel to a hundred dark-skinned Hawaiians in 1850. "As they all sat around the mat and heard the voice of this missionary from Utah, they were transfigured before George Q. Cannon, and he saw ninety-seven of them become white and three of them remained dark," Neff related. Cannon "did not understand ... why it was that three of them would remain dark and all the rest should become light. He received a partial answer to this manifestation when it was learned that ninety-seven of those people ... joined the Church ..., while three of them never did."[30]

Given the ubiquity of such teachings, perhaps it is not surprising that whiteness theology became entrenched in popular LDS culture. In *Seek*, a popular LDS quiz game published in 1958, the designers posed several questions reinforcing this theology. "True or False," one question asked, "the Lamanites are promised that if they repent and accept the gospel their skin color will eventually become white again." Another question asked: "Name the descendants of Lehi who were cursed with dark skin because of their wickedness." Similarly, the award-winning Broadway musical *The Book of Mormon*, which debuted in 2011, describes LDS whiteness teachings, albeit from a satirical perspective. The show's creators, Trey Parker and Matt Stone, depict two naive and unsuspecting (white) missionaries sharing the "white and delightsome" scripture in 2 Nephi 30: 6 with dark-skinned Ugandans embroiled in war. The scripture was supposed to comfort them, but the opposite occurred: "How is this supposed to make things better for us?" a Ugandan sneered.[31] Also significant, in *Book of Mormon Stories*, a popular children's book, the authors reaffirm a link between skin color and conduct, informing young readers that "Laman and

---

30. Cannon's experience recounted by Neff in the April 1927 session of general conference. In *Conference Report* (Salt Lake City: Church of Jesus Christ of Latter-day Saints, 1927), 49–50. Cannon would later serve as a counselor in the First Presidency. See also Hokulani K. Aikau, *A Chosen People, A Promised Land: Mormonism and Race in Hawai'i* (Minneapolis: University of Minnesota Press, 2012), 43.

31. Transcript of *The Book of Mormon* musical (2011), www.scribd.com/doc/237052798/The-Book-of-Mormon-Script, 67. For a discussion of the musical, see J.B. Haws, *The Mormon Image in the American Mind: Fifty Years of Public Perception* (New York: Oxford University Press, 2013), 242–46.

Lemuel's followers ... became a dark-skinned people. God cursed them because of their wickedness."[32]

Such teachings, naturally, affected black Latter-day Saints, who found whiteness theology in LDS scripture demeaning. Darius Gray, a black LDS man, recalled that "The Book of Mormon talked about Lamanites and Nephites primarily Lamanites often having dark skin and being out of favor with God. I wanted to know how that related to me."[33] Another black LDS man, David Jackson, found the Book of Mormon deeply troubling, particularly the passages which "explain why the Lamanites received dark skins and a degenerate status."[34] Isaac Thomas, another black LDS man, complained about sermons he had heard in sacrament meeting "about being white and delightsome while others are black and loathsome and sinful."[35] Wain Myers, an outspoken black LDS man, expressed anguish after hearing missionaries quote from the Book of Mormon informing him he was cursed. He wondered how the church could teach racism "from the heart of the book it said was another testament of Jesus Christ."[36] Darron Smith, a black LDS scholar, lamented how the Book of Mormon created an institutional framework "where whiteness operates in opposition to people of color." The "white and delightsome" and "dark and loathsome" binaries, Smith opined, allowed Latter-day Saints to view people of color as "deviant and inferior."[37] In similar fashion,

---

32. *Seek: LDS Quiz Game* (Salt Lake City: Bookcraft, 1958; reissued 2003); my thanks to Courtney A. Harris for this reference. No author listed, *Book of Mormon Stories: Beginning Reader* (Salt Lake City: Church of Jesus Christ of Latter-day Saints, 1997), 26.

33. Gray oral history with Gregory A. Prince, Jan. 17, 2002, Box 22, Folder 2, Gregory A. Prince Papers, Special Collections, Marriott Library. See also Darius Gray oral history with Elizabeth Haslam and Dennis Haslam, Dec. 1, 1971, Box 1, Folder 7, African American Oral History Project, 1971–73, ibid.

34. Jackson, Letter to Dennis Gladwell, Aug. 13, 1995, Matthew L. Harris files (courtesy of David Jackson). For more on Jackson and LDS racism, see Harris and Bringhurst, *Mormon Church and Blacks*, 122–31.

35. Thomas, "Convert to High Priest: A Journey Before and After the Revelation," in Cardell K. Jacobson, ed., *All God's Children: Racial and Ethnic Voices in the LDS Church* (Springville, Utah: Bonneville Books, 2004), 58.

36. Myers (with Kelly L. Martinez), *Baptist Preacher to Mormon Teacher* (Springville, Utah: Cedar Fort, Inc., 2015), 41–42.

37. Smith, "Unpacking Whiteness in Zion: Some Personal and General Observations," in Newell G. Bringhurst and Darron T. Smith, eds., *Black and Mormon* (Urbana: University of Illinois Press, 2004), 153–54.

Wynetta Martin, the first black woman to join the LDS Tabernacle Choir, demurred when a fellow Latter-day Saint asked her if she "would change [her] skin to white if [she] had the chance." After politely saying no, Martin explained, "I have a built-in tan which cannot be removed unless our Father in Heaven takes a part in the transformation."[38]

Despite unease among black Latter-day Saints, some LDS leaders continued to proclaim that blacks would lose their "dark pigment" through conversion and righteous living. When Apostle Joseph Fielding Smith declared to LDS religious educators in 1954 that "we know of cases" where the "dark skin [of negroes] really has disappeared," he was not speaking metaphorically. For Smith, there were actual, tangible examples of black Latter-day Saints whose skin color turned lighter after converting to the church.[39] He further asserted that the "curse of Cain"—or "skin of blackness"—would be removed after the rest of God's children received "the holy priesthood." Here he echoed the teachings of Brigham Young, Wilford Woodruff, and other LDS leaders, holding that black skin was fluid and finite. If blacks lived worthy, Smith reasoned, God would lift the curse and make them pure again. They could even inherit the "celestial kingdom."[40]

---

38. Martin, *Black Mormon Tells Her Story: "The Truth Sang Louder Than My Position"* (Salt Lake City: Hawkes Publication, 1972), 71. This essay focuses on black Mormons, but it is important to note that Latter-day Saint Native Americans and Latinos were also troubled at how the church racialized them. For this point, see "Lacee A. Harris, "To Be Native American—and Mormon" (1985), in Givens and Neilson, eds., *Columbia Sourcebook of Mormons*, 254–60; Claudia L. Bushman, *Contemporary Mormonism: Latter-day Saints in Modern America* (Westport, Connecticut: Rowman and Littlefield, 2006), 102–03; Garrett, *Making Lamanites*, 104–06; Ignacio Garcia, "Empowering Latino Saints to Transcend Historical Racialism," in Gina Colvin and Joanna Brooks, eds., *Decolonizing Mormonism: Approaching A Postcolonial Zion* (Salt Lake City: University of Utah Press, 2018), chap. 8.

39. Smith, "Discussion after Talk on Racial Prejudice," 22. For more on Smith's views on race and lineage, see Matthew L. Harris, "Mormons and Lineage: The Complicated History of Blacks and Patriarchal Blessings, 1830–2018," *Dialogue: A Journal of Mormon Thought* 51 (Fall 2018): 108–09.

40. Smith, *Way to Perfection*, 106–07; Smith, *Answers to Gospel Question*, 2:178. See also Young sermon of August 19, 1866, George D. Watt et al., eds., *Journal of Discourses*, 26 vols. (Liverpool, England:1854–86), 11:272; and Wilford Woodruff sermon of September 16, 1877, G. Homer Durham, ed., *The Discourses of Wilford Woodruff* (Salt Lake City: Bookcraft, 1990), 163; First Presidency (George Albert Smith, J. Reuben Clark, David O. McKay), Statement of 1949, in Harris and Bringhurst,

As these teachings permeated LDS culture in the last half of the twentieth century, critics scoffed at how Latter-day Saints racialized themselves. In 1953 a journalist expressed disdain for the LDS teaching that "Negroes were originally white" but were then cursed for refusing "to accept God."[41] A 1959 commission investigating civil rights in Utah noted that the "Negro is not admitted to barber shops ... [and] beauty parlors ... and teaches that by righteous living, the dark-skinned races may again become 'white and delightsome.'" That same year a *Time Magazine* journalist commented on the commission's report, noting that the "Mormon interpretation of the curse of Canaan ... together with unauthorized, but widely accepted statements by [Mormon] leaders in years past, has led to the view among many Mormon adherents that birth into any race other than white is a result of inferior performance in pre-earth life."[42]

Rank-and-file members echoed a whiteness theology as well. Following journalist Clare Boothe Luce's nationally syndicated column averring that Mormonism holds "the human dignity of the Negroes in low esteem," a Latter-day Saint informed her that it "is our understanding that the negro will, in due time of the Lord, have his dark skin coloring taken from him; that in keeping with God's divine justice his limitations will be removed."[43] Similarly, a white politician in Utah courted the black vote by informing them that their "curse would be removed, in time, because God was going to turn them white again." Such expressions were also

Mormon Church and Blacks, 66; McConkie, *Mormon Doctrine*, 477; Henry D. Moyle, "What of the Negro?" Address to the French East Mission, Geneva, Switzerland, Oct. 30, 1961, CHL. By contrast, Apostle Mark E. Petersen took a contrary view from Apostle Joseph Fielding Smith. Petersen reasoned that he knew of "no scripture having to do with the removal of the curse from the Negro." Petersen, "Race Problems As They Affect the Church," 17.

41. J. A. Rogers, "Was Ezra Taft Benson's Decision Influenced by His Mormonism," *Pittsburgh Courier*, Oct. 10, 1953.

42. "Utah Advisory Committee," *The National Conference and the Reports of the State Advisory Committees to the U.S. Commission on Civil Rights, 1959* (Washington, DC: U.S. Government Printing Press, 1960), 379–80; "Mormons and Civil Rights," *Time Magazine* 73 (Apr. 13, 1959): 96.

43. "Clare Boothe Luce Says Romney '64 Deadlock Choice," *Arizona Republic*, Sept. 1, 1963; unidentified writer, Letter to Clare Boothe Luce, May 24 [1964], Box 21, Folder 4, Paul R. Cheesman Papers, Perry Special Collections.

widespread at Brigham Young University, the church's flagship educational institution. In the 1960s a BYU student interviewed dozens of students for a research project and discovered that they had been taught Mormonism's distinct whiteness teachings. "I've heard it said, I don't recall where or from whom," one respondent noted, "that if the Negro joins the Church, his skin will gradually become more light in color, the curse of Cain becoming less strong upon him. I've never seen a Negro to whom this has happened, so I don't know if it is true or not." Another respondent explained: "The motif of the Indian or Negro's skin lightening in color upon joining the Mormon Church is not uncommon in the author's experience."[44]

Yet, as troubling as the stories are, neither critics nor practicing Latter-day Saints mischaracterized LDS racial teachings. Since the founding of the church in 1830, Mormon leaders have consistently linked dark skin with evil and whiteness with purity, much as some white Protestants did in the eighteenth and nineteenth centuries.[45] There are examples in historical literature where white people claimed that dark-skinned people experienced

44. D. H. Oliver, a non-LDS black man from Salt Lake City, recounted the story about the white politician courting the black vote. In Oliver, *A Negro on Mormonism* (Salt Lake City: D. H. Oliver, 1963), 11. For the BYU study, See Stephen D. Taylor, "Mormon Folklore: The Negro A Study of Beliefs and Stories," written for William Wilson's English 391 Folklore class, 1969, 12–13, copy in Perry Special Collections.

45. For two insightful treatments of Mormon whiteness, particularly as it relates to nineteenth-century Mormonism, consult Mueller, *Race and the Making of the Mormon People,* and Reeve, *Religion of a Different Color.* Also see W. Paul Reeve, "All 'Mormon Elder-Berry's' Children: Race, Whiteness, and the Attack on Mormon 'Anglo-Saxon Triumphalism,'" in Patrick Q. Mason, ed., *Directions for Mormon Studies in the Twenty-First Century* (Salt Lake City: University of Utah Press, 2016), 152–75. Protestant Christians also associated black people with the lineage of Cain and Ham, and dark skin with sin. For this point, see David Brion Davis, *The Problem of Slavery in Western Culture* (Ithaca, New York: Cornell University Press, 1966); Stephen R. Haynes, *Noah's Curse: The Biblical Justification of American Slavery* (New York: Oxford University Press, 2002); Molly Oshatz, *Slavery and Sin: The Fight Against Slavery and the Rise of Liberal Protestantism* (New York: Oxford University Press, 2012); David M. Goldenberg, *The Curse of Ham: Race and Slavery in Early Judaism, Christianity, and Islam* (Princeton, New Jersey: Princeton University Press, 2003); Grace Elizabeth Hale, *Making Whiteness: The Culture of Segregation in the South, 1890–1940* (New York: Random House, 1998); Chappell, *A Stone of Hope*; Harvey, *Freedom's Coming*; Harvey, *Christianity and Race in the American South*; Noll, *God and Race*; Botham, *Almighty God Created the Races.*

a skin transformation after they embraced Christ's redemption. Historian John Turner notes, for example, that "some European and white American Protestants speculated that the offspring of African converts to Christianity would grow progressively whiter, physically as well as morally."[46]

One of the clearest examples of LDS racial tropes came from John Taylor, the third president of the LDS Church, who taught that "that the devil should have a representation upon the earth" through the lineage of Cain and Ham. Likewise, Bruce R. McConkie linked "negroes" with the "Devil" in *Mormon Doctrine* and promised that God would change their black skin after converting to Mormonism. "Negro blood," he insisted, would be "purged out of a human soul by baptism," facilitated by "the receipt of the Holy Ghost and personal righteousness." No less controversial, in 1969 church officials sought a dark-skinned person to represent Satan in the temple ceremony while at the same time invited a white man with Caucasian features to represent Jesus.[47] Some LDS leaders,

---

46. Turner, *The Mormon Jesus: A Biography* (Cambridge, Masschusetts: Harvard University Press, 2016), 251. See also Jon F. Sensbach, *Rebecca's Revival: Creating Black Christianity in the Atlantic World* (Cambridge, Massachusetts: Harvard University Press, 2005), 167, 197–99; Winthrop D. Jordan, *White Over Black: American Attitudes Toward the Negro, 1550–1812* (Chapel Hill: University of North Carolina Press, 1968), 215, 258–59; Rebecca Anne Goetz, *The Baptism of Early Virginia: How Christianity Created Race* (Baltimore: Johns Hopkins University Press, 2012), chap. 5. For an emphasis on whiteness in Protestant Christian theology, see Colin Kidd, *The Forging of Races: Race and Scripture in the Protestant Atlantic World, 1600–2000* (Cambridge, England: Cambridge University Press, 2006); Derek Chang, *Citizens of a Christian Nation: Evangelical Missions and the Problem of Race in the Nineteenth Century* (Philadelphia: University of Pennsylvania Press, 2010)); Katharine Gerbner, *Christian Slavery: Conversion and Race in the Protestant Atlantic World* (Philadelphia: University of Pennsylvania Press, 2018); and Edward J. Blum and Paul Harvey, *The Color of Christ: The Son of God and the Saga of Race in America* (Chapel Hill: University of North Carolina Press, 2012).

47. G. Homer Durham, ed., *The Gospel Kingdom: Writings and Discourses of John Taylor* (Salt Lake City: Bookcraft, 1987), 103; McConkie, *Mormon Doctrine*, 102 (subheading); McConkie, Memorandum to Spencer W. Kimball, 1977, Matthew L. Harris files (courtesy of Edward L. Kimball). For LDS officials seeking a dark-skinned Latter-day Saint to represent Satan in the temple ceremony, see David John Buerger, *The Mysteries of Godliness: A History of Mormon Temple Worship* (San Francisco: Smith Research Associates, 1994), 169; and BYU religion professor Spencer Palmer's interview with Buerger, Aug. 1, 1979, who noted that "several LDS Polynesians" complained about using someone with "black skin" to play Satan. After one of the Polynesians rejected the role, Palmer, a white man, got the part (my thanks to

moreover, taught that blacks would be white in the afterlife[48]—this despite the First Presidency declaring in 1944 that "nothing has yet been revealed" regarding "the color of the Negro when he comes forth in the resurrection."[49] Finally, some LDS leaders supported eugenics at the turn of the twentieth century, clearly implying, in the words of one writer, a "Mormon Whiteness."[50]

By the late twentieth century, however, the church began to distance itself from its controversial racial theology. After years of relentless criticism during the turbulent civil rights years, leaders

---

Signature Books for providing a transcript of the interview). For the color of Jesus in Mormon theology, see Turner, *Mormon Jesus*, chap. 9; Blum and Harvey, *Color of Christ*, 84–85, 147–48, 253–55; Kidd, *Forging of the Races*, 237; Noel Carmack, "Images of Christ in Latter-day Saint Visual Culture, 1900–1999," *BYU Studies* 39 (2000): 19–59; Matthew O. Richardson, "Bertel Thorvaldsen's *Christus*: A Mormon Icon," *Journal of Mormon History* 29 (Spring 2003): 72–83.

48. LDS convert Elijah Abel, a black man, received a patriarchal blessing in 1836, in which the patriarch blessed him that he "shalt be made equal to thy brethren and thy soul be white in eternity," in Harris and Bringhurst, *Mormon Church and Blacks*, 27. Similarly, a black LDS woman, Jane Manning James, received a patriarchal blessing in 1844 stating that her lineage was through "Cainaan the Son of Ham" but that God could remove the curse "and stamp upon you his own lineage" (my thanks to Max Mueller for providing a copy of Manning's blessing). See also Matthias F. Cowley, *Wilford Woodruff: History of His Life and Labors* (Salt Lake City: Deseret News, 1909), 587, for LDS church president Joseph F. Smith's sermon at Manning's funeral when he blessed her that she would be "a white and beautiful person" in the resurrection. For a trenchant discussion of Manning and Mormon whiteness theology, see Mueller, *Race and the Making of the Mormon People*, 147–52; and Quincy D. Newell, *Your Sister in the Gospel: The Life of Jane Manning James, a Nineteenth-Century Black Mormon* (New York: Oxford University Press, 2019).

49. First Presidency Secretary Joseph Anderson, Letter to W. N. Montgomery, Aug. 3, 1944, in "Manuscript of Council of the Twelve Minutes and First Presidency statements on the Negro," 12, Box 64, Folder 5, Spencer W. Kimball Papers.

50. Two recent published articles shed light on Mormon eugenics. See Joseph R. Stuart, "'Our Religion Is Not Hostile to Real Science': Evolution, Eugenics, and Race/Religion-Making in Mormonism's First Century," and Cassandra L. Clark, "'No True Religion without True Science': Science and the Construction of Mormon Whiteness," both in *Journal of Mormon History* 42 (Jan. 2016): 1–43, 44–72. Mormons were one of many groups supporting the eugenics movement at the turn of the century. For a brief explanation of eugenics in the United States, including laws that supported it, consult Jill Lepore, *The Mansion of Happiness: A History of Life and Death* (New York: Alfred A. Knopf, 2012), 82–93. The Supreme Court upheld a state statute supporting eugenics in *Buck v. Bell* (1927). See William E. Leuchtenburg, *The Supreme Court Reborn: The Constitutional Revolution in the Age of Roosevelt* (New York: Oxford University Press, 1995), 5–25; and Adam Cohen, *Imbeciles: The Supreme Court, American Eugenics, and the Sterilization of Carrie Buck* (New York: Penguin, 2016).

made modest attempts to tone-down LDS whiteness teachings.[51] In 1978, some six weeks after the June priesthood revelation, President Spencer W. Kimball instructed apostles not to teach that "the Negro" was denied the priesthood for being "less valiant in the previous existence" or because of "dark skin." "We just don't know what the reason was," Kimball said.[52] Kimball also consented to modifications in the Book of Mormon to change the problematic phrase "white and delightsome" to "pure and delightsome."[53] Correspondingly, church leaders dropped "the reference to the devil having a black skin" when they revised the temple ceremony in 1990. Twenty years later church officials removed the phrase "skin of blackness" in the chapter heading in 2 Nephi (Book of Mormon) to describe the "curse" God put on the sinful Lamanites. Finally, in 2013, the "Race and Priesthood" essay affirmed that black skin is not "a sign of divine disfavor or curse."[54]

Nonetheless, well into the twenty-first century, some Latter-day

---

51. Harris and Bringhurst, *Mormon Church and Black*, 79–81; Bringhurst, *Saints, Slaves, and Blacks*, 173–74; Haws, *Mormon Image in the American Mind*, 50–71; Matthew L. Harris, "Mormonism's Problematic Racial Past and the Evolution of the Divine-Curse Doctrine," *John Whitmer Historical Association Journal* 33 (Spring/Summer 2013): 102–07.

52. As Apostle LeGrand Richards explained to Wesley Walters and Chris Vlachos in an interview on August 16, 1978, CHL. A copy of the transcript is also in Perry Special Collections and Special Collections, Marriott Library. A published version of the interview may be found in Wesley P. Walters, *Interview with Mormon Apostle LeGrand Richards Concerning 1978 Negro "Revelation,"* Aug. 16, 1978 (Phoenix: Ex-Mormons for Jesus, 1978).

53. In 1981, according to Edward Kimball, President Kimball changed "language that righteous Lamanites would become 'a white and delightsome people' to 'a pure and delightsome people,' consistent with Joseph Smith's editorial changes in the 1840 edition." Kimball's son noted that "the change made clear that the primary issue was moral purity, not color" (Kimball, *Lengthen Your Stride* [Working Draft], 470). See also Douglas Campbell, "'White' or 'Pure': Five Vignettes," *Dialogue: A Journal of Mormon Thought* 29 (Winter 1996): 119–35; Royal Skousen, *The Book of Mormon: The Earliest Text* (New Haven, Connecticut: Yale University Press, 2009), 754; John Dart, "'Curse' Idea Upsets Some Indian Mormons: But Many Are Converted Despite Dark-Skin Teachings," *Los Angeles Times*, Feb. 10, 1979; "Mormons Altering Indian Prophecy," *New York Times*, Oct. 1, 1981; and "Mormons No Longer Promise 'White' Skin to Indians," *Los Angeles Times*, Sept. 30, 1981.

54. For the temple reference, see Keith E. Norman, "A Kinder, Gentler Mormonism: Moving Beyond the Violence Of Our Past," *Sunstone*, Aug. 1990, 10. For changes to the chapter subheading in 2 Nephi, see Peggy Fletcher Stack, "Church Removes Racial References in Book of Mormon Headings," *Salt Lake Tribune*, Dec. 20, 2010. See also "Race and Priesthood" essay.

Saints continued to associate white skin with righteousness. A black LDS woman, for example, expressed anguish at being told by a white LDS woman that she would be white in the resurrection and thus difficult to recognize in the next life. "You're so sweet," the white woman enthused, "but I don't know how I'm going to recognize you in the celestial kingdom, because I just can't visualize you white. … So you'll [have to] recognize me. … You'll have to come find me."[55] At BYU, a disgruntled student explained in the campus newspaper how he "listened to one of BYU's most popular [Book of Mormon] teachers describe our central scripture as 'black and white.' I doubt there is a single reader of this letter that doesn't already know which side he said is good and which is evil," the student complained. "When my teacher acknowledged that he too had sinned, he called it 'the black in myself.'" The student further lamented that he had "sat in classes on this campus where tenured, highly-rated professors teach that blacks will be whites when they reach heaven."[56] At the same time, a black LDS woman reported: "I have been a member [for] nine years and have been told many times on many different occasions how I'll be white in heaven or how my skin is a sin/curse."[57] Likewise, at a conference entitled "What It Means to Be a Non-White Mormon in America," dark-skinned Latter-day Saints bristled when recounting stories in

---

55. As recounted in Margaret Young and Darius Gray's film *Nobody Knows: The Untold Story of Black Mormons* (2008), transcript published in "Nobody Knows: The Untold Story of Black Mormons—Script," *Dialogue: A Journal of Mormon Thought* 42 (Fall 2009): 120–21.

56. Tristan Call, Letter to the editor, *BYU Daily Universe* (student newspaper), Jan. 23, 2008. As late as 2012, some BYU professors embraced Mormonism's controversial racial teachings. On this point, see Harris and Bringhurst, *Mormon Church and Blacks*, 136–39; and Haws, *Mormon Image*, 272. BYU students also touted LDS racial teachings. See Eugene England, "Are All Alike Unto God? Prejudice Against Blacks and Women in Popular Mormon Theology," *Sunstone* 15 (Apr. 1990): 18; Darron T. Smith, "These House-Negroes Still Think We're Cursed: Struggling against Racism in the Classroom," *Journal of Culture Studies* 19 (July 2005): 439–54; Eugene England, "Becoming a World Religion: Blacks, the Poor—All of Us," *Sunstone* 21 (June-July 1998): 58; Lynn K. Wilder, *Unveiling Grace: The Story of How We Found Our Way Out of the Mormon Church* (Grand Rapids, Michigan: Zondervan, 2013), 123–27; Carrie A. Moore, "LDS Black Seek Inclusion among Utahns," *Deseret News*, Nov. 17, 2001; Jacobson, *All God's Children*, 62.

57. Phylicia Rae Jimenez, Facebook blog, *Dialogue: a Journal of Mormon Thought* (Mar. 29, 2017): www.facebook.com/Dialoguejournal.

which white Latter-day Saints told them "their complexion would get whiter if they were righteous."[58]

As these teachings percolated throughout the LDS community, particularly on blog sites and social media, some Saints publicly denounced them. Mette Ivie Harrison, a white LDS woman, provided a blunt appraisal for *The Huffington Post* in a piece entitled "Is White Supremacy Inherent to Mormon Doctrine?" Harrison criticized LDS racial teachings, finding it "deeply troubling ... to read passages in the Book of Mormon and wonder how the term 'white' is meant to be understood if it is not about skin color. If this is all metaphorical, as I would like to claim then why does it sound so racist?" She wished that Latter-day Saints would stop "talking about skin color as a way of determining the worth of a person's soul—or their righteousness."[59]

Janan Graham-Russell, a black LDS woman, offered another criticism, condemning institutional racism in the LDS Church in a sharply-worded essay in *The Atlantic* magazine. In "Choosing to Stay in the Mormon Church Despite Its Racist Legacy," Graham-Russell explained that "the upper male and female leadership of the LDS Church remains largely white and American. While these leaders may be perfectly efficient in their roles," she admitted, "the persistent racial disparity suggests that the previous restrictions [on black people], and the ambiguity regarding their origins, still influence the pool from which the highest-ranking members of the Church are selected."[60]

---

58. Stack, "Sunstone Conference Asks What It's like to Be Mormon and Non-White," *Salt Lake Tribune*, July 7, 2015; "2015 Theology From the Margins Conference: Personal Narratives on Being a Non-White Mormon in America," *Sunstone*, Mar. 16, 2016: www.sunstonemagazine.com/2015-theology-from-the-margins-conference-personal-narratives-on-being-a-non-white-mormon-in-america. Race and Mormonism has been a hot topic of late. See, for example, *Journal of Mormon History* 41 (July 2015), which devotes an entire issue on the subject. Also see Aikau, *A Chosen People*; Garrett, *Making Lamanites*; Reeve, *Religion of a Different Color*; Mueller, *Race and the Making of the Mormon People*; and Newell, *Your Sister in the Gospel*.

59. Mette Ivie Harrison, "Is White Supremacy Inherent to Mormon Doctrine?" *The Huffington Post*, June 18, 2016: www.huffingtonpost.com/mette-ivie-harrison/is-white-supremacy-inhere_b_7614052.html.

60. Janan Graham-Russell, "Choosing to Stay in the Mormon Church Despite Its Racist Legacy," *The Atlantic*, Aug. 28, 2016: www.theatlantic.com/politics/archive/2016/08/black-and-mormon/497660.

Graham-Russell also criticized LDS leaders when they approved a racially insensitive song for the church's Young Women's program. Written by an Asian Latter-day Saint girl in 2016, the song "White" reaffirmed LDS racial themes depicting white as pure and black as sinful. "This song is very inappropriate," Graham-Russell stated. "I get the [doctrinal] idea but more care should be taken with anything involving the word 'white' and the LDS church because of its history and the present experiences of black members. It is symptomatic," she continued, "of not having honest conversations about race and what has been said about whiteness and blackness in our history."[61] Andrew Spriggs, a black LDS blogger concurred, adding: "The word 'white' is probably no good for Mormons, because we know Mormons have a heritage of associating whiteness (meaning purity) with whiteness (skin color). The church needs to focus on other analogies to restoration from sin," he stated, "because it's not a hypothetical to note that the church has believed that dark skin itself was a sin one needed to be cleansed from."[62]

In 2017, during businessman-turned-politician Donald Trump's racially-charged US presidency, LDS whiteness theology became an issue again when a white LDS housewife made national headlines for tweeting under the hashtag "whiteculture." Fusing Mormon scripture with an alt-right ideology, LDS convert Ayla Stewart unabashedly excoriated the Black Lives Matter social-protest movement, condemned racial diversity, and retweeted posts from Ku Klux Klansman David Duke. In addition, she criticized two prominent black Latter-day Saint women and

61. Graham-Russell, as quoted in Peggy Fletcher Stack, "LDS Church Yanks Song 'White' after Lyrics Fell Flat with Mormons of color," *Salt Lake Tribune*, Dec. 13, 2016.

62. Spriggs, "Whiteness in the 2017 LDS Mutual Theme" (blog), *Wheat and Tares,* Dec. 9, 2016: www.wheatandtares.org/2016/12/09/whiteness-in-the-2017-lds-mutual-theme. Church leaders heard the criticism and took swift action. "The song is being pulled pending further review," LDS spokesman Eric Hawkins noted. Yet pulling the song did not allay Graham-Russell's concern. "It's a cyclical process," she explained. "Something like this is said/published, people respond to it, and the piece in question is removed, only for it to happen again and again. The effort to build bridges to communities of color has to be more than optics." Hawkins and Graham-Russell, both quoted in Stack, "LDS Church Yanks Song."

created additional unease when she agreed to speak at a neo-Nazi rally in Charlottesville, Virginia.[63] *Newsweek*, *Slate*, and *Harper's* magazines revealed Stewart's extremist views to a national public, thus exposing the underside of LDS racial teachings.[64] The LDS Church promptly released an official statement critical of "White supremacist attitudes" as "morally wrong and sinful," adding, "Church members who promote or pursue a 'white culture' or white supremacy agenda are not in harmony with the teachings of the Church." The church's vigorous denunciation of Stewart pleased many black Latter-day Saints who "celebrated" and "even wept for joy" as their church leaders "pointedly disavowed groups that promote white supremacy."[65]

Such stories disclose a palpable anguish for many black Latter-day Saints, yet regrettably the "Race and Priesthood" essay does not repudiate whiteness theology, thereby missing an opportunity to heal what is ostensibly an open wound for many people of color in the church. The essay also fails to nuance the richness

---

63. Tamu Smith and Zandra Vranes, the two black LDS women in question, are best known for their blog *Sistas in Zion* and their book *Diary of Two Mad Black Mormons: Finding the Lord's Lessons in Everyday Life* (Salt Lake City: Ensign Peak, 2014). For the neo-Nazi rally in Virginia, see Louis P. Nelson and Claudrena N. Harold, eds., *Charlottesville 2017: The Legacy of Race and Inequality* (Charlottesville: University of Virginia Press, 2018).

64. Conor Gaffey, "How a Charlottesville Speaker Forced the Mormon Church to Condemn White Supremacists," *Newsweek,* Aug. 17, 2017: www.newsweek.com/charlottesville-mormons-white-supremacists-651747; Ruth Graham, "The Mormon Church Condemned White Supremacists, and this Mormon White Supremacist Mom Is Very Mad About It," *Slate,* Aug.18, 2017: www.slate.com/blogs/xx_factor/2017/08/18/the_mormon_church_condemned_white_supremacists_and_this_mormon_white_supremacist.html; Seyward Darby, "The Rise of the Valkyries: In the Alt-Right, Women Are the Future, and the Problem," *Harper's Magazine,* Sept. 2017: www.harpers.org/archive/2017/09/the-rise-of-the-valkyries/4. See also Peggy Fletcher Stack, "Mormon Blogger Trumpets Alt-Right Racial Views, but Is Out of Tune with Her Religion, *Salt Lake Tribune,* Apr. 2, 2017; Joshua Rhett Miller, "This Young Mom Is the Face of Mormonism's Hateful Alt-Right," *New York Post,* Mar. 31, 2017.

65. "Church Releases Statement Condemning White Supremacist Attitudes," *LDS Newsroom,* Aug. 15, 2017: www.lds.org/church/news/church-releases-statement-condemning-white-supremacist-attitudes?lang=eng; Peggy Fletcher Stack, "Black Mormons Applaud as LDS Church Condemns White Supremacy as 'Morally Wrong and Sinful,'" *Salt Lake Tribune,* Aug. 15, 2017. Stewart backed away from the neo-Nazi rally when it turned violent. See Gaffey, "How a Charlottesville Speaker Forced the Mormon Church to Condemn White Supremacists."

and complexity of the Book of Mormon—to clarify ambiguous passages of race in LDS scripture. This omission is important, for LDS scripture affirms both a message of inclusion for people of color ("All Are Alike Unto God") and a message of exclusion, marked by curses and future promises that dark-skinned people will one day become "white and delightsome."[66] Thus, the essay presents an incomplete view of race in LDS scripture. This is not a minor quibble. During much of the twentieth century, LDS leaders appealed to the Pearl of Great Price and the Book of Mormon as proof texts to justify the temple and priesthood ban.[67] Furthermore, the essay's omission of whiteness theology is problematic in that the 1978 revelation ending the ban did not attempt to modify interpretations based on these canonical works in light of the new policy change.[68]

Finally, the essay omits reference to the most important publications ever written about Mormons and blacks. This includes Stephen G. Taggart's *Mormonism's Negro Policy: Social and Historical Origins*, Lester Bush's seminal *Dialogue* article "Mormonism's Negro Doctrine: An Historical Overview," Newell Bringhurst's

---

66. On the ambiguity in the Book of Mormon as it relates to race, see Givens, *Wrestling the Angel*, 173; Bushman, *Rough Stone Rolling*, 97–98, 107–08, 288–89; Mauss, *All Abraham's Children*, 115–18; and Hickman, "The *Book of Mormon* as Amerindian Apocalypse." For deeper context to Mormon whiteness teachings, see Joanna Brooks, *Mormonism and White Supremacy: American Religion and the Problem of Racial Innocence* (New York: Oxford University Press, 2020).

67. LDS officials considered the Book of Abraham to be the main "proof text" justifying priesthood denial, but they sometimes associated the Book of Mormon with their racial teachings. See, for example, Petersen, "Race Problems—As they Affect the Church"; McConkie, *Mormon Doctrine*, 108, 554; Brooks, *L.D.S. Reference Encyclopedia*, 328; Alvin R. Dyer, "For What Purpose?" speech to LDS missionaries, Mar. 18, 1961, Oslo Norway, CHL; John A. Widtsoe, "Notes on the Negro," c. 1941, Box 227, Folder 4, John A. Widtsoe Papers, CHL; "Minutes of President Alvin R. Dyer on the visit of Roy A. Cheville, and the Negro Question," Sept. 10, 1969, Box 70, Folder 5, David O. McKay Papers, Special Collections, Marriott Library; William E. Berrett, "Race Problems," address to Brigham Young University Religious Education Faculty, July 10, 1956, CHL. For appeals to the Book of Abraham to justify the ban, see First Presidency, Minutes, Mar. 1, 1968, Box 67, Folder 3, David O. McKay Papers; Smith, *Way to Perfection*, 98–111; Smith, *Doctrines of Salvation*, 1:64–66; Llewlyn R. McKay, ed., *Home Memories of President David O. McKay* (Salt Lake City: Deseret Book Co., 1956), 226–31; Kimball, *Lengthen Your Stride*, 310–14; McConkie, *Mormon Doctrine*, 102, 107–08, 314, 476–77; Harris and Bringhurst, *Mormon Church and Blacks*, 35–40, 44–50, 55–62.

68. Harris and Bringhurst, *Mormon Church and Blacks*, 118.

Saints, Slaves, and Blacks: The Changing Place of Black People Within Mormonism, and Armand Mauss's *All Abraham's Children: Changing Mormon Conceptions of Race and Lineage.*[69] Other important works are also ignored, notably, Lester E. Bush and Armand L. Mauss's *Neither White nor Black: Mormon Scholars Confront the Race Issue in a Universal Church*, Newell G. Bringhurst and Darron T. Smith's *Black and Mormon*, and Gregory A. Prince and William Robert Wright's *David O. McKay and the Rise of Modern Mormonism.*[70] In short, the essay shuns virtually every major work of scholarship that has ever been published relating to the black-LDS priesthood and temple ban.[71]

Strengths and Reactions

Such problems notwithstanding, there is much to praise in the "Race and Priesthood" essay. For the first time in LDS discourse, the church has denounced its anti-black teachings, disavowing by name doctrines the church once taught as authoritative: the divine curse, the sinful conduct of black people in a premortal life, and the sin of interracial marriage. Second, leaders have now acknowledged that the ban resulted from the prevailing racism of Brigham Young's era rather than divine revelation—thus moving away from earlier characterizations that "we don't know how it began or why it began."[72] Third, the essay marks the first time

---

69. Stephen G. Taggart, *Mormonism's Negro Policy: Social and Historical Origins* (Salt Lake City: University of Utah Press, 1970); Lester E. Bush, Jr., "Mormonism's Negro Doctrine: An Historical Overview," *Dialogue: A Journal of Mormon Thought* 8 (Spring 1973): 11–68; Bringhurst, *Saints, Slaves, and Blacks*; Mauss, *All Abraham's Children*. For the influence of Taggart and Bush on LDS racial policy, see Harris and Bringhurst, *Mormon Church and Blacks*, 92–96.

70. Lester E. Bush and Armand L. Mauss, eds., *Neither White nor Black: Mormon Scholars Confront the Race Issue in a Universal Church* (Midvale, Utah: Signature Books, 1984); Bringhurst and Smith, eds., *Black and Mormon*; Prince and Wright, *David O. McKay and the Rise of Modern Mormonism*.

71. The one exception is Edward L. Kimball, "Spencer W. Kimball and the Revelation on Priesthood," *BYU Studies* 47 (Spring 2008): 5–85, which the essay quotes four times. However, the essay does not utilize the fuller and nuanced version of Kimball's work discussing his father's priesthood revelation in *Lengthen Your Stride*, chaps. 20–24.

72. The church first advanced this position in a 1969 First Presidency statement, published in the *Church News*, Jan. 10, 1970, 12; and *Improvement Era* 73 (Feb. 1970): 70–71. Church leaders first taught the "we don't know" rationale during the civil rights movement when critics strongly denounced the priesthood and temple ban. For

that leaders have attributed the ban to someone other than Joseph Smith.[73] Fourth, the essay admits the ban was both a temple and priesthood restriction, rejecting the popular perception that it applied solely to priesthood ordination. Finally, the essay acknowledges that black men held the priesthood during the early days of the church, clearly implying that Joseph Smith's position on black priesthood ordination was more permissive, inclusive, and progressive than Young's. This assertion marks a dramatic reversal from earlier church positions when leaders either denied outright or minimized altogether black ordination.[74]

---

this analysis, see Harris, "Mormonism's Problematic Racial Past and the Evolution of the Divine-Curse Doctrine," 107–08. For BYU professors advancing this position, see Joseph Fielding McConkie, *Answers: Straightforward Answers to Tough Gospel Questions* (Salt Lake City: Deseret Book Co., 1998), 30; Robert L. Millet, *Getting at the Truth: Responding to Difficult Questions about LDS Beliefs* (Salt Lake City: Deseret Book Co., 2004), 63.

73. For years, LDS leaders and Church Education System instructors averred that Joseph Smith instituted the ban. See the First Presidency statements of 1949 and 1969 in Harris and Bringhurst, *Mormon Church and Blacks*, 66, 81–83. See also Smith, *Way to Perfection*, 110; Kimball, ed., *Teachings of Spencer W. Kimball*, 449; Milton R. Hunter, *Pearl of Great Price Commentary* (Salt Lake City: Bookcraft, 1951), 141; Marcus H. Martins, *Blacks and the Mormon Priesthood: Setting the Record Straight* (Orem, Utah: Millennial Press, 2007), 9–10; Juan Henderson, "A Time for Healing: Official Declaration 2," in (no editor listed) *Out of Obscurity: The LDS Church in the Twentieth Century* (Salt Lake City: Deseret Book Co., 2000), 154.

74. For much of the twentieth century, LDS leaders were ambivalent about acknowledging priesthood ordination among black converts during the early years of the church. LDS Church historian Andrew Jenson stoked the controversy when he published a four-volume book entitled *Latter-day Saint Biographical Encyclopedia* (Salt Lake City: Andrew Jenson History Co., 1901–36). In the entry on Elijah Abel, one of the earliest black Mormons to receive the priesthood, Jenson acknowledged the ordination (3:577). This prompted a flurry of letters from the grassroots to LDS church headquarters. Some LDS officials acknowledged Abel's ordination, though they called it "exceptional" (Joseph Anderson [Secretary to First Presidency], Letter to Dorothy Woods, Oct. 24, 1947, Box 49, Folder 19, Richard D. Poll Papers, Special Collections, Marriott Library), while others denied it outright, claiming that the "story that Joseph Smith [had] ordained a Negro and sent him on a mission is not true" (Joseph Fielding Smith, Letter to Eulis E. Hubbs, Mar. 5, 1958, Box 9, Folder 7, Joseph Fielding Smith Papers). Some LDS apostles asserted that when the ordination was discovered, it "was declared null and void by the Prophet himself and ... by the next three presidents who succeeded the Prophet Joseph" (Harold B. Lee, "Doing the Right Things for the Right Reasons," BYU Devotional Address, Apr. 19, 1961, *BYU Speeches of the Year* [Provo, Utah: BYU Extension Services, 1961], 7). First Presidency counselor J. Reuben Clark planned to address the topic in general conference in 1954 and was prepared to acknowledge that "[t]here was one and possible two colored men upon whom the priesthood was confirmed in the very early days of the Church

Reaction to the essay has been mixed, especially from the church's small, but noteworthy black community. Darius Gray, a black member of some fifty years and a founding member of the church's Genesis Group called it "'an absolutely marvelous document' of great clarity and sensitivity." "It should be viewed as an official comment" from the top LDS leaders, he added.[75] Another long-time black Latter-day Saint, Catherine Stokes, was equally effusive, stating, "Hallelujah," in proclaiming the document "a Christmas gift to each and every member of the church—black, white, or whatever ethnicity."[76] Another black Saint Don Harwell, head of the Genesis Group at the time, praised the document for renouncing "the silliness that blacks were fence-sitters and less valiant (in the premortal existence), all the things that some [church] members used to justify the racism."[77] Bryndis Roberts, an African

---

before the Brethren understood the scriptures on the subject" (Clark, untitled general conference address, "Draft #3, Sept. 13, 1954, Box 210, "Negro and the Church" Folder, J. Reuben Clark Papers). However, for undisclosed reasons, he did not deliver it, probably because the Quorum of the Twelve and the First Presidency were divided on the subject. See also LDS Church President David O. McKay who noted that "in the days of the Prophet Joseph Smith one of Negro blood received the Priesthood. Another in the days of Brigham Young received it and went through the Temple. These are authenticated facts but exceptions" (McKay, Journal, Jan. 17, 1954, Box 32, Folder 3, David O. McKay Papers). Stephen G. Taggart, *Mormonism's Negro Policy*, and Lester E. Bush Jr., "Mormonism's Negro Doctrine," were the first LDS scholars to discuss black priesthood ordination. Since those seminal studies were published, a number of other important works have appeared, most notably Newell G. Bringhurst, "Elijah Abel and the Changing Status of Blacks Within Mormonism," *Dialogue: A Journal of Mormon Thought* 12 (Summer 1979): 22–36; Bringhurst, *Saints, Slaves, and Blacks*, chap. 3; Connell O'Donovan, "The Mormon Priesthood Ban and Elder Q. Walker Lewis: An Example for His More Whiter Brethren to Follow," *John Whitmer Historical Association Journal* 26 (2006): 47–99; Connell O'Donovan, "Brigham Young, African Americans, and Plural Marriage: Schism, Race, and the Beginnings of Black Priesthood Denial," in Newell G. Bringhurst and Craig L. Foster, eds., *The Persistence of Polygamy: From Joseph Smith's Martyrdom to the First Manifesto, 1844 to 1890* (Independence, Missouri: John Whitmer Books, 2013), 48–86; W. Kesler Jackson, *Elijah Able: The Life and Times of a Black Priesthood Holder* (Springville, Utah: Cedar Fort, 2013); Russell W. Stevenson, "'A Negro Preacher': The Worlds of Elijah Abels," *Journal of Mormon History* 39 (Spring 2013): 165–254; Stevenson, *For the Cause of Righteousness*, 228–49; Reeve, *Religion of a Different Color*, 106–39, 193–210.

75. Tad Walch, "LDS Blacks, Scholars Cheer Church's Essay on Priesthood," *Deseret News*, June 8, 2014.

76. Peggy Fletcher Stack, "Mormon Church Traces Black Priesthood Ban to Brigham Young," *Salt Lake Tribune*, Dec. 16, 2013.

77. Walch, "LDS Blacks, Scholars Cheer."

American Relief Society president in her local LDS congregation, offered a more cautious assessment: "I do not believe [the church] has done nearly enough to rid itself of the stain of exclusionary practices of the past." She wished the church would:

> Issue the Race and Priesthood essay as a letter from the First Presidency, an Official Declaration, or a proclamation.
> 1. Have that official document translated into all the languages that the Church uses to communicate with its worldwide membership.
> 2. Read it at General Conference and make it clear that neither the ban nor the justifications for the ban came from God.
> 3. Direct that it be read from the pulpit in every ward, branch, "cluster" ... and mission in the world.
> 4. Incorporate it into all levels of the Church's curriculum and teachings.[78]

Millennial Latter-day Saints were even more circumspect. Alexis Henson, a BYU student, stated that she was "super excited" when the statement was first issued but some six months later expressed her frustration at its limited exposure to the rank-and-file church membership, lamenting "nobody even knows about it." Fellow student Devan Mitchell claimed that certain church members who "had seen the essay haven't accepted it," further stating, "We might still need something a little more if we still have people defending" past racial theories used to justify the priesthood restriction which he termed "folklore."[79]

Several African American Latter-day Saints lamented that the essay did not admit wrongdoing or apologize for the ban. Darron Smith, a professor at the University of Tennessee and author of three books on blacks and Mormonism, urged the church to add an addendum and issue a formal apology.[80] Julienna Viegas-Haws, a BYU graduate and African American woman, observed that the

---

78. Bryndis Roberts, "African American Mormon Convert: LDS Church Needs to 'Make Amends' for Past Racism" (blog), *Flunking Sainthood,* Mar. 19, 2015: www.janariess.religionnews.com/2015/03/19/african-american-mormon-convert-lds-church-needs-make-amends-past-racism.

79. Ibid.

80. Darron T. Smith, "The Mormon Church Disavows Its Racist Past But Still Offers No Apology" (blog), *Huntington Post Religion,* Dec. 16, 2013: www.huffingtonpost.com/darron-t-smith-phd/the-mormon-church-disavow_b_4440244.html.

essay "falls short of a formal apology from the First Presidency for the hurt caused by the racism that produced the temple and priesthood ban," adding: "the church continues to suffer from institutional amnesia regarding the temple and priesthood ban and the hurt it has caused. I fear we are making similar mistakes today towards other groups. Our failure to remember can only result in a painful repetition of the past." Mica McGriggs, another African American BYU student, explained: "without an apology (which the essay lacks), no true healing can be found. An apology would be a balm for many."[81]

Some white Latter-day Saints were equally adamant about an apology. Brad Kramer, a graduate student at the University of Michigan, affirmed: "You can't repent, as a person, a people, or a church, of something that you refuse to acknowledge was a sin," he explained on Facebook. "This was a great and grievous sin, with ruinous consequences, that we collectively allowed ourselves to commit in God's name. And to the degree that we still blame God for our sin, we are still culpable in it and cannot truly heal from it."[82] Gina Colvin, an outspoken Latter-day Saint woman from New Zealand, put it even more starkly: "The lives of faithful people both black and white were destroyed, upended, devastated by this doctrine. There are generations and generations of Black and Colored folk who have had to wonder who they are in God's eyes because church leaders sustained a discourse that blatantly positioned them as inferior. They need an apology. ... They deserve an apology."[83]

---

81. Viegas-Haws, "LDS Church Could Speed Healing if It Noted June 8 Each Year," *Salt Lake Tribune*, June 20, 2015; McGriggs, as quoted in Carol Kuruvilla, "6 Questions With a Black Mormon Feminist" (blog), *Huffington Post Religion*, Sept. 3, 2015: www.huffingtonpost.com/entry/6-questions-with-a-black-mormon-feminist_ 55e75b1ee4b0b7a9633b833c. See also Mica McGriggs, "The Continuing Effects of the Priesthood Ban," *Sunstone*, Summer 2015, 24–25.

82. Kramer, quoted in Peggy Fletcher Stack, "On 37th Anniversary of Priesthood Ban's End, Black Mormons Say Race Issues Still Need Attention," *Salt Lake Tribune*, June 14, 2015.

83. Colvin, "Mormons, Mandela, and the Race and Priesthood Statement" (blog), *KiwiMormon*, Dec. 8, 2013: www.patheos.com/blogs/kiwimormon/2013/12/ mormons-mandela-and-the-race-and-priesthood-statement. See also Kristy Money and Gina Colvin, "LDS Church Should Go Further to Disavow Racist Priesthood Ban," *Salt Lake Tribune*, Dec. 21, 2014.

LDS scholars also provided insights, most prominently Washington State University sociology professor emeritus Armand L. Mauss, who was consulted during the crafting of the document. Mauss stated that he "was delighted to see it" and praised the church for its "new and greater level of candor and transparency." He felt personally "vindicated after fifty years and various encounters with stake presidents for promulgating" misinformation justifying the priesthood ban.[84] Similarly, Paul Reeve, the Simmons Professor of Mormon Studies at the University of Utah and a contributor in drafting the document, hoped that the information in the essay would have a "direct impact ... in the pews of Mormon congregations," adding: "You continue to hear stories of people citing or clinging to old racist teachings, and so the hurt and harm of those teachings can hopefully start to fade and diminish." Patrick Mason, at the time the Howard W. Hunter Chair of Mormon Studies at Claremont Graduate University who also consulted on the essay, declared it a "statement ... welcomed by [church] members concerned about outside charges of racism," showing that "the church has repudiated that past" and "we can move on from that troubled part of our legacy."[85]

Distinguished LDS scholar Richard L. Bushman, author of *Rough Stone Rolling*, an acclaimed biography of Joseph Smith, also weighed in on the implications of the document. He characterized it as "written as a historian might tell the story [and] not as a theological piece, trying to justify the practice." By depicting the priesthood ban "as fitting the common practices of the day," Bushman commented that it was "something that just grew up and, in time, had to be eliminated." But "accepting that," Bushman added, "requires a deep reorientation of Mormon thinking," noting that "Mormons believe that their leaders are in regular communication

84. Armand Mauss, Email to Tad Walch, Dec. 13, 2013, copy provided by Mauss in an email to me. Portions of Mauss's statements were contained in Walch, "LDS Blacks, Scholars Cheer."

85. As quoted in Walch, "LDS Blacks, Scholars Cheer." Reeve explained his role in crafting the document in Rick Bennett, "Paul Reeve's Role in Race Essay," *Gospel Tangents Podcast*, Feb. 27, 2017: www.gospeltangents.com/2017/02/27/paul-reeve-wrote-the-race-essay. Mason explicates his views on the "Race and Priesthood" essay in *Planted: Belief and Belonging in an Age of Doubt* (Salt Lake City: Deseret Book Co., 2015), 109–10.

with God, so if you say [Brigham] Young could make a serious error, it brings into question all of the prophet's inspiration." Black LDS writer Marvin Perkins, co-author of the DVD series *Blacks and the Scriptures,* echoed similar concerns, stating: "The disavowal says to the church and the world, 'Everything we taught you justifying the restriction is wrong.' But what would be ideal would be for every member to be as well-versed regarding the truths of the priesthood ban and scriptural truths regarding skin color and curses as they are with the Joseph Smith story and the First Vision. We need it repeated over and over in church curriculum in manuals and over the pulpit. That's the way this will be resolved."[86]

Final Thoughts

The "Race and Priesthood" Gospel Topics essay is the best official expression to date concerning LDS racial teachings. The essay should be praised—even celebrated. But it stops short of full disclosure. In its defense, the LDS hierarchy had to walk a delicate line acknowledging past teachings while protecting earlier leaders from charges of doctrinal error.[87] Thus, the "Race and Priesthood" essay offers neither a full disclosure of LDS racial teachings nor provides an avenue for healing by offering an apology in recognition of the pain caused by the church's institutionalized racism. The essay does not acknowledge—or attempt to explain—the continuing presence of whiteness teachings in LDS scripture and discourse.

Nevertheless, the essay is a major milestone in LDS ecclesiology. Latter-day Saints now have an authoritative document to cite when they encounter fellow Saints who promote anti-black and other racist teachings or attribute the ban or such racism to God. Equally important, the essay rejects past racist teachings, declaring unequivocally that God does not privilege or punish people based on skin color or prior conduct in a pre-mortal life. This overdue

---

86. As quoted in Peggy Fletcher Stack, "Mormon Church Traces Black Priesthood Ban to Brigham Young."

87. Historian Richard Bushman noted the precariousness of the position when he observed, "Mormons believe that their leaders are in regular communication with God, so if you say [Brigham] Young could make a serious error it brings into question all of the prophet's inspiration." Quoted in Stack, "Mormon Church Traces Black Priesthood Ban to Brigham Young."

admission is welcome news. It is proof that LDS teachings are evolving—and that they will continue to evolve as Latter-day Saints seek to make the church more inclusive for people of color.

11. THE CONTINUING CONTROVERSY OVER THE BOOK OF ABRAHAM

Stephen C. Taysom

In 2013, a Latter-day Saint named Jeremy Runnells was undergoing a faith crisis. In the spring of that year, he wrote a lengthy letter to a member of the LDS Church's CES (Church Education System) laying out the reasons for his loss of faith and asking if the CES officer could answer any of the theological, scriptural, or historical issues that Runnells addressed. The letter almost immediately spread via the Internet, reportedly provoking additional faith crises as well as sharp apologetic responses. Among the many topics that Runnells's letter broached, and which local church leaders quickly found themselves trying to explain to worried congregants, was the Book of Abraham. Runnells asked more than a dozen questions, mostly dealing with the discrepancies between the papyri material Joseph Smith claimed to have translated and the translation of that same material by non-LDS Egyptologists. In fact, at the same time that the "Letter to a CES Director" was going viral, University of Chicago Egyptologist Robert Ritner translated the "Joseph Smith papyri" and published his scholarly translation.[1] He concluded that Smith's Book of Abraham bears no resemblance to the texts from which he claimed to have translated it. This was not new. In 1912, Episcopal Bishop Franklin S. Spaulding sent the images, or facsimiles, accompanying the Book of Abraham text, along with Smith's interpretations of them, to a panel of distinguished academics for comment. The comments were harsh. Each dismissed the material as common and Smith's

---

1. Robert K. Ritner, *The Joseph Smith Papyri: A Complete Addition* (Salt Lake City: Signature Books, 2013).

translations as absurd. As long as there have been criticisms of the Book of Abraham, there have been responses from apologists. In Spaulding's day, the job fell to men like John Widtsoe, B. H. Roberts, and Jan Sjodahl.[2] Although erudite and eloquent, these men were not Egyptologists.

In the late 1960s, fragments of the original papyrus related to the Book of Abraham were found in New York City and obtained by the LDS Church. This development led later defenders to learn the languages and culture of ancient Egypt. The first Mormon to do so was Hugh W. Nibley, who had taken a leave of absence from BYU to study under Egyptologist Klaus Baer at the University of Chicago's Oriental Institute. Others, such as Yale-trained Egyptologist John Gee, would follow. The Runnells letter and the Ritner book and the responses they generated from apologists are the latest battles in a war that has raged over the Book of Abraham since the late nineteenth century, but they came at a moment in which the LDS Church was moving toward addressing problematic areas in church history. Given the long history of contention over the Book of Abraham, and the newly stoked fires, it made a great deal of sense for the church to include an essay on the Book of Abraham in its online Gospel Topics series. This chapter explores the Book of Abraham controversy by introducing the reader to the Book of Abraham itself through a discussion of its history, content, and context, then moving to a discussion of the LDS Church's essay, and concluding with a review of some of the major historiographical landmarks in the history of the controversy.

The Book of Abraham: History, Translation, Content

The concept of what constitutes "scripture" is a contentious one both within and among religious traditions. Not all religious traditions situate scripture as a touchstone for doctrine, policy, and ritual, although the Abrahamic faiths absolutely do. Typically, the process of deciding to include a text in the canon of scripture is as much political as it is religious. Religions, because they are social and cultural entities, are interested in various forms of power.

---

2. The responses of these men to Spaulding's *Joseph Smith as Translator* appeared in the February 1913 issue of the church's *Improvement Era* magazine.

Granting a text scriptural status within the Abrahamic traditions elevates that text, and all of its subtexts, above contestation. The story of how the New Testament was created provides the classic model of this process. The texts that became what we know as the New Testament represented a tiny percentage of the documents produced and studied by various types of early Christianity. The decision about what to put in and what to keep out was driven by the need to select only those texts that supported the particular theological and ecclesiastical structures of the group doing the selecting. Over time, the mechanics of the process tended to evaporate, leaving believers with the impression that the New Testament, and the Old Testament as well, was one coherent text that sprung forth from the mind of God. So, too, with the Koran. Eventually, many Christians, Jews, and Muslims viewed these scriptures not only as divine and authoritative, but also literal and inerrant. Joseph Smith's approach to scripture opened the canon again, making space for a potentially unlimited corpus of authoritative, sacred writings. The Book of Abraham is an example of one such new book of scripture.

The Book of Abraham is unique, and uniquely controversial, among these books because it is the only text "translated" by Smith for which we have the original source material. Smith claimed to have translated the Book of Mormon from a set of ancient metal plates that disappeared when he completed the translation; Smith said that the material in the Book of Moses came to him through a process of direct revelation, and that he did not work with an original source at all. By contrast, Smith produced the Book of Abraham from a set of documents that came with some mummies that he and his followers acquired from a man named Michael Chandler in the 1830s. Purchasing mummies may strike modern readers as strange, but in the nineteenth century the United States and much of Europe was is in the throes of "Egyptomania." Napoleon and other European leaders and adventurers spent much of the nineteenth century stocking their national museums with Egyptian antiquities. Figures such as the British Museum's E. A. Wallis Budge exploited Egypt's status as a contested colonial battleground to claim and export ancient treasures of all kinds. Mummies held a particularly powerful sway over European and American imaginations, and in the absence of effective laws regulating the removal and sale of human remains from Egypt, opportunities to purchase them were not in short supply.

The story of the Book of Abraham is anything but clear. This confusion both contributes to and derives from the controversy that continues to smolder around the nature of the text. The Book of Abraham generates such intense debate because, in the minds of many of the participants in the controversy, Smith's entire prophetic identity rises and falls with the legitimacy of the Book of Abraham. So there are really two strands to this narrative. The first is the story of the Book of Abraham's production and reception during Smith's lifetime. In the 1820s, a brilliant Frenchman, Jean Francois Champollion, claimed to have cracked the code of Egyptian hieroglyphic language. His seminal work, *Précis du Système Hiéroglyphique des Anciens Egyptiens,* was published in 1827. In this book, Champollion argued, correctly, that the ancient Egyptian written language was formed by a combination of ideographic and phonetic signs.[3] Although Champollion's work with Egyptian linguistic forms began before the Book of Abraham was published, it took many years before this work gained acceptance by scholars. No less prestigious institution than the British museum claimed as late as the 1840s that "hieroglyphs remained a mystery." The production of the Book of Abraham occurred in the twilight era of the Egyptian mysterium during which "pharaonic antiquities could be little more than curious objects about whose history one could only speculate."The controversy, however, arose largely because some of the material that Smith used in his translation resurfaced long after it had become "possible to read what the artifacts had to say about themselves, their makers, and the context in which they were made."[4] The materials that Smith received from Chandler could be translated and this translation could, in turn, be compared, and contrasted, with what Smith

---

3. *Cracking the Egyptian Code: The Revolutionary Life of Jean-Francois Champollion* (New York: Oxford, 2012).

4. Elliott Colla, *Conflicted Antiquities: Egyptology, Egyptomania, Egyptian Modernity* (Durham, North Carolina: Duke University Press, 2007), 96.

produced. This inaugurated the ongoing debate about the nature of the relationship between the papyri Smith had and the English text that he published as the Book of Abraham.

The Book of Abraham controversy begins with the papyrus scrolls that Smith used to produce the Book of Abraham. We have a good idea about where the papyri came from, but we have a much less clear idea about where they ended up. All parties agree that Smith came to own various ancient Egyptian artifacts and texts in the mid-1830s. In 1835, Smith and most of the members of his church resided in the village of Kirtland in northeast Ohio. Chandler had been travelling throughout the eastern United States, displaying and selling mummies he had acquired. By the time he arrived in Kirtland, Chandler had only a few mummies left. In Smith, Chandler found an eager buyer, and he sold several mummies to Smith in the summer of 1835. Smith loved ancient things, in large part because he believed that he was in the process of restoring the original religion of the ancient biblical patriarchs. Smith could not pass up the opportunity to own Egyptian artifacts given the connection described in the Old Testament between the patriarch Abraham and the ancient land of Egypt. As it happened, the mummies themselves proved of little interest to Smith. Much more important were the mysterious scrolls that accompanied the mummies. Egyptian hieroglyphics had yet to be deciphered, and this, coupled with their pictographic quality, lent an irresistible air of mystery to Egyptian texts. Smith began working with the textual materials in the fall of 1835, but he did not publish his "translation" of the materials until 1842. By then, Smith and the church had relocated to Nauvoo, Illinois, where he would remain until his murder in the summer of 1844. The material that would eventually be canonized as the Book of Abraham appeared first in the LDS newspaper *Times and Seasons* in March 1842, along with certain images from the papyrus scrolls, images that Smith called "facsimiles" and which he numbered 1–3.

Smith claimed that, within the two papyrus scrolls and the various smaller fragments that he acquired from Chandler, were stories not only about Abraham but also about Joseph, as well as other individuals. Of course, the only material that was actually translated and published was that portion that dealt with Abraham. It was, perhaps, inevitable that Smith would produce revelatory material dealing with Abraham. The Book of Abraham's publication in 1842 is clearly linked with Smith's evolving theological ideas. By the 1840s, when the Book of Abraham was published in serial form, Smith had come to believe that he had divine authority to restore the ancient covenant made between God and Abraham. This was made explicit in the language of the Mormon "sealing ceremony" which Smith pronounced on individuals for whom he performed wedding ceremonies of both the monogamous and polygamous varieties. The ceremony, among other things, promised that those entering into this "new and everlasting covenant of marriage" became the recipients of the blessings of "Abraham, Isaac, and Jacob." Clearly, Smith's interest in Abraham was central to his theological project, and the focus on Abraham and the Abrahamic covenant grew increasingly intense in step with Smith's interest in the covenants of the Mormon temple, especially the marriage covenant. It is not clear what impact the Book of Abraham had on readers in Nauvoo. There is no evidence of any internal skepticism about the content of the book, or of Smith's ability to translate ancient religious records. Like the Book of Mormon, this "new" ancient text served as further proof of Smith's calling as a prophet and as a source for new theological ideas that would eventually exert deep and powerful influence over the course of Mormon history and theology.

The book opens with a story of Abraham and his father. Abraham's father was a favorite of ancient Jewish writers, who produced numerous midrashim detailing his exploits. Generally, he is portrayed in that literature not only as an idol-worshipper, but also as an idol-dealer, making and selling images of various gods. In Smith's Book of Abraham, Abraham's father is far more sinister. Abraham recounts that his "fathers" have turned their backs on the one true God, the god first introduced in the Garden of Eden, and that priests had taken up what the book describes as an Egyptian practice of human sacrifice. Much to the chagrin of his father, Abraham wanted to claim the true priesthood bestowed by the one true God. Rather than allow this, Abraham's father apparently gave his son to the priests, who duly prepared to kill him as an offering to one of the many gods whom they worshipped in their apostate religion. At the last minute, Abraham is rescued by an angel of God and hears the voice of the one true God, who identifies himself as Jehovah who tells Abraham that he has come to take him away from his father's house. The story then describes the covenant that Jehovah makes with Abraham, in language similar to that found in the Hebrew Bible. Smith's Abraham is taught by Jehovah about astronomy and the creation of the earth.

Most significantly, from a theological perspective, is Abraham's vision of the life of human spirits before being born into mortality. Abraham is shown a scene of God gathering what he calls "intelligences" and "organizing" them into anthropomorphic spirit form. These spirits were then grouped according to rank, and God informs Abraham that his spirit was among the "noble and great ones" who were chosen as spirits to come to earth to play important roles in God's plan for humans. It is at this point that three other important theological ideas are introduced. First, the concept of "estates." According to the Book of Abraham, the intelligences cum spirits who chose to come to earth passed a major hurdle and "kept their first estate." A life faithfully lived on earth would mean that an individual kept her "second estate" and would merit eternal glory. Second, the idea that Satan's origins are found in his unsuccessful attempt to come to earth as God's son and his subsequent failure to keep his "first estate," first introduced in the Book of Moses, is reinforced in the Book of Abraham. Here, then, Smith produces a text that places ancient Judaism and Christianity in the same story by introducing Abraham to the "redeemer of the world," just as Smith had done with Moses more than a decade earlier. Finally, there is an extremely brief mention of "that race [descended from Ham] which preserved the curse in the land." After Smith's death, Brigham Young introduced a policy forbidding persons of black African ethnicity or descent from holding the priesthood and participating in temple rituals. Later some Latter-day Saints, most prominently church apostle/president Joseph Fielding Smith, pointed to the Book of Abraham as a scriptural basis for this exclusion.

In Nauvoo, Smith placed a heavy emphasis on the material aspect of the Egyptian relics acquired in Kirtland. Visitors to Smith's home could view the papyrus fragments as well as the mummies, although he apparently charged twenty-five cents to view these "curiosities." During the 1840s, many more Mormons, and others, would have been exposed to the physical artifacts than to the text itself, a fact that carries some potentially significant implications. In choosing to display mummies and papyrus scrolls, Smith was forging a physical connection between himself and the mystical worlds of Egypt, on the one hand, and of the biblical patriarchs, on the other. Thus Smith used material culture to reify two of his most important identities: God's chosen keeper and administrator of the restored Abrahamic covenant and a seer with the power to unlock antiquity's greatest mysteries and in antebellum America, nothing seemed more mysterious and meaningful than ancient Egypt.

The LDS Church fragmented after Smith's murder in June 1844, with the vast majority of Mormons accepting Brigham Young as Smith's legitimate successor and eventually following him west to what would become Utah. Smith's wife, Emma, and their children remained in Nauvoo, and so did the Egyptian artifacts. In 1851, the Book of Abraham was republished in pamphlet form by Franklin Richards, then president of the LDS Church's British Mission, as part of a new collection called the Pearl of Great Price. In 1878, the First Presidency assigned Orson Pratt to revise the collection and publish it under the official auspices of the LDS Church. Two years later, the Pearl of Great Price, including the Book of Abraham, was presented to the general membership of the church, who voted to canonize the collection. While the text itself, including three images from the papyrus scrolls that had been published along with the scriptural translation since its initial appearance in the *Times and Seasons*, thus became part of the official canon, the papyrus scrolls themselves disappeared into history. The Smith family apparently sold the artifacts in 1856, and interested parties generally assumed that some of the scrolls had made their way to Chicago where they were destroyed in the Chicago fire of 1871. In 1966, officials at the Metropolitan Museum of Art in New York City revealed that they possessed in their collections artifacts labeled "papyrus fragments of hieratic Books of the Dead, once the property of Mormon leader Joseph Smith."[5] Working through University of Utah professor Aziz Atiya, the museum sold/transferred the materials to the LDS Church.

"Translation and Historicity of the Book of Abraham"

The church's Gospel Topics essay is an important document on the ongoing history of the Book of Abraham, due in no small part to the essay's attempt to shift the grounds of the debate. The essay concedes that "Mormon and non-Mormon Egyptologists agree that the characters on the fragments do not match the translation given in the Book of Abraham." Yet the essay maintains that the Book of Abraham is ancient, authentic, and scriptural by emphasizing five major points. I will briefly list the arguments and then discuss each in detail. First, there are no surviving eyewitness accounts of the translation process, making it "impossible to reconstruct" Smith's translation procedures. Second, the material obtained from the collection at the Metropolitan Museum of Art represents only a small percentage of the original papyri, thus ostensibly rendering any relationship between the text of the Book of Abraham and the fragments in the church's possession "a matter of conjecture." Third, the essay argues that Smith never translated things in the traditional sense of that term, but rather used supernatural gifts to draw English text from ancient sources. According to the essay, there is no reason to believe that the translation process of the Book of Abraham differed significantly from the methods Smith used to translate the Book of Mormon. Fourth, the text of the Book of Abraham contains details about the ancient world that would have been impossible for Smith to have known. Finally, the essay asserts that, ultimately, the status of the Book of Abraham as ancient scripture can only be established through faith and a witness from the Holy Ghost.

The first two points make what one might consider an "agnostic" move. That is, they have the effect of decreasing falsifiability

---

5. "Review of the Year 1947," *Metropolitan Museum of Art Bulletin* 7/1 (1948): 17, quoted in John Gee, "Editors Introduction," in Hugh W. Nibley, *An Approach to the Book of Abraham* (Salt Lake City: Deseret Book Co., 2009), xxv.

by increasing or emphasizing the areas for which no evidence of any kind exists. Specifically, the essay points out two areas about which little is known: the translation process Smith used and the materials that Smith translated.

Let us begin with the second point first. One of the major bones of contention in the Book of Abraham debate is whether or not the materials obtained from the Metropolitan Museum were the same ones Smith described using in his translation of the Book of Abraham. Almost as soon as the papyrus fragments from the Met surfaced, now known popularly as comprising a portion of the Kirtland Egyptian Papers, it became clear that the text of the Book of Abraham could not possibly be derived from the characters on those papyrus fragments. (I use KEP to refer hereafter to the papyri.) The church entrusted the translation of the documents to Hugh Nibley, professor of religion at Brigham Young University. Nibley felt that LDS responses to previous challenges made by Egyptologists to the historicity of the Book of Abraham had been non-existent because the "Mormons, untrained in Egyptology [were] helpless to question on technical grounds the assertions of such experts."[6] Nibley, while a linguist and scholar, had only studied ancient Egyptian writings for a short time and was barely proficient but took to the task with a will. Even so, it quickly became evident to Nibley that the KEP bore no resemblance at all to Smith's translation. This criticism, as the church's essay notes, predated the re-discovery of the KEP by a century or more. The "facsimiles" and their interpretations accompanied the first publication of the Book of Abraham, and have been included with it ever since. Egyptologists recognized the pictures as being parts of common Egyptian funerary texts, such as the Book of the Dead, and they knew that such texts had nothing whatever to do with Abraham. Although the facsimiles continue to prove controversial, they were only the tip of the iceberg. When the KEP emerged and were translated, this seemed like an obvious victory for the critics of the Book of Abraham. If the Egyptian documents and their translation did not match the Book of Abraham, then, it would seem, Smith had

---

6. Hugh W. Nibley, *An Approach to the Book of Abraham* (Salt Lake City: Deseret Book Co., 2009), 41.

simply invented his "translation." But defenders of the Book of Abraham were not willing to surrender on this point. One of the main challenges faced by defenders of the Book of Abraham with regard to papyrus is that Smith himself repeatedly claimed that he was translating from papyrus and that the papyrus he was working with contained Abraham's writings. Without these assertions linking the Book of Abraham with a physical piece of papyrus, the defenders could easily have claimed that Smith received the entire Book of Abraham through revelation without the use of a text, just as he had done with the Book of Moses in 1830. Smith's insistence on linking the Book of Abraham with a papyrus scroll, however, necessitated a more sophisticated defense.

Nibley, and the church, took the position that the scraps of papyrus in the KEP did not match descriptions from those who had seen the materials Smith worked with. Smith, they argued, was known to have worked with a "long scroll." Critics, in turn, argued that a long scroll could easily be rendered into smaller fragments, a practice that was common when scholars and museums dealt with long scrolls. In his 1982 book, *By His Own Hand Upon Papyrus*, former Mormon Charles Larson summarized what continues to be the critics' position: "two things became clear to those working with the papyri. First, two key papyri fragments belonged together to form one piece. And second, these fragments could be linked to the Book of Abraham."[7] Defenders of the Book of Abraham took the opposite approach. Nibley, who admitted in 1970 that the hope, presumably on the part of both critics and defenders, was that the translation of the Met fragments would lead to a "quick decision" and settlement of the Book of Abraham question, "were blasted when it became apparent on the one hand that those documents do not contain the Book of Abraham, and on the other that the connection between [them] and the Book of Abraham is anything but clear."

Later, LDS Egyptologists would agree with Nibley. Yale-trained John Gee gathered and analyzed statements of eyewitnesses of the scrolls and concluded that based on, *inter alia*, the size and

---

7. Charles Larson, *By His Own Hand Upon Papyrus*, (Cedar Spring, Michigan.: Inst for Religious Research), 1982. Electronic version available here: www.mit.irr.org/his-own-hand-upon-papyrus-part-2.

description of the scrolls the eyewitnesses saw, that "the Book of Abraham was located elsewhere" than on the KEP. Kerry Muhlestein, a UCLA-trained Egyptologist employed by BYU, summed up the position of the apologists in a 2010 essay. "Those who saw the papyri in Joseph's day," Muhlestein asserted, "agreed that the long roll was the source of the Book of Abraham. Because we know this roll was destroyed in the Chicago fire, assumptions that the Book of Abraham came from the Metropolitan Museum fragments run contrary to contemporary eyewitness accounts. Judging from these accounts, it seems the Book of Abraham came from the scroll, not the fragments."[8] The church's 2013 echoes this view, claiming that it is "futile to assess Joseph's ability to translate the papyri … since … it is likely that much of the papyri accessible to Joseph when he translated the Book of Abraham is not among those fragments." By arguing that the actual documents used by Smith to produce the Book of Abraham have not yet been discovered, defenders need not concede anything with regard to Smith's claims of a correlation between the materials he bought from Chandler and the text of the Book of Abraham. More importantly, defenders can harmonize Smith's claims to have derived the Book of Abraham from an ancient Egyptian text with the conclusion that the KEP and the Book of Abraham text have no linguistic relationship.

The other appeal to agnosticism made in the church's essay centers on Smith's translation process. This is a slightly less complex issue than that of the papyrus. There is no question that Smith maintained an unusually capacious understanding of the term "translation." He believed that he had a God-given gift to produce texts, in English, that were originally written in unknown languages, written in known languages, texts not written at all (as in the case of the Book of Moses), from metal plates, papyrus, and even on material that was shown him in vision. The church's 2013 essay maintains that "the Lord did not require Joseph Smith to have a knowledge of

---

8. Kerry Muhlestein, "Egyptian Papyri and the Book of Abraham: Some Questions and Answers," *Religious Educator* 11:1 (2010), available at www.rsc.byu.edu/archived/volume-11-number-1-2010/egyptian-papyri-and-book-abraham-some-questions-and-answers; accessed Aug. 4, 2016.

Egyptian. By the gift and power of God, Joseph received knowledge about the life and teachings of Abraham." Critics, however, point to a set of documents located with the papyri as part of the KEP that indicated Smith's attempt to create and use traditional linguistic tools in his translation of the Egyptian papyri

The documents at issue are called the *Egyptian Alphabet and Grammar*, and they appear to contain Egyptian symbols along with phonetic equivalents.[9] In 1966, Jerald and Sandra Tanner, Christian critics of the LDS Church, published these materials. The implication that critics drew from these texts is that Smith was pretending to create translation apparatus for Egyptian, and that the entire enterprise exposed him as a fraud. One critic summed it up this way: "the book turned out to be nothing but page after page of nonsensical gibberish. Though it had apparently succeeded at one time in impressing unsophisticated minds, the work was unable to withstand the scrutiny of experts."[10] As with the translation of the KEP papyri, even LDS scholars had to agree with the critics. In 1968, Nibley dismissed the *Egyptian Alphabet and Grammar* documents as something produced by Smith "in a moment of privacy," engaging in a "little speculation on his own hands and knees in the front room of the [Nauvoo] Mansion house with the papyri spread out around him on the floor" and without any real value.[11] By 1971, however, Nibley had adjusted his opinion and had adopted the position that defenders of the Book of Abraham continue to maintain, namely that Smith did not actually produce the alphabet and grammar document and that he did not use it to produce the Book of Abraham.[12] Nibley's shift came in response to Richard P. Howard, Church Historian of the Reorganized Church of Jesus Christ of Latter Day Saints, which also bases its claims on Joseph Smith. In an interview with the *New York Times* and in a published article in

---

9. For the publication of the *Egyptian Alphabet and Grammar*, along with other Book of Abraham documents, see Robin Scott Jensen and Brian M. Hauglid, eds., *Revelations and Translations, Volume 4: Book of Abraham and Related Manuscripts* (Salt Lake city: Church Historian's Press, 2018).

10. Larson, *By His Own Hand*, www.mit.irr.org/his-own-hand-upon-papyrus-part-2.

11. Hugh W. Nibley, "Prolegomena of any Study of the Book of Abraham," *BYU Studies* 8, 2 (Winter 1968): 176.

12. Hugh W. Nibley, "The Meaning of the Kirtland Egyptian Papers," *BYU Studies* 11, 4 (Summer 1971): 350–99.

the journal *Courage*, Howard set forth what would become known as the "modus operandi" theory, arguing that Smith's use of the alphabet and grammar was his "modus operandi" in "determining [the] contents" of the Book of Abraham.[13] Nibley challenged Howard to use the alphabet and grammar to produce English text from Egyptian writing, suggesting that such a feat would be impossible and that, therefore, Smith could not have done so. Nibley's challenge to Howard ignored the real point that critics of the Book of Abraham were making with the modus operandi theory, namely that Smith used the alphabet and grammar as a way to lend credence to a fictitious and imagined translation. Other defenders followed Nibley's lead but developed more sophisticated arguments. Most recently, John Gee argued that, not only was the alphabet and grammar produced entirely by Smith associate W. W. Phelps, but that it could not have been created before January 1836.

Like so many things in the Book of Abraham debate, the devil is in the smallest of details. Just as Nibley's initial argument found sophisticated defenders in later years, so did the modus operandi theory. Historian Christopher Smith argued, using a methodical and close reading of the Book of Abraham text itself, that Joseph Smith relied on the alphabet and grammar to produce parts of the Book of Abraham, especially the first three verses of the first chapter of the Book of Abraham in 1835.[14] Because apologists and critics alike agree that the alphabet and grammar could not possibly have been helpful in translating Egyptian, evidence that Joseph Smith both created it and used it as part of his translation process poses serious problems for the book's defenders. John Gee thus seeks to undermine Christopher Smith's assertions about both authorship of the alphabet and grammar and the timing of the documents creation. According to Gee, no evidence exists tying

---

13. Richard P. Howard, "The 'Book of Abraham' in Light of History and Egyptology," *Courage* (Apr. 1970): 38. The Community of Christ, then the RLDS Church, does not accept the Book of Abraham as scripture. This, obviously, makes their approaches to Joseph Smith's translation menthods different from LDS approaches. See www.cofchrist.org/scripture-in-community-of-christ for a description of the Community of Christ canon.

14. Christopher C. Smith, "The Dependence of Abraham 1:1–3 on the Egyptian Alphabet and Grammar," *The John Whitmer Historical Association Journal* 29 (2009): 38–54.

anyone but Phelps to the creation of the alphabet and grammar, and because the alphabet and grammar employs a transliteration system that was not introduced to the Mormon community until January 1836, "it must date after the later system was taught."[15] If that is true, and if the agreed upon dating of the translation of some of the Book of Abraham to 1835 is indeed correct, then not only was the alphabet and grammar useless, but Joseph Smith could not have even *pretended* to have used it in his production of the Book of Abraham.

Although most of the debates surrounding the KEP lack nuance, two pieces, at least, attempted to take a more complex view of the issue. Samuel Brown argued that Phelps most likely did produce the alphabet and grammar documents, but that he did so with the consent and under the supervision of Joseph Smith, and that Smith apparently trusted Phelps's linguistic ability.[16] Brian Hauglid, a professor at Brigham Young University, believes, contrary to what Nibley and Gee have argued, that Phelps did not create the alphabet and grammar on his own, and he argues that Joseph Smith possibly experimented with the KEP while producing the Book of Abraham. Although Hauglid takes a somewhat tentative approach, he cautions that any attempt to separate Smith's obvious interest in Egyptian language from the translation process of the Book of Abraham "would likely do violence to ever reaching a better understanding of the historical context" of the Book of Abraham's production.[17] Brown's article is useful for our purposes because it is one of the few pieces dealing with the Book of Abraham that is not designed either to discredit or shore up Joseph Smith's prophetic claims. Hauglid's piece demonstrates that, even, among apologists working for the church today, there are disagreements about these issues.

We can now move on to the third main assertion in the church's

---

15. John Gee, "Joseph Smith and Ancient Egypt," in Lincoln H. Blumell, Matthew J. Grey, and Andrew H. Hedges, eds., *Approaching Antiquity: Joseph Smith and the Ancient World* (Salt Lake City: Deseret Book Co., 2015), 440–41.

16. Samuel Brown, "The Translator and the Ghostwriter: Joseph Smith and W.W. Phelps," *Journal of Mormon History* 34, 1 (Winter 2008): 26–62.

17. Brian M. Hauglid, "The Book of Abraham and the Egyptian Project," in Blummell et. al., *Approaching Antiquity*, 501–502.

2013 essay, the claim that Mormonism's founding prophet translated the Book of Abraham via supernatural means. In order to bolster this argument, the essay seeks to link Smith's production of the Book of Mormon and the Book of Moses with the Book of Abraham. In arguing for uniformity of process, the essay attempts to blunt or even circumvent the critical problems involving the KEP once and for all. The essay makes the case that a statement from a revelation in which Joseph Smith was told by God, in relation to the Book of Mormon, that Smith could "not write that which is sacred save it be given you from me" also "can be applied to the Book of Abraham." The basic point here is that no matter what the papyri say or do not say, Smith's Book of Abraham was somehow bolstered by, extended by, enriched by, or completely consisted of divine revelation. The papyrus scrolls, according to this view, acted as a material vehicle that prompted some sort of revelatory experience which, in turn, resulted in the production of the Book of Abraham. This is sometimes referred to as the "catalyst" theory because the papyrus acted as a catalyst for the reception of revelation. In 2013, the LDS Church issued a new edition of its scriptures, and an important shift in describing the Book of Abraham. Before 2013, the official language in the published Book of Abraham stated that the book was "a translation from some Egyptian papyri"; the 2013 edition (and to the present) now describes the text as an "inspired translation of the writings of Abraham."

Although not a huge shift, the change in wording does add an important new dimension. "Inspiration" is now comingled with "translation" in such a way that any deviation from the modern Egyptological translation of the papyrus fragments may be explained, to believers at least, as the result of catalytic inspiration.[18] Obviously, those who do not accept Smith's prophetic claims, see this move as nothing more than an effort to salvage credibility in the eyes of believers. Although this is a fair point, it must be remembered that, while Smith did apparently attempt to translate the Egyptian characters in a traditional manner, contemporary

---

18. For a more detailed discussion of the catalyst theory, see David E. Bokovoy, *Authoring the Old Testament* (Draper, Utah: Greg Kofford Books, 2014), 165.

accounts clearly attest that he claimed to be getting some sort of revelation as well. This is not, in other words, a new invention by apologists, although the emphasis on the role of revelation has grown stronger. Also, as with all of the church's essays, this one is aimed at believing Latter-day Saints who may be troubled by what they are reading about the Book of Abraham. Foregrounding inspiration over translation thus provides some breathing room for those who wish to maintain belief in the historical and religious legitimacy of the Book of Abraham. The cost of this is that the church's essay downplays the important differences between the modes of "translation" used for the Book of Mormon, the Book of Moses, and the Book of Abraham. That there are differences is undisputed. There is, for example, no "Book of Moses controversy" to speak of. What is the difference? Smith claimed that the Book of Moses came via direct revelation, independent of any text, and thus one's acceptance or rejection of this material is thus strictly a matter of faith. The Book of Mormon case is similar. Even though Smith claimed to have had access to ancient records and used these to produce the Book of Mormon, the textual material itself is not extant and the language Smith claimed he read on the plates is a heretofore unknown Hebrew-Egyptian hybrid. The Book of Moses and the Book of Mormon thus ostensibly share complete freedom from secular falsifiability and dwell almost exclusively in the realm of faith. The Book of Abraham, however, presents a more complex case that requires more sophisticated defenses.

The first three points made in the essay are, as I noted earlier, grounded in an agnostic epistemology. That is, they are all about highlighting the significant gaps in what we know, and what can be proven, about the Book of Abraham. The fourth point takes a different tack, seeking to make the case that in at least one area of secular learning, namely the history of the ancient Near East, the Book of Abraham fares well. As with almost all of the other points, Hugh Nibley was the first person to try to make this case. In fact, in 1981 he produced a substantial book, *Abraham in Egypt*, designed to make one simple argument: the Book of Abraham contains things about the ancient world that no modern person knew until after the death of Joseph Smith. As we have seen, early in the 1970s, Nibley abandoned any contention that the KEP had any value in understanding the Book of Abraham. He turned instead to the text of the Book of Abraham itself. As Nibley described the situation,

> there are two propositions regarding the Book of Abraham that none can deny. The one is that Joseph Smith could not possibly have known Egyptian as it is understood today. The other is that the Prophet has put down some remarkable things in the pages of the Book of Abraham. Why should we waste time on proposition number 1? It is proposition 2 that provides us at last with firm ground to stand on—and none of the critics has given it a moment's thought.[19]

This is an interesting statement for a number of reasons. First, it is jarring to see how summarily Nibley has dismissed any interest in Smith's efforts to work with the Egyptian language. Critics naturally would have seen such a move as an admission of defeat. Nibley, however, wants to draw attention to what he says the critics have ignored, namely that "what Joseph Smith tells us about Abraham ... can now be checked against a large corpus of ancient writings, unavailable to Joseph Smith."[20] And, according to Nibley, the Book of Abraham and the ancient apocryphal Abraham literature that he cites, check out nicely. Geographical, religious, political, and other features of the world described in the Book of Abraham are, according to Nibley, consonant with what non-LDS scholars and ancient sources tell us about Abraham's world.[21] Not only did Nibley see antiquity in Mormonism, he saw Mormonism in Egyptian antiquity. In 1975, Nibley published *The Message of the Joseph Smith Papyri: An Egyptian Endowment*. This lengthy, dense book argues that the Egyptians practiced rituals that closely resemble the LDS temple endowment.

On this score, later defenders of the Book of Abraham adopted Nibley's pattern. In the July 1988 issue of the LDS Church's

---

19. Hugh W. Nibley, *Abraham in Egypt*, 2nd ed. (Salt Lake City: Deseret Book Co., 2000), 155. The book was originally published in 1981, and republished in 2000 as part of the "Collected Works of Hugh Nibley" series.

20. Ibid.

21. Hugh W. Nibley *The Message of the Joseph Smith Papyri: An Egyptian Endowment* (Salt Lake City: Deseret Book Co., 1975).

Ensign magazine, Michael Rhodes, an Oxford-educated Egyptologist who taught in BYU's Department of Ancient Scripture, repeated Nibley's argument, almost verbatim when he wrote that "in reality, the actual method Joseph Smith used is far less important than the resulting book of scripture he produced. But here the Prophet's critics prefer to ignore the evidence of the text itself. The Book of Abraham should be evaluated on the basis of what it claims to be: a record of Abraham."[22] Rhodes then informs the reader that the Book of Abraham is teeming with authentic ancient information. Note that Rhodes also follows Nibley's lead in chastising the critics for failing to engage with this point. The implication seems to be that critics will not enter into a debate that they know they will lose.

The church's 2013 essay cites several pieces of evidence to support the assertion that the Book of Abraham bears the marks of antiquity, including the prevalence of human sacrifice, capital punishment for those who agitated against the religious order of Egypt or its territorial holdings, the use in the Book of Abraham of the previously unknown term "Olishem" which was subsequently discovered in epigraphic form in Syria, possible parallels between Elkenah as described in the Book of Abraham and the Canaanite god El, and Abraham's father's ancient reputation as an idolater.

It is true that critics have remained largely, although not completely, silent on the matter of the evidence for antiquity in the Book of Abraham itself. Certainly, critics have had far less to say about these issues than about the translation questions. Part of this may be a lack of substantial evidence for rebuttal. It may also stem from the critics' belief that their work on the translation problems so thoroughly discredited the Book of Abraham's claim to an ancient identity that any engagement with its content is as unnecessary as it is uninteresting. There are some scholars critical of the Book of Abraham who have ventured into the fray, however. The most recent example is a brief essay published along with Ritner's translation of the KEP that takes up the challenge offered by

---

22. Michael D. Rhodes, "Why Doesn't the Translation of the Egyptian Papyri Found in 1967 Match the Text of the Book of Abraham?" *Ensign*, July 1988, at www. lds.org/ensign/1988/07/i-have-a-question?lang=eng; accessed Aug. 11, 2016.

Nibley and Rhodes. Christopher Woods, Ritner's colleague at the University of Chicago, challenged the apologists' argument about the location of the city of Ur. The current scholarly consensus, Woods points out, is that ancient Ur was located in Babylon and, therefore, outside of the Egyptian cultural sphere of influence. The current state of knowledge about ancient Near Eastern religious practice, according to Woods, "poses grave difficulties for the account given in the Book of Abraham." In particular, Woods notes that "there is no evidence whatsoever for the cults of the purported Egyptian gods described in the narrative or for established Egyptian religious practices more generally in the city [of Ur]."

Much of the apologetic material relies on taking the view that Ur was farther north, and not in Babylon at all. In fact, the church's essay acknowledges the scholarly consensus about the Mesopotamian Ur in a footnote, but seeks to blunt this by claiming that "cogent arguments have been made for a northern location within the realm of Egyptian influence." The "cogent arguments" that the essay then cites as evidence for an Ur that supports the Book of Abraham's claim to antiquity come from Nibley and another BYU professor, Paul Hoskisson. So, at least with regard to the apologetic arguments about ancient religious life at Ur and their consonance with the Book of Abraham, one must accept that the Ur described in the Book of Abraham is not the Ur recognized by the vast majority of scholars, but is rather the Ur recognized only by those who already accept the Book of Abraham as scripture. For readers unconvinced of Joseph Smith's prophetic calling, this circular reasoning is neither helpful nor persuasive. Again, however, it is worth remembering that these are essays designed to provide faithful doubters with some measure of comfort via plausibility, and in that regard this portion of the essay, in my opinion, is relatively successful.

Ritner, for whom Woods wrote his piece on the location of Ur, has emerged as the most important critic of the Book of Abraham since 1912. Never before has the Book of Abraham attracted a critic who is so well-educated, highly accomplished, and confrontational in almost equal measure. During his time as a professor at Yale, Ritner had a role in the education of John Gee, one of the foremost apologists for the LDS Church on the Book of Abraham.[23] For reasons that remain unclear, but which have been speculated about endlessly on internet message boards, Gee and Ritner had a falling out that apparently devolved into an ongoing personal animus. Ritner publicly denigrated Gee in print, writing that "unlike ... all of my other Egyptology students, Gee never chose to share drafts of his publications with me to elicit scholarly criticism," and that Gee's articles on the Book of Abraham do not "reflect the standards of Egyptological proof that I required" as a professor.[24] Whatever the reason, Ritner, who teaches at the Oriental Institute at the University of Chicago, felt obliged to involve himself in the Book of Abraham controversy after "several years of (often anguished) requests," apparently by individuals undergoing some sort of faith crisis and looking for answers about the Book of Abraham. Ritner obliged by publishing a translation of the Joseph Smith Papyrus documents in which he deals, by his own admission, "often bluntly" with "published criticism by Mormon apologists (often vituperative)."[25] In the prestigious *Journal of Near Eastern Studies*, Ritner described the Book of Abraham as a "pastiche of Genesis." Ritner appears to object to what he sees as an attempt to throw a scholarly cloak over "outlandish nonsense," his term, particularly when it comes from one of his own former students.[26]

The final point made by the church's essay is that the Book of Abraham can only be completely validated via a spiritual witness. When writing to in-group readers who accept the basic premise that the LDS Church is the one true church of God and that things like the Holy Ghost and revelation exist, such a claim is

---

23. As of 2017, Gee is the William Bill Gay Research Professor of Egyptology at the Neal A. Maxwell Institute for Religious Scholarship at Brigham Young University. Among his many works include "Abraham in Ancient Egyptian Texts," *Ensign*, July 1992, 60; "Two Notes on Egyptian Script," *Journal of Book of Mormon Studies* 5:1 (1996): 162–176; *A Guide to the Joseph Smith Papyri* (Provo, Utah: Foundation of Ancient Research and Mormon Studies, 2000); *An Introduction to the Book of Abraham* (Provo, Utah: Religious Studies Center at Brigham Young University and Deseret Book Co., 2017).

24. Robert K. Ritner, "'The Breathing Permit of Hor,' Thirty Years Later," *Dialogue: A Journal of Mormon Thought* 33, 4 (Winter 2000): 103.

25. Ritner, *The Joseph Smith Egyptian Papyri*, 9.

26. Robert K. Ritner, "'The Breathing Permit of Hor' Among the Joseph Smith Papyri," *Journal of Near Eastern Studies* 62, 3 (2003): 161.

a valid rhetorical move. No one would expect non-believers to accept this as legitimate academic argument. It is, however, a legitimate *devotional* argument. The overall message of the Book of Abraham essay is to argue that no academic argument marshaled against the Book of Abraham is fatal, that there are plausible, academically valid defenses against them sufficient to create room for an informed faith, but a faith that must ultimately rest on spiritual–supernatural–affirmation.

Conclusion

I am not a scholar of near-eastern antiquity nor of Egyptology. I am, however, trained as a historian of religion. I am interested in the ways in which religion(s) interact with culture(s). One of the great ironies of religion is that in order to be successful, at least from a sociological perspective, a religious tradition must both deftly adapt and change to maintain its place within its larger cultural web as well as maintain the appearance of eternal changelessness. This is not an easy task. The LDS Church's essay on the Book of Abraham, although aimed at believers going through some degree of faith crisis, is useful for scholars of religion interested in these dynamics of religio-cultural interaction. Clearly, the LDS Church has produced an environment in which scholarly achievement has been harnessed to devotional defenses in sophisticated and powerful ways. As important as what the LDS Church chose to do with the Book of Abraham is what it chose *not* to do. It could have chosen, for example, to distance itself from the Book of Abraham along the lines of what some forms of mainline Christianity have done with the Bible. That it acted in the opposite direction speaks as much to its future engagements with controversy as to its past interactions.

12. "MOTHER IN HEAVEN"
A FEMINIST PERSPECTIVE

Caroline Kline and Rachel Hunt Steenblik

The doctrine of Heavenly Mother holds enormous potential for LDS women, though this potential has been largely unrealized. Unlike most other Christian traditions which affirm a genderless, amorphous deity, the Church of Jesus Christ of Latter-day Saints posits a sexed, embodied Heavenly Mother and Father. The existence of this embodied female deity is crucial for LDS women, since She stands as the eternal exemplar of LDS women's own divine destinies. If Heavenly Mother exists, Her human daughters will have the potential to exist as female deities in the eternities. However, despite the ennobling potential of Heavenly Mother teachings within the LDS Church, She has been largely ignored in LDS liturgy, rhetoric, and worship. LDS leaders model and encourage members to refer to and pray to "Heavenly Father," and Heavenly Mother is absent from temple rituals, the vast majority of church leaders' sermons, and almost all church curriculum, Mormon scripture, and, in general, the consciousness of most LDS members. She thus inhabits an ambiguous position, as a deity purportedly equal in holiness and glory to God the Father, but overwhelmingly wrapped in a cloak of invisibility and silence.[1]

Since the 1970s and 1980s, LDS feminists have worked to elevate Heavenly Mother in the consciousness of church members, understanding that She stands as a potentially powerful symbol of female empowerment and equality. In the 1990s and 2000s, the church excommunicated LDS feminist theologians

---

1. In this essay, we adopt a style that differs from the other essays in the present compilation and capitalize all divine nouns and pronouns to reflect the usage adopted in the Gospel Topics essay on Heavenly Mother.

Margaret Toscano and Janice Allred after they refused to cease publishing articles on Heavenly Mother.[2] These ecclesiastical disciplinary actions, combined with direction from President Gordon B. Hinckley in 1991 not to pray to Heavenly Mother, made the subject of Heavenly Mother something of a taboo topic among orthodox Latter-day Saints. With the rise of LDS internet discussion forums in the early 2000s, however, discussions of Heavenly Mother and Her contested position, role and status have proliferated as well as more personal stories of members yearning and reaching for Her in their lives.

Given Heavenly Mother's ambiguous position and the many fraught questions surrounding Her—is She truly God, equal to God the Father? If so, why is She so absent from our rhetoric, let alone our worship? Why are we not encouraged to develop relationships with Her?—it makes sense that the institutional church composed a (very brief) Gospel Topics essay on the subject of Heavenly Mother, entitled "Mother in Heaven," in the fall of 2015.[3] This essay is a much-needed contribution that is useful in some respects but leaves unresolved several important questions about Heavenly Mother's role, status, and near invisibility in LDS worship and rhetoric.

Useful Contributions

The fact that the "Mother in Heaven" essay was written at all and published on LDS.org, with the explicit approval of the highest leaders of the church, helps to remove the unofficial taboo status from discussions of Heavenly Mother. Citing David L. Paulsen and Martin Pulido's wide-ranging *BYU Studies* article on historical teachings of Heavenly Mother, the "Mother in Heaven" essay implicitly affirms one of the major points of the Paulsen-Pulido article—that there is no doctrinal basis for LDS silence about the

---

2. See Peggy Fletcher Stack, "A Mormon Mystery Returns: Who is Heavenly Mother?" *Salt Lake Tribune*, May 16, 2013. Margaret Toscano discusses these excommunications in "Margaret M. Toscano," Ann Braude, ed., *Transforming the Faiths of Our Fathers: Women Who Changed American Religion* (New York: Palgrave Macmillan, 2004), 157–71.

3. "Mother in Heaven," Gospel Topics essay (Oct. 23, 2015): www.churchofjesuschrist.org/study/manual/gospel-topics-essays/mother-in-heaven?lang=eng.

Mother God.[4] Moreover, this Gospel Topics essay explicitly affirms LDS teachings about Heavenly Mother as "cherished and distinctive," and refers to them as "the doctrine of Heavenly Mother," lending official sanction to LDS beliefs in Heavenly Mother.[5]

With this Gospel Topics essay, which explicitly refers to "a Heavenly Mother" (upper case) rather than the more general "heavenly parents" or "a heavenly mother" (lower case), the institutional church is positioning Heavenly Mother as on par, in some sense, with Heavenly Father. The essay begins with an assertion of humans on earth as spirit children of "a Heavenly Father and a Heavenly Mother." Using this language and punctuation throughout the essay, the writers implicitly reject older notions of Heavenly Father and multiple heavenly mothers.[6] This is an important step forward in discussions and understanding of female deity, because the specter of a polygamous Father God surrounded by a cadre of subordinate deified wives has haunted the minds of generations of LDS women. In contrast, this essay features a quote by Susa Young Gates, which positions "the divine Mother" as "side by side with the divine Father."[7] By using this particular language about Heavenly Mother, the essay promotes an image of a monogamously married deified couple, equal in worth and glory.

The "Mother in Heaven" essay also reviews the origins of the

---

4. David L. Paulsen and Martin Pulido, "'A Mother There': A Survey of Historical Teachings about Mother in Heaven," *BYU Studies* 50, 1 (2011): 73, 75.

5. Gordon B. Hinckley also referred to Heavenly Mother teachings as "doctrine" in 1991: "Logic and reason would certainly suggest that if we have a Father in Heaven, we have a Mother in Heaven. That doctrine rests well with me." Hinckley, "Daughters of God," *Ensign*, Nov. 1991: www.churchofjesuschrist.org/study/general-conference/1991/10/daughters-of-god?lang=eng. Two First Presidency statements (cited in the Gospel Topics essay) offered support by including teachings on Heavenly Mother: 1909's "The Origin of Man" and 1995's "The Family: A Proclamation to the World."

6. Linda P. Wilcox similarly noted capitalization and its relationship to the question of multiple heavenly mothers, with her example (taken from an LDS Department of Seminaries and Institute manual) both illustrating what she called "the church's style" of capitalizing "Heavenly Father" while not capitalizing "heavenly mother," and suggesting "the possibility of multiple heavenly mothers." Wilcox, "The Mormon Concept of a Mother in Heaven," in Maureen Ursenbach Beecher and Lavina Fielding Anderson, eds., *Sisters in Spirit: Mormon Women in Historical and Cultural Perspective* (Urbana: University of Illinois Press, 1987), 72.

7. Susa Young Gates, "The Vision Beautiful," *Improvement Era* 23, 6 (Apr. 1920): 542.

doctrine of Heavenly Mother. Spending two of its six paragraphs on historical references to Heavenly Mother by church leaders, the essay explains that while we do not have hard evidence that Joseph Smith taught this doctrine, we do have compelling secondary and tertiary evidence that he told women like Zina Diantha Huntington that they would someday meet their Heavenly Mother. The essay also nicely credits and quotes famous early LDS women like Eliza R. Snow and Susa Young Gates for expressing and explicating the doctrine of Heavenly Mother.[8]

The writers of the essay chose to feature nine quotes from church leaders about the existence and role of Heavenly Mother. Five of these quotes are general and simply affirm Heavenly Mother's existence or the fact that humans are spirit children of divine parents.[9] The four other quotes give us marginally more information about Heavenly Mother. Susa Young Gates's quote, as mentioned above, positions Heavenly Mother as a co-equal with God the Father. Apostle M. Russell Ballard's quote ("We are part of a divine plan designed by Heavenly Parents who love us") emphasizes that a loving Heavenly Mother played a role in designing the plan of salvation.[10] Apostle and later President Harold B. Lee's quote points to a Mother God whose love and concern eclipse that of earthly parents, and he implied that Heavenly Mother (along with other divine influences) "is working to try and help us when we do all that we can."[11]

One of the last quotes in the "Mother in Heaven" essay derives from Gordon B. Hinckley's 1991 talk, in which he cautions members against praying to Heavenly Mother. "The fact that we

---

8. Eliza R. Snow, "My Father in Heaven," in "Poetry, for the Times and Seasons," *Times and Seasons* 6 (Nov. 15, 1845): 1039; "O My Father," no. 292, in *Hymns of The Church of Jesus Christ of Latter-day Saints* (Salt Lake City: Church of Jesus Christ of Latter-day Saints, 1985), 292.

9. Snow, "My Father in Heaven"; "The Origin of Man," *Improvement Era* 13, 1 (Nov. 1909): 78; "The Family: A Proclamation to the World," *Ensign* or *Liahona*, Nov. 2010, 129; Rudger Clawson, "Our Mother in Heaven," *Latter-day Saints' Millennial Star* 72, 39 (Sept. 29, 1910): 620; Dallin H. Oaks, "Apostasy and Restoration," *Ensign*, May 1995: 84.

10. M. Russell Ballard, When *Thou Art Converted: Continuing Our Search for Happiness* (Salt Lake City: Deseret Book Co., 2001), 62.

11. Harold B. Lee, "The Influence and Responsibility of Women," *Relief Society Magazine* 51, 2 (Feb. 1964): 85.

do not pray to our Mother in Heaven in no way belittles or denigrates her," the essay quotes Hinckley.[12] While every other quote in the "Mother in Heaven" essay emphasized Heavenly Mother's involved role as partner to Heavenly Father in the godly duties of loving humans, planning for their salvation, and working to help them, Hinckley clearly positions Heavenly Mother as having a different role than Heavenly Father, one that is more removed and distant than that of the involved Father God with whom LDS members are encouraged to commune. Thus the essay's comment about Latter-day Saints not praying to Heavenly Mother firmly positions Heavenly Mother as "other"—separate, shadowy, and distinct in role. It problematizes the previous quotes which emphasized similarities between Heavenly Parents, rather than differences. This is a sobering but necessary part of the essay, because it highlights the institutional church's ambiguous rhetoric on and treatment of Heavenly Mother. She is equal and involved in Her concern, status, and salvific planning, yet we are to only commune with God the Father, because that is "the pattern set by Jesus Christ," and, in practice, rarely include her in our LDS God rhetoric.[13]

The essay's treatment of the church's doctrine of Heavenly Mother is startlingly brief, a mere six paragraphs.[14] However, despite its brevity, the essay accomplishes a number of important tasks, in our feminist perspective. Namely, it affirms her existence (and even capitalizes her name), downplays the possibility of multiple "heavenly mothers," affirms her somewhat equal status, and steers away from folk doctrinal explanations about Heavenly Mother being too sacred to discuss. This essay therefore lays groundwork for more inclusive LDS God rhetoric in the future.

---

12. Hinckley, "Daughters of God."

13. In his 1991 talk, Hinckley likewise justified not praying to Heavenly Mother because there was no record in the standard works of Jesus praying to anyone other than Father in Heaven. He may have been inspired by early LDS Apostle Orson Pratt, who wrote, "Jesus prayed to His Father, and taught His disciples to do likewise; but we are nowhere taught that Jesus prayed to His Heavenly Mother." *The Seer* (Washington, DC: Orson Pratt, Oct. 1853), 159.

14. The average number of paragraphs of all of the other Gospel Topics essays is twenty-five; the next shortest one has thirteen paragraphs.

Contestable Claims

Despite the essay's calling to our attention church leaders' views affirming Heavenly Mother, there are a couple of statements near the end of the essay which are contestable. The penultimate paragraph states, "Latter-day Saints direct their worship to Heavenly Father, in the name of Christ, and do not pray to Heavenly Mother." It then quotes, as previously noted, a portion of President Hinckley's 1991 address, "Daughters of God": "The fact that we do not pray to our Mother in Heaven in no way belittles or denigrates her."[15] The essay, however, does not include Hinckley's other remarks in his 1991 talk about praying to Heavenly Mother, specifically his statement, "In light of the instruction we have received from the Lord Himself, I regard it as inappropriate for anyone in the Church to pray to our Mother in Heaven."[16] Also omitted is the sentence directly preceding the quoted portion, in Hinckley's original speech, "I suppose those ... who use this expression and who try to further its use are well-meaning, but they are misguided."[17]

This is notable, because as LDS Church member Aaron Taylor writes, the Gospel Topics rendition differs from Hinckley's prescriptive statement from twenty-five years earlier. The Gospel Topics essay features, in the words of Taylor, "a descriptive statement and not a prescriptive one. It doesn't say that we *should not* pray or *must not* pray to Heavenly Mother. It doesn't say that if we pray to Heavenly Mother, we'll face Church discipline. It just says that we *do not* pray to her. It's descriptive and it's false. I know Mormons who pray to Heavenly Mother."[18]

Indeed, as Hinckley himself indicated in his 1991 talk, some Latter-day Saints pray to Heavenly Mother. While this form of worship is unusual among orthodox members, essays, blog posts, and interviews with Latter-day Saints depict various members'

---

15. Hinckley, "Daughters of God."
16. Ibid.
17. Ibid.
18. Aaron Taylor (a.k.a. Ziff), "Latter-day Saints ... Do Not Pray to Heavenly Mother," *Zelophehad's Daughters* (blog), Nov. 2, 2015: www.zelophehadsdaughters.com/2015/11/02/latter-day-saints-do-not-pray-to-heavenly-mother.

experiences praying to and communing with God the Mother. In a 2012 article Margaret Toscano discusses LDS women who have experienced visions of Heavenly Mother, sometimes after praying to Her.[19] Caroline Kline describes an LDS woman's experience reaching out to Heavenly Mother and communing with Her.[20] Additionally, Edward Jones, recalling his own experience of praying to Heavenly Mother in a moment of extreme personal strife, asserts that Heavenly Mother led him back to activity in the church. He further states that "I speak to Her everyday, as if she were standing next to me. ... In the great day of judgement, I cannot imagine that the Heavenly Mother will condemn me for reaching out to Her to save my life."[21] Thus, while the Gospel Topics essay's assertion that church members do not pray to Heavenly Mother may be true generally, it is not entirely accurate.

At least one prominent LDS woman offered a prayer to Heavenly Mother: second General Relief Society President, Eliza R. Snow, known in her day as Zion's "Presidentess," "Poetess," "Priestess," and "Prophetess." Her prayer is in the form of her poem turned hymn, "O My Father," quoted toward the beginning of the Gospel Topics essay as "the most notable expression of the idea [of Heavenly Mother]." LDS Church historian Jill Mulvay Derr notes that Snow's first volume of poetry published in 1856 featured this poem on page one. However, it was titled "Invocation, or the Eternal Father and Mother." Derr remarks that this title reflected Snow's "growing eagerness to bear personal witness of the place of woman within the eternal scheme."[22] The poem's 1856 title further suggests that Snow herself viewed her words as

---

19. Margaret Toscano, "Movement from the Margins: Contemporary Mormon Women's Visions of the Mother God," in Laurence Lux-Sterritt and Claire Sorin, eds., *Spirit, Faith and Church: Women's Experiences in the English–Speaking World, 17th–21st Century* (Newcastle upon Tyne: Cambridge Scholars Publishing, 2012), 207–26.

20. Caroline Kline, "Mormon Feminist Blogs and Heavenly Mother: Spaces for Ambivalence and Innovation in Practice and Theology," in Gina Messina-Dysert and Rosemary Radford Ruether, eds., *Feminism and Religion in the 21st Century: Technology, Dialogue, and Expanding Borders* (New York: Routledge, 2015), 34–46.

21. Edward Jones, "How Heavenly Mother Saved My Life," *Rational Faiths* (blog), Mar. 14, 2013: www.rationalfaiths.com/how-heavenly-mother-saved-my-life.

22. Jill Mulvay Derr, "The Significance of 'O My Father' in the Personal Journey of Eliza R. Snow," *BYU Studies* 36 (1996–97): 105. Snow's poem was originally published as "My Father in Heaven," in *Times and Seasons*, Nov. 15, 1845, see fn8.

a prayer to both Heavenly Parents. We see this in the last stanza as well, as Snow directly addressed Heavenly Father and Heavenly Mother: "Father, Mother, may I meet you/ in your royal courts on high?/ Then, at length, when I've completed/ all you sent me forth to do/ with your mutual approbation/ let me come and dwell with you."[23] Snow's poem showcases a reaching toward Heavenly Mother that has characterized several Saints' lives. Because the essay writers quoted this very poem/hymn earlier in the "Mother in Heaven" essay, and because of the accessible blog posts and personal stories of Latter-day Saints reaching out to Heavenly Mother in prayer, their choice to state unequivocally that Saints do not pray to Heavenly Mother is an interesting one. Taylor, for his part, finds the descriptive rather than prescriptive language a hopeful shift in rhetoric, as he regards it as "easier to change a descriptively stated norm than a prescriptively stated one."[24]

Also problematic is the essay's assertion that "we have been given sufficient knowledge to appreciate the sacredness of this doctrine and to comprehend the divine pattern established for us as children of heavenly parents."[25] While it may be true that we have enough knowledge to appreciate the sacredness of this doctrine, it is debatable that "we have been given sufficient knowledge to comprehend the divine pattern established for us as children of heavenly parents."[26] For example, the essay's use of the term "the divine pattern" is not entirely clear. Is it the general pattern of males and females forming unions together? Or is it the pattern of the godly union of exalted male and female? If it is the latter, many Latter-day Saints have indeed had difficulties comprehending this union, given that half of that union is overwhelmingly absent from church leaders' and church members' discourse. A number of prominent LDS writers have expressed their yearning for Heavenly Mother and their confusion as to why She is so overwhelmingly absent from church leaders' rhetoric about deity. Carol Lynn Pearson's searing poem, "Motherless House," gives voice to

---

23. Snow, "O My Father," in *Hymns*, 292.
24. Taylor, "Latter-day Saints … Do Not Pray to Heavenly Mother."
25. "Mother in Heaven," Gospel Topics essay.
26. Ibid.

the profound sense of loss some Saints feel at Heavenly Mother's absence from their lives. Pearson manifests no sense of having been given sufficient knowledge of our Heavenly Parents' union, roles, and relationship to their mortal children. She writes, "Who could have done this?/ Who would tear an unweaned infant/ From its Mother's arms/ And clear the place of every souvenir?" She concluded, "I am a child—/ Crying for my Mother in the night."[27]

LDS women like Pearson yearn for more information about and acknowledgment of Heavenly Mother and feel acute bewilderment about their own status in the eternities, given Heavenly Mother's shadowy and unheralded role. Hannah Wheelwright, co-editor of *Mormon Feminism: Essential Writings*, has written about her faith crisis stemming from lack of knowledge about Heavenly Mother, and consequently her own role in the eternities.[28] She states her concerns as follows:

> Though I would never have been able to articulate it at the time, it was frustrations and anger at Heavenly Mother that most tormented me during the darker times of my faith journey … I was very bitter that the deity I was supposed to (logically) look up to as the role model for my gender was nothing but a hoped-for-shadow in the annals of the church to which I belonged. Nothing but a few scanty references and warning about it being inappropriate to pray to her. There was plenty of evidence for past worship of the feminine divine, but my religion, which had such potential to be at the forefront of revealing new doctrine about Her, our Mother in Heaven, had ignored Her.[29]

Other LDS feminists have lamented the lack of current information on Heavenly Mother because knowledge of Heavenly Mother is integral to our salvation. Margaret Toscano explains:

> Joseph Smith in the King Follett Discourse emphasizes the importance of knowing God if we are to know ourselves: "If men do

---

27. Carol Lynn Pearson, "Healing the Motherless House," in Maxine Hanks, ed., *Women and Authority: Re-emerging Mormon Feminism* (Salt Lake City: Signature Books, 1992), 232–33.

28. Joanna Brooks, Rachel Hunt Steenblik, and Hannah Wheelwright, eds., *Mormon Feminism: Essential Writings* (New York: Oxford University Press, 2015).

29. Hannah Wheelwright, "The Talk I Would Have Given," *Young Mormon Feminists* (blog), June 24, 2013: www.youngmormonfeminists.org/2013/06/24/the-talk-i-would-have-given.

not comprehend the character of God, they do not comprehend themselves." In the same discourse Joseph quotes John 17:3 and paraphrases it thus: "If any man does not know God … he has not eternal life; for there can be eternal life on no other principle." If God is male and female, then eternal life is connected with knowing her as well as him. And knowledge of the Mother is crucial for women and men alike to know themselves as eternal beings.[30]

Toscano's point is a profound one. If, as the LDS Church posits, God is not only a Heavenly Father, but also a Heavenly Mother, then, as Joseph Smith said, it is essential to our eternal salvation to know and comprehend both God the Mother and Father. How does one learn to comprehend God the Mother, when explicit references to Her are absent from scripture and the vast majority of church discourse? How does one learn to comprehend God the Mother when there are norms against praying to Her and establishing relationships with Her?

The complacency of the last paragraph of the "Mother in Heaven" Gospel Topics essay, which states that although information about Heavenly Mother is limited, we have been given "sufficient knowledge to comprehend the divine pattern," misses the mark for Saints who want and need more than a divine pattern. As Ashley Mae Hoiland writes in response to the essay,

> I need a mother. I don't need the notion of a mother, or even the appreciation for a mother. I need a mother that comes with me in the middle of the night to take care of a child. I need a mother who nurtures my intellect and challenges me to do more. … [M]y knowledge is not 'sufficient." I suppose it is sufficient if all I am to know is that my Heavenly Mother had many children and is married to my Father in Heaven, both qualities I do love and respect, but I am not sufficed there. … I need more than a pattern to follow, I need a mother.[31]

---

30. Margaret Toscano, "Put on Your Strength O Daughters of Zion: Claiming Priesthood and Knowing the Mother," in Hanks, ed., *Women and Authority,* 427. Similarly, in Joseph Smith's "Lectures on Faith," Smith taught that one has to know God's true nature and attributes in order to obtain exaltation. Smith, "Lecture 3: On Faith": www.rsc.byu.edu/archived/lectures-faith-historical-perspective/lectures-faith-1990-edited-version/lecture-3.

31. Ashley Mae Hoiland, "We Need a Mother," *By Common Consent* (blog), Oct. 23, 2015: www.bycommonconsent.com/2015/10/23/we-need-a-mother.

Hoiland believes that this essay is a wonderful opening to the topic, but feels that the last paragraph mutes the discussion with its brief statement implying that sufficiency in comprehending a pattern is enough. The "Mother in Heaven" essay, unfortunately, for many Latter-day Saints yearning to know more about Heavenly Mother, provides no suggestion that we might learn more about Her in time, given the church's emphasis on continuing revelation and personal revelation. Rather, the final emphasis of the essay reinforces the notion that we have enough information about Heavenly Mother, rather than that we do not have everything and more may someday come forth.

Unexplored Issues

The "Mother in Heaven" essay succeeds in accomplishing certain purposes—namely, acknowledging that Heavenly Mother exists as an involved counterpart to Heavenly Father. It further dispels the taboo that we should not speak of Her. However, there are many issues that the writers chose not to address, despite the fact that they could have done so. One of those is simply why this doctrine of Heavenly Mother matters. As mentioned in the introduction, the LDS belief in sexed, embodied Gods, male and female, is a distinctive and, for many Saints, ennobling aspect of LDS doctrine. That humans, male and female, may someday in the eternities retain some celestial form of their sexed bodies, live with their spouses, and perpetually grow, evolve, and learn until they ultimately become deified peers of embodied Heavenly Parents is an exciting and unique aspect of LDS thought.

This vision of the afterlife, along with its change, growth, and embodied activity, stands in stark contrast to most other Judeo-Christian traditions which envision God as disembodied, sexless, and changeless.[32] Because Latter-day Saints believe that gender is eternal, it matters very much to women's vision of

---

32. See Rosemary Radford Ruether and Camille Williams, "A Dialogue on Feminist Theology," in Donald W. Musser and David L. Paulsen, eds., *Mormonism in Dialogue with Contemporary Christian Theologies* (Macon, Georgia: Mercer University Press, 2007), 251–302. For more on the classical conception of God as changeless and disembodied, see the first two chapters of Carol Christ, *She Who Changes: Re-imagining the Divine in the World* (New York: Palgrave Macmillan, 2004).

their own eternal future and identity that they have a Mother in Heaven, actively participating in the work of salvation.[33] If Heavenly Mother was utterly absent from the LDS belief system and non-existent as women's ultimate exemplar of their own eternal destinies, LDS women would be contemplating an eternity in which there was no space for their own perfected and deified female selves. The importance of this doctrine to women's eternal identity and purpose cannot be understated. As Apostle Neal A. Maxwell said, the doctrine of Heavenly Mother is one of the "truths that [is] most relevant and most needed in the times in which [we] live."[34] Sadly, Maxwell's acknowledgment of the importance of Heavenly Mother has not led to the incorporation of Her into the church's religious rhetoric or liturgy. This unique LDS doctrine, for example, is not emphasized in the Sunday school curriculum, the Church Education System manuals, or in scripture. It is indeed an extremely rare LDS general conference or church block that sees one single mention of Heavenly Mother.[35]

The essay might also have addressed (or at least footnoted) the history and context of Heavenly Mother and how the LDS conception of a female deity relates to other faith traditions. Unlike some of the other Gospel Topics essays which review the development of LDS thought (i.e., "Race and the Priesthood") or place it in a wider context (i.e., "Becoming Like God"), this essay ignores both how the discourse on God the Mother has evolved

33. "All human beings—male and female—are created in the image of God. Each is a beloved spirit son or daughter of heavenly parents, and, as such, each has a divine nature and destiny. Gender is an essential characteristic of individual premortal, mortal, and eternal identity and purpose." "The Family: A Proclamation to the World," *Ensign*, Nov. 1995, 102.

34. Maxwell, "The Reality of the Living Prophets," in Neal A. Maxwell, *Things as They Really Are* (Salt Lake City: Deseret Book Co., 1978).

35. Notably, on October 3, 2015, Apostle Jeffrey R. Holland used the phrase "Mother in Heaven" in general conference for the first time since Gordon B. Hinckley's 1991 address, "Daughters of God." Holland's pronouncement: "To Mother Eve, to Sarah, Rebekah, and Rachel, to Mary of Nazareth, and to a Mother in Heaven, I say, 'Thank you for your crucial role in fulfilling the purposes of eternity.'" Holland, "Behold Thy Mother," *Ensign*, Nov. 2015, 50. Perhaps signaling the beginning of a shift towards incorporating more acknowledgment of Heavenly Mother, March 2016's general women's session of conference included one mention of Mother in Heaven and one mention of heavenly parents, both by Neill F. Marriott. "What Shall We Do?" *Ensign*, May 2016, 10–12.

over time and how it fits into wider theology on the divine feminine.[36] Referencing Linda Wilcox's pioneering work—which the essay does not do—would have been helpful in historically and contextually situating Heavenly Mother discourse.[37] Wilcox first discusses a divine female in the broader stage of world religions before examining its inception within Mormonism. Like the "Mother in Heaven" Gospel Topics essay, Wilcox notes that Joseph Smith likely taught the doctrine, but explains that with scant scriptural basis for Heavenly Mother, early church leaders largely inferred the existence of a Heavenly Mother.[38] Tracing the development and shifts in Heavenly Mother discourse over the years, she suggests that Latter-day Saints during the turn of the twentieth century appealed to Heavenly Mother to promote women's rights, while many twentieth-century leaders appealed to Heavenly Mother to reinforce woman's role as mother.[39] Wilcox concludes that early LDS writers have used Heavenly Mother discourse to promote whatever vision of womanhood they advocated at the time. Wilcox asserts that "for the moment, Mother in Heaven can be almost whatever an individual Mormon envisions her to be. Perhaps, ironically, we thus set her up, despite herself, to fill the most basic maternal role of all—that of meeting the deepest needs of her children, whatever they might be."[40]

Also missing from the essay are many prominent early Latter-day Saints—including Brigham Young, Orson Pratt, and John Taylor—who believed in heavenly mothers, rather than a Heavenly Mother.[41] Taylor, for example, wrote, "Knowest thou not that

---

36. "Race and the Priesthood," Gospel Topics essay: www.churchofjesuschrist. org/study/manual/gospel-topics-essays/race-and-the-priesthood?lang=eng; "Becoming Like God," Gospel Topics essay: www.churchofjesuschrist.org/study/manual/ gospel-topics-essays/becoming-like-god?lang=eng.

37. Greater reliance on the Paulsen and Pulido article would also have been welcome, particularly its history (and rebuttal) of the notion of sacred silence regarding Heavenly Mother.

38. Wilcox, "The Mormon Concept of a Mother in Heaven," 65–67.

39. Ibid., 67–70.

40. Ibid., 74.

41. Brigham Young, "Self-Government—Mysteries—Recreation and Amusements, not in Themselves Sinful—Tithing—Adam, Our Father and Our God," *Journal of Discourses*, 1 (Apr. 9, 1852): 50: www.jod.mrm.org/1/46 ; Orson Pratt, *The Seer*, Oct.1853, 1:158.

eternities ago thy spirit, pure and holy, dwelt in thy Heavenly Father's bosom, and in his presence, and with thy mother, one of the Queens of heaven, surrounded by thy brother and sister spirits in the spirit world, among the Gods?"[42] That this essay instead emphasizes only one (capitalized) Heavenly Mother indicates a rejection of these earlier ideas about God the Father producing spirit offspring with multiple deified women. The fact that the essay ignores the possibility of heavenly mothers is a positive development for many Saints who find the notion of multiple heavenly mothers—and thus eternal polygamy, including eternal gestation and parturition—disturbing. Still, it is surprising that the essay did not address multiple heavenly mothers, given that other Gospel Topics essays have forthrightly discussed thorny historical issues. The essay veers away from such controversial practices and ideas, other than the brief discussion of prayers to Heavenly Mother.

Also missing from the essay is a larger discussion of Heavenly Mother's role. The essay mentions only a few roles: She is a co-equal with Heavenly Father, a co-designer of the plan of salvation, and a loving and attentive parent. As David Paulsen and Martin Pulido find, since the 1840s, there have been hundreds of references to Heavenly Mother in LDS discourse by church leaders, a number which pales in comparison to the thousands, if not millions, of references to God the Father by church leaders over the same period.[43] More could therefore have been said about Heavenly Mother's character, status, or actions. For instance, Susa Young Gates' depiction of Mother in Heaven standing side by side with Father in Heaven could have been reinforced by other quotes from church leaders that likewise envision Heavenly Mother as a glorified, holy, present counterpart to Heavenly Father. Apostle Melvin J. Ballard stated, "No matter to what heights God has attained or may attain, he does not stand alone; for side by side with him, in all her glory, a glory like unto his, stands a companion, the Mother of his children. For as we have a Father in heaven, so also

---

42. John Taylor, "Origin, Object, and Destiny of Women," *The Mormon*, Aug. 29 1857, reprinted in *Young Woman's Journal*, ed. Susa Yung Gates (Salt Lake City: Young Ladies Mutual Improvement Association of Zion, 1896–97), 8:412.

43. Paulsen and Pulido, "A Mother There," 76. They report finding 600 sources that reference Heavenly Mother since 1844.

we have a Mother there, a glorified, exalted, ennobled Mother."[44] Bruce R. McConkie, later an apostle, likewise envisioned Heavenly Mother as a being of "like glory, perfection, and holiness," similar to God the Father, and Apostle James E. Talmage envisioned God the Mother as sitting next to God the Father, "crowned with glory and majesty."[45] Finally, speaking of both Heavenly Mother and Heavenly Father, and firmly placing the former as an instigator of the plan of salvation, Chieko Okazaki, a general church officer, pronounced that it was with "increased love, mingled with pride and grief" that "[Heavenly Mother and Heavenly Father] accepted the willing offer of Jesus Christ."[46] While most of these references to Heavenly Mother's actions and roles are incidental to larger discussions about Heavenly Father and do not fully elaborate or articulate the doctrine of Heavenly Mother, they provide added authoritative heft to the notion that Heavenly Mother is a present deity positioned directly beside God the Father.

These discussions might have been included in the essay. Indeed, it would be helpful to provide more historical context and additional authoritative weight to the points the authors tried to emphasize. There are still other omissions that are unsurprising given that they introduce difficult and potentially unsettling theological questions or imply the need for a consideration of change in practice or teachings. One of these omissions, touched upon earlier, is the negative ramifications of not acknowledging and knowing Heavenly Mother. As Margaret Toscano and Janice Allred point out, how can women begin to comprehend themselves if they cannot develop a richer sense of who their God the Mother is?[47] How can Latter-day Saints achieve salvation without

44. Melvin J. Ballard, "His Discourses," in *Sermons and Mission Services of Melvin Joseph Ballard*, ed. Bryant S. Hinckley (Salt Lake City: Deseret Book Co., 1949), 205.

45. Bruce R. McConkie, *Mormon Doctrine*, 2nd edition (Salt Lake City: Bookcraft, 1966), 516–17; James E. Talmage, "The Eternity of Sex," *The Young Woman's Journal*, Oct. 25, 1914), 603.

46. Chieko N. Okazaki, "Grace and Glory: Strength from Our Savior," in Dawn Hall Anderson and Susette Fletcher Green, eds., *Women in the Covenant of Grace: Talks Selected from the 1993 Women's Conference Sponsored by Brigham Young University and the Relief Society* (Salt Lake City: Deseret Book Co., 1994), 243–44.

47. Toscano, "Put on Your Strength," 427; Allred, "Toward a Mormon Theology of God the Mother," in Janice Allred, *God the Mother and Other Theological Essays* (Salt Lake City: Signature Books, 1997), 42–43.

knowing Her? Moreover, what other ramifications are there if we perpetuate this wall of silence Saints have built up on the topic of Heavenly Mother? Toscano explains that cultural silence about Heavenly Mother and incessant depictions of God as male, as well as a heavy focus on males in authoritative positions in the church, lead to girls and women not only having difficulty envisioning themselves as Gods in embryo, but also lead to girls and women seeing no space for themselves as spiritual leaders or theologians.[48] This consequently reinforces the idea "that to men alone belongs the power to teach, define, and explore what the LDS religion is."[49] Ultimately, Toscano argues that male dominated structures of power within the LDS Church determine what has theological legitimacy—and important subjects like Heavenly Mother therefore too often get relegated to "the trash bin of theology and culture."[50]

Another unsurprising omission—but one which is fundamental and on which practicing Saints would benefit from clarification—is the question of Heavenly Mother's status in the Godhead. Is She completely outside the Godhead? And if so, what implications does this have for Her status as deity? Is She not God in any way, and thus is the "God" the Latter-day Saints refer to only God the Father, or perhaps at times the tri-part God consisting of the Father, Son, and Holy Ghost? Or is She half of the "God" portion of the tri-part Godhead? While church authorities' rhetoric often implies that "God" is Heavenly Father (as the first Article of Faith might be interpreted as suggesting), there are counter-narratives to this understanding of God within the LDS Church. Nineteenth-century apostle Erastus Snow claimed that "God" is the combination of deified male and female. He stated, "There can be no God except he is composed of the man and woman united, and there is not in all the eternities that exist, nor ever will be, a God in any other way. I have another description: There never was a God, and there never will be in all eternities, except they are made of these two component parts; a man and a woman; the

---

48. Margaret Toscano, "Is There a Place for Heavenly Mother in Mormon Theology: An Investigation into Discourses of Power," *Sunstone*, July 2004, 16.

49. Ibid., 19.

50. Ibid., 21.

male and the female."[51] This view of God consisting of both Heavenly Mother and Heavenly Father is compelling for many Saints, particularly feminist ones. LDS feminist Joanna Brooks embraces Snow's notion of God, saying, "It is Mormon doctrine that God is not only a Heavenly Father but a Heavenly Father and a Heavenly Mother." She explains, "If doctrine holds that only the married are exalted to Godhood, then it follows quite rationally that God is a married couple."[52] LDS theologian Eugene England seemed to agree, suggesting that "we would more accurately and profitably read the scriptural references to 'God' as meaning God the eternal partnership of Heavenly Father and Heavenly Mother," and that "they have a more perfect unity even than that of God and Christ and the Holy Ghost, and so the word God implies both of them, at least as much as it denotes the three beings in the classical Christian trinity called 'God.'"[53] Janice Allred's vision of God falls nicely in line with Snow's as well, as she argues that God is indeed the divine couple of Heavenly Mother and Heavenly Father.[54] She however, envisions an even more expansive role for Heavenly Mother. Not only is She half of the God portion of the Godhead, but She is also, Allred argues, acting in the role of the Holy Ghost.[55] This idea is appealing to some LDS feminists

51. Erastus Snow, "There is a God—Communion With Him an Inherent Craving of the Human Heart—Man in His Image—Male and Female Created He Them—Spirit and Flesh—Mortal and Immortal," *Journal of Discourses* 19 (Mar. 3, 1878): 270: www.jod.mrm.org/19/266. Harold B. Lee also implied that the God in Genesis 1:26–27 includes both Mother and Father God: "Could there have been a Father in Heaven without a Mother? ... While still keeping that question in mind, think of the significant statement contained in the scriptures describing the creation of man. 'And God said, Let us make man in our image, after our likeness. So God created man in his own image, in the image of God created he him; male and female created he them.' If you consider carefully those in whose image and likeness male and female were created, I wonder if you will not also discover the organizers of intelligences in the world of spirits." "Plan of Salvation," in Clyde J. Williams, ed., *Teachings of Harold B. Lee* (Salt Lake City: Deseret Book Co., 1996), ebook edition.

52. Joanna Brooks, "Ask Mormon Girl: Why Do We Not Talk About Heavenly Mother?" *Ask Mormon Girl* (blog), June 19, 2012: www.askmormongirl.wordpress.com/2012/06/19/ask-mormon-girl-why-do-we-not-talk-about-heavenly-mother.

53. Eugene England, "Becoming Bone of Bone and Flesh of Flesh," in Mary E. Stovall and Carol Cornwall Madsen, eds., *As Women of Faith: Talks Selected from the BYU Women's Conferences* (Salt Lake City: Deseret Book Co., 1989), 107.

54. Allred, "Toward a Mormon Theology of God the Mother," 55.

55. Ibid., 59.

who embrace the idea of an active, comforting, communing, immanent Mother God, standing with them in times of trial and directing them toward the right. While these Saints believe it is important to envision Heavenly Mother as part of the Godhead, most church leaders have been silent on the issue, thus leaving space for some LDS theologians to envision Her as outside the Godhead—or ignore Her existence entirely.[56] Therefore, an explicit discussion or clarification of Mother in Heaven's status and role in the Godhead—and a clarification that "God" does indeed (or does not) mean the combined unit of Heavenly Father and Heavenly Mother—would have been helpful contributions to the discussion.

Finally, the essay does not address the implications of a Heavenly Mother doctrine for LGBTQ people. Beliefs in exaltation and a gendered godhood firmly place LDS cosmology within a stark heteronormative framework. It leaves little room for gay Saints to envision themselves eternally with loving same-sex partners. LDS religion scholar Taylor Petrey discusses the heteronormative and gender essentialist assumptions inherent within Heavenly Mother discourse, and proposes ways to accommodate within the LDS Church options beyond the heteronormative.[57] Petrey creates theological space for same-sex relationships by displacing "biological reproduction as the sole way of imagining kinship as well as the model for celestial (pro)creation."[58] Petrey's work is important because it seriously grapples with the ways the LDS Church's embodied God the Mother and Father marginalize people who do not fit within traditional gender binaries. That these implications for LGBTQ Saints are not addressed in the Gospel Topics essay is not surprising. The church does not want to draw attention to the way this doctrine marginalizes a substantial

---

56. See Blake Ostler, *Exploring Mormon Thought: The Attributes of God* (Salt Lake City: Greg Kofford Books, 2001). Toscano mentions in "Is There a Place for Heavenly Mother" that Ostler never once in his 485-page book addresses the subject of Heavenly Mother or God's gender, and that he uses the male pronoun for God throughout his book.

57. Taylor G. Petrey, "Rethinking Mormonism's Heavenly Mother," *Harvard Theological Review* 109, 3 (July 2016): 315–41. See also Taylor G. Petrey, "Toward a Post-Heterosexual Mormon Theology," *Dialogue: A Journal of Mormon Thought*, 44, 4 (Winter 2011): 106–41.

58. Petrey, "Toward a Post-Heterosexual Mormon Theology," 128.

minority of members and erases possibilities of their limitless potential as gay individuals.[59] However, given the stark implications of the Heavenly Mother doctrine for LGBTQ people, we would be remiss if we did not mention it here.

Final Thoughts

The Gospel Topics essay accomplishes a couple of very important purposes—particularly in regard to dismantling cultural silence on Heavenly Mother and also legitimizing as authoritative church doctrine some positive and ennobling quotes about a (capitalized, singular) Heavenly Mother. But it might have gone farther, specifically establishing the importance of the doctrine, giving greater historical context on this important issue, and articulating more clearly and thoroughly Heavenly Mother's status and role within the framework of LDS thought and life. However, the authors chose not to address these issues, perhaps fearing that a more thorough examination would only lead to difficult questions and implications. Indeed, the essay's two ending paragraphs give a sense of muting the topic, with their emphasis on sufficiency with what limited information we have, rather than the possibility that someday we might know more.

The essay, while a notable starting place, sparks more questions about Heavenly Mother than it satisfies. The essay mentions that Latter-day Saints do not pray to Heavenly Mother (a point that should be nuanced), but it never explains why. Why would God the Mother or Father blame humans for reaching out to deity and attempting to feel Her love and guidance? How could such an action be considered immoral? Admittedly, it has been far more historically common among Christians to address prayers to a (usually metaphorically male) Father in Heaven. But given the LDS belief in both a literal Mother and Father God, why is communing with both Heavenly Parents inappropriate? This is a

---

59. This may not seem to be an omission to most LDS given that many Saints envision homosexuality as a condition that will be healed in the next life. However, to LGBTQ Saints and allies who envision their gender and sexual orientation as an intrinsic part of their identity, this lack of conversation about the implications for gay Latter-day Saints would indeed be an omission.

logical conundrum that is not satisfied with facile references to Mormons only praying the way Jesus prayed.

Another question the essay raises is how we can acknowledge Heavenly Mother's godhood. The essay quoted Apostle Rudger Clawson saying, "We honor woman when we acknowledge Godhood in her eternal Prototype."[60] Yet if She is almost entirely absent from church leaders' discourse and official written material (the essay being a major exception), how can Latter-day Saints ever break free from cultural silence about Heavenly Mother so as to actually acknowledge Her godhood? Might this essay indicate a shift towards a new era of discourse about God the Mother, an era in which our church leaders, followed by its members, begin to include Her more substantially in their God-talk? There is some reason to hope, as General Young Women leader Neill F. Marriott mentioned Heavenly Mother twice in the March 2016 general women's conference session.[61]

Another related question is how Heavenly Mother can be acknowledged and discussed in the most productive and least constricting way. Some LDS feminists fear that Heavenly Mother discourse from church leaders will reify gender roles. Consequently, they are wary of Her inclusion in our God discourse. Rachel Whipple writes, "I am glad that we haven't been told as much about our Heavenly Mother as our Heavenly Father. ... We are not limited in seeking Her, the feminine divine, by constraints set out by the visions of men."[62] Other LDS feminists

---

60. "Mother in Heaven," Gospel Topics essay.

61. Neill F. Marriott, "What Shall We Do?" The first mention of Heavenly Mother was via a quotation from Orson F. Whitney: "All that we suffer and all that we endure, especially when we endure it patiently, ... purifies our hearts ... and makes us more tender and charitable, ... and it is through ... toil and tribulation, that we gain the education ... which will make us more like our Father and Mother in heaven." The second more oblique mention was in her conclusion: "Our high responsibility is to become women who follow the Savior, nurture with inspiration, and live truth fearlessly. As we ask Father in Heaven to make us builders of His kingdom, His power will flow into us and we will know how to nurture, ultimately becoming like our heavenly parents."

62. Rachel Whipple, "Why I'm Glad Heavenly Mother Is as yet Uncorrelated," *Times and Seasons* (blog), May 15, 2013: www.timesandseasons.org/index.php/2013/05/why-im-glad-heavenly-mother-is-as-yet-uncorrelated. Other feminists echo Whipple's point. Emily Gilke Palmer says this about Heavenly Mother,

even question the utility of this doctrine of Heavenly Mother at all, given the fact that Heavenly Mother in practice seems so removed from Her earthly children. Is She choosing to not be a more active part of our lives? Or was this chosen for Her? Either way, the implications can be frightening. As Sheila Taylor opines "If Heavenly Mother exists, what we have is a divine role model for women which may be more disturbing than no role model at all—one in which women are silenced to the point of invisibility, in which they seem to disappear altogether into the identity of their husbands."[63] A universe without a Heavenly Mother, even with the challenge of not having a female divine role model, may be more palatable than one in which the female divine role model is subsumed into the male and silenced.

This brief six-paragraph Gospel Topics essay standardizes a conception of a singular Heavenly Mother who plays some sort of role in heaven and in our lives. However, it leaves many questions unanswered. On the one hand, the brevity of this treatment is disappointing in that it fails to answer important questions about Her status in the Godhead and Her relationship to Her earthly children. Such limited attention to Her communicates a woeful underestimation of Her importance. On the other hand, the brief essay centering only on Her represents a watershed moment. As such it stands as the most authoritative exposition of Mother in Heaven ever produced within the LDS Church because it bears the official imprimatur of the church. But, at the same time, that it is only six paragraphs, the shortest of all Gospel Topics essays, is itself emblematic of Her continued marginal status.

Ultimately, the rhetoric of the essay positions Her as a kind of co-equal to Heavenly Father in some ways, but this sense of Her as a truly equivalent partner to God the Father is undercut by both affirmations that we do not commune with Her in prayer and by

---

"Part of what is so lovely about the unknown and the lack of doctrine [about Heavenly Mother] is that you're free to find definition and meaning yourself." Palmer, in Anna Marie Killian's *Her*, Mar. 2016: www.annamkillian.com/her-1/eb787l1oh5v1w2mwcnvokrusp3n9mh.

63. Sheila Taylor (a.k.a. Lynette), "Why I Don't Want to Believe in Heavenly Mother," *Zelophehad's Daughters* (blog), Nov. 7, 2007: www.zelophehadsdaughters.com/2007/11/07/why-i-don%E2%80%99t-want-to-believe-in-heavenly-mother.

its inferences that what limited information we have about Her is enough. This treatment of Heavenly Mother—rhetorically asserting a kind of equality in this essay, but in practice maintaining a clear patriarchal privilege in regard to its overwhelming emphasis on God the Father—mirrors other larger patterns in church discourse regarding gender. Eve too has, over the years, been slowly embraced rhetorically as equal partner to Adam by church leaders, while she simultaneously and puzzlingly remains subordinated to Adam in their expositions.[64] Wives in church discourse have seen a similar trend, as narratives of equal partnership with their husbands coexist simultaneously with narratives of men presiding.[65] The essay may thus be understood as contributing to the larger trend among LDS leaders to rhetorically embrace the female as equal while keeping subordinating structures in place.

Nevertheless, in asserting Heavenly Mother standing "side by side" with Heavenly Father and in implicitly rejecting old cultural ideas of the propriety of a "sacred silence" about Her, the essay opens up possibilities that church discourse about Heavenly Mother may someday become less taboo. With the essay, there is new space to envision and hope for a gradual lifting up of the Mother in a uniquely LDS discourse that acknowledges Her Godhood and highlights Her active participation in the godly work of loving and guiding humans on earth.

---

64. Caroline Kline, "The Mormon Conception of Women's Nature and Role: A Feminist Analysis," *Feminist Theology* 22, 2 (2014): 186–202.

65. Caroline Kline, "Saying Goodbye to the Final Say: Mormon Male Headship Ideologies," in Patrick Q. Mason and John G. Turner, eds., *Out of Obscurity: Mormonism Since 1945* (New York City: Oxford University Press, 2016), 214–33.

13. "JOSEPH SMITH'S TEACHINGS ON PRIESTHOOD, TEMPLE, AND WOMEN"
A CRITIQUE

Margaret M. Toscano

In 2013 officials of the Church of Jesus Christ of Latter-day Saints began to publish a series of Gospel Topics essays to ensure that "accurate information from many different sources" would be available for Latter-day Saints to study in order to be "well informed about Church history, doctrine, and practices." The church's official web site states that it "places great emphasis on knowledge." But the church apparently also worries that people will access harmful and untrue information about it, its history, and its mission. Consequently, a stated central purpose of the Gospel Topics essays is to counter "questionable and often inaccurate sources" available on the internet.[1] In what follows, I critique the church essay titled "Joseph Smith's Teachings on Priesthood, Temple, and Women," concluding that it omits important evidence and thus misdirects its readers about LDS women's right to priesthood ordination.

It is not surprising that the church published its essay on women and priesthood near the time the LDS Ordain Women movement first made its appearance in March 2013.[2] The group's mission statement asserts that its purpose is "to articulate issues of gender

---

1. At www.lds.org/topics?lang=eng&old=true.

2. For the inception and development of the LDS Ordain Women movement, see Margaret M. Toscano, "The Mormon 'Ordain Women' Movement," in Gina Messina-Dysert and Rosemary Radford Ruether, eds., *Feminism and Religion in the 21st Century: Technology, Dialogue, and Expanding Borders,* (New York: Routledge, 2015), 153–66. Also see Gordon Shepherd, Lavina Fielding Anderson, and Gary Shepherd, eds., *Voices for Equality: Ordain Women and Resurgent Mormon Feminism* (Salt Lake City: Greg Kofford Books, 2015). Ordain Women is an activist group that has organized a number of publicized events.

inequality" in the LDS Church and "to call attention to the need for the ordination of Mormon women to the priesthood."[3] Over the past few decades, a number of scholars have published works that forefront and rely on Joseph Smith's 1842 Nauvoo Relief Society speeches as crucial theological and historical justification for women's ordination to priesthood in the Mormon tradition.[4] In these speeches, Smith declared his intention to put women in possession of the priesthood and to make the members of the Relief Society "a kingdom of priests as in Enoch's day—as in Paul's day."[5] But most LDS have remained unaware of these statements and the scholarship that has examined them. Knowledge, however, is growing, as evidenced by the testimonies appearing in the personal "Profile" section of the Ordain Women web site, as well as in the scholarly source material referenced on www.ordainwomen.org.[6]

Importantly, the church essay admits that many members will be surprised by the priesthood language Smith used to describe women's place in the church, which indicates most members are still unaware of the existence of historical evidence for women's ordination in the Mormon tradition. The thesis of the church essay is that Smith's statements about women and priesthood do not mean what they seem to mean. To make this central point, the essay employs the technique of "gaslighting," that is, the rhetorical or psychological technique of making someone believe that what they have observed or read or understood was an illusion, a flickering of light that clouds one's vision and judgment.[7] The church

---

3. See www.ordainwomen.org.

4. See Margaret and Paul Toscano, *Strangers in Paradox: Explorations of Mormon Theology* (Salt Lake: Signature Books, 1990), 143–220; D. Michael Quinn, "Mormon Women Have Had the Priesthood since 1843," in Maxine Hanks, ed., *Women and Authority: Re-emerging Mormon Feminism* (Salt Lake: Signature Books, 1992), 365–409; Linda King Newell, "The Historical Relationship of Mormon Women to Priesthood," in ibid., 23–48.

5. "Discourse, March 31, 1842, as reported by Eliza R. Snow," 22, Joseph Smith Papers, accessed Jan. 20, 2017, at www.josephsmithpapers.org/paper-summary/discourse-31-march-1842-as-reported-by-eliza-r-snow/1?highlight=kingdom%20of%20priests%20as%20in%20Enoch%27s%20day.

6. The Nauvoo Relief Society minutes became available online with the publication of the Joseph Smith Papers in 2012: www.josephsmithpapers.org/paperSummary/nauvoo-relief-society-minute-book.

7. The term "gaslighting" comes from Patrick Hamilton's 1938 stage play *Gas Light*, later adapted for film in 1944 by George Cukor. Scholars began to use the

essay seeks to convince readers that (1) Smith never ordained women to priesthood and never intended to do so, (2) the temple priesthood does not confer authoritative keys or have any efficacy in the church organization, (3) the Relief Society was never intended to be a priesthood organization, and (4) anyone who thinks otherwise is under a misperception and misguided. The purpose of the church essay is to show that Smith's words, views, and actions with respect to women and priesthood exactly correspond with those of LDS Church leaders today.

In taking this stance, the essay ignores significant scriptural and historical evidence that indicates the opposite, namely, that (1) Smith intended the Relief Society to be a women's priesthood organization; (2) he viewed the temple priesthood as the fullness of the Melchizedek priesthood restored by Elijah—a priesthood that encompasses all the church orders of priesthood together with their keys, powers, and rights; and (3) he intended a group or quorum of anointed men and women holding temple priesthood fullness to govern the church. The evidence for this alternate view, though not abundant, is significant. Because the church essay presents only documents and arguments supporting the view that only men have the right to priesthood offices and to govern the church, the essay misrepresents information anachronistically to compel the conclusion that the view of current LDS Church leaders on the question of women and priesthood is identical to Smith's. Moreover, the essay writers reinforce their interpretation by putting the historical evidence within the framework of current gender role divisions promulgated in the church, asserting that this represents the revealed eternal relationship between men and women. The church essay also obscures all inequities between men

---

term in psychological literature in the 1960s. See R. Baron and J.A. Whitehead, "The Gas-Light Phenomenon," *The Lancet* 293 (1969): 1258–60. More recently, scholars are using the term to examine social justice issues. See Tuesda Roberts and Dorinda J. Carter Andrews, "A Critical Race Analysis of the Gaslighting Against African American Teachers," in Dorinda J. Carter Andrews and Frank Tuft, eds., *Contesting the Myth of the Post Racial Era: The Continued Significance of Race in U.S. Education,* (Bern, Switzerland: Peter Lang, 2013), 69–94; also see Rachel McKinnon, "Epistemic Injustice," *Philosophy Compass* 11, 8 (July 28, 2016): www.onlinelibrary.wiley.com/wol1/doi/10.1111/phc3.12336/full.

and women by emphasizing only the positive roles women can play in the church today.

Overview

The church essay is presented in four parts. Part one, the "Early Latter-day Saint Understanding of Priesthood," insists that the first Mormons viewed priesthood very much as did Christians in other denominations, namely, as "ordination to ecclesiastical office and authority to preach and perform religious rites"; and, as in other churches, this authority was held by "men alone." By revelation, the LDS understanding was expanded beyond the view of ordination of men trained for the ministry to extend to lay men, but not women. Divine messengers called and appointed Joseph Smith to the Melchizedek priesthood that bestowed the "right of presidency," the right to "administer in spiritual things," and the "right to officiate in all the offices of the Church."[8] Later, in 1836, more angelic messengers conveyed keys to Smith "that would enable church members to receive temple ordinances." The Latter-day Saints were then commanded to build a temple where the "power of godliness" could be revealed.[9] "The culminating ordinances of the priesthood were to be found in the temple and would help prepare men and women to enter into God's presence."[10]

Part two focuses on "Joseph Smith and the Nauvoo Relief Society." When the women of Nauvoo wanted to form a benevolent society to help those in need, Smith told them he had "something better" for them.[11] The essay argues that the Relief Society was different from the common women's groups of that time for a special reason, namely, "because it was established by a prophet who acted with priesthood authority to give women authority, sacred responsibilities, and official positions within the structure of the Church, not apart from it." At this point the essay alerts contemporary LDS that they might find "unfamiliar" at least two aspects

---

8. The church authors reference D&C 27 and 107. I use double quotation marks to indicate this.

9. D&C 84 is referenced.

10. At www.lds.org/topics/essays?lang=eng, 1–2.

11. This is Sarah Granger Kimball's recollection about the founding of the Relief Society (fn16 in church essay).

of Smith's teachings to the Relief Society: (1) his use of what is now thought of as priesthood language to describe women's roles in the church, and (2) his "endorsement of women's participation in giving blessings of healing." In the first instance, the essay argues that Smith was simply using priesthood terminology in a different way than LDS do today. In the second instance, subsequent prophets have clarified through revelation that it is proper only for men with the Melchizedek priesthood to administer healing blessings since they alone "'hold the priesthood of God and have the power and authority to administer to the sick in the name of Jesus Christ.'"[12] The essay's main point is to reinforce the current church teaching that no matter what the historical sources seem to say, "neither Joseph Smith, nor any person acting on his behalf, nor any of his successors conferred the Aaronic or Melchizedek Priesthood on women or ordained women to priesthood office."[13]

Part three, "Priesthood and the Temple," insists that the priesthood language and promises of Smith to the Relief Society relate only to the administration of temple ordinances. Though Smith said he was going to make the women of the Relief Society a "kingdom of priests," the essay counters that he was merely referring to those women and men who would enter into an "order of the priesthood" and become a "kingdom of priests" when they receive their temple endowments. The essay asserts: "Temple ordinances were priesthood ordinances, but they did not bestow ecclesiastical office on men or women." The essay then proceeds to explain that temple ordinances brought new understanding about the "interdependent relationship of women and men." Through temple sealings, husbands and wives may become like their heavenly parents. If they are true to their covenants, they will be exalted in heaven above. But temple priesthood does not give authority in the church below, the essay argues.[14]

Part four, "Women and Priesthood Today," summarizes the main points of the essay and insists that women's relationship to

---

12. This is a statement of LDS Church President Heber J. Grant in 1926, at www.lds.org/topics/essays?lang=eng, 4.

13. At www.lds.org/topics/essays?lang=eng, 2–4.

14. At www.lds.org/topics/essays?lang=eng, 4–6.

priesthood has remained constant from Smith's day to the present. This is manifest, the essay argues, by the following: (1) men are ordained to priesthood offices, but both men and women enjoy the spiritual power and blessings of the priesthood; (2) both men and women "officiate in sacred ordinances in temples"; and (3) men and women "can obtain the highest degree of celestial glory only by entering together into an order of the priesthood through the temple sealing ordinance."[15]

Critique: Framing the Issues

The church essay interprets the historical evidence for the purpose of demonstrating a clear continuity on the crucial question of women's relationship to priesthood, namely that women have never been ordained to church offices nor held priesthood keys from the days of Joseph Smith to the present. The essay is meant to assure LDS people that the church is led by revelation through living prophets who have not deviated from the original teachings of the church's founding prophet. Therefore, the place of women within the organization today reflects God's will, the same yesterday, today, and, presumably, forever. To achieve this conclusion, the writers of the essay adopt a very positive tone, asserting an interpretation that seems self-evident from the historical sources. Their arguments appear complete and thorough. They make no mention in six pages of text or in seven pages of footnotes of any dissenting arguments or scholarship regarding their central theme.[16]

The essay's objective is reinforced by its frame, which begins and ends on the theme of the "many opportunities for service" LDS women enjoy in the church, both at the local level and "the Churchwide level." The essay reminds readers that women can preach sermons in local congregations and even in general conference; can serve full-time missions; like men, they can "perform and officiate in holy rites" in temples; can "lead organizations that minister to families, other women, young women, and children"; can "participate in priesthood councils"; and can teach history and

---

15. Ibid., 6–7.

16. The church essay does not quote from scholarship published by Signature Books, *Sunstone*, or *Dialogue: A Journal of Mormon Thought*.

theology in the church's education system.[17] The essay then states that, notwithstanding all these opportunities, questions do arise sometimes about why only men are ordained to priesthood—a statement implying that women raising this question might be ungrateful, a sentiment that echoes many speeches of church leaders since the 1970s that admonish women to focus on their blessings and opportunities rather than complain about not having priesthood authority.[18]

It must be observed, however, that the list of what women lack is both significant and omitted. The church essay does not point out that whatever LDS women can do in the church is always circumscribed and directed by men because of the priesthood structure that directs the organization. Men decide when, where, and how women function in the church, and also how church resources are distributed to them. Women never preside over men. A twelve-year-old deacon has more priesthood authority in the church than his mother.[19] LDS women never ordain LDS men, call men, interview men, or supervise men. Women cannot sit on church disciplinary councils even when a woman is being disciplined. Only men administer the saving ordinances of the gospel. However, women can and do transmit temple ordinances to other women, but again it is in a framework controlled by male

---

17. At www.lds.org/topics/essays?lang=eng, 1.

18. Gordon B. Hinckley, later fifteenth president of the church, advised women not to ask why they do not have priesthood, but rather to "dwell on the remarkable blessings" they have ("Ten Gifts from the Lord," *Ensign*, Nov. 1985, at www.lds.org/general-conference/1985/10/ten-gifts-from-the-lord?lang=eng). Patricia Holland told women: "The question is how we fulfill our responsibilities, not who has what role" ("A Woman's Perspective on the Priesthood," *Ensign*, July 1980, at www.lds.org/ensign/1980/07/a-womans-perspective-on-the-priesthood?lang=eng). Bruce C. Hafen, in "Women, Feminism, and the Blessings of the Priesthood," told women they can do all that men can do except what relates to "administering the gospel and governing all things" (*BYU Speeches of the Year*, Mar. 29, 1985, at www.speeches.byu.edu/speakers/bruce-c-hafen).

19. It can be argued that the temple priesthood a woman holds with her husband outranks that of her son, though a son with Melchizedek priesthood can give healing blessings in the home, but the mother cannot. Apostle Boyd K. Packer said the temple ceremony does not bestow priesthood ("The Temple, the Priesthood," *Ensign*, May 1993, 20). Dallin H. Oaks said temple priesthood only relates to the home not to the church ("Priesthood Authority in the Family and the Church," *Ensign*, Nov. 2005, 24–27), which would mean a deacon has priesthood authority in the church, but his mother does not.

priesthood. Changes in the temple ceremony made in January 2019 have created more equity between women and men because both genders now make the same covenants together as individuals, eliminating the male as intercessor between the woman and God. Moreover, negative language of female obedience to husbands has been removed from the temple ceremony, which has positive implications for women's status in the church at large.[20]

On October 2, 2019, the church announced that women can now serve as witnesses for baptisms and temple sealings, which has been met with enthusiastic approval by both mainstream and feminist LDS women.[21] Such changes in the temple and other ritual practices are moving the church closer to the interdependent ideal expressed in the church essay. However, it should be noted that the larger inequities that remain for women are due to the fact that they do not have priesthood and men do. In October 2019, the church also announced that "Young Women presidents may take a greater role in counseling young women," which may have come as a response to women's complaints about the possible inappropriateness of young women confessing to adult male leaders. But this directive also states that the "bishop maintains his role as a 'common judge' on ecclesiastical matters and the organization leaders work under his direction."[22] Since hearing confessions is seen as one of the bishop's priesthood functions, this role cannot be assumed by a woman leader even though she can give counsel. This distinction illustrates why priesthood ordination remains at the center of discussions about gender equity in the church. The church's hierarchical priesthood structure ensures that men always preside over women in the church. In fairness, it must be stated

---

20. See Peggy Fletcher Stack and David Noyce, "LDS Church changes temple ceremony; faithful feminists will see revisions and additions as a 'leap forward,'" (*Salt Lake Tribune*, Jan. 2, 2019, at www.sltrib.com/religion/2019/01/02/lds-church-releases).

21. See Jana Reiss, "Why It's Important that Mormon Women Can Now Be Official Witnesses to a Baptism," (*Religion News Service*, Oct. 2, 2019, at www.religionnews.com/2019/10/02/why-its-important-that-mormon-women-can-now-be-official-witnesses-to-a-baptism).

22. See Tad Walch,"October 2019 General Conference: Here Are All the Changes that Were Announced," (*Deseret News*, Oct. 5, 2019, at www.deseret.com/2019/10/5/20899428/general-conference-changes-mormon-lds-october-2019).

that LDS men are also subordinate to and directed by those men with greater authority in the priesthood hierarchy. But the larger point remains. All LDS women as a class are subordinate to all LDS men as a class.

The church essay ignores the historic and expanded roles women played in the nineteenth and early-twentieth-century church, where women not only gave healing blessings but controlled their own organizations' funds and budgets, publications, and programs to a much greater degree than they do today.[23] The essay also ignores the male-centered history of the LDS hierarchy since the days of Brigham Young.[24] It does not acknowledge the ongoing controversy over whether the temple endowment has transmitted priesthood keys to women since the time of Joseph Smith to the present.[25] It ignores other pertinent historical information that disrupts the assumption of priesthood and doctrinal continuity. For example, at the beginning of the twentieth-century, there was a subtle battle between male church leaders and those women who had been present at the 1842 founding of the Relief Society. The question was whether the women and their organization were to be "called *in* the order of the Holy Priesthood" or "called *by* the Holy Priesthood." The argument was not petty. The difference is significant, as the women knew. To be "called *in* the order of the Holy Priesthood" means that the Relief Society is a priesthood organization in its own right with women having authority to govern their own organization apart from male priesthood holders. But to be "called *by* the Holy Priesthood" means that women's

23. See Linda King Newell, "A Gift Given, a Gift Taken: Washing, Anointing, and Blessing the Sick Among Mormon Women," *Sunstone* 6 (Sept.-Oct. 1981): 16–22; Jill Mulvay Derr, Maureen Ursenbach Beecher, and Janath Russell Cannon, *Women of Covenant: The Story of Relief Society* (Salt Lake City: Deseret Book Co., 1991), 23–180; and Vella Neil Evans, "Empowerment and Mormon Women's Publications," in Hanks, ed., *Women and Authority*, 49–68.

24. Whether this history is also misogynistic is a matter of opinion. But Quinn says it is in "Women Have Had Priesthood," 378–85. For Brigham Young's complex views on women, see John G. Turner, *Brigham Young: Pioneer Prophet* (Cambridge, Massachusetts: Harvard University Press, 2012), 157–61, 377–82.

25. In "Retrieving the Keys: Historical Milestones in LDS Women's Quest for Priesthood Ordination," in Shepherd et al., eds., *Voices for Equality*, 137–66, I argue that from Brigham Young to the present there has been a cover-up about the implications of Joseph Smith's revelations on women's relationship to the temple.

individual authority is subordinate to men's and that the Relief Society is only an auxiliary to the central authority of the male priesthood quorums.[26]

Early Latter-day Saint Understanding of Priesthood

Part one of the essay on how priesthood was understood at the time of Joseph Smith begins with the conventional narrative promulgated by the church, namely, that there was a general apostasy after the deaths of the ancient apostles and that the central purpose of the founding of Mormonism was to restore true priesthood authority and keys to Smith and, from him, to LDS Church leaders and male priesthood holders, who alone possess God's authority today. The essay claims Smith taught this view. But this is not as clear as leaders have suggested. From a careful examination of the words of Smith and the scriptural texts he produced, it is evident that he did not emphasize a universal apostasy in the same way as his successors.[27] What Smith emphasized was an absence of fullness. He assumed that some truth and authority had been present throughout the history of Christianity, but he believed his calling was to restore and bring together a fullness of Christ's divine truth and power. Smith said: "The dispensation of the fullness of times will bring to light the things that have been revealed in all former dispensations, also other things that have not been before revealed. He shall send Elijah the prophet &c., and restore all things in Christ."[28]

---

26. The *Woman's Exponent* from 1892 to 1911 shows the women's resistance and inevitable capitulation. For change in language, see "Relief Society Jubilee," *Woman's Exponent* 20 (Apr. 1, 1892), 141, and "Official Announcement," *Woman's Exponent* 39 (Jan. 1911): 44.

27. The main scriptural texts used to show Joseph Smith's (i.e., the Lord's) belief in the general apostasy are D&C 1:11–17, D&C 112, and the First Vision in JS-H. Both D&C 1 and 112 may be interpreted to describe the general state of wickedness in Smith's day (or any day), not the specific apostasy of Christianity, which is not mentioned. D&C 1:21–23 state two of the several purposes of the Mormon restoration: "That faith also might increase in the earth," and "That the fullness of my gospel might be proclaimed." Both purposes imply that faith and Christ's gospel were already present, but need to be increased. Though Smith was told in the First Vision that he should join none of the Christian sects and that "they were all wrong," this could mean that Smith's mission was to stand apart from these denominations to bring forth something different.

28. "Discourse, October 3, 1841, as reported by *Times and Seasons*," 578, Joseph Smith Papers, at www.josephsmithpapers.org/paper-summary/discourse-3-october-

The LDS understanding of apostasy is important to my critique because the church's emphasis on the restoration of true priesthood authority is a crucial subtext in the church essay, undergirding their entire argument about women's relationship to priesthood and the centrality of priesthood authority to the institutional church's claim to legitimacy.[29] If, as the church essay assumes, LDS Church leaders are the only ones with God's authority to administer the gospel and its ordinances, then they are also the only ones who have the right to say what priesthood means, who is called and ordained to use it, and how. But a number of early church records strongly suggest that Smith viewed the priesthood transmitted through the temple endowment not only as a source of individual spiritual empowerment but also as encompassing all the keys of the priesthood that function in the institutional church.[30] For Smith, the purpose of the priesthood was not simply to create and maintain the church. Rather, the purpose of the church was to bring all people into the priesthood after the "Order of the Son of God," that is, into a priestly relationship with God, so that all men and women might "speak in the name of God" (D&C 1:20).

While the church essay asserts that the "culminating ordinances of the priesthood were to be found in the temple and would help prepare men and women to enter into God's presence,"[31] it nevertheless obscures the point that women, as well as men, receive the fullness of the Melchizedek priesthood through the temple ordinances in order to bring those individuals before God at the veil.[32] If Smith revealed that both men and women who are a part

---

1841-as-reported-by-times-and-seasons/2?highlight=dispensation%20of%20fulness%20of%20times%20will%20bring%20to%20light. For a collection of Joseph Smith's speeches with primary sources, see *The Words of Joseph Smith: The Contemporary Accounts of the Nauvoo Discourses of the Prophet Joseph Smith*, ed. Andrew F. Ehat and Lyndon W. Cook (Provo, Utah: BYU Religious Studies Center, 1980).

29. D&C 1:30, describing "the only true and living church upon the face of the whole earth," is a crucial scripture for the church's position. But it is complicated by scriptures like D&C 86:8–11 that say "the priesthood has remained" in certain people through their lineage and they will be "a savior unto my people."

30. See *Strangers in Paradox*, 143–53.

31. At www.lds.org/topics/essays?lang=eng, 2

32. This seems to be the import of D&C 84. For a documented interpretation of Joseph Smith's teachings on the meaning of the fullness of the Melchizedek priesthood, see Toscano and Toscano, *Strangers in Paradox*, 179–208.

of the "kingdom of priests" constituted by the temple endowment can speak in the name of the Lord, then the notion of priesthood authority as defined and taught by the church today is undercut.

Joseph Smith and the Nauvoo Relief Society

Part two of the church essay focuses on the importance of Smith's speeches at the founding of the Relief Society in Nauvoo, Illinois, in 1842. The essay quotes Sarah Granger Kimball's report that Smith told the women he had something "better" for them than offered in the typical women's charitable institutions of their time. The essay interprets this to mean that the Relief Society was "established by a prophet" who gave women authority within the church, under the direction of men. The essay states: "Revelatory developments in Nauvoo afforded women new opportunities to participate in the Church and expanded Latter-day Saints' understanding of the eternal relationship between men and women."[33] The essay proceeds to dismiss the importance of any terms or practices from the nineteenth-century that could equalize women's relationship with men and instead focuses on how the Relief Society provided women an official organization and therefore official roles and opportunities within the institutional church in Nauvoo. And the writers see this as expansive for women. But if the women's organization and the significance of their church offices were, as the essay purports, under the direction of men's priesthood authority, this seems to be no different from other religious groups in the nineteenth-century. In other groups, too, women saw themselves as having "sacred responsibilities," but their spiritual gifts were still under the direction of men.[34] If women have only delegated authority from men, which is believed to reflect the "eternal relationship" between men and women, then this is surely not a better or more expansive view of gender relationships, but rather the same structure of male leadership that prevailed in the nineteenth-century church, as it has done in other patriarchal religions.

---

33. At www.lds.org/topics/essays?lang=eng, 2.

34. The church essay footnotes (13, 15) several fine histories (e.g., by Ann Braude and Catherine Brekus) of women's roles in other American religious traditions in the nineteenth century, 8. "Sacred responsibilities" comes from church essay, 3.

The church essay emphasizes the "auxiliary" nature of the Relief Society, saying it was never "apart from" the structure of the church, thus ignoring the work of scholars who have explored the relative independence of the Relief Society until the 1970s. Such scholars recognize that the Relief Society always functioned within the church under general male guidance; but they also demonstrate that it had much greater autonomy prior to the advent of church correlation (an institutional change beginning in the 1960s that eliminated the autonomy of the Relief Society and other church auxiliary organizations).[35] The essay does not mention that Brigham Young disbanded the Relief Society for more than twenty years (between 1844 and 1867), nor does it explain how this action might have curtailed rather than expanded opportunities for women after it was re-established as a subordinate church auxiliary organization.[36]

The church essay explains away as insignificant any language Smith used that could suggest he intended women to possess the same priesthood conferred on men. For the essay's authors, the two most troubling terms in Smith's vocabulary are "keys" and "ordination." Smith told the Relief Society in Nauvoo: "I now turn the key to you in the name of God and this Society shall rejoice, and knowledge and intelligence shall flow down from this time."[37] The essay gives only the first clause of this quotation before explaining that the nineteenth-century church "used the term keys to refer at various times to authority, knowledge, or temple ordinances."[38] In other words, the essay posits that "keys" is a vague term with no priesthood significance. And yet the term was significant enough

---

35. *Women of Covenant* is the most thorough study.

36. See First Council of the Seventy Minutes and Early Records, Book B, 1844–48 (Mar. 9, 1845), 78, quoted in *Women of Covenant*, 63, which discusses the disruption of the Relief Society, 59–82. For a treatment of women's responses to this disruption, see Laurel Thatcher Ulrich, *A House Full of Females: Plural Marriage and Women's Rights in Early Mormonism, 1835–1870* (New York: Alfred Knopf, 2017), especially xvii, 127–28, 180.

37. "Nauvoo Relief Society Minute Book," p. [40], Joseph Smith Papers, at www.josephsmithpapers.org/paper-summary/nauvoo-relief-society-minute-book/37?highlight=I%20now%20turn%20the%20key%20to%20you%20in%20the%20name%20of%20God%20and%20this%20society.

38. Joseph Smith's second phrase is: "this is the beginning of better days, to this Society."

for LDS Church leader B. H. Roberts to alter the historical record and change Smith's language from "I now turn the key *to you*" to "I turn the key *in your behalf*" [my italics]. This change appeared in Roberts's 1908 edition of the *History of the Church*.[39] Scholars attribute the original change to George A. Smith, who worked on Joseph Smith's history in 1854.[40] Both George A. Smith and B. H. Roberts seemed to understand and resist the priesthood implications for women of Joseph Smith's statement, or they would not have changed his words to ensure that there are no such "misunderstandings" that might suggest that women can hold priesthood keys apart from men.[41] While it is true that Joseph Smith used the term "keys" to refer to temple rituals, his usage is consistent with his view that priesthood rights are conferred by the temple rituals, which are the keys to administer ordinances and give laws to God's people.[42] The church essay acknowledges that Smith said he would "ordain" women to preside over the Relief Society, but then declares that this has no priesthood significance because it simply refers to women being set apart to church callings. The essay further asserts that, while women did preside in their organizations, it was only by virtue of "delegated priesthood authority" given by men.

The essay quotes an 1880 speech of third LDS Church President John Taylor, in which he explained that when he helped ordain to Emma Smith, Joseph Smith's wife, and her counselors to lead the Relief Society in Nauvoo, "the ordination then given did not

39. Joseph Smith Jr. et al., *History of the Church of Jesus Christ of Latter-day Saints,* ed. B. H. Roberts, 6 vols., 1902–12, Vol. 7, 1932 (rpt., Salt Lake City: Deseret Book Co., 1976), 4:607. I checked the original 1908 edition against the 1976 reprint, and they match in wording and page numbers.

40. See Dean C. Jessee, "The Writing of Joseph Smith's History," *BYU Studies* 1, 4 (Summer 1971): 458.

41. Dallin H. Oaks reinforced this interpretation in 1992 when he announced in conference that "No priesthood keys were delivered to the Relief Society" ("The Relief Society and the Church," *Ensign,* May 1992, 36).

42. Joseph Smith relevant sermons: Oct. 5, 1840 (at www.rsc.byu.edu/archived/words-joseph-smith-contemporary-accounts-nauvoo-discourses-prophet-joseph/1840/5-october);Aug.27,1843(atwww.rsc.byu.edu/archived/words-joseph-smith-contemporary-accounts-nauvoo-discourses-prophet-joseph/1843/27-august); Mar. 10, 1844 (Wilford Woodruff Journal, at www.catalog.churchofjesuschrist.org/assets?id=09e6d1b1-cd59-41d4-bc46-e3d74899ceac&crate=0&index=217).

mean the conferring of the Priesthood upon those sisters."[43] The authors, however, fail to relate that Taylor's statements form part of a larger disagreement between church leaders and temple-endowed LDS women during this period. Women endowed during Smith's lifetime, such as Bathsheba Smith and Eliza R. Snow, knew that they had received priesthood ordinations in the temple and that their anointings there had significance for the way they functioned in the Relief Society and church.[44] Taylor's assertion that Emma Smith's election as president of the Relief Society did not confer priesthood on her obscures relevant facts. Though true on one level, Taylor's statement ignores Emma Smith's anointing 'to the fullness of the Melchizedek priesthood through her endowment (sometime in 1842) and her election and ordination to the presidency of the Anointed Quorum on September 28, 1843.[45]

This omission encapsulates the central disagreement between some scholars and the official position of the church today. The open question is whether the temple endowment bestows "real" priesthood on women and men, and, if so, whether this priesthood can or should have any authority or efficacy within the ecclesiastical structure of the church, including the Relief Society.[46] Because the church essay does not disclose crucial statements and actions of Joseph Smith, readers are not able to make informed

43. At www.lds.org/topics/essays?lang=eng, 3–4; original statement in "R.S. Reports," *Woman's Exponent* 9, 7 (Sept. 1, 1880): 55.

44. See Quinn, "Women Have Had Priesthood," 369–378.

45. Devery S. Anderson and Gary James Bergera, eds., *Joseph Smith's Quorum of the Anointed 1842–1845: A Documentary History* (Salt Lake City: Signature Books, 2005), 25–26.

46. Jonathan Stapley's 2018 book, *The Power of Godliness: Mormon Liturgy and Cosmology* (New York: Oxford University Press), pages 26–33, adds important questions and sources to the on-going debate about the relationship between ecclesiastical and temple priesthood. Stapley develops the term "cosmological priesthood" to distinguish nineteenth-century concepts of priesthood from current views about priesthood in the church. He also criticizes authors in books such as *Women and Authority* (edited by Maxine Hanks, including one of my essays) of presentism for using the past to justify current ordination. In my 1984 essay "The Missing Rib," and in the priesthood chapters from *Strangers in Paradox*, I argue that Joseph Smith's views of priesthood are more expansive and "cosmological" than is evident in current LDS practice. Stapley himself does not deal with Smith's discourses on the fullness of the priesthood, Smith's complex interpretation of Elijah's mission, and the importance of the Quorum of the Anointed.

interpretations of their own as to whether Smith's speeches to the Relief Society of Nauvoo about priesthood are consonant or dissonant with current church teachings. Their essay obfuscates the issues by alleging Smith's language was loose. The authors insist that "Joseph's actions illuminate the meaning of his words: Neither Joseph Smith, nor any person acting on his behalf, nor any of his successors, conferred the Aaronic or Melchizedek priesthood on women or ordained women to priesthood office."[47] This assertion is misleading and anachronistic because it is made in the absence of significant and voluminous evidence indicating the opposite about the interrelationship between Smith's actions and words on women and priesthood.[48]

The first body of omitted evidence consists of Smith's contemporary statements. These show (1) what he meant by giving women the priesthood through the endowment, and (2) how he saw women's priesthood as central for their authority to govern the Relief Society and to exercise spiritual gifts, including healing the sick. The Manuscript History of the Church records Smith's lecture to the Relief Society on April 28, 1842, in which he told the women that they "would come in possession of the privileges, blessings, and gifts of the Priesthood, and that the signs should follow them, such as healing the sick."[49] The word "privileges" here is important because it implies women's right to exercise priesthood as well as receive its blessings. The church essay undercuts the power and authority of women to give healing blessings by insisting that Smith only acknowledged healing blessings by

---

47. See www.lds.org/topics/essays?lang=eng, 3.

48. See Toscano and Toscano, *Strangers in Paradox*, 179–97; Paul Toscano, *The Serpent and the Dove: Messianic Mysteries of the Mormon Temple* (Create Space Independent Publishing, 2nd ed., 2015), 103–32; Quinn, "Women Have Had Priesthood"; Newell, "Historical Relationship of Women and Priesthood"; Carol Cornwall Madsen, "Mormon Women and the Temple: Toward a New Understanding," in Maureen Ursenbach Beecher and Lavina Fielding Anderson, eds., *Sisters in Spirit: Mormon Women in Historical and Cultural Perspective* (Urbana: University of Illinois Press, 1987), 80–110; Anderson and Bergera, *Joseph Smith's Quorum of the Anointed*, 1–49.

49. Apr. 28, 1842, "History, 1838–1856, volume C-1 [2 November 1838–31 July 1842]," 1326, Joseph Smith Papers, at www.josephsmithpapers.org/paper-summary/history-1838-1856-volume-c-1-2-November-1838-31-july-1842/500?highlight=would%20come%20in%20possession%20of%20privileges%20blessings%20and%20gifts%20of%20Priesthood.

women that arise upon their faith in Jesus rather than upon their priesthood authority. Not only do his full statements to the Relief Society contradict this interpretation, but LDS women who were present in Nauvoo later connected Smith's priesthood promises with their right to administer to the sick.

Bathsheba Smith said that "Joseph gave us everything, every order of the priesthood" and "instructions that they could administer to the sick."[50] The church essay quotes Eliza R. Snow (Relief Society president in the mid- and late nineteenth century) to support the idea that it is inappropriate for women to use priesthood in healing blessings: "Women can administer in the name of JESUS, but not by virtue of the Priesthood."[51] However, this statement is taken out of the larger context of Snow's teachings that show she believed only endowed women should heal by the authority of the priesthood they possessed through the temple ritual.[52] The essay concludes that though all women can give such faith blessings, the official and pre-ferred approach is for women, whether temple-endowed or not, to abstain from blessing others in deference to blessings given by male priesthood holders.[53] Here the essay asserts that the present pol-icy changes by continuing revelation what Smith taught, unlike the focus of the rest of the essay, which denies such changes.

The second body of omitted evidence consists of Smith's full instructions to the Nauvoo Relief Society. He told the women that they should organize their society according to the pattern of the priesthood, that they "should move according to the ancient Priest-hood," and that "he was going to make of this society a kingdom of priests as in Enoch's day—as in Paul's day."[54] It is evident from later

---

50. Pioneer Stake Relief Society minutes, June 9, 1905, Church History Library, Church of Jesus Christ of Latter-day Saints, Salt Lake City; *Woman's Exponent* 34 (July-Aug. 1905): 14.

51. At www.lds.org/topics/essays?lang=eng, 4.

52. Zina D. Young concurred with this belief. See *Woman's Exponent* 13 (Sept. 15, 1884): 61; and *Woman's Exponent* 17 (Apr. 15, 1889): 172.

53. For a historical treatment of healing practices and their decline among nine-teenth- and early-twentieth-century LDS women, see Linda King Newell, "Gifts of the Spirit: Women's Share," in Beecher and Anderson, eds., *Sisters in Spirit*, 111–49.

54. Nauvoo Relief Society minutes, footnoted above. The church authors do later quote the phrase "kingdom of priests" in the temple section, but they remove it from its larger context as Joseph Smith gave it to the Relief Society.

records of the women who heard these promises that they understood the words to mean both that they would receive priesthood
through their endowments and that the Relief Society was part of
the "Order of the Priesthood." In the summer of 1905 Bathsheba
Smith reviewed the original Nauvoo Relief Society minutes as the
society's current president who also presided over women's temple
work. She reported in the *Woman's Exponent*: "[Joseph] said ... he
wanted to make us, as the women were in Paul's day, 'A kingdom
of priestesses.' We have the ceremony in our endowments as Joseph taught."[55] Later in the fall, along with her counselors in the
general presidency of the Relief Society, Bathsheba Smith declared
in the *Woman's Exponent* that Joseph Smith had told the women
in Nauvoo that the purpose of founding the Relief Society was to
make "complete the organization of the Church by organizing the
women in the order of the Priesthood."[56]

The connections Bathsheba Smith made are crucial: the endowment ceremony constitutes endowed women as priestesses in their
own right, thus fulfilling Joseph Smith's promise at the founding
of the Relief Society to make them "a kingdom of priestesses," or
"priests." This is why these women understood the Relief Society to
be an order of the priesthood necessary to complete the organization
of the church itself. Relating Joseph Smith's priesthood promises
to the Relief Society leadership structure supports the view that
women's priesthood has an ecclesiastical function. But in January
1906, just two months after Bathsheba Smith had published her
strong statement in the *Woman's Exponent,* the Relief Society presidency made a "Correction" in that same publication, stating they
were mistaken when they reported the original record as stating
their organization was "in the order of the priesthood." Rather, they
are simply called "by the priesthood."[57] One year later LDS Church
President Joseph F. Smith declared that a "wife does not hold the
priesthood in connection with her husband"; she only "enjoys the

---

55. *Woman's Exponent* 34 (July-Aug. 1905): 14.

56. *Woman's Exponent* 33 (Nov. 1905): 36. Bathsheba Smith is quoting Sarah M.
Kimball, who read this statement on March 17, 1892, at the Jubilee celebration of
the founding of the Relief Society, which was published in "Relief Society Jubilee,"
Woman's Exponent 20 (Apr. 1, 1892): 141.

57. *Woman's Exponent* 34 (Jan. 1906): 44.

benefits thereof," but she is allowed to bless their children with her husband, though he must act as "mouth."[58] This wrangling over Joseph Smith's language and intentions reveals a process of pressure from male leaders that required female leaders of the Relief Society to diminish their view of the priesthood promises of Joseph Smith, a concession reluctantly given by those women.[59]

The third body of omitted information relates to Joseph Smith's statements regarding the nature of the priesthood to be restored by the prophet Elijah. Smith stated clearly that the organization of the priesthood and church was not complete or in its proper order until Elijah came to restore the fullness of the Melchizedek priesthood.[60] He connected this restoration by Elijah not just with family sealings but with the temple endowment as it relates to the fullness of the priesthood. Smith said: "Why send Elijah[?] because he holds the keys of the Authority to administer in all the ordinances of the priesthood and without the authority is given the ordinances could not be administered in righteousness."[61] And yet official LDS doctrine claims that the restoration of the priesthood in the church centers on the angelic visitations of John the Baptist and Peter, James, and John, and that Elijah only has to do with sealing ordinances. But Joseph Smith said differently: "Now for Elijah. The spirit, power, and calling of Elijah is, that ye have power to hold the key of the revelations, ordinances, oracles, powers and endowments of the fullness of the Melchizedek Priesthood and of the kingdom of God on the earth; and to

---

58. *Improvement Era* 10 (Feb. 1907): 308. Quinn documents church leaders' inconsistent and changing language to describe women's relationship to priesthood, in "Women Have Had Priesthood, 356–85. Brigham Young both talks about women having priesthood themselves and also only in connection with their husbands.

59. Ulrich notes that Eliza R. Snow carried the Nauvoo Relief Society minute book to Utah and that "she used it to remind her closest associates of the promises they had received in Nauvoo" from Joseph Smith, in *House Full of Females*, xvii.

60. "History, 1838–1856, volume C-1 [November2, 1838–July 31, 1842] [addenda]," 18 [addenda], Oct. 5, 1840, Joseph Smith Papers, at www.josephsmithpapers.org/paper-summary/history-1838-1856-volume-c-1-2-November-1838-31-july-1842/553?highlight=when%20priesthood%20is%20restored%20with%20all%20its%20authority

61. "Instruction on Priesthood, 5 October 1840," p. 9, Joseph Smith Papers, at www.josephsmithpapers.org/paper-summary/instruction-on-priesthood-5-october-1840/17.

receive, obtain, and perform all the ordinances belonging to the kingdom of God."[62]

The fourth area of omitted information consists of Smith's many statements that connect the temple endowment with the bestowal of the fullness of the Aaronic and Melchizedek priesthoods upon the women and men who receive it. His statements show that he saw this temple priesthood as not different in nature from the church priesthood but as more authoritative and empowering.[63] For Smith, all the orders of the priesthood are connected; they are one and united and hold all the keys: not only of the Melchizedek and Aaronic orders, but of those belonging to Abraham, Moses, Elias, Elijah, and the Messiah too. He said that "all priesthood is Melchizedek; but there are different portions or degrees of it."[64] Likewise, all priesthood is Messianic because all levels are "after the order of the Son of God" (D&C 107:1–5)[65] The fullness of the priesthood conferred in the temple bestows the keys to govern the church and administer all the ordinances, as well as to hold the keys of knowledge and revelation.[66] Women and men are invested with the fullness of the Aaronic and Melchizedek (and Messianic) priesthoods in the temple ceremony; and both men and women together as a group are told that with the white temple robe placed on the right shoulder (to symbolize the fullness of the Melchizedek priesthood), they each may officiate in all of the ordinances of the gospel.[67] This general

---

62. Wilford Woodruff Journal, Mar. 10, 1844, in Ehat and Cook, eds., *Words of Joseph Smith*, 329.

63. See Toscano and Toscano, *Strangers in Paradox*, 151–53.

64. From William Clayton's Private Book, in Ehat and Cook, eds., *Words of Joseph Smith*, 59. This corresponds with descriptions of the power of the Melchizedek priesthood in D&C 84 and 107.

65. Also see "The Nature and Purpose of Priesthood," in Toscano and Toscano, *Strangers in Paradox*, 147–53.

66. Paul Toscano in *The Serpent and the Dove*, 52–58, sees church priesthood, which he calls "chapel" priesthood, as provisional and encompassed by the permanent, non-provisional temple priesthood, which is more inclusive. Joseph Smith did not fully address the question of how lines of authority can be established within the church context to avoid disorder if temple priesthood is higher (thus the succession crisis discussed below), though D &C 81:2 sets forth an order under the president of the church. Paul Toscano addresses this in *Serpent*, 133–42.

67. The common LDS practice requiring men to have the Melchizedek priesthood to participate in temple ordinances implies that women must have it too. The

statement refers not just to temple ordinances, but to gospel ordinances from baptism to the second anointing.[68]

The church essay states that Smith never conferred Melchizedek priesthood on women, but this ignores what he taught as essential doctrine: "Those holding the fulness of the Melchisedic priesthood are kings and Priests [and by implication queens and priestesses] to the most high God, holding the keys of power and blessings ... that Priesthood is a perfect law of Theocracy, and stands as God, to give laws to the people, administering endless lives."[69] During Smith's lifetime, the fullness of the Melchizedek priesthood was also referred to as "the highest order of Priesthood," implying that it encompassed all of the lower priesthoods in the church.[70] Brigham Young recorded in his diary that his wife Mary A. Young was admitted to the highest order of the priesthood on November 1, 1843.[71] Such language was used often in Nauvoo to refer to men and women receiving their endowments individually, even before they were sealed in marriage or received their second anointings.[72]

The fifth area of omitted information in the church essay relates to Emma Smith's anointing and ordination to the highest priesthood, and to her election and installation as co-president of the so-called Anointed Quorum, along with her husband, Joseph Smith. The Anointed Quorum, also Holy Order, Quorum

---

fact that women of African origin were not allowed to receive their temple endowments until after the 1978 revelation that extended priesthood to men in this group implies the same thing.

68. This meaning is especially evident when connected with Joseph Smith's statements about Elijah and the Melchizedek priesthood quoted above.

69. Aug. 27, 1843, "History, 1838–1856, volume E-1 [1 July 1843–30 April 1844]," 1,708, Joseph Smith Papers, at www.josephsmithpapers.org/paper-summary/history-1838-1856-volume-e-1-1-july-1843-30-april-1844/80?highlight=perfect%20 law%20of%20theocracy.

70. Quinn lists forty-eight women who received their endowments and second anointings in Nauvoo before the opening of the temple, in "Women Have Had Priesthood," 394–96. Anderson and Bergera also list forty-eight women as members of the Quorum of the Anointed/Holy Order while Joseph Smith was alive, xxxix.

71. Brigham Young Diary, Nov. 1, 1843, in Anderson and Bergera, eds., *Joseph Smith's Quorum of Anointed*, 32.

72. This means that women were ordained to priesthood apart from their husbands and marriage. The second anointings did not bestow priesthood but sealed all priesthood blessings unprovisionally.

of the Anointed, or simply Quorum, was comprised of endowed men and women who met together in Nauvoo during the last few months of Joseph Smith's life.[73] That Emma Smith was ordained to the fullness of the Melchizedek priesthood is affirmed by scholars, but her role as joint-president of the Quorum of the Anointed is seldom acknowledged. This role can be implied from the record of the event, set forth in the September 28, 1843, minutes of the Quorum of the Anointed: "Baruk Ale [Joseph Smith] was by common consent & unanimous voice chosen president of the Quorum & anointed and ordained to the highest & holiest order of the priesthood (& Companion D[itt]o)."[74] If the terms listed apply to Joseph Smith as we understand them today, then they apply equally to Emma Smith, who is the "companion" in this reference.[75] The "ditto" indicates that the same language was used in her anointing as was used in Joseph Smith's, and that she was ordained with him to the presidency of the Quorum. This evidence belies the church essay's assertion that women have never held office in the church. Interestingly, Brigham Young stated later in 1845 that women "never can hold the keys of the Priesthood apart from their husbands."[76] This could imply that Young understood the significance of Emma's ordination in 1843—that she had keys giving her the right to preside over the Anointed Quorum; but his statement also implies that her claim died with Joseph Smith.

The sixth area of omitted information revolves around the mission and function of the Anointed Quorum. Was it a real priesthood quorum? Though it has sometimes been viewed simply as a prayer circle, there is sufficient evidence to establish that

---

73. Anderson and Bergera provide the documentary evidence for this quorum, its members, and functions from over a dozen primary sources.

74. From "Meetings of Anointed Quorum," quoted in Anderson and Bergera, eds., *Joseph Smith's Quorum*, 26. Smith was commonly called Baruk Ale. Joseph Smith's diary has "(and companion)" without the "Ditto," quoted ibid. Though the online Joseph Smith Papers has not published this diary entry yet, there is an "Interim Content" reference to this event, but it omits the "(and companion)" at the end of the sentence.

75. Scholars have always interpreted the "companion" as Emma Smith. See Andrew F. Ehat, "Joseph Smith's Introduction of Temple Ordinances and the 1844 Mormon Succession Question," MA thesis, Brigham Young University, 1982, 94–96.

76. From Council of Seventy Minutes, Mar. 9, 1845, quoted in Quinn, "Women Have Had Priesthood" 373.

its functions went beyond a prayer group because it was constituted as an ongoing priesthood body that held regular meetings
in which the members discussed doctrine and consulted and
voted about issues affecting the church.[77] In *The Mormon Hierarchy: Origins of Power*, historian D. Michael Quinn asserts that
the Anointed functioned as the highest priesthood quorum in
Nauvoo at the end of Smith's life, though only for a few months.
Quinn gives as evidence the fact that Smith used the Anointed
Quorum as a "forum for political strategy," having them vote and
approve a "Petition to Congress" and "a proclamation to the kings
of the earth."[78] The role membership in the Anointed Quorum
assumed for Brigham Young and other members of the Quorum
of the Twelve during the trial of Sidney Rigdon is crucial evidence
that these men saw the Quorum as a functioning church priesthood quorum in Nauvoo, giving them the right to succeed Joseph
Smith.[79] Brigham Young, Heber C. Kimball, W. W. Phelps, and
others announced that they had "higher authority" than Sidney
Rigdon because of their second anointings and membership in the
Anointed Quorum.

All of these six bodies of evidence omitted in the church essay
show that Smith actually did things during his life that give a
context for interpreting his words regarding women and their
priesthood roles within the church structure. He wanted the
Relief Society to be organized in the pattern of the priesthood;
he described the temple anointings as conferring the fullness of
the Melchizedek priesthood that encompasses all other orders
of the ecclesiastical priesthood; he saw this as the fulfillment of
Elijah's restoration of priesthood that would make the church organization complete; he ordained women to the fullness of the
priesthood to fulfill this promise; and he included women in a

---

77. I first made this argument in "The Missing Rib: The Forgotten Place of
Queens and Priestesses in the Establishment of Zion" at Sunstone Symposium, Salt
Lake City, Aug. 1984, printed in *Sunstone*, July 1985, 16–22; see expanded view, "A
Kingdom of Priestesses," in Toscano and Toscano, *Strangers in Paradox*, 179–97.

78. Quinn, *Mormon Hierarchy: Origins of Power*, 114–16 (143–263 detail the
whole succession crisis). Quinn shows how the Quorum also met after the death of
Joseph Smith to consider William Marks's position in the church (149).

79. Toscano, *The Serpent and The Dove*, 106–14.

priesthood quorum at the end of his life. Though debatable, the evidence is sufficient to challenge the church essay's assertion that what we see in the church today was what Joseph Smith established in Nauvoo.

Priesthood and the Temple

In the section on "Priesthood and the Temple," the church essay emphasizes yet again its central idea that all the priesthood language used by Joseph Smith in relation to women refers only to them receiving their temple endowments: "Temple ordinances were priesthood ordinances, but they did not bestow ecclesiastical office on men or women." When Smith told the women he was going to make them a "'kingdom of priests,'" the essay insists he was "speaking of the relationship of all the Saints to the temple," not to the ecclesiastical priesthood that manages the church. Thus, the "kingdom of priests" refers to the special "order of the priesthood" that relates to both endowed men and women as they function in sealed family units with the potential to be like their heavenly parents.[80]

The essay acknowledges that the "order of the priesthood" women (along with men) enter through their temple covenants fulfills God's promise that the Saints would be "endowed with power from on high" (D&C 38:32). This power comes through the temple endowment and brings personal revelation, as well as increased faith and knowledge; and it is "available to adult members regardless of marital status."[81] The essay explains this fulfills the promise made in D&C 84:20 that it is through the ordinances that "the power of godliness" is manifest. It is odd that the authors make this connection for all endowed people in the church, whether male or female, single or married, because the larger context of D&C 84:19 clearly connects ordinances and the power of godliness with the "greater priesthood" that administers the gospel and holds "the key of the mysteries of the kingdom, even the key of the knowledge of God." The whole of D&C 84 has always been understood to refer to the Melchizedek priesthood authority

---

80. See www.lds.org/topics/essays?lang=eng, 5.
81. Ibid.

that manages the church and holds the keys of administration to govern every aspect of the church's mission.[82] The fact that the line between church priesthood and temple priesthood becomes blurry as soon as D&C 84 is invoked shows the underlying issue emphasized in my critique. While church leaders deny that the "order of the priesthood" bestowed in the temple has anything to do with ecclesiastical priesthood, this distinction is not at all clear in the statements and revelations of Joseph Smith, including D&C 84. Without the interpretations of church leaders, the more compelling reading of the evidence, I believe, is that the two priesthoods overlap, with the ecclesiastical priesthood embraced and fulfilled by the temple priesthood.

By equating "the order of the priesthood" of the temple with eternal marriage, the church essay both reinforces and reinterprets leaders' long-standing debates over women's relationship to the priesthood as revealed in the temple rituals and sealings. In the past, some leaders said that women who are sealed in the temple hold the priesthood "in connection" with their husbands in a home or eternal family context, with the husband still presiding, while other leaders have denied even this priesthood connection.[83] Still, the quibbling acknowledges what many endowed members see as obvious: women wear the garments of the priesthood in the temple and participate in what are called priesthood ordinances. The question arises, even for those unaware of Smith's statements on the topic, about what kind of priesthood women have through the temple. The explanation usually given is the one emphasized in the church essay, namely, that temple priesthood is the "order of the priesthood" referred to in section 131 of the Doctrine and Covenants, stating that for a man to obtain the highest level of the

---

82. See "Melchizedek Priesthood" in Daniel H. Ludlow et al., eds., *The Encyclopedia of Mormonism*, 5 vols. (New York: Macmillan, 1992), at www.eom.byu.edu/index.php/Melchizedek_Priesthood.

83. See my chronology in "Retrieving the Keys" that traces and documents changes from Brigham Young to the present. Young acknowledged women's priesthood but subordinated them to male leaders; in the 1880s women were said to hold priesthood in connection with their husbands; Joseph F. Smith said women were only recipients of the blessings of the priesthood; and Dallin H. Oaks acknowledged priesthood partnership in the home between men and women, but not in the church. See also Newell, "Mormon Women and Priesthood," and Quinn, "Women Have Had Priesthood."

celestial kingdom, he must enter into the order of priesthood that is connected "to the new and everlasting covenant of marriage."[84]

The church essay explains that the "ultimate destiny of faithful men and women" is to become like their heavenly parents.[85] Moreover, the marriage sealing joins couples together in a way that reflects the relationship of the heavenly parents, which implies it is necessary to have both males and females to reflect the image of God. The writers explain that Smith's "revelations and ordinances imparted new understanding of the interdependent relationship of women and men"[86] by quoting Newel K. Whitney, the Presiding Bishop in Smith's day: "'Without the female all things cannot be restor'd to the earth. It takes all to restore the Priesthood.'"[87]

These statements about the union of men and women reflecting the divinity of the heavenly parents and about the centrality of women for the full restoration of priesthood seem promising for the equality and status of women in the church.[88] But several problems emerge upon closer examination, which all center on the question of what is meant by "interdependent." Does it imply an equality of status and authority? If the eternal relationship between men and women is defined by the church's 1995 Proclamation on the Family, and this is seen as the true reflection of the eternal relationship between the Heavenly Father and Mother, then the heavenly parents as a model of equality is undercut. While the Proclamation on the Family argues for an "equal partnership"

---

84. The church essay emphasizes that singles as well as married people enter into the temple covenant society and that every person will have the opportunity to be sealed in marriage. For her experience of priesthood power as a single female leader in the church, see Sheri L. Dew, *Women and the Priesthood: What One Mormon Woman Believes* (Salt Lake City: Deseret Book Co., 2013).

85. See www.lds.org/topics/essays?lang=eng, 5.

86. Ibid.

87. May 24, 1842, "Nauvoo Relief Society Minute Book," p. [58], Joseph Smith Papers, at www.josephsmithpapers.org/paper-summary/nauvoo-relief-society-minute-book/55?highlight=without%20the%20female%20all%20things%20cannot%20be%20restor%27d.

88. Scholars interested in promoting equality for LGBTQ people in the church ask whether a heterosexual couple as the highest representation of godliness excludes LGBTQ people from fully reflecting the image of God. See Taylor Petrey, "Toward a Mormon Post-Heterosexual Theology," *Dialogue: A Journal of Mormon Thought* 44, 4 (Winter 2011): 106–41.

between mothers and fathers, it undermines such a relationship by describing men's primary role as "presiding" and women's primary role as "nurturing."[89] And the Proclamation, like the Gospel Topics essay, never mentions the Heavenly Mother independently from the Father. She is only one of the "heavenly parents" in both cases.[90] The brief Gospel Topics essay on "Mother in Heaven" emphasizes the phrase "heavenly parents" throughout, which implies more of a dependent relationship with the Heavenly Father than an interdependent one. The Father is seen as a power on his own, or with the other two male entities in the Godhead, as the supreme divine power (without the Heavenly Mother) in most official church texts.[91]

The priesthood-holding husband as the one who presides in the eternal family is reinforced by the recent changes in the temple ceremony. Though these changes have eliminated most negative language regarding women, as well as introduced more equitable covenants (as noted above), there are two new elements in the endowment that promote patriarchal marriage and patriarchal priesthood. Although men are still ordained to become priests to God, as in the past, women do not receive a similar promise. They are not ordained to become priestesses to God, but rather priestesses in the new and everlasting covenant. This is surely better than being ordained as priestesses to their husbands, which was the previous wording that put women clearly in an eternally subordinate role or position to men. But the new promise is vague. Is it referring to the new and everlasting covenant of marriage as described in D&C 131? This seems likely since the new marriage ceremony in

---

89. "The Family: A Proclamation to the World," lds.org, at www.lds.org/topics/family-proclamation?lang=eng&old=true. See Margaret Toscano's analysis of the Proclamation in "Are Boys More Important than Girls? The Continuing Conflict of Gender Difference and Equality in Mormonism," *Sunstone*, June 2007, 19–29. See also Janice Allred, "Feminist Gender Theology," in Shepherd et al., eds., *Voices for Equality*, 82–86.

90. It is significant that in official church discourse the phrase "heavenly parents" is never capitalized.

91. David L. Paulsen and Martin Pulido document more than 600 references to the Heavenly Mother in official LDS discourse since 1844, in "'A Mother There': A Survey of Historical Teachings about Heavenly Mother," *BYU Studies* 50, 1 (2011): 71–97. For a response, see Margaret Toscano, "Heavenly Motherhood: Silences, Disturbances, and Consolations," *Sunstone*, Mar. 2012, 70–78.

the temple tells men to preside in love and kindness. While there is also more equality now in the marriage ceremony, nevertheless, if men are supposed to preside, even in love and kindness, the relationship is still patriarchal on some level. Why not create more equity by making both men and women "priests" to God to fulfill Joseph Smith's promises to the Nauvoo Relief Society? There is some evidence that in Nauvoo before Smith's death that women were ordained, not as priestesses to their husbands, but as "priestesses unto God." Though the sources are not conclusive, they are strong.[92] Making women priestesses in the new and everlasting covenant reinforces the church essay's interpretation that "the order of the priesthood" in the temple is only about temple marriage, not about the fullness of the priesthood in the larger sense as Smith's statements imply. Thus, recent changes reinforce the idea that women do not receive priesthood in the temple in any real sense.

Women and Priesthood Today

The last section returns to the frame that begins the church essay. It is significant that the writers do not resort to the argument that motherhood is women's primary role, or to the line that motherhood is women's compensation for not getting the priesthood.[93] This shows that some church officials are listening to some women's complaints, even if they do not acknowledge the complaints. The writers of the church essay wisely emphasize instead "the numerous positions of leadership and service" that women perform within the ecclesiastical structure.[94] After restating the list of things women can do in the church today that begins the essay, it states: "In these and other ways, women exercise priesthood authority even though they are not ordained to priesthood office. Such

---

92. Four main pieces of evidence reinforce each other: (1) Heber C. Kimball's Nauvoo diary, dated Feb. 1, 1844 (in Anderson and Bergera, eds., *Joseph Smith's Quorum*, 54); (2) Phineas Richards's diary of Jan. 22, 1846; (3) Daniel Tyler's article in the *Juvenile Instructor*, May 15, 1880 (these last two quoted in Quinn, "Women Have Had Priesthood," 368, 393); and (4) Emma Smith's ordination to the fullness of the priesthood, since her ordination is described as the same as Joseph's with the "Ditto."

93. While Dew does not make the typical equation, she does emphasize motherhood as women's "high privilege" in *Women and the Priesthood*, 136–54.

94. At www.lds.org/topics/essays?lang=eng, 6.

service and leadership would require ordination in many other religious traditions."[95] This re-emphasizes the idea that Joseph Smith expanded the roles of LDS women from what other churches had and have, but it fails to acknowledge organizations that have ordained women and expanded their roles in the last forty years, such as the LDS sister church, the Missouri-headquartered Community of Christ (before 2001, the Reorganized Church of Jesus Christ of Latter Day Saints).[96] The ending of the church essay implies that the priesthood authority women have in the church is equal to what men have: "In ecclesiastical callings, temple ordinances, family relationships, and quiet, individual ministry, Latter-day women and men go forward with priesthood power and authority. This interdependence of men and women in accomplishing God's work through His power is central to the gospel of Jesus Christ restored through the Prophet Joseph Smith."[97]

The church essay does reflect a change that has evolved in the last few years in official discourse about women's relationship to priesthood. Whereas in the past women were usually said simply to be the recipients of the blessings of the priesthood, now they are described as exercising priesthood power and authority. LDS female leaders, in an April 2013 interview, emphasized the blessings of the priesthood women receive but also said that women exercise the power of the priesthood.[98] A year later, in his April 2014 general conference talk, Apostle Dallin H. Oaks further expanded women's priesthood power. His address, which is footnoted three times in the Gospel Topics essay, acknowledges that women have both the power and authority of the priesthood but still not the keys or offices. Oaks emphasizes that the authority women have

---

95. Ibid.

96. See Robin Kinkaid Linkhart, "Ordination of Women: The Community of Christ Story," in Shepherd et al., eds., *Voices for Equality*, 185–99. It is ironic that the Community of Christ, which has never included the temple endowment in its practice with its implied priesthood ordination for women, still ordained women to priesthood on the basis of social justice and the equality of Christ's gospel, while the LDS Church rejects the idea.

97. At www.lds.org/topics/essays?lang=eng, 6–7.

98. The interview with LDS women leaders happened the same week Ordain Women was launched; see www.mormonnewsroom.org/article/women-leaders-insights-church-leadership.

is delegated authority deriving from the priesthood authority of male leaders and that such delegated priesthood authority has a limited scope only relating to women's church callings while they serve in them.[99] Priesthood authority never resides in women themselves. Importantly, these changes in language occurred during the well-publicized first year of the LDS Ordain Women movement. But this kind of emphasis on the power and authority that women have through their gospel covenants and righteous participation in the church has continued as an important theme in official church discourse since that time. For example, President Russell M. Nelson in the women's session of the October 2019 general conference told the women of the church that "the priesthood is just as relevant to you as a woman as it is to any man. Because the Melchizedek Priesthood has been restored, both covenant-keeping women and men have access to '*all* the spiritual blessings of the church' [D&C 107:18]." Importantly, Nelson still distinguishes between the power that women have from their covenants, whether gospel or temple, and that of men "who bear the priesthood."[100]

The evolving church discourse about women exercising priesthood power and authority is an important development for women's empowerment in the LDS Church. It shows what seems like a promising trend. But without priesthood ordination, offices, and keys, women's authority is always subordinate to men's authority and power. Most people would concede that the all-male First Presidency, Council of the Twelve, other general authorities, regional representatives, stake presidencies, and bishoprics have more priesthood power and authority than any of the women in the church. A stake president has more priesthood authority and ecclesiastical power than the general president of the Relief Society. And it is the men in important leadership positions who have the authority to define church doctrine, to decide church policies, and to determine how church resources are used on both a general

---

99. Dallin H. Oaks, "The Keys and Authority of the Priesthood," *Ensign,* May 2014, 49–52.

100. Russell M. Nelson, "Spiritual Treasures," *Ensign,* Nov. 2019, www.churchofjesuschrist.org/study/ensign/2019/11/36nelson?lang=eng.

and local level, even when women are granted some input in councils and committees. And since it is the First Presidency and the Quorum of the Twelve who are sustained as prophets, seers, and revelators, it is only men who speak authoritatively as the mouthpieces of God. No woman, no matter how gifted, charismatic, or worthy, can ever fill this role. So women's "priesthood" power can never be as powerful or authoritative as men's because it lacks the structural and symbolic substance, which makes women more dependent on men for spiritual blessings than interdependent with them in using the priesthood. Pictures from recent general conferences reinforce this situation; a sea of male leaders dominates the visual field in conference pictures. And ironically, even in President Nelson's talk to women about their equal access to God's spiritual power, the two pictures that accompany his address in the *Ensign* depict men alone as the givers and receivers of the Aaronic and Melchizedek priesthood restoration events in Joseph Smith's day.

The church essay makes the church organization sound much more egalitarian than it is when it describes the interdependence of women and men on a general level as they go about their "ecclesiastical callings" and "quiet, individual ministry." The hierarchical nature of the LDS Church is very much understated in the essay, which gives the feeling of a communitarian, empowered body of saints working together in equality. Perhaps this describes the experience of many women and men in the church, but obviously there are many who disagree. The church essay says: "Priesthood defines, empowers, ennobles, and creates order."[101] This may be the ideal, but the hierarchical order of the LDS priesthood also disempowers and diminishes for many people, as is evidenced by discussions on the internet and also in current scholarship.[102]

Whatever is true about Smith's doctrine and actions regarding women, the church essay gives a sugarcoated view of men's and women's functions and interactions in the contemporary church

---

101. Ibid.

102. For a compilation of LDS feminist writings that highlights important internet discussions from the last decade and also positions them in a historical and scholarly context, see Joanna Brooks, Rachel Hunt Steenblick, and Hannah Wheelwright, eds., *Mormon Feminism: Essential Writings* (New York: Oxford University Press, 2016), esp. 226–92 for internet entries and references.

organization. It states that women and men both "go forward with priesthood power and authority" to work in an interdependent way to bring about God's purposes in the world. It is true that the work of men and women in the church is certainly "interdependent" in the sense that without both women and men the jobs that need to be done in every LDS Church community could not be accomplished. But this is not the same as saying that men and women have equal or equivalent authority and power within the structure of the church, which seems to be an implication of the essay.[103] While the church essay seems to exalt women's right to use priesthood power and authority, it also undermines it at the same time. By saying that women have power and authority but no offices or keys, church leaders effectively bar women from using priesthood in many significant ways within the church structure, especially since all of women's callings are done under male supervision, never vice versa.

Conclusion

One positive effect of the church essay is that its writers take seriously the statements and actions of Joseph Smith, which is not always the case in a church that privileges the words of living leaders over dead ones. Since the past is always a helpful lens through which to view and analyze the present, the Gospel Topics essays can serve as a beginning point for fruitful discussions. However, the essay on "Joseph Smith's Teachings on Priesthood, Temple, and Women" uses a gaslighting technique to obscure the historical information from Smith's life and work that justifies the priesthood ordination of women in the LDS Church. Likewise, the essay omits any information in the church's current practices that disadvantage women. In both cases, the church essay creates an illusion that shuts down opposing views on both the past and the present. In this critique, I present missing evidence and alternative interpretations so that readers are better able to formulate their own conclusions.

---

103. The idea that women have the power of the priesthood but not the right to any priesthood office is at variance with D&C 121 that condemns any effort to separate the power of the priesthood from the rights of the priesthood.

AFTERWORD

Armand L. Mauss

At the end of their introduction, the editors of this volume assure us that each contributor to it is "an experienced and thoughtful scholar," many of whom "have written widely on religious thought in general and Mormon history in particular." After reviewing their work here, I would certainly concur in that assessment. Indeed, I have known of the work of all them for some years, and I regard many of them as personal friends. Yet, as with any authors, these had certain key points to make and ideas of their own to emphasize, which did not always seem to recognize adequately the more limited intentions of those who wrote the original thirteen Gospel Essays. Nevertheless, I would judge all of these critiques as worthy of consideration by the leaders and scholars of the Church of Jesus Christ of Latter-day Saints, mainly for what they reveal about the *human* element in the history of the Church.[1] Although implicit claims about divine guidance, or the absence thereof, might occur in the Gospel Essays, such claims are simply not at issue in this afterword or, as far as I can tell, in any of the critiques either.

I assume that some sort of general template or editorial guidelines were provided for these critiques. They were certainly not identical in format, but each one was introduced in some way with descriptive material that provided an historical and/or intellectual context for the original Gospel Essay—and thus derivatively for the

---

1. In this afterword, when I use the word "Church" with an initial capital, I shall always be referring to the Church of Jesus Christ of Latter-day Saints. When I use "Gospel Essay(s)" (or sometimes simply "Essay"), again with initial capital, I shall always be referring to one or more of the thirteen Gospel Topics essays published on-line by the Church and discussed in the present collection. When I use the terms "critique(s)" or "critic(s)," I shall be referring to one or more of the contributions of the authors in this collection (with perhaps rare and obvious exceptions).

present author's own critique. Then the importance and strengths of each Gospel Essay were identified, often in quite generous terms. Finally, the critique assessed what the author regarded as the weaknesses, oversights, selective or misleading statements, inadequate treatments, or missed opportunities of the Gospel Essay under discussion. Although each of these three components could be found in each critique, they were not always presented in separate or discrete sections but were sometimes distributed around the text. Of course, it was primarily in its discussion of the weaknesses and inadequacies of a given Gospel Essay that a critic might comment quite extensively on his or her own special intellectual interest.

———

One of the special assets of this collection is the introduction itself, offered by the editors Matthew L. Harris and Newell G. Bringhurst. It grabs the reader's attention immediately with a surprisingly thorough account of the process that some have dubbed the "Swedish Rescue Mission," beginning with the 2010 meeting in Stockholm, where the LDS Church Historian and Assistant Historian met with several hundred Swedish Latter-day Saints. The purpose of the meeting was to deal with questions and issues from the history of the Church that had produced a faith crisis for many Swedes, especially after the publicity given the personal crisis reported by Hans Mattsson, a Swedish Area Authority of the Church. The editors attribute the decision to publish the Gospel Essays largely to this Stockholm episode and derivative developments, aided and abetted by the widespread influence of four or five websites. The full story of what emerged from the Stockholm encounter has a rather interesting *dramatis personae* involving some surprising participants, not all of whom could be considered Church leaders in any sense. From my own reading and personal contacts, I had known about the general outline of this episode, but the editors here succeeded in fleshing out the story with some surprising details—all well documented. They devote about two-thirds of the introduction to that account, and the rest to explaining the politically sensitive process, within the Church, of producing and distributing the Gospel Essays.

Although this introduction finds the immediate context for such faith crises in the rise of the Internet, I would have expected some acknowledgment of the importance of the *Church's own retrenchment policies* during the decades *preceding* any Internet access, when the Church enforced a kind of "circle the wagons" policy, explicitly resisting the very kind of transparency now apparently acceptable. An early casualty of this retrenchment era was Leonard J. Arrington (1917–99), appointed Church Historian in 1972—the first trained academic to receive such an appointment—and the founder, in effect, of what came to be called the New Mormon History. Arrington's appointment, and the early publications of some of his younger associates, soon drew the ire of a group of conservative senior apostles, with the result that Arrington was soon replaced as Church Historian and his entire operation and personnel were scaled down and moved to Brigham Young University.[2] During this period, even faithful scholars (including a few of Arrington's own colleagues) were sanctioned, often severely, for publishing on precisely some of those troubling issues that were later exposed on the internet—usually under much less friendly auspices.[3] One wonders if the impact from the Internet exposés would have been so damaging if the Church had instead welcomed the research and candid publications of its own scholars on such topics during those pre-Internet years.

———

In my reading and rereading of the critiques in this volume, I sensed certain themes that seemed to recur, whatever specific Gospel Essays might have been under consideration. Given the space available, I will discuss only three of these. First will be the *political constraints* faced by the authors of these Essays. All the

---

2. Several important publications in recent years review this and other important episodes in Arrington's career. The latest and most thorough is Gary James Bergera, ed., *Confessions of a Mormon Historian: The Diaries of Leonard J. Arrington, 1971–1997* (Salt Lake City: Signature Books, 2018), 3 vols.

3. Discussed in my "Authority and Dissent in Mormonism," pp. 386–405, in Terryl L. Givens and Philip L. Barlow, eds., *The Oxford Handbook of Mormonism* (New York: Oxford University Press, 2015), as well as in numerous other publications during recent decades, many of which, in fact, are cited in some of the critiques herein.

critiques pointed out inadequacies or missed opportunities in the Gospel Essays. Many of these criticisms, it seemed to me, would draw a ready concurrence not only from some Church leaders, but especially from the Essay authors themselves, who did not enjoy the luxury of venting their own special concerns and interests about the topic, as the critics were free—or even expected—to do. A couple of the critics did express some recognition of the Essay authors' predicament with phrases like "walking a tightrope"; but, in general, there seemed but little acknowledgment of what the editors' introduction itself made clear—namely, that the entire process was fraught with political sensitivity in the decision-making at every stage, starting with the very selection of the Essay topics themselves; the authors to be consulted and assigned; and just when, where, and how the Essays would be disseminated, even among the variety of Church auspices available. As the introduction makes clear, the decision for a limited and gradual distribution (or "soft rollout"), was intended to shield some of the more sheltered Saints from the sudden spiritual shock of unwelcome discoveries; but the result was a rather uneven distribution of the Gospel Essays. Some of the more curious and enterprising members thus discovered the Essays (on less prominent Church websites) before other members did—even before many of the local priesthood leaders did. In the introduction, the editors mention several cases of misunderstanding and hurt feelings resulting from this slow and spotty distribution, and it would not be difficult to imagine many other unintended consequences.

One form of political constraint that drew special disdain in several of the critiques was the studied avoidance, in the citations and footnotes of the Gospel Essays, of publications that had originally appeared in the quarterly *Dialogue: A Journal of Mormon Thought*, an independent scholarly journal founded by young Latter-day Saint intellectuals more than fifty years ago. During those decades, some of the most ground-breaking and enduring articles in the history of Mormon scholarship were published in *Dialogue*, including many that would have strengthened the footnotes in the new Gospel Essays. A similar boycott is evident in the lack of citations to certain scholars, no matter how competent or relevant, whose work or public *personas* had acquired the taint of controversy in one way or another.[4] The point here is not that the citations in the Gospel Essays were generally inadequate or misleading (though that complaint appeared occasionally against some of the critiques). Nor can the authors of the Essays be faulted for relying often on primary sources from the Church's own archives, and/or on secondary sources from Church publications (e.g., *Ensign, BYU Studies*) if such citations were relevant to the points under discussion. Certainly many other (non-Church) primary and secondary sources (e.g., *Harvard Theological Review*) were also cited in the Essays—including a few from other Mormon-focused but independent publications that have sometimes published controversial material (e.g., *Journal of Mormon History* and Signature Books). Yet the avoidance in the Church Essays of citations to even the most thorough and important scholars on key topics, and to so substantive and well-established a periodical as *Dialogue*, suggests the heavy hand of ecclesiastical politics.[5]

A second theme that seemed to recur among the critiques—though in various ways—was around the issue of *Church doctrine*: What is doctrine? How can we tell? Where does it come from? How and why does it change? Even official pronouncements on such questions have never proved definitive.[6] Some four decades

4. I glanced carefully through the footnotes for all thirteen of the Church Essays and found *only one* citation to *Dialogue: A Journal of Mormon Thought* (within note 21 of the essay on "Plural Marriage and Families in Early Utah"). The boycotted scholars in question (including about half of the authors in the present collection) tended to be among those involved in controversies during the Church's "retrenchment" era—i.e., during the second half of the twentieth century.

5. Only two examples of many that could be cited on this point would be Lester E. Bush, "Mormonism's Negro Doctrine: An Historical Overview," *Dialogue: A Journal of Mormon Thought* 8, 1 (Spring 1973): 11–68; and D. Michael Quinn, "LDS Church Authority and New Plural Marriages, 1890–1904," *Dialogue: A Journal of Mormon Thought* 18, 1 (Spring 1985): 9–105.

6. One prominent pronouncement was offered in July 1954, apparently in response to a controversy that had occurred during a conference that summer of faculty in the Church Education System. See J. Reuben Clark's "When are the Writings or Sermons of Church Leaders Entitled to the Claim of Being Scripture?" in *Church News*, July 31, 1954, and reprinted in *Dialogue: A Journal of Morn Thought* 12, 2 (Summer 1979): 68–81. A long and preachy sermon, it concludes by emphasizing the exclusive role of

ago, I proposed that "doctrine" in the Church, as an historical matter, can be seen in *four categories* along a scale ranging from most to
least authentic: *canonical, official, authoritative,* and *folklore.*[7] These
are not necessarily permanent categories for any given doctrine,
which might be folklore at one particular historical period but become official at a later period (and vice-versa, as occurred—in both
directions—with the doctrine about black people).[8] All four categories, in fact, are susceptible to fluctuation in their doctrines across
time, as they are influenced by developments in the Church or in
the surrounding society—or both—and by generational changes
and shifting concerns among the apostolic leadership. Presumably
the demotion of a doctrine from the canonical level to a lower one
would be quite rare, but theoretically it could happen. Yet it always
takes time for a doctrine to migrate (or drift) totally from one
category to another, and while the migration is occurring, a given
doctrine can become a source of contention among members (or
observers) who hold varying assessments of its authenticity.

Doctrine might originate in a variety of ways. In the Latter-day
Saint experience, of course, *historical claims* have often been the
basis for declaring certain teachings as formal doctrines—including, for example, the entire 1838 First Vision narrative of Joseph
Smith, as presented in the current version of the Pearl of Great
Price (canonized in 1880). Indeed, as we now know—and is clear
from David J. Howlett's essay herein—this canonized account of
the First Vision was not the first or even the second version in
the historical record, but it was selected for inclusion in the PGP,
along with many other accounts of Smith's various early visionary experiences, for largely *doctrinal* reasons (e.g., the nature of
the godhead *contra* the conventional Trinitarian teachings in the

---

the president of the Church, "when moved upon by the Holy Ghost," but along the
way concedes that a president might not always be so moved. What Clark here calls
"scripture" seems to include both canonical and official categories of doctrine.

7. See pp. 32–34 in my "The Fading of the Pharoah's Curse," *Dialogue: A Journal
of Mormon Thought* 14, 3 (Fall 1981): 10–45.

8. While not employing the categories I have suggested here, Gordon and Gary
Shepherd have amply demonstrated statistically the variations across decades in the
prominence given to various Church doctrines preached in general conferences: Gordon Shepherd and Gary Shepherd, *A Kingdom Transformed: Early Mormonism and the
Modern LDS Church* (Salt Lake City: University of Utah Press, 2016), second edition.

Catholic and Protestant traditions), and are thus part of the "work" that Howlett finds the various versions do in this Gospel Essay. In fact, periodic doctrinal innovations can be underway more or less constantly in the Latter-day Saint experience, but because they often occur too slowly and gradually to be apparent to the membership across a given generation or two, they are eventually identified only by historical research. A good example of this point (if perhaps a minor one) can be seen in the increasing prominence given to the salvific importance of the Garden of Gethsemane in the doctrine of Atonement.[9]

Several of the critiques in this collection touch on the issue of *doctrinal innovation* in one way or another. Perhaps the most obvious example is the chapter by Caroline Kline and Rachel Hunt Steenblik, who appreciate the apparent removal of a "taboo" in the recent history of the Church against public teaching or discussions about the Mother in Heaven.[10] Nevertheless, they identify several important "contestable claims" and "unexplored issues" that make the Church Essay seem unduly dismissive in its concluding observation that although "our present knowledge about a Mother in Heaven is limited ... we have been given sufficient knowledge" about the sacredness of the doctrine and the "divine pattern established for us as children of heavenly parents." For these two feminist critics, the Church Essay (and the Church generally) offer but little to those "many Latter-day Saints yearning to know

---

9. See John L. Hilton III and Joshua P. Barringer, "The Use of Gethsemane by Church Leaders, 1859–2018," *BYU Studies Quarterly* 58, 4 (2019): 49–76. I had long wondered how Gethsemane came to be considered part of the atonement process; I was a young adult before I ever encountered the idea in Church teachings.

10. As indicative of the end of the taboo, they cite in particular the 2011 article by David L. Paulsen and Martin Pulido, "'A Mother There': A Survey of Historical Teachings about Mother in Heaven," *BYU Studies* 50, 1:70–97. As welcome as this article was (to me, as well as to the authors of this critique), I must confess that I found somewhat disingenuous a passage early in that article (75–76) where Paulsen and Pulido claim that their research has "cast doubt" on earlier claims that "a sacred silence has always surrounded" the Heavenly Mother doctrine, and that her "ascribed roles have been marginalized or trivialized"—as though Latter-day Saints have never felt any constraints in discussing the topic. However, as Kline and Steenblik point out, precisely just such a "sacred silence" on the subject had been enforced during the late twentieth century by the excommunications of feminist theologians in the Church who persisted in writing about it. Indeed, during that same "retrenchment" era, I doubt that *BYU Studies* itself would have considered publishing this very article.

more about Heavenly Mother ... [without even a] ... suggestion that we might learn more about Her in time, given the Church's emphasis on continuing revelation and personal revelation." This observation, like much of the critical essay as a whole, amounts to a call for an important doctrinal *innovation*—namely, for the Mother in Heaven doctrine to be elevated to canonical status through the Church's formal revelatory process.[11]

Perhaps a less dramatic example of the potential for doctrinal innovation occurs in the critique by Craig L. Blomberg ("Are Mormons Christian?"), who sees in the work of some LDS scholars (e.g., Stephen Robinson and Robert Millet) certain rearticulations underway of Church doctrines about grace, works, and the sufficiency of the Atonement. These point to the "genuinely Christian nature" of the Church, says Blomberg, and if such modifications continue in the same direction, the younger generations of Saints and Evangelicals might yet be able to reach each other across the "wide divide." Sometimes doctrinal innovation depends on the *outcome of contending interpretations* across a "divide" of sorts even within the Church, as opposing caucuses of Church leaders and/or scholars might promote (perhaps for decades at a time) one versus another doctrinal understanding. One thinks, for example, of the long-running argument between Brigham Young and Orson Pratt over the so-called Adam-God theory.[12] A more recent example may be seen in the engaging historical critique by John-Charles Duffy, who reviews the alternating dominance among Church

---

11. The review in the Paulsen and Pulido article suggests that the Heavenly Mother doctrine has historically migrated between the categories of "authoritative" (but not actively taught) and "official," so its elevation to canonical status would probably require a process something like that which produced the 1978 revelation on race and priesthood. Whatever might be the aspirations of Church feminists for such an elevation of the Heavenly Mother doctrine, the apostolic leaders will always prove vigilant in maintaining their own special prophetic prerogatives in declaring a given doctrine *canonical*, resisting any intimations of internal or external public pressure in the process.

12. David John Buerger, "The Adam-God Doctrine," *Dialogue: A Journal of Mormon Thought* 15, 1 (Spring 1982): 14–58. As John G. Turner's essay herein makes clear, similarly contested meanings of the doctrine of "blood atonement" underlie important episodes of violence in Mormon history, at least during the mid-nineteenth century. Happily neither of these two doctrines from Brigham Young's time has survived to gain doctrinal standing in the contemporary Church.

leaders and scholars between a "read translation" theory versus a "composed translation" theory to explain the process by which Joseph Smith rendered the Book of Mormon in English.

Indeed, throughout the history of the Church, other doctrinal disputes have resulted from different understandings of what Joseph Smith *really meant* by some of the language he used (or was attributed to him by scribes). These disputes were not often highly contentious, at least, not publicly, but they have had winners and losers, as indicated by whether and when a given doctrinal position has gained "official" standing (or, perhaps, at least, "authoritative" in some instances). As just indicated, the actual meaning of "translation" in the case of the Book of Mormon has been argued among and between Latter-day Saints of presumably equal competence and faithfulness for decades. More recently, the meaning of "translation" has also raised important questions about the doctrinal authenticity of the Book of Abraham, as Stephen C. Taysom's critique explains. He shows in some detail how the Church was forced, after the 1960s, to abandon its original claims, such as Joseph Smith's ability to translate ancient Egyptian. The Gospel Essay in question has therefore (understandably) "shift[ed] the grounds of the debate" versus its non-Mormon critics to claims that are less subject to falsifiability, acknowledging that ultimately "the Book of Abraham can only be completely validated via a spiritual witness."[13]

Of course, quite aside from the meaning(s) of "translation," there are many other ambiguities, with important doctrinal implications, in the writings attributed to Joseph Smith. One of the most important of these is discussed at some length by Margaret M. Toscano in her trenchant critique of the Gospel Essay on Smith's teachings

---

13. Taysom does not refer specifically to the closing paragraph in this Church Essay, but when I read that paragraph in the Essay, I was struck by the intellectual and spiritual space that it implicitly offers to those Saints who might doubt the historicity of *any* "ancient scriptures" (including much of the Bible), while still embracing them as divinely inspired. Note these observations at the end of that Gospel Essay: "The veracity and value of the book of Abraham [and perhaps by implication the Book of Mormon?] cannot be settled by scholarly debate ... [about] translation and historicity. The book's status as scripture lies in the eternal truths it teaches and the powerful spirit it conveys. ... The truth of the book of Abraham is ultimately found through careful study of its teachings, sincere prayer, and the confirmation of the Spirit."

about priesthood, temple, and women. At issue in this critique is what Smith *really meant* when he wrote and spoke in Nauvoo, Illinois, about women's roles in the priesthood. For Toscano, there is little or no ambiguity about the matter: Smith intended the Relief Society to be a women's priesthood organization with women presumably ordained to priesthood offices, such as bishop, elder, or priest, etc. He clearly ordained women to the *temple priesthood*, which was the fullness of the priesthood, brought by the ancient prophet Elijah, through which the entire Church was eventually to be governed. Such a scenario would have developed more fully if Smith had not been murdered in Illinois. Toscano recognizes that the evidence for her view is "not abundant but significant," and has largely been ignored in this Church Essay.[14]

Along with such cases of doctrinal innovation, contention, and migration, the *demotion* of a doctrine down the "authenticity" scale also takes time and can be confusing. For example, Richard Sherlock seems offended at the efforts of some Church leaders to distance themselves from doctrines that have long been identified as authentically "Mormon" but heretical to other Christians. In particular, the ideas that (a) as man is God once was, and that (b) as men become gods they will rule their own kingdoms, seemed to be treated dismissively by President Gordon B. Hinckley and by the authors of the Gospel Essay in question ("On Becoming Gods"). Sherlock finds this tactic "misleading." Kline and Steenblik too noticed (more approvingly) that the related idea of "multiple heavenly mothers" (multiple wives of individual men ruling their own kingdoms), was among those "thorny historical issues … veer[ed] away from" in the Gospel Essay on Heavenly Mother. Even though deliberate avoidance of such "thorny" issues might be regarded as "misleading" by critics, another way to understand such a tactic is

---

14. Interestingly, Gary James Bergera (writing on a totally different Gospel Essay—early polygamy) emphasizes the importance of *memory* problems in trying to reconstruct what Joseph Smith (or anyone else) *really* said or did during previous events, citing the work of (e. g.,) scholars Loftus and Schacter. Then, citing LDS scholars Prince and Harrell, Bergera points, in fact, *specifically* to problems with "Smith's understanding of any relationship between *Elijah* and the performance of various priesthood ordinances … [since that understanding] … evolved gradually ex post facto and never developed as clearly or fulsomely as later LDS teaching suggests" (italics added).

to see it as part of the normal historical "drift" as such teachings are quietly demoted, perhaps ultimately to the bottom category (folklore) or even to complete oblivion.

––––––

The third and final theme that seems prominent to me in this collection is the *concern with equality* in both the doctrines and the practices of the Church. This issue recurs among the critiques quite naturally because it recurs among the Gospel Essays themselves, many of which try to address the various forms of *inequality* that remain in the modern Church itself. To the critics, the Church's rationales or explanations might seem misleading or otherwise inadequate, but at least the Church is recognizing the issue as problematic for its own organizational and doctrinal integrity. Many Latter-day Saints seem to feel that the Church is already correcting the inequalities remaining in its historical heritage, some of which were simply derivative from the surrounding American heritage more generally. After all, the 1978 revelation on priesthood removed a major obstacle to equality for members of black African ancestry, and certain language changes in the current version of the Book of Mormon have attempted to destigmatize the aboriginal peoples called "Lamanites." Furthermore, during recent years, many changes have been made in both policy and liturgy to enhance the roles, prominence, and power of female Church members.

The critics in this volume, however, find all such recent changes as abjectly inadequate if the ultimate goal is true equality among all the children of our heavenly parents. Where race is concerned, Matthew L. Harris ("Race and Priesthood") identifies many examples indicating that a fundamental "whiteness theology" has remained "entrenched in popular LDS culture," no matter how progressive some of the Church's more recent policy changes might seem. This traditional preoccupation with whiteness, furthermore, has often been discussed in very literal terms, as, for example, when Church leaders have predicted that the skin color of dark-skinned converts could actually turn white—or, at least, much lighter—as they join the Church and grow in righteousness.

Such notions have affected both popular and official definitions and treatment not only of peoples of African descent but especially the American aboriginal peoples (Indians) even down to the present era.

Thomas W Murphy and Angelo Baca ("Book of Mormon and DNA Studies") adopt the "decolonizing methodology" of modern social science to demonstrate powerfully what will be necessary for Latter-day Saints truly to understand these aboriginal peoples and to embrace them as equals in the divine family. While these authors credit the Church with finally acknowledging the lack of DNA evidence for the Israelite origins of the Lamanites, the Book of Mormon nevertheless still contains conflicting messages, in which "all are alike unto God," but yet "also represents dark skin as a curse from God" that can be removed only through righteous behavior (as that is defined in the scripture). This message "has its roots in the colonial ideology" of the white settlers, whose "narratives ... have privileged the authority of colonizers over the bodies and voices of the colonized." The Church itself, whatever its scriptural rationale, was acting, of course, on that same "colonial ideology" as it settled Utah. Yet, since the Gospel Essay itself concedes that "the primary purpose of the Book of Mormon is more spiritual than historical," one sees a hint that perhaps the Church is becoming more open to non-historical interpretations that might offer some common ground not only with its more skeptical scholars, but also with "those who approach the Book of Mormon from an Indigenous perspective" (see my comment in note 13, above, on the Book of Abraham Essay).

Of course, the equality issue arises also in the critiques dealing with the relationships between men and women in the Church, both historically and currently. The critiques taking on this issue most directly are those by Toscano and by Kline and Steenblik (already cited above in connection with issues of *doctrine*).[15] However,

---

15. Certainly, the equality issue underlies the whole checkered history of *plural marriage* in the Church. The three critiques here of the relevant Gospel Essays, by (respectively) Gary James Bergera, George D. Smith, and Newell G. Bringhurst, are all very well done, but I have chosen not to focus on them in my discussion of equality here. The topic of plural marriage, both in these critiques, and in the original Gospel Essays to which they are responding, requires special attention of its own.

the Church Essay on Joseph Smith's teachings about women, observes Toscano, "obscures all inequities between men and women by emphasizing only the positive roles women can play in the church today." The Church, furthermore, continues to insist, "no matter what the historical sources seem to say, ... [that] neither Joseph Smith, nor any of his successors conferred the ... Priesthood on women or ordained women to priesthood office."[16] Aside from the issue of priesthood ordination, the Church Essay ignores the many "expanded roles women played" in the Church during the nineteenth century and even later, when they largely controlled the funds, budgets, publications, and programs of their own auxiliary organizations, and, in spiritual matters, periodically gave healing blessings. The Essay instead emphasizes recent changes in the Church to elevate publicly the importance of women's current (if historically lesser) ecclesiastical roles and leadership, including especially in the priesthood work of the temple. The facts thus remain even in the contemporary Church that "all of women's callings are done under male supervision, never vice-versa," so that all "women as a class" are subordinate to all "men as a class."

In their critique of the Church Essay on Heavenly Mother, Kline and Steenblik, while obviously in agreement with much of Toscano's critique, nevertheless take a much more positive and upbeat tone—and understandably so, given the very recent willingness in the Church leadership to end an earlier period of "cultural silence" about Heavenly Mother in Latter-day Saint discourse and to (re)emphasize "as authoritative church doctrine" the traditional teachings about her in Church literature. One question posed and discussed by these authors is why does this doctrine matter? Why, I would add, does it matter particularly in the present discussion of equality between Latter-day Saint men and women? Kline and Steenblik acknowledge, citing Toscano, that since the male Church leaders determine what matters in theology, their seeming embrace of the *divine* female as equal might be

16. Of course, this complaint would be more impressive if there were any known case in these "historical sources," especially in Smith's own lifetime, of a woman ever having been ordained to an office like bishop or elder in the Relief Society, or in the ordinary *operational priesthood* of the Church, where such specific offices have so far been reserved only for male members.

mostly rhetorical, for the "subordinating structures" of the Church itself remain in place. Yet whatever equality might or might not occur in the *mortal* Church, the *theology* about a mother in heaven, minimal as it now seems, is extraordinarily important to women's aspirations about life in celestial eternity. Given the traditional Latter-day Saint concept that "God" actually refers to heavenly parents—a divine Father and Mother—then the ultimate destiny of humans, male and female, is to "retain some form of their sexed bodies, live with their spouses, and perpetually grow, evolve, and learn" in the pattern of the Heavenly Parents themselves. If the divine Father, in his various roles, is the model for mortal men to follow, then surely a greater understanding of the divine Mother's roles is *equally* important for mortal women. It is not surprising, then, that many women feel a strong yearning for fuller doctrine on this "distinctive" and "ennobling" Latter-day Saint tradition. Inadequate as the Church Essay might be in many respects, the authors see in it "new space to envision and hope for a gradual lifting up of the Mother in a uniquely LDS discourse that acknowledges Her Godhood and highlights Her active participation in the godly work of loving and guiding humans on earth."

———

In these critiques, I saw a spirit of good will and constructive intentions. Some of them might have had their own "axes to grind" in the process, but I thought that the authors genuinely reflected a desire to see improvements in future Church Essays, and perhaps even in updated versions of some of those already published. The editors, at the end of their own introduction, observed that some of the Essays have already been "silently revised since they were first published," a process that will presumably continue. It would be truly fascinating to find evidence in future Church Essays of the constructive influence of these critiques.

CONTRIBUTORS

Angelo Baca is a cultural activist, scholar, filmmaker, and currently a doctoral student in anthropology at New York University. He is the cultural resources coordinator at Utah Diné Bikéyah, a nonprofit organization dedicated to the defense and protection of culturally significant ancestral lands. The National Parks Conservation Association recently designated him as one of "10 Under 40" dynamic cultural activists who make up the association's Next Generation Advisory Council. He has published a widely read op-ed in the *New York Times. Shash Jaa': Bears Ears* is Angelo Baca's latest award-winning film about the five tribes of the Bears Ears Inter-Tribal Coalition that worked together to protect 1.9 million acres of Utah wilderness through a national monument designation. His work reflects a long-standing dedication to both Western and Indigenous knowledge.

Gary James Bergera is managing director of the Smith–Pettit Foundation and company director of Signature Books, both of Salt Lake City. He is author of *Conflict in the Quorum: Orson Pratt, Joseph Smith, Brigham Young*; co-author of *Brigham Young University: A House of Faith*; editor of *Line Upon Line: Essays on Mormon Doctrine, The Autobiography of B. H. Roberts*, and *Statements of the LDS First Presidency: A Topical Compendium*; and co-editor of *Joseph Smith's Quorum of the Anointed: A Documentary History, 1842-1845*, and *The Nauvoo Endowment Companies: A Documentary History, 1845-1846*. Most recently, he edited the Leonard J. Arrington diaries, published in three volumes as *Confessions of a Mormon Historian*. Bergera's publications have received awards from the Dialogue Foundation, the John Whitmer Historical Association, the Mormon History Association, and the Utah Historical Society. He currently serves on the editorial boards of the *Journal of Mormon History* and the *John Whitmer Historical*

Association Journal; and previously was managing editor of *Dialogue: A Journal of Mormon Thought.* He is the 2018 recipient of the Leonard J. Arrington lifetime achievement award from the Mormon History Association.

Craig L. Blomberg is Distinguished Professor of New Testament at Denver Seminary in Littleton, Colorado. He holds the PhD in New Testament from the University of Aberdeen, Scotland. Blomberg is the author of fifteen books and has co-authored or co-edited ten more, along with more than 150 journal articles or chapters in multi-author works. His books include four on the historical reliability and interpretation of parts or all of the Bible (esp. the Gospels), two on interpreting and preaching the parables, three commentaries (on Matthew, 1 Corinthians and James), a textbook on Jesus and the Gospels and another on Acts through Revelation, a handbook on exegetical method, and three books on material possessions in the Bible. He is a member of the Committee on Bible Translation for the New International Version and on the committee tasked with producing the 35th anniversary edition of the NIV Study Bible.

Newell G. Bringhurst is an independent scholar and Professor Emeritus of History and Political Science at College of the Sequoias in Visalia, California. Bringhurst received his PhD in American History from the University of California at Davis. He is the author/editor of thirteen books published since 1981. His most recent are *The Mormon Quest of the Presidency: Eleven Mormons who Ran for President from 1844 to 2012* (2008, original ed., 2011, enlarged, expanded ed.), co-authored with Craig L. Foster; and the co-editor (with Craig L. Foster of a trilogy under the title *The Persistence of Polygamy.* The three are: *Joseph Smith and the Origins of Mormon Polygamy* (2010); *From Joseph Smith' s Martyrdom to the First Manifesto* (2013) and Fundamentalist Mormon Polygamy from 1890 to the Present (2015). Also published in 2015 was *The Mormon Church and Blacks: A Documentary History* co-edited with Matthew L. Harris. He is a long-time member of the Mormon History Association, having served as its president in 1999-2000. He is also the member of the John Whitmer Historical Association, of which he served as president from 2005 to 2006.

John-Charles Duffy is an Assistant Teaching Professor in the Department of Comparative Religion at Miami University (Ohio), where he teaches courses on religion in U.S. history and culture. Duffy received his PhD in Religious Studies from the University of North Carolina at Chapel Hill. He is the coauthor of *Mormonism: The Basics* (Routledge, 2016) and has published articles on Mormon intellectual and cultural history in several venues.

Matthew L. Harris is Professor of History at Colorado State University-Pueblo. He holds a PhD in American History from the Maxwell School of Citizenship and Public Affairs at Syracuse University. Harris is the author and/or editor of several books, including most recently *The Mormon Church and Blacks: A Documentary History* (University of Illinois Press 2015); *"Watchmen on the Tower": Ezra Taft Benson and the Making of the Mormon Right* (University of Utah Press, forthcoming, 2020); and *Thunder on the Right: Ezra Taft Benson in Mormonism and Politics* (University of Illinois Press, 2019). He has won numerous awards at Colorado State University-Pueblo, including the Provost's Award for Teaching Excellence, the Student's Choice Award for Teaching and Service, and two awards for Scholarly and Creative Excellence.

David J. Howlett is a Visiting Assistant Professor of Religion in the Department of Religion at Smith College in Northampton, Massachusetts. He earned his PhD in Religious Studies from the University of Iowa and has authored numerous studies dealing with the theory and practice of religion, Mormonism, and religion and culture. His book *Kirkland Temple: The Biography of a Shared Space* (University of Illinois, 2014) earned distinction for the "best first book" from Mormon History Association and the John Whitmer Historical Association. More recently, Howlett coauthored *Mormonism: The Basics* (Routledge, 2016). He has also authored several articles in the *Journal of Mormon History*, *Dialogue: A Journal of Mormon Thought*, and the *John Whitmer Historical Association Journal*. Howlett is an eighth-generation member of the Community of Christ and serves as one of three volunteer World Church Historians for the church.

Caroline Kline earned her PhD in religion at Claremont Graduate University. Her areas of interest revolve around the intersections of Mormon and feminist theology and the study of contemporary Mormon women's communities. She is the co-founder of the Mormon feminist blog, The Exponent. Her publications include "The Mormon Conception of Women's Nature: A Feminist Analysis," in the Journal of Feminist Theology and "Saying Goodbye to the Final Say: The Softening and Reimagining of Mormon Male Headship Ideologies," in Out of Obscurity: Mormonism Since 1945, edited by Patrick Mason and John Turner. She co-edited with Claudia Bushman the book Mormon Women Have Their Say: Essays from the Claremont Oral History Collection. Her dissertation examines the oral histories of Mormon women of color in the United States, Botswana, and Mexico.

Armand L. Mauss is professor emeritus of sociology and religious studies at Washington State University. He retired there at the end of the last century, and during the current century, he has continued a long career of teaching and publishing in the field of Mormon Studies. He is the author of *The Angel and the Beehive: The Mormon Struggle with Assimilation* (1994), *All Abraham's Children: Changing Mormon Conceptions of Race and Lineage* (2003), and *Shifting Borders and a Tattered Passport: Intellectual Journeys of a Mormon Academic* (2012).

Thomas W Murphy teaches in the Department of Anthropology at Edmonds Community College in Washington state. He holds a PhD in Anthropology from the University of Washington and specializes in Mormons and Native Americans, environmental sustainability, and science and religion. His work on DNA and the *Book of Mormon* has been covered in the *Los Angeles Times* and *Christianity Today* and his award-winning research has appeared in many journals, including the *Journal for the Scientific Study of Religion*, *Ethnohistory*, *Journal of Mormon History*, *Review of Religious Research*, *Dialogue: A Journal of Mormon Thought*, and *Sunstone*.

Richard Sherlock has three degrees from Harvard University in theology and philosophy. He has taught in Massachusetts, Tennessee, and New York. Before coming to Utah State University (Logan), he was professor of moral theology at Fordham University. His work has appeared in the *American Journal of Medicine*, *American Journal of Jurisprudence*, *Interpretation*, *Journal of Religious Ethics*, and other periodicals. His co-edited work with Carl Mosser, *The Mormon World*, is forthcoming from Routledge.

George D. Smith is a businessman, co-founder of Signature Books, which specializes in Mormon and Western-American studies, and founder of the Smith–Pettit Foundation. He received degrees from Stanford University and New York University and has served on the boards of the Commonwealth Club of California, the Graduate Theological Union in Berkeley, the *Kenyon Review*, the Leakey Foundation, and National Public Radio, and has acted as elections monitor for The Carter Center in China and Central America, and for women's advocacy in Africa. He is the award-winning author of several books on Mormon history, as well as of articles published in the *Journal of Mormon History*, the *John Whitmer Historical Association Journal*, *Free Inquiry*, and *Dialogue: A Journal of Mormon Thought*.

Rachel Hunt Steenblik is a PhD student in philosophy of religion at Claremont Graduate University and has a BA in philosophy from Brigham Young University and an MS in library and information science from Simmons College. She contributed to the research and publication of an article in *BYU Studies* entitled "'A Mother There': A Survey of Historical Teachings about Mother in Heaven." She also authored *Mother's Milk: Poems in Search of Heavenly Mother for By Common Consent Press*, co-edited *Mormon Feminism: Essential Writings* for Oxford University Press, and writes at The Exponent blog.

Steven C. Taysom holds a PhD in the History of Religion from Indiana University and is currently Associate Professor of Philosophy and Comparative Religion at Cleveland State University. He has published numerous articles on American religious history and a book about Shaker and Mormon boundary maintenance strategies. He is completing a scholarly biography of LDS Church President Joseph F. Smith (forthcoming from the University of Utah Press).

Margaret M. Toscano is Associate Professor of Classics and Comparative Studies and Department Chair of World Languages and Cultures at the University of Utah. She received her PhD from the University of Utah in Comparative Literature. Her research centers on myth, religion, and gender in both ancient and modern contexts. She also works on the reception of classical culture in film and has published articles about the HBO-BBC series *Rome*. She is the co-editor (with Isabel Moreira) of the book *Hell and Its Afterlife: Historical and Contemporary Perspectives*, released first in 2010 and now in paperback by Routledge. She has published extensively on Mormon feminism for over thirty years. She co-authored (with her husband Paul) the book *Strangers in Paradox: Explorations in Mormon Theology* (Signature Books, 1990) and more recently her chapter "Retrieving the Keys: Historical Milestones in LDS Women's Quest for Priesthood Ordination" appeared in the 2015 book *Voices for Equality*, published by Kofford Books.

John G. Turner is Professor of Religious Studies at George Mason University and writes and teaches about the place of religion in American history. Turner holds a PhD in American History from the University of Notre Dame and a Masters of Divinity from Louisville Presbyterian Theological Seminary. He is the author of several books about the history of religion in the United States, mostly recently *The Mormon Jesus: A Biography* (Harvard University Press, 2016) and *Brigham Young: Pioneer Prophet* (Harvard University Press, 2012).

376

INDEX